TED
TEMPLEMAN

A PLATINUM PRODUCER'S LIFE IN MUSIC

Ted Templeman as told to Greg Renoff

Copyright © Ted Templeman, 2020

Published by ECW Press
665 Gerrard Street East
Toronto, Ontario, Canada M4M 1Y2
416-694-3348 / info@ecwpress.com

To the best of his abilities, the author has related experiences, places, people, and organizations from his memories of them. In order to protect the privacy of others, he has, in some instances, changed the names of certain people and details of events and places.

Editor for the Press: Michael Holmes
Cover design: VAiN Eudes, Whitespace
Background image: © Shane Brown
Front cover photograph of Ted Templeman: © Rhino Entertainment Company, a Warner Music Group Company
Author photo: © Shane Brown

LIBRARY AND ARCHIVES CANADA
CATALOGUING IN PUBLICATION

Title: Ted Templeman : a platinum producer's life in music / Ted Templeman as told to Greg Renoff.

Names: Templeman, Ted, 1942– author. Renoff, Greg, 1969– author.

Identifiers: Canadiana (print) 20200183524 Canadiana (ebook) 20200183532

ISBN 978-1-77041-483-9 (softcover)
ISBN 978-1-77305-480-3 (PDF)
ISBN 978-1-77305-479-7 (ePUB)

Subjects: LCSH: Templeman, Ted, 1942– I LCSH: Sound recording executives and producers — United States — Biography. I LCSH: Musicians — United States — Biography. I LCSH: Rock music — United States — History and criticism. I LCGFT: Autobiographies.

Classification: LCC ML429.T287 A3 2020 DDC 781.66092—dc23

PRINTED AND BOUND IN CANADA

PRINTING: MARQUIS   5   4   3

TED
TEMPLEMAN

For my children,
Teddy and McCormick Templeman

The members of Van Halen and I receive gold record awards for *Van Halen II* in the office of Warner Bros. Records' head Mo Ostin, summer 1979 (from left to right): Michael Anthony, David Lee Roth, me, Edward Van Halen, Mo Ostin, and Alex Van Halen. RHINO ENTERTAINMENT COMPANY, A WARNER MUSIC GROUP COMPANY.

CONTENTS

ACKNOWLEDGMENTS

Many people helped bring this book to fruition. Donn Landee generously shared his memories and his unpublished photographs. Dick Scoppettone and Ed James, Ted's bandmates in Harpers Bizarre, clarified a number of obscure points in the band's history. Mike Wilson and his archival staff at WEA uncovered many key images and documents related to Ted's career. Vain Eudes conjured up a beautiful cover concept, Shane Brown snapped a great headshot of me, and Jeremy Steffen color corrected and repaired many of the images that appear in this book. For their unwavering support of this project, thank you to Jeffrey Curran, Bob Diforio, Andy Harris, Jeff Hausman of the Van Halen News Desk, Rob Heinrich, Jeff Hendrickson, Brian Kehew, Jan Velasco Kosharek, Chris McLernon, David Schnittger, Gita Varaprasathan, Matt Wake, and Matt Wardlaw. Ted and I also appreciate the efforts of the ECW Press team, particularly Jessica Albert, Susannah Ames, Jack David, Michael Holmes, and Laura Pastore. Lastly, thank you to Ted's colleagues at WEA and to all the engineers, session musicians, and artists who worked alongside Ted in the studio so everyone else could listen to the music.

GREG RENOFF

Chapter 1

PACIFIC

Lots of people are named after relatives, but it's a funny thing when your parents aren't sure if that person is living or dead when you're born. You see, my parents, Robert and Evelyn, named me after my father's younger brother, Edward J. "Ted" Templeman. As I grew up, my parents explained to me how I became his namesake. And in turn, my uncle Ted would give me glimpses into the hellish ordeal he experienced during the Second World War.

Like me, my uncle Ted was a Santa Cruz boy. He was the youngest of three brothers. His oldest brother, Ken; my dad, Robert; and Ted all were really close, and they all joined the military during the war years. Ted, in fact, quit school in the eleventh grade and enlisted in the Navy on Independence Day, 1940. I think the three of them felt inspired to serve their country because they'd emigrated from Canada just a few years earlier.

After my uncle Ted completed boot camp in September 1940, he'd serve on a heavy cruiser, the USS *Houston*, which, in late 1941, was stationed in the Philippines.

When the Japanese attacked Pearl Harbor, Navy brass ordered the *Houston* to sail for the Dutch East Indies. Good thing too, because the Japanese almost immediately launched an overwhelming air assault on the Philippines.

After holding her own in some smaller engagements, the *Houston*'s luck ran out in late February 1942. During the Battle of Sunda Strait, a larger Japanese naval force attacked her and a number of other Allied ships in the waters just north of Java.

My uncle and his crewmates fought like hell but their ship was torpedoed and set aflame by naval gunfire. The *Houston* proceeded to keel over and sink. My uncle didn't like talking about his wartime experiences, but he told me what haunted him for the rest of his days was watching, helplessly, as scores of his shipmates burned to death. More than half the crew died when the *Houston* sank in the early morning of March 1.

My uncle Ted, along with eighteen other survivors, huddled in the darkness, hanging onto wreckage and each other in the rolling seas. Shortly after daybreak, a Japanese barge happened upon them; its crew then pulled them from the water. After having them strip-searched, the ranking Japanese officer had second thoughts about taking them prisoner. He suddenly ordered them back into the sea at gunpoint. Most of the guys didn't even have time to grab their life jackets. But the Japanese did show some mercy, giving them a small raft to transport the guys too injured to keep swimming. My uncle was one of the men who treaded water and hung onto the raft.

Adrift again, a few hours later the group encountered a sailboat manned by local fishermen sympathetic to the Allied cause. They threw the exhausted sailors a line and towed them to the Java shoreline.

After resting on the beach, my uncle and his party plunged into the jungle, hoping to link up with the Dutch forces that they knew were operating on the island. That plan came to grief when a group of armed Javanese allied with the enemy captured them

My uncle, Edward J. Templeman, 1941. He spent almost all of World War Two as a prisoner of war after he survived the March 1942 sinking of the USS *Houston*.
GREG RENOFF COLLECTION.

and handed them over to the Japanese. My uncle Ted was a prisoner of war. He was nineteen years old.

About two weeks after the battle, the terrible news about the *Houston*'s fate reached the States. Around the same time, the Navy sent Ted's parents (my grandparents), Earl and Minnie, a telegram telling them that their son, along with every other member of the ship's crew, was now considered missing in action. His parents, my mother (who was already pregnant with me) and father, and the rest of the extended family prayed for a miracle but feared the worst.

Much happier news came on October 24, 1942, when I was born in Santa Cruz. (Years later, Carl Scott, who managed my band Harpers Bizarre, changed my birthdate and those of my bandmates to later years because he wanted us to appear younger to our fans, so websites like Wikipedia often give my birthday as 1944.) Like my uncle, I would be called Ted, despite the name Edward J. Templeman II appearing on my birth certificate. My mom and dad later told me they named me after him because deep in their hearts they thought he was dead.

In later years my uncle would tell me about what he endured in captivity. For the first few weeks he and the other *Houston* survivors were held in camps in Java. The Japanese didn't tend to their wounds and underfed them. He told me beatings were a daily occurrence.

In October 1942 the Japanese moved him and a number of other Americans to Singapore and then eventually to Burma. The Japanese forced prisoners at my uncle's camp to work on the infamous Burma Railway project, laying railroad line through the jungle. Before dawn each day their guards would herd them along a path from their camp to construction sites, where they'd toil until night fell. They'd then stagger back, dead tired, to their camp, with their guards forcing the feeblest of the prisoners to keep pace with the others. My uncle confided in me about one event during those marches that particularly traumatized him. A little girl came alongside the line of prisoners and started walking near him. Out of sympathy she handed a piece of bread to the man in line in front of my uncle. A guard, without flinching, then shot her in the head.

In the Burma camp, they lived on moldy rice and consumed starvation rations. My uncle said the guards would throw these little crumbs of rice on the ground and they'd all scramble to pick them up and eat them. They gave them fetid fish pulsing with maggots. So they had to fend for themselves to get sufficient calories to survive. They'd eat the snakes that would coil up in the rafters of their huts and whatever other living things they could get their hands on. He told me that one time he was so ravenous that he ate a live spider. The prisoners eventually got hold of a monkey that came to serve as their food tester. They'd cut a piece off of a snake and feed it, raw, to the monkey. If the monkey didn't die, they'd eat the snake meat too.

He said the Korean guards, who worked in the camp for the Japanese, were the worst aspect of his captivity. They were huge and mean and treated the prisoners worse than the Japanese did. He said there was a big, stinking latrine pit in the camp. To punish the prisoners, the guards would submerge their heads in the raw sewage, sometimes until they died. My uncle told me they did this for their own amusement. Other times they'd simply kick men to death. Guys got sick and died of everything from diseases like dysentery to infected wounds that went untreated. Many were killed while doing the dangerous construction work. All of it was awful, unspeakable stuff that he rarely wanted to discuss. I do recall, however, that one time he did raise the subject was in connection with the 1957 movie *The Bridge on the River Kwai*, which dramatized the plight of Allied prisoners held by the Japanese. He thought it romanticized the horrors he and his compatriots endured while building the "Death Railway" for the Japanese.

In late December 1943, my family's prayers were answered. A postcard, written in what appeared to be my uncle's handwriting, arrived at his parents' home in Santa Cruz all the way from Moulmein, Burma. It contained the sentence, "Let me know about the family and Evelyn." Since the note used my mother's name, the military and the rest of my family knew it was almost certainly from him rather than a Japanese forgery. My mom told this story many times over the years.

In 1944 the Japanese relocated my uncle and a number of other prisoners to Bangkok. That summer he mailed another letter home, which thanks to the Red Cross made it to Santa Cruz from Thailand, albeit eight months after it was written. He'd survived years in captivity, but the war still wasn't over, and he still wasn't home.

I was no older than a toddler during the war, but my earliest memories involve it. My uncle Ken was a sergeant major in the Army Air Corps and flew on B-29s. He never talked to me about the war, but my mom used to tell me that Ken found out after the war that, while on bombing missions in the Far East, he'd flown right over one of the places where my uncle Ted was imprisoned. Ken had an important job; he worked on the Norden bombsight for his bomber group. I learned later that the Norden was a top-secret project, which explains why when he'd come to our house on Kennan Street in Santa Cruz, he'd arrive in an army jeep with a driver and a guard armed with a rifle. The two soldiers would escort him into the house. It was all very military.

I also remember hearing, seemingly every day, the low rumbling roar of B-29s soaring overhead. I'd look up and see their aluminum airframes shimmering in the sunlight as they flew in formation. They were awesome to behold. And I recall nights where we had to darken the house lights for mandatory blackouts because of possible Japanese air attacks. One thing that also sticks out is a train trip to San Diego my mother and I took to see my dad, who was serving on a Navy sub chaser. I was very young and don't remember a lot about it, but it was one hell of a long trip from Santa Cruz.

After the Japanese surrendered, my uncle was freed in Thailand. He then traveled to Calcutta, India, and from there the Army Air Force flew him to Washington, D.C. I learned later from my parents that he couldn't come home right away because he needed to regain his strength, so he was hospitalized for a few weeks in Bethesda, Maryland.

Finally, on October 3, 1945, he arrived home in Santa Cruz. He'd traveled the last leg of his journey by Greyhound bus. He'd been gone from home for five years. It was a *big* deal when he came back; something like one out of four guys who survived the sinking of the *Houston* didn't survive captivity.

My uncle Ted remained a mild-mannered, soft-spoken guy throughout his life, but to be honest, I don't know if he ever really recovered from the trauma.

Before the war ended, our family grew with the addition of my sister, Roberta, who was born in 1945. We're only two and a half years apart in age, and we were really close as kids. Soon after her birth, my father was discharged from the Navy. Back home, he resumed working at a local nursery. My father loved plants, and he'd continue to work there for decades to come.

Still, my father's real passion was music. He played guitar and harmonica. My mother, too, was a musician. She played saxophone, clarinet, and piano, and for years she gave piano lessons in Santa Cruz. They also played together in a band called the Bob Templeman Quartet, along with a sax player and a drummer.

Music was in a lot of ways the family business. My maternal grandfather, John J. Anderson, and my grandmother Sarah owned John Anderson Music on Walnut Avenue in Santa Cruz. It had three separate departments: pianos, which paid the store's bills, band instruments, and radios and records. My mom, even before I was born, worked there with my grandfather. She ran its band instrument department.

Despite my grandparents' well-established roots in the Santa Cruz community, at some point before I was born my grandfather bought two hundred acres in the rugged, wooded hills of nearby Felton. My grandmother, it turns out, had developed tuberculosis. The doctors thought the clear mountain air would be good for her health, so he built a house up there for her. He'd join her in Felton on weekends. Otherwise he'd spend the workweek living in an apartment above his store. Unfortunately, she succumbed to the disease before I was born.

The Bob Templeman Quartet, circa 1955. Featuring my mother on piano and my father on guitar, my parents' group played lots of community events in Santa Cruz during the fifties. GREG RENOFF COLLECTION.

Around 1946 or so, my grandfather gifted my parents something like twenty acres of his Felton holdings, so my parents decided to build a house near his and move from Keenan Street. I was about five years old.

I can remember when our new home was under construction. One of my other uncles worked for a cement plant and helped build a well on the property. One day, he and his men placed dynamite and blasting caps in the ground. We ducked down behind his truck as his workers touched a wire to a battery. *Boom!* All these tree stumps and dirt went flying in the air. Hearing that explosion and seeing the blast was great fun for me as a kid. The house itself was small, but it was solid, considering that it was a cabin built by hand in the middle of the woods.

Moving up there was a big adjustment after living in Santa Cruz. In town, you had paved roads, sidewalks, stores, telephones, and lots of neighbors. Now my family was living in the woods with my grandfather. Still, we weren't alone. There was another family, the Hoopers, living on the same hill. They were great people. Mrs. Hooper was a woman of letters, a Berkeley graduate who taught at the Felton School we attended. She had four children, two of whom were the same ages as me and my sister. We spent a lot of time with the Hooper clan.

In some senses, life in the woods was idyllic. My grandfather's land felt endless to me. As a kid, two hundred acres seemed like two thousand. We laid out our own baseball diamond in a clearing. There was a wonderful swimming hole. The property had three redwood groves, which were beautiful. We'd walk through them on the soft carpet of needles. The trees were so dense that when sunlight dappled the forest floor it looked like an Impressionist painting. There were verdant clusters of pines, some standing on hills that overlooked the town of Felton. When you stood at the highest points on the property you could see all the way to Santa Cruz, some seven or so miles away. I tell people that Roberta and I grew up, scrappy and shoeless, in the trees. This gorgeous landscape was our playground.

My sister and I had some great, albeit mischievous, adventures. We'd leave our property and go onto the grounds of a nearby Christian camp. We'd wade into the San Lorenzo River and swim to the camp's dock, upturning the rowboats the campers used. We'd trespass on land owned by the rich people who kept vacation retreats near our property and swim in their pools.

One of our other favorite pastimes was traveling along what we called the "Trail through the Trees." It was an elevated path consisting of thick vines and limbs that must have been twenty or so feet above the ground. It was a great way to navigate the dense forest.

We'd use the trail to sneak onto a nearby orchard. One sundrenched afternoon Roberta and I were sitting in the shade, eating some juicy apples we'd picked off the trees. All of a sudden we heard these whizzing noises. We looked around and saw dust kicking up from the ground and bark flying off the trees, right near our heads. The orchard's owner was shooting at us! We scrambled away, racing along the trail back to our house. We grabbed our .22 rifles and went back to the orchard. We flopped on our bellies, and crawled forward until we spotted the property owner. It's hard to believe when I think back on it, but Roberta and I opened fire on him. He shot back, and we exchanged gunfire for a minute or so. It's a miracle, honestly, that no one was injured or killed. But I was given my first .22 for my tenth birthday and wasn't afraid to use it.

Learning to shoot was part of life in the woods. We encountered lots of dangerous, scary animals, so keeping guns handy was just a normal thing to us. There were rattlesnakes all over the place. I watched one day as my mother blew the head off of one from a good distance with her .22. There was a population of rats on the hill that we wanted to keep out of the houses and our gardens. We'd send our dogs to dig into the nests they built in the twisted roots of big trees. When the rats scrambled out of their holes and up the trunks to get away from the snarling dogs, we'd shoot the rodents.

Still, there was an animal that scared me more than snakes and rats. There were mountain lions in the woods. During the night, they screamed. Their cries sounded just like a woman in anguish. It was very unnerving.

I was crawling through the underbrush on the way to a place we called "Cave Mountain" when I came face to face with one. I was so scared I could barely breathe. It was moth-eaten and scroungy, and it looked just as frightened as me. I froze, paralyzed, immediately aware that I didn't have my two dogs or my rifle with me for protection. After what seemed like an eternity, it turned tail and bounded off through the woods. I sat in the same spot, shaking and terrified, for a long time.

Something else up there scared the hell out of my sister and me. When my grandfather died in 1953, he left a house on his property to one of my mother's uncles, a big mean alcoholic who stayed drunk most days. The scenes that went down when he was drinking were horrible. He'd fist-fight with his friends or other relatives who drank like he did. At family gatherings, he bellowed out drunken refrains of "San Antonio Rose" or "On the Road to Mandalay." You never knew what he was going to do next. I learned to walk on eggshells around him to avoid attracting his attention. It was a nightmare.

To their credit, my parents never drank. I think that may have had something to do with my youthful distaste for alcohol, an aversion that served me well — while it lasted.

Beyond the animals and my alcoholic uncle, there were other downsides to living in the mountains. For example, if it rained hard when we went to town, maybe for groceries, we'd sometimes come back to find the gravel-and-dirt road up the hill washed out. My dad would park the car on the road. Leaving us in the car, he'd trudge up the hill to retrieve another car, which was parked near our house. He'd drive down the muddy road to the washout. We'd take our groceries out of the one car, splash across the wash, put them in the other car, and go back up to the house. On a couple of other occasions, the Hooper family's well went dry, so my father would get in his truck and go and get a big tank of water for them. Rural living back then wasn't as romantic as in most people might imagine.

Still, my sister and I did spend a lot of time in town. I started attending the Felton School in the late 1940s. While in elementary school I found that I had a couple of talents. I came in first at the school's tap dancing contests. I also excelled at sprinting, winning cash prizes at school events when there were races. As a result, my family and the Hoopers nicknamed me "Speed."

Academically, I was a good student who became an avid reader at a young age. My mom was a big influence on me in that area. The first novel I read was *Wuthering Heights*. The second was *The Great Gatsby*. In fact, I was Gatsby for Halloween in the fifth grade. I had my mom make me a white suit. It looked great, but the problem was when I wore it to school that year, none of the other kids knew what a Gatsby was!

I also got into poetry as a child. My mom introduced me to Shelley, Keats, and Byron. I read a lot of John Masefield, e.e. cummings, and T.S. Eliot. To this day, I write poetry just to get my own thoughts on paper.

Upon reflection, I think I became so interested in books because of the things that came with my uncle's drinking. Reading gave me an escape from the craziness that went on when he was deep in the bottle.

My one uncle aside, I had a lot of good family role models. I greatly admired my uncles Ted and Ken and spent a lot of time with them in the years right after the war. They remained in the service, and what I remember best from their visits to our home when I was young is that they always had brand-new cars. That made me think the military took good care of these guys, because they seemed financially comfortable. Meanwhile, my parents always bought used cars. As a kid who was becoming car-crazy, I loved riding in my uncles' shiny new Oldsmobiles and Pontiacs. Their influence helped start my lifelong love affair with chrome, steel, and leather.

My grandfather, too, was a big inspiration. I respected him for many reasons, but I was especially impressed by the fact that he was a self-made businessman. In the early 1920s, he went to work for a Santa Cruz music and radio retailer called Howe's Music. He saved up his money until he could afford to purchase a Baldwin piano franchise. Then he could buy them direct from that company and sell them for a good markup. In 1939, he opened his first store, John Anderson Music, in Santa Cruz.

His store's record department became the place where I was first exposed to Black music. My grandfather had this selection of older records from Okeh Records, which in the early part of the century was a big label for Black artists. He encouraged me to play these "race records" on the store's phonograph. To be honest, I didn't even know who most of these artists were, but not many people in Santa Cruz other than my grandfather did either. At the time the town was very white, so nobody bought these records. When he saw I liked this kind of music, he'd save the records that didn't sell and give them to me. They were 78s. Lots of them were singles, but some were albums. One song I especially remember hearing at that time was Louis Jordan's "Caldonia." It's a jump blues tune that came out in 1945 on Decca. (It's got a killer piano groove.) So my grandfather's the person who turned me onto Black music.

At the same time he was expanding my musical horizons, he was going to pains to teach me about the history of race and popular music. He'd tell me about racist themes embedded in other songs that had been part of American culture when he was a kid — minstrel music. He explained that those songs mocked Black people and parodied their music. That's a big reason why he encouraged me to look at and listen to the Okeh records he stocked. They were all Black artists, not whites imitating Blacks for laughs.

His bigger goal, though, was to teach me the truth about race. He'd tell me that Black people and white people were all of one race — the human race. He hated prejudice of any kind. In fact, I remember my grandfather threw a customer out of his store after the man made an anti-Semitic remark about another Santa Cruz merchant. His lessons about the ugliness of religious or racial hatred stuck with me forever.

Because he had an apartment above the store, I spent a lot of one-on-one time with him. I'd walk over to his store after school and listen to music or walk upstairs and hang out in his residence. After he passed away, my parents inherited the store. My mom ran it after he died. I missed him deeply, but because the business stayed in the family, I continued to spend a lot of time there in the years that followed.

Musical instruments, like records, grabbed my interest. My grandfather was good on a lot of instruments, especially piano. Since my mother was an accomplished pianist, she thought I should learn to play as well. So I took lessons from a well-known local teacher named Loren Cox. He had played in bands around Santa Cruz. I used to go to his studio to take lessons. I hated them: honestly, I don't think he taught me much beyond the basics.

Luckily, I had another person in my life who, unlike my piano teacher, made playing music seem fun. Like my uncle Ken, my mother's nephew — my cousin — Eddie Root was in the Air Force. He and my mother were close, so much so that I called him my uncle. Everything he did seemed cool to me, and so he became my mentor and role model. He hated cigarettes, so naturally I never smoked, and never have. He used to take me to China Ladder Beach. We'd descend the steep cliff that overlooked the Pacific to catch fish and swim in the surf. Because he had been in the Air Force, I had ambitions as a kid to be a military pilot. He took me to the baseball diamond and taught me how to field a grounder. He played high school football, so I gravitated to the sport even though I wasn't big in stature.

But most importantly, Eddie inspired me to get into jazz. My cousins, my mom, and my dad were all fans as well, but once Eddie started teaching me about jazz I embraced it. He played trumpet, a fact that immediately made it a much cooler instrument than piano in my young mind. In fact, sometimes he sat in with my parents' band, the Bob Templeman Quartet.

Still, it seems fitting that my mom, my dad, an aunt, and Eddie took me to see the Chet Baker Quartet, headed by the legendary jazz trumpeter, on July 21, 1954, at the Santa Cruz Civic

Auditorium. This was my first jazz concert. I remember we sat in the cheap seats at the back of the big auditorium, and by the time the house lights went down, it was obvious that most of the tickets hadn't been sold. The small crowd was comprised of jazz aficionados and a surprisingly large number of young women. I now know that the handsome Baker was kind of like a screen idol among his female fans.

Since we were in the back, it was hard for me to see. But the music carried clearly to the back of the hall. Along with Baker's unbelievable playing, the thing that stood out to me was Russ Freeman's gorgeous piano. The Baker recordings that I had heard to that point were on records by the Gerry Mulligan Quartet. That group didn't have any piano or guitar. On this night, with Freeman on piano, Baker played over chords, giving his music a more intricate sound than recordings that featured Mulligan and Baker playing only with a bassist and drummer.

This experience stuck with me. Apart from my amazement at the way all of his young female fans swooned at his every move, Baker's tone, cool and airy, really got under my skin. I immediately started searching for the "Bernie's Tune" single by the Gerry Mulligan Quartet, which featured Baker. Before I found that record, my parents got me my first horn, a Conn Connstellation. I'd take it to my grandfather's record store, where I listened to Baker recordings, along with those by trumpeters Harry James and Rafael Méndez. I'd play along to these records, trying to copy their melodious lines. I was becoming obsessed with the trumpet.

When I started camping out at the music store's instrument department with my horn, I met jazz cats who came in to buy reeds, sheet music, or guitar strings. I learned a lot from listening to them talk and trying out different instruments. John Anderson Music was the great place to soak up the lingo, the look, and the culture of jazz from working musicians.

Before long, my trumpet practice began to pay off. In early 1955, when I was in seventh grade, I performed a solo in a Veterans of Foreign Wars talent show at the Santa Cruz Civic Auditorium. I didn't win in my category, but it was a good experience to play in front of a large crowd in a big hall. Soon after, I played in a trio with Loren Cox at a Chamber of Commerce dinner. Also, when I was in eighth grade, my high school band teacher encouraged me to accompany him on piano at a Kiwanis dinner or two. I played a song by Méndez, and the ragtime standard "The Twelfth Street Rag." We also played Pérez Prado's "Cherry Pink and Apple Blossom White," which was a big hit around that time. It has a little dip in it that is hard to do for some horn players, but I didn't find the song particularly difficult to play. It just seemed like it was to the audience and my teacher. I was becoming a performer.

Eddie, God bless him, kept taking me to concerts. I saw pianist Stan Kenton and his orchestra a number of times, most notably at Fort Ord on Monterey Bay in the late spring of 1955. Kenton became a *huge* influence on me. During these years his band featured monster players like trumpeter Maynard Ferguson, trombonist Kent Larsen, bassist Eddie Safranski, guitarist Sal Salvador, and drummer Stan Levey. I particularly loved his records with the trumpeter brothers Pete and Conte Candoli. His arrangements were always innovative, and his use of percussion, too, would have a major impact on me. I played the hell out of his version of "The Peanut Vendor." It's brimming with timbales, claves, and maracas, and helped make me a percussion freak as a producer.

Eddie also took me to shows in Carmel-by-the-Sea that summer. That town was so, so cool. It was a short drive from Santa Cruz. We'd get there in the afternoon and walk the downtown streets. Back then it was just a little arts community with almost no tourist trade. There were all these funky little shops, including some great hi-fi equipment places.

Two shows I saw with Eddie in Carmel-by-the-Sea particularly stand out in my mind. In June, we went to see the Dave Brubeck Quartet at the Sunset Auditorium. The support act for Brubeck was Mort Sahl, a pioneer in stand-up comedy. My thirteen-year-old mind grasped almost nothing he discussed. But since the crowd seemed to know the appropriate times to chuckle, laugh, and guffaw, I assumed I was watching a sophisticated show with a literate bunch of people.

When Brubeck came on, though, the sound off the stage exploded like an atomic bomb. Brubeck hummed along to all of his piano solos, and his band was unbelievably tight.

Over the years that followed, I'd see Brubeck a few more times. At a subsequent performance, Eddie took me to the stage entrance so I could meet Brubeck and his drummer Joe Morello. I don't remember what I said to them, but I was thrilled beyond belief to shake their hands.

Brubeck's playing, in particular, made piano cool to me and pushed me to take the instrument more seriously. After getting the sheet music from the music store, I learned to play the Brubeck classic "The Duke" the way he performed it on *Jazz: Red Hot and Cool*. It was the first piano piece I ever played from reading sheet music.

What also stuck with me from the first time I saw Brubeck was how hip all of the guys in his band dressed. At the time, most music-crazy guys my age tried to dress like Elvis. They wore jeans or blue pants with thin suede belts and regular dress shoes with laces. Over time I'd change my own style to have a different vibe. Because Brubeck wore glasses, I went to an optometrist and had him make me some horn-rim glasses with non-prescription glass in them. I'd wear them with Ivy League shirts, olive drab army sweaters with khaki pants, and penny loafers in order to stand out from the crowd. When you grow up in a rustic setting like I did, you yearn to become a dazzling urbanite. Kids my age thought I was a little strange, but I loved jazz, and they had no idea about jazz culture and music. I read the jazz critic Ralph J. Gleason's columns in the *San Francisco Chronicle*, a habit I'd maintain in the years that followed. My peers didn't have any interest in the stuff he wrote about. They were too busy listening to white pop music.

That year, 1955, ended in disastrous fashion for the city of Santa Cruz. In the days before Christmas it rained steadily for something like a week. The San Lorenzo River rose higher and higher. I joined in with everyone else to fill sandbags in an effort to hold back the encroaching water, but it was all for naught. On December 22, the river overflowed and flooded downtown. A few people died and the destruction was horrible. I vividly remember seeing cars drifting, like logs in a river, along Pacific Avenue. When the water finally receded and we could get back into the music store, there was an ugly brown watermark on the walls at least four feet high. The pianos were washed around the showroom, waterlogged and ruined. That damp, muddy river smell, even after the cleanup, seemed never to go away. The flood of 1955 was a nightmarish experience for everyone who lived through it.

When I was about thirteen, I got my first real job. I worked at a dairy farm owned by the Scaroni family. The farm was operated by the three Scaroni brothers, Bill, Arnold, and Johnny, and their sister Katie, who'd inherited the property from their parents. Their property stood on some hilly oceanfront property about eight miles north of Santa Cruz. It was a rite of passage in my family to work there, because all of my cousins, and even my uncle Eddie, had done the same. I worked there over the next two or three summers. Because the property was a good distance from my home, I lived on the farm during the summer.

My workday began at six in the morning. The three brothers had already been at it since five, milking the cows. We'd all then sit down to breakfast, which Katie prepared. Her cooking was incredible. She'd serve us eggs fried in butter, thick slices of bacon, toast, and fried potatoes.

After we ate, my job was to catch and hitch the team of draft horses. One of them was named Punch, I remember. It was a harder task than you'd think — they didn't come when you called their names. I had to lure them with carrots and then hook them up to a hay wagon.

Then all of us would get on this wagon. We'd cross Highway 1, go way up in the hills, above the ocean, and they would pitch this hay onto the wagon. Arnold was blind but could throw hay with a pitchfork into the wagon bed in an amazingly accurate way. Once the wagon was full, I'd drive the team back down to the barn with the load of hay. After arriving at the barn, they'd put the hay up while I unhitched the horses from the wagon and walked behind them, driving them into the paddock. It wasn't very glamorous work, but I loved it.

Lunch was next. It was a full meal with Swiss steak, or another meat dish, with potatoes. We'd then hitch up the wagon again and head back into the fields for another load of hay. We'd head back, unload again, and ride over the fields one final time. Before we'd get to work pitching hay again, everyone would take a siesta. We'd lie down and put our hats over our faces. Then we'd do another run and that would be it. The evening meal was light.

Over time I became buddies with Bill. He was a bit of a curmudgeon, but I liked him. He had a girlfriend named Lena who worked at a bar called the Laguna. After work, he often took me along to this place. I'd sit there and hear the latest accounts of the knife fights among the town's community of Filipino fieldworkers or some drunken incidents from the previous evening. He'd then drive us back to the ranch.

On the days I didn't go to the Laguna I had free time before bedtime to wander their huge, beautiful oceanfront property. It was a half-mile of rocky beach and towering cliffs. At the time

I didn't think much about it, but they'd built their ranch house without a view because in those days, a family wanted to be protected from the ocean storms. In later years Californians rarely thought in such practical terms when they owned property right on the Pacific.

There was little that got in the way of the daily routine on the farm, which, like all agricultural work, is very regimented. I remember, however, one day that we did deviate from the day's schedule. We heard that a rampaging escaped bull had slammed into a pickup truck on the property, rolling it onto its side. We all took a break that day to go over and see this dented, upended truck.

A major event in my young life, which certainly upended our workday routine, came when I got into a brawl with another farm worker named Sonny Landino. It was the most ferocious fistfight of my life. He was huge, probably twice my size. But once we started scrapping I fought him like a crazed terrier. We tore at each other for some time, but at the moment the Scaroni brothers broke it up, I was getting the best of him. I had him in a chokehold and was punching him in the face.

The truth of the matter is that I was lucky to have gotten the upper hand, but to the brothers, it was a clear knockout. They loved to tell people about this fight, and the tale got taller every time they told another neighbor. For years they'd bring it up. It became the biggest story on the ranch since the bull knocked over the pickup.

Once fall rolled around, I'd be back at home and going to school. Since I couldn't spend every afternoon camped out at my grandfather's store spinning records, I started listening to the radio more avidly. Although we lived some seventy or so miles south of Oakland, at night I could pick up the signal from an AM radio station called KWBR. I'd hear all of these soulful R&B songs — things you wouldn't normally hear on pop radio. I'd write down the names of the tunes I liked, or just try to remember them. Sometimes I could buy the records at the store, but since there wasn't any demand for R&B records in Santa Cruz, I didn't always find what I was looking for.

There were two songs that I had no trouble remembering. One was "Try Me" by James Brown. That song hit me like a sledgehammer. I couldn't believe how great it was. The second was "Fever" by Little Willie John; that one really resonated with me too. The latter became a huge hit in 1956, the same year I started attending San Lorenzo Valley High School. Without a doubt, my enthusiasm for the R&B hits of the day came easily since my grandfather had exposed me to the music of Black artists from earlier decades.

Around the same time, the movie *Blackboard Jungle* became a sensation. I loved the Bill Haley & His Comets hit "Rock Around the Clock" that appeared in it. I started paying more attention to the hit charts and I learned to love pop music, especially since the ubiquitous love themes in the lyrics reminded me of whichever girl I had a crush on at the time. All of this acted to derail my jazz obsession a bit, but if you'd asked me about my musical identity in 1956, I'd still have told you I was a jazz player.

By 1957, I'd started working part-time as a copy boy at the *Santa Cruz Sentinel*. I got the job through my friends Fred and Bruce McPherson. Their family owned the newspaper.

Early the next year, Fred, Bruce, and I came up with the idea to save money so we could go to Hawaii to surf. A few months later we packed up our boards and our trunks and went over on a prop plane, a DC-6B. It was a thirteen-hour flight from Oakland to Honolulu. We stayed for a week or so and had a great time. Along with riding our boards, we body-surfed Makapu'u Point. We returned on a Constellation, a faster plane, which made the return trip shorter.

On the beach in Hawaii, 1958. TED TEMPLEMAN COLLECTION.

My horizons were expanding.

Chapter 2

JAZZBO

I've always kept myself busy. That was no different in high school. To be honest, I spread myself a little too thin during those years. I was working at John Anderson Music and then at the *Santa Cruz Sentinel*. I also occasionally worked with my father at the nursery — which I hated.

Along with trying to keep up academically, I was playing three sports at San Lorenzo Valley High, so I could earn my varsity letters. My days of being the fastest kid in school had come and gone, so even though I made varsity track, I didn't do the team much good. I wasn't very good at basketball either and spent a lot of time sitting on the bench. In fact, during games, I used to quietly hope that the score remained close or even that we'd fall behind so I wouldn't have to play.

Football, however, was another story. Even though I wasn't a big kid, I played defensive guard. To get ready for football season, a friend and I would smash our forearms into the wooden doors of the barn on the Felton property. We'd walk away bruised, but it got us ready for practice.

Nonetheless, I wasn't prepared to utterly sacrifice my body for the sport. In those days, face masks on football helmets only had one horizontal bar, so it was common to get poked in the eye or smacked in the chin. I had a special mouthpiece made, because I played trumpet for the high school band and I didn't want to lose my teeth on the bottom of some pile. Still, I wasn't afraid to mix it up, and I loved the physicality of the sport.

Eventually, I made varsity in football. I wasn't good enough to be a starter, so I used to sub in for other players. I remember the very first time I got to play in a varsity game, our team was losing a close one to King City High School. When I got in the huddle, I was nervous. I heard the play call from our captain. I stuck my hand in the dirt and waited for the snap. When the play started, my mind went blank. I'd forgotten my assignment. Everyone was in motion, blocking and running, and I didn't know what I was supposed to do. Suddenly, the ball carrier fumbled. I saw the football tumbling and bouncing right by my feet. I jumped on it, recovering the fumble. My teammates all embraced me. It was a total accident, but still it felt great to be the hero at that moment.

By the time I graduated, I had lettered in the three sports. At the time, that seemed like I'd accomplished an important goal. Music, though, was my main priority. Still, you wouldn't have known it from my stint in high school band. I was good enough to be first chair trumpet, but because I kept screwing around at band practice, I got demoted to second chair, or even third chair. I got thrown out and then reinstated in the band three times. I played in the marching band too, which you had to do if you were a member of the concert band. I thought it was all a big drag.

I goofed off a lot at band practices because I was much more interested in jazz and R&B. I went to watch jazz shows in San Francisco or Carmel whenever possible and remained glued to my radio to hear the latest pop hits. I'd also get my fill of music by picking up afternoon and weekend shifts at my parents' music store. I didn't like selling reeds, sheet music, and guitar strings, but it gave me time to start messing around on the drums, which I really took to, thanks to my love for Joe Morello of the Dave Brubeck Quartet.

Around 1957, I met a teenager named Cornelius Bumpus at the music store. Corny, as he liked to be called, stood out immediately because he was Black. At the time, Santa Cruz was lily white — his family was just about the only Black family in town. He was a sax player, and he'd come in with his mom. She bought him his first saxophone at the store, and later, he'd come in without her to buy reeds. We started talking and it turned out we both listened to R&B, at night, on Oakland radio. He told me about James Brown and I started telling him about Little Willie John. He also liked jazz. Since we listened to the same stuff, we immediately hit it off and became close friends.

Around that same time I joined, of all things, a group that specialized in Portuguese music called the Johnny Mello Band. It featured Johnny Mello on saxophone, two cousins, Bruce and Gene Bettencourt, on drums and accordion respectively, and me on trumpet. I didn't really enjoy this gig, but the money was good and I already knew from personal experience that playing music, regardless of what kind, was a lot more satisfying than a lot of other jobs.

Most of our appearances were at big community events like weddings and festivals. Sometimes we played parties at the Portuguese Hall in Santa Cruz. I remember that the kitchen there served this great-tasting Portuguese *sopa*. It came in a bowl with linguiça sausage and bread saturated in the broth. We also sometimes played at awards dinners for local fraternal organizations like the Shriners or the Masons.

Most often, though, we gigged a long ways out of town. We'd pile into Johnny Mello's car — he had a brand new '57 Chevy — and ride over the Pacheco Pass on Highway 152 to the San Joaquin Valley so we could perform in places like Gustine, Turlock, and Fresno.

Our sets consisted mostly of standards of the day, interspersed with some ethnic tunes. One we played was "Bate O Pé," a traditional Portuguese dance song. Gene played its bass line and chords on the accordion, while Johnny and I played the song's melodies on the sax and trumpet. When it was all over, we'd squeeze back into Johnny's car and head back to the coast. We'd arrive back in Santa Cruz in the wee hours of the morning. Needless to say, getting up for school the next day wasn't easy and I was exhausted from a schedule that included school, sports, work, and gigging.

Anytime I thought about cutting back on work, I resolved against it, because I always had my eye on things I wanted to buy for myself. I wanted to keep upgrading my hip Ivy League wardrobe. As a life experience, growing up in the woods made for a unique and exciting childhood. But on the other hand, it caused no end of embarrassment to me when I started the social part of life that begins in junior high school. Teenagers can be cruel to each other, and I was looked at as kind of a hick by the cooler kids. So making sure I had the latest fashions was important to me.

My musical interests and ambitions likewise drove my spending. I wanted and purchased a hi-fi system. In addition, I bought good trumpets, a banjo, the right trumpet mouthpieces, and a guitar. (My father got me started on guitar by teaching me chords.) I could get things at wholesale prices from my family's music store, but they were still expensive.

Most of all, though, I wanted a car. In fact, I purchased my first, a Studebaker convertible, around this time. I bought it before I had my license. Since I couldn't drive legally on public roads, I drove it around the Felton property on its dirt roads. My parents weren't worried at all when I did that because I'd first learned to drive when I was about twelve. I'd practiced on my parents' trucks, grinding the gears as I mastered the manual transmission, rumbling along the tree-lined roads.

I had also begun practicing the drums seriously. Even though trumpet was my main instrument and I still considered myself a jazz guy, I really caught the drummer's bug after I heard the propulsive beat on Jerry Lee Lewis's "Whole Lotta Shakin' Goin' On" when it came out in early 1957. It changed my life. It had such soul and such a rock 'n' roll feel. I loved its dynamics; the way it quiets down in the middle and then just builds to a powerful ending. To this day, it still kicks ass.

I started drum lessons at the store to learn how to play properly. But over the course of my first year of playing, like a lot of

My beginnings as a drummer, circa 1955. TED TEMPLEMAN COLLECTION.

musicians, I adapted standard techniques to fit what felt comfortable to me. For example, I found my own way of holding the left stick so I could really slam the snare.

Now at this time, to the best of my knowledge, there were no rock groups in Santa Cruz or anywhere nearby, so I knew I'd have to start my own. Around 1958, I met a pianist named Bill Davis. He was a hell of a good player. We paired up, calling ourselves the Dukes of Rock & Roll. We then added a sax player named Alan Ross, and later a guitarist named Ed Penniman, who played a Fender guitar through a Fender amp. We never found an electric bass player in town, so we went without a bassist. We could've found an upright acoustic bass player, but we never sought one out. We played so loudly that an unamplified bass would've been inaudible over the din.

In the beginning, we didn't have a singer either, but that didn't stop us from playing covers of the rock 'n' roll hits of the day. One of the songs we did — which I loved — is a cult classic, "White Port Lemon Juice," by the Four Deuces.

We started getting gigs too. We played middle school dances, parties, and even managed to get on the bill for a rock show at the Santa Cruz Civic Auditorium. That was a cool night. By this time, our lineup had changed — we had a new guitar player named Don Stewart and had added a vocalist named Bob Cecil.

In early 1959, we got what we thought was going to be a big break for us. I don't remember how this came to happen, but we got invited to appear on a Sacramento TV show. In the end, being on the air amounted to nothing — it didn't get us anywhere.

On the same day we were on the show, the jazz singer Anita O'Day was also going to be on. But for whatever reason her drummer didn't show up at the studio, so I was asked to fill in at the last minute. I was thrilled because, well, it was Anita O'Day and I was a big fan. I loved her *Anita* album — the one where she's on the cover surrounded by foliage. Her version of "No Moon at All" from that record was just phenomenal.

It was all kind of a blur, but what I do remember is that soon after I met her, I realized she was drunk. That made for a really bizarre experience — trying to learn the song before the cameras came on and seeing her in that condition. I guess I did okay, because I got asked to fill in again for her drummer one other time, I think in San Jose. She was toasted again, even worse than she'd been on the TV show in Sacramento.

In June 1960 I graduated high school. Since I was still working at the newspaper and gigging around the area with the Mello band, I enrolled as a part-time student at Cabrillo Junior College in Santa Cruz. While I was there, I met a fellow jazz aficionado, an acoustic bassist named Chris Poehler. We quickly became friends, in no small part because he was one hell of a musician and a jazz purist. I'd go down to his parents' place, which was on the water in nearby Rio del Mar. His mom would make us olive sandwiches and we'd rehearse tunes in the hopes that we could start playing live.

Soon after, I tracked down Corny, who'd also enrolled at Cabrillo. He partnered with us and a drummer whose name I've forgotten, and we formed a jazz quartet. He played tenor sax and I played trumpet. Our instruments blended really well together right from the start. The first song we worked up together was "Bernie's Tune" as performed by the Gerry Mulligan Quartet with Chet Baker. We copied it note for note, including the solos, and even worked out the counterpoint that those guys did. My tone revealed Baker's influence on my playing. It was kind of breathy and soft.

We practiced and got good enough as a unit to where we could start getting gigs. I loved the musical freedom that we had as a quartet. Because we didn't have a piano or guitar player, no one held down the chords. For instance, if you have a piano or a guitar playing an A minor 7, and as a trumpeter or saxophonist, you play "outside" of that chord, it stands out like a sore thumb. You have to stay within the framework of those chords. But if you're playing bebop, and there's no chord playing, you can whack around in there. The two of us, we really had a great time when we performed. I would play with Corny off and on all the way through college.

In August 1962, I met a girl named Kathleen Tone. She was driving around Santa Cruz with her friends and we were introduced to each other. I was thrilled to meet her because she'd caught my eye at football games; she was a cheerleader for a rival high school. Subsequently, I'd go see her at the Santa Cruz Boardwalk, where she worked selling french fries to tourists and locals. Kathi and I would date, on and off, throughout the 1960s.

That fall, I had the chance to go on the trip of a lifetime to Europe with my friend Mike Miller and my sister. At this point, I'd never traveled the continental United States outside of California, so I was very excited for the coming adventures. I was nineteen years old.

My sister, Mike Miller, and I first traveled to Sacramento to link up with Mike's parents. The three of us then rode in the backseat of his parents' Thunderbird. I remember the first night we stayed in Wyoming, the second in Iowa, the third in Ohio, and then we drove all the way to New York City. It was quite a treat to see the country this way, even though we didn't linger anywhere for long. We crossed the continent in three and a half days. Mike's father didn't take it slow, that's for sure.

After we arrived in Manhattan, we checked into the Waldorf Astoria, where we'd stay for the next couple of days. One highlight for me was seeing my first Broadway play, *I Can Get It For You Wholesale*, with Elliott Gould and Barbra Streisand. Her star was just starting to rise — I don't think she'd even made a record yet — but I distinctly remember her singing and acting were great.

On the docks in New York, Roberta, Mike, and I said goodbye to Mike's parents, who'd not be accompanying us overseas. We then boarded the *Queen Mary* and sailed to the UK. If memory serves, my one-way ticket was about $140 for steerage — the cheapest ticket you could buy. One thing that stands out in my mind is that a crew member took us down to see the massive engine room on the ship.

After traveling through England we went to Scotland. I'd started keeping a diary at this point and in one entry, I wrote: "Today, I met an older woman. I talked to her for a while. She's 29 years old." When we were in Edinburgh, we read in the newspaper that Queen Elizabeth II and the Duke of Edinburgh, Prince Philip, planned to visit the city. We convinced an official of a bank along their route to let us stand on the bank's balcony and watch them enter a nearby cathedral. To see the Queen of England up close like that was memorable.

Once we'd spent a week or so in Scotland, the three of us set out to explore Europe more fully. We sailed from Newcastle to Norway. During the journey, the North Sea was so rough that the crew had to strap us into our bunks so we wouldn't tumble onto the floor while we slept. We sailed to Bergen, Norway. On the way into port, we saw the gorgeous fjords along the coast. I loved Norway. In fact I even got to celebrate my twentieth birthday in Bergen.

That October, the Cuban Missile Crisis began. We'd see the newspaper headlines, and even if we couldn't understand every word, it was clear the world was on the brink of nuclear war. It made for an unnerving backdrop to our big adventure.

After we left Norway, we traveled by train through Sweden, Denmark, and Holland. Inspired by Arthur Frommer's popular guidebook *Europe on Five Dollars a Day*, we decided to travel the continent.

In Amsterdam, Mike bought a Volkswagen bus and we started touring Europe. We first headed into France. We went to Paris and stayed in a three-dollar-a-night place near the train station, the Gare du Nord. After Paris, we drove along the coast of northern France, headed toward Spain.

Near the Spanish border we stopped in a lovely French coastal town called Biarritz. It was quaint and scenic and had what the Germans call *gemütlichkeit*, which means this nice, warm feeling.

Here, though, our Europe on the cheap approach to travel caught up to us. When we arrived at our hotel, the innkeepers served us bowls of soup. When I picked up my spoon, I saw the soup had rancid grease floating on it like an oil slick. Since the innkeepers were sitting at the table with us, we had to eat it and smile. It had a horrible taste. Then when we got in our rooms, we discovered they had dirt floors. It was an awful night.

We headed into the Pyrenees and into Spain. We were driving across the mountains, in winter, in a VW bus. We'd struggle to climb these icy roads, and sometimes, the bus slid backwards because of ice and snow, on roads that lacked guardrails in places. It was dangerous, but we were young and fearless.

Once we got out of the mountains, things got a lot less stressful. In Spain, I bought three Ramirez guitars, one for me, one for Kathi, and one for Roberta. We bought the guitars in part so we could sing and play while traveling. Folk music was all the rage then, so we felt inspired by these new acts, like Pete Seeger and Peter, Paul and Mary. Mike Miller and I played guitar together, and my sister, who had a great voice, sang. Other times, I played the banjo and Mike played the guitar. We'd all latched onto a romantic dream inspired by our youth. We thought we could support ourselves like troubadours, busking our way across the continent, and extend our trip indefinitely. I will tell you that we didn't quite do as well, financially, as we'd hoped. We still ended up staying in youth hostels and budget hotels.

Eventually, we traveled through Barcelona before making a beeline for the French Riviera. We stayed in Cannes before driving into Italy. In Rome, our VW got broken into and everything we had in it was stolen. Luckily we kept our instruments in our room, so we didn't lose them.

We then headed south, along the west coast of Italy. Once we got to the Naples province, we hiked up to the crater rim of Mount Vesuvius. We could see the glowing magma. It was amazing. We visited Pompeii. Next came the city of Naples, the island of Capri, and Florence. After a couple days in Venice, we went over the Brenner Pass into Austria and then onto West Germany and traveled to Munich. Once there Roberta and I parted ways with Mike, who headed home. We stayed with our childhood friend, Harriet Hooper, who grew up with us on the hill back in Felton. She'd married an army officer who was a West Point graduate. In fact, he showed me around the army base where he was stationed. I also took a somber tour of the Dachau concentration camp, which is located right outside of Munich.

Before we left West Germany, Roberta and I made two final stops. We went skiing in the Alpine town of Kitzbühel and toured the Neuschwanstein Castle in Bavaria.

After that, we went to Frankfurt for a Lufthansa flight home. We touched down in Greenland to refuel before arriving back in the States, a few months after we'd left. It was quite an adventure.

Chapter 3

FEELIN' GROOVY

One constant during my childhood was the ocean. My friends and I spent as much time as possible in the surf. Although my life got busier as I grew up, I still made a point to get my beach time.

On Friday, July 19, 1963, I body-surfed at Little Wind and Sea, a secluded spot favored by locals. I hung out with friends until after midnight and then drove home along a two-lane blacktop, Graham Hill Road, in my black 1959 Corvette. The road was dark and deserted. Engine humming, the car sliced through the light fog that drifted out of fields and forests. I drove fast but not recklessly. I turned the radio dial, searching for songs.

Almost home, I rounded a curve, headlights banishing darkness. Then I saw it. It was big, a brown animal lying across the road, motionless. I downshifted and braked hard. Its head rose up. It was a horse, now desperately trying to find its footing on the slick asphalt. I turned the wheel. The car slid and fishtailed.

When the collision happened, the horse's awful scream blended with the sickening crunch of the car coming apart.

I wasn't wearing a seat belt. I remember sailing, tumbling through the air, a white and yellow light exploding in my eyes, then darkness.

When I awoke, my head throbbed. Disoriented, I felt branches clawing at my face and arms. Disentangling myself, I shifted my weight, only to feel myself starting to fall. I'd landed in the middle of an oak tree, some ten feet off the ground.

After a couple of minutes, I felt able to lower myself out of the tree. Crouching on my hands and knees, I wondered if I could walk. I could see the glow of the headlights of my wrecked car up a small rise. I'd ended up in a weedy gully alongside the road. I tried to stand, then decided against it. I crawled up the dirt-and-gravel roadbed to the blacktop.

Following the light, I fixed my eyes on my Corvette. It was wedged against a wooden sign for a nearby state park, its fiberglass body cracked and splintered, windshield shattered, engine smoking. Over the ringing in my ears, I could hear the horse's agonized cries. Flesh bloodied and legs broken, it was in its death throes.

I sprawled out on the shoulder, trying to clear the cobwebs. I'm not sure how much time elapsed, but eventually headlights approached. I staggered to my feet, hands on my knees. I mustered the energy to wave. The car slowed almost to a stop, then rapidly accelerated. I couldn't believe it, because I needed help, badly. I sat back down. Soon after, I first felt the pulsing from a slice near my hairline. I touched my cheek and neck. They were sticky. Later I'd realize that that the ghastly sights of the dying horse and my crimson face had spooked the driver.

At least one other car passed me.

Eventually, the California Highway Patrol found me. One of the officers put a rag on my head to staunch the bleeding. The other shot the horse in the head. They then drove me to the hospital and called my parents.

Once the sun came up, I got a better sense of my condition. My left leg was dragging behind me when I walked. After the doctors examined me, they said I had a cerebral contusion, or a "bruise on the brain."

It took me a long time to recover. I had persistent headaches and sleep problems, and my leg healed slowly. Even after my limp disappeared and the headaches got better, I didn't sleep as well as I did before the accident. That's true to this day.

When I was a student at Cabrillo — this was in 1963 — I saw two guys my age playing folk songs around town. One of them, a blond guy, played upright bass while the other, a dark-haired guy, played acoustic guitar. They'd perform at mixers and beach parties. They called themselves the Cabbage Patch Trio even thought they were a duo. Maybe that was supposed to be funny, not sure. They played all of these Kingston Trio songs and, for laughs, some Smothers Brothers tunes. I was impressed with their singing and playing.

The first time I saw them, though, one song they did really got my attention. The guitarist sang "Ya Got Trouble" from *The Music Man*. That film had just come out in theaters and was a huge hit, so everyone knew that song. But almost *nobody* knew all the lyrics. It's not a verse-chorus-verse pop song — memorizing the lyrics was akin to memorizing Lincoln's Gettysburg Address. But he just rattled off every word, singing note-perfect, all while playing acoustic. His performance really blew me away. It was clear these guys weren't just nailing down a bunch of songs from a musician's fake book.

I chatted with them a bit after a gig. The two guys were both named Dick — Scoppettone and Yount. The latter, who played upright bass, looked familiar. He told me that before he'd teamed up with Scoppettone and formed the Cabbage Patch Trio, he'd played guitar for my old friend Cornelius Bumpus's band, Corny & the Corvettes. That's where I'd seen him before.

After the guitarist introduced himself, I learned that his father was James J. Scoppettone, a Santa Cruz municipal judge and a heavy hitter in local politics. I think we also talked about the fact that I'd played drums in the Dukes.

At the time, I was still kind of a jazzbo. To be sure, I played my piano all the time. I played quite a bit of guitar and banjo, dabbled in some folk stuff, and of course had played rock with the Dukes. But I mostly played jazz on my trumpet.

Folk music, though, didn't really set me afire like rock 'n' roll and pop music did. I think that's why I locked in on Scoppettone's performance of "Ya Got Trouble." It was a pop song, albeit straight out of musical theater. But he'd done it so well that it made me think that playing pop music could be challenging and exciting.

Very late in 1963, I got a call from the two of them. They told me they'd traded in their acoustics for electrics and wanted to start a rock band. It turned out we'd all heard the Beatles; the British Invasion was just beginning. I dragged my drums over to Yount's parents' house, and we played as a trio: Yount on bass, me on drums, and "Scap," as we called him, on guitar and lead vocals. We clicked and right then and there formed a group.

Soon after, we added a second guitar player to pair with Scap, Ed James. He was just a kid, maybe sixteen at the time, but loved rock 'n' roll just like the rest of us, so he fit right in. The four of us called ourselves the Tikis.

We rehearsed, built a repertoire of covers, and got ourselves some regular gigs. We played in Palo Alto at a hip eatery called St. Michael's Alley. We played as far away as the Bay Area. We used to go up even farther north, gigging in Mendocino County. We'd load up Yount's station wagon in the afternoon and take Highway 17 north to Ukiah and Clearlake. We'd perform, cram all of our gear back into the car, and drive south. We'd get back in town in the dead of the night.

Getting dressed for an early Tikis gig, 1964 (*from left to right*): me, Ed James, Dick Scoppettone, and Dick Yount.
GREG RENOFF COLLECTION.

We also came up with our own unique stage look. We wore white shirts, skinny ties, and dark blazers, but instead of suit pants, we wore Bermuda shorts that matched our blazers. On our feet, we sported white calf-high socks and penny loafers. It seemed like a good idea at the time.

Nearer to home, we played country club weddings, high school dances, and fraternity parties at Santa Clara University. Probably our highest profile regular gig was at a locally famous venue down on the Santa Cruz Beach Boardwalk called the Cocoanut Grove. It was a dance hall — a big band hotspot as far back as when my parents were teenagers. Benny Goodman and Gene Krupa played there. By the sixties, big band music had run its course so the owner booked rock 'n' roll bands.

As we built a following and bigger circuit of places for us to gig, we started to make good money. I could afford nice gear, new drums. The insurance money from the Corvette, along with my band income, paid for my next car, a Jaguar XK-E.

Playing in the Tikis was electrifying fun, but I had to consider my priorities. In 1964, I could have transferred from Cabrillo, a junior college, to University of California, Santa Barbara, an excellent four-year school. But enrolling there meant moving 250 miles away from Santa Cruz. That would have meant the end of the Tikis for me.

So I decided to make the best of it at Cabrillo so I could stay in the Tikis. I'd exerted minimal academic effort in high school and wanted to make the most of my education going forward, so I didn't sign up for a cupcake schedule. At Cabrillo, I took philosophy, invertebrate and vertebrate zoology, physiology, inorganic and organic chemistry. My senior year in high school I'd read historian William Shirer's *The Rise and Fall of the Third Reich*, and then subsequently I'd visited Dachau during our trip to Europe. In fact, I'd gotten so interested in German history by this time that I took German as my foreign language.

I usually got pretty good grades despite the difficulty of my coursework.

I liked college, but it was hard too, because we were practicing and gigging at night. I'd go to class in the morning, but most nights of the week, my head didn't hit the pillow until just a few hours before sunrise. I was wiped out. But when you're dedicated to music, you can't give it up. It's part of your being.

At the time, our main competition for the plum gigs was Corny & the Corvettes. In some ways, we were neck and neck with them in and around Santa Cruz. In fact, we used to trade off sets at the Grove with them.

But musically, Corny's group was miles ahead of us. Now don't get me wrong. The Tikis were a solid band. We were good at what we did and we had a lot of fans. We played the hits of the day, including lots of Beatles songs, very well.

But Corny & the Corvettes were the kings. They were slick and talented. They played great, moved great, and looked great. Corny sang lead and played sax; the rest of the band included a second sax player, a guitarist, a bassist, and a drummer. And what a drummer! Johnny Craviotto was a *killer*; he'd go on to

Stepping out from behind the drum kit to sing lead for the Tikis while onstage at the Cocoanut Grove in Santa Cruz, September 1964. GREG RENOFF COLLECTION.

We'd have fun onstage by switching instruments on a few tunes. I play bass while Yount sings, James plays guitar, and Scoppettone plays drums at the Cocoanut Grove, January 1965. GREG RENOFF COLLECTION.

Singing lead from behind the drums at the Cocoanut
Grove, January 1965. Starting in 1967, I'd give up my role
as drummer while becoming one of our two lead vocalists, after John Petersen, formerly of the Beau Brummels,
joined Harpers Bizarre. GREG RENOFF COLLECTION.

Doing double duty at the Grove as both drummer and
percussionist, drumstick in one hand and maracas in the
other, January 1965. GREG RENOFF COLLECTION.

play with Neil Young and Moby Grape. They performed James Brown songs and all these R&B hits. They'd pack the Grove's dance floor. Meanwhile, we'd be playing these sappy love songs. In my mind, it wasn't much of a competition.

Along with gigging and practicing, Scap and I started to write songs. He had a great voice and endless ideas. We'd bounce things off each other at my house, sing melodies to each other, and when we came up with things we liked, we made these primitive demos with my reel-to-reel recorder.

As we wrote, I started to study hit songs in a more disciplined fashion. I'd sit with my friends and wear out the grooves on my Motown records. Looking back, I realize now that these were my first efforts to think like a producer. Finding my favorite records became more than just deciding whether I liked a melody or rhythm. I started thinking about percussion, bass sounds, vocal mixes — in other words, how these songs were constructed in the studio before they ended up on vinyl.

The more I studied Motown's records and read about the label, the more I came to understand the importance of Motown's owner, a producer in his own right, Berry Gordy. You didn't need to be the smartest record man around to know that if you're seeing the same producer's name on the label of your favorite hits, that person's doing something right.

He was a fabulous producer. He just knew how to oversee those things and get them right with everyone from Marvin Gaye to the Supremes. When I'd pick up trade papers and read about the label, I'd think about their talent pool, all flowing through Detroit, where Gordy and his staff did their recording, in the basement of a house, incidentally. What a genius. He knew the value of a great song and had an uncanny ear for talent — he just had an instinct for that stuff. He was a natural.

I also became a huge fan of Gordy's songwriting, production, and arrangement team of Lamont Dozier and the brothers Brian and Eddie Holland, Holland–Dozier–Holland. They had all of these huge Motown hits, songs you couldn't get out of your head and seemed to reach out of the speakers and grab you.

One of the first songs that had that effect on me was Mary Wells's 1963 smash, "You Lost the Sweetest Boy." The drumbeat-and-piano intro is the perfect hook, especially when accompanied by an almost gospel background vocal part, courtesy of the Supremes. Then there's the beat. It churns forward, propelled by sax licks and a perfect pairing of tambourine and drums. The other notable feature about this song is its great lyric, one that resonates with anyone who's been part of a love triangle. But like so many other Motown hits about love and longing, the song sounds upbeat even though the lyrics are about heartbreak.

Another Holland–Dozier–Holland song I never got sick of is Martha and the Vandellas' "Heat Wave." This record had a huge impact on me. The piano, drums, and the sax all working together are magic. I loved its up-tempo shuffle groove and its infectious background vocals.

Their work with the Supremes, though, may have been their greatest achievement. That group had something like ten No. 1 hits. "Stop! In the Name of Love" is probably my favorite, but I loved "Back in My Arms Again" too. They were such an incredible act. You've got Diana Ross — she's a singer who always stood out when you were turning the dial in the car — singing with these other girls, Mary Wilson and Florence Ballard, who just supported her masterfully. With these songs, everything from the lyrics to the orchestration engendered such a sense of excitement and fueled my earliest ambitions to try to write hits and produce records.

During these years I'd play these records over and over. As I took them apart in my head, I thought about how Holland–Dozier–Holland built their hits from the ground up, because they were the arrangers as well as the writers. They'd start out with these great basic tracks — drums, bass, guitar, and sax — and then they'd add vibes and strings to sweeten things up. They were masters of getting the right combinations of instruments. The melodies were invariably infectious. And underneath it all, they had these pumping rhythms going at these spot-on tempos. It was like they had an intuitive feel for crafting hits.

In the fall, I think because the Tikis had gotten on the radar of some DJs at San Jose's KLIV radio station, we got hired to open for the Beach Boys at the San Jose Civic. The gig, which happened on October 16, 1964, was a game changer. At that time, the Beach Boys were riding high in the wake of their first No. 1, "I Get Around," and they were in competition with the Beatles for the hearts and minds of teenage rock fans. I remember that *A Hard Day's Night* had just come out that past summer. So to get this gig was a heady achievement for four guys from Santa Cruz. We played a quick set; the crowd liked us. Some girls even screamed and grabbed their heads as we sang.

We stayed backstage after our set so we'd be able to see the Beach Boys from the side of stage. The Beach Boys came out, tuned up, and the audience came apart. Because of our vantage point, we couldn't see the crowd; we could only hear it in full throat. The band came out and just *killed*.

Now at the time, it wasn't too hard to wow a crowd if you had a hit. Over the years, we played with a lot of bands with images and stage shows that outstripped their musicianship by a mile. Sure, the Beach Boys had All-American good looks. But they could *all* sing and play well and their live sound was superb. I remember they all used Fender instruments and amps. Carl Wilson played lead through his Bandmaster. Brian plugged into this incredibly great-sounding Bassman. His sound just filled the room. And Dennis was one hell of a live drummer. He could really slam hard and kept an incredibly even groove. Later on, I found out that he hadn't played on most of their studio output, but as I'd learn, playing in the studio was a whole different deal than playing on stage. In sum, seeing these guys live, absorbing everything from their unsurpassed body of songs to their wonderful live performances, was a life-changing experience for me.

A week later, on the 23rd, we played with the Beach Boys again, a bit outside of San Jose proper, at Foothill College in Los Altos Hills. It was less of a zoo backstage, so we hung around with them a bit in their dressing room before the show. I watched as Brian gathered all the guys up and got them in a circle around him. He was the only one with an instrument in hand; he had his Fender Precision plugged into a little amp. While he played, they sang their most beautiful songs, like "In My Room" and "Surfer Girl," one after another. They'd vocally build the root and the chord. If someone's pitch wavered, Brian spotted it immediately and got him back in tune. He was dialing them in and got them ready to go onstage. It was mind-blowing. Before I witnessed this warmup, I would've said that vocally, the Beach Boys couldn't compete with the Four Freshmen, a vocal-quartet act of the fifties that had been a big influence on the Beach Boys. But after hearing the Beach Boys sing right in front of me, I thought, wow, they are vocally *better* than the Four Freshmen. At the time that was the highest praise I could bestow on a vocal group. And it wasn't lost on me that this was in a cramped dressing room on a college campus. Brian was so on top of it; it just all clicked for me at that moment about how this young guy could write all of these incredible songs and melodies. He was so brilliant and so focused.

By early 1965, we'd committed to trying to get a record deal. We'd written a couple dozen songs to this point. We'd demoed up a few of them in a local studio, including a song I wrote with Scap called "Lost My Love Today." I sang lead on it. That was the first song on this five-song tape we sent out to places like Capitol and RCA. A couple of times we got a letter in the mail from a label, asking us to come down to Los Angeles and audition. In the end, we'd get turned down.

One of those auditions sticks in my mind because it taught me a valuable lesson. We got a call back from Columbia. That label was one of the biggest in America, so we were thrilled. The A&R guy who heard our tape invited us to play for the label at a Los Angeles studio. We came as soon as they'd have us. Now I don't recall which song we started off with, but it wasn't "Lost My Love Today." I was behind the drums, like I always was, and Scap was singing this other song. He was, after all, our default lead singer. We're settling in, starting the final verse of the first song, and the Columbia A&R rep stands up, waves his arm, and stops us dead. He says, "Hey, how come you don't sound like your demo?"

None of us knew what to say.

"You know, 'Lost My Love,' the first song on the tape?"

That hadn't even crossed my mind. He'd probably played the tape, heard the first song, liked it, and wanted more songs like that one. And so they passed on us. After the fact, I realized that one of the things they were attracted to was the *sound* of my voice. It's the same thing as when I listened to a Supremes song. There's a certain familiar hook you're expecting to hear. I'm not comparing my vocal abilities to those amazing ladies. As a vocalist, I'm very limited. What I'm trying to say is that when I sang, I was distinctive and recognizable. Even today, if I sing, I *sound* unique. That's what the Columbia guy had latched onto, and we blew it by not giving him what he was expecting. That was a painful lesson, but an important one for me and my future endeavors.

In February 1965, the Beau Brummels, a brand-new group out of the Bay Area, scored a national hit with "Laugh, Laugh." Every time we turned on Top 40 radio, we'd hear their song. They featured acoustic guitars and harmonica on the track, which to me, with its Beatles drumbeat, sounded like a blend of folk and pop. At the time, it was an innovative sound. Their success gave us a sense of hope for getting a deal, even though we'd gotten nothing but one no after another from record companies.

We saw that they'd signed with a newly formed company,

Autumn Records, out of San Francisco. Because the Beau Brummels had become so huge, we really wanted to be on Autumn. Then we found out that the two main DJs at San Francisco's KYA, "Big Daddy" Tom Donahue and Bobby Mitchell, owned Autumn. Since the two of them had demonstrated they knew how to break a band, their label immediately went to the top of our list. In addition, we figured, rightly or wrongly, that an up-and-coming company might be more receptive to a little band from Santa Cruz than the majors in Los Angeles and New York.

Over the next few months, we sent Autumn our demos. We called Autumn and KYA, leaving Mitchell and Donahue message after message, inquiring when we could audition. Scap and I would drive into San Francisco and drop by, unannounced, at the Autumn office. By that point, Autumn was doing well enough that Donahue and Mitchell had also hired a young, smart, ambitious guy named Carl Scott to help run Autumn's affairs. Scott, who was in the office every day, likely got sick of dealing with us, but we were nothing if not persistent.

In May, Autumn finally agreed to give us a tryout. Some years later, we learned from Carl that Mitchell and Donahue hadn't had some sort of epiphany about our potential. They thought we were an unremarkable band and didn't like our "Beatles on the Beach" image, but our relentlessness had eroded their ability to say no to us.

When we auditioned, Donahue and Scott, who were both heavyset guys, kind of waddled into the room as we tuned up. They sat back, arms crossed, as we played our best songs for them. When we finished, Donahue asked us if we wanted a deal. He didn't have to ask twice!

We were ecstatic. At the time, signing with Autumn was a big deal. The Beau Brummels were on a roll; they now had a second hit single, "Just a Little." Autumn, in addition, had R&B singer Bobby Freeman, best known for his 1958 hit "Do You Want to Dance," on their roster. We learned that Mitchell and Donahue had

Cutting early demos with Tikis, early 1965. These studio sessions — my first — came just before the Tikis signed a deal with Autumn Records.
GREG RENOFF COLLECTION.

a concert production operation as well. With Scott as point person, Autumn put on concerts at the Cow Palace that featured not only the label's own acts, like the Beau Brummels and Freeman, but also the Animals, the Coasters, Roy Orbison, the Temptations, the Shirelles, and the Supremes. Even after Donahue and Mitchell, who would both leave KYA to run their label, went off the airwaves and thus lost their ability to talk up these shows on KYA, these concerts remained very successful.

Around June, Donahue told us that he'd booked a studio session for us at a San Francisco facility called Coast Recorders. This was the same studio where the Beau Brummels and the Kingston Trio had recorded. We'd be making a real record. It felt like we'd arrived.

Autumn's house producer was a musician and Bay Area DJ named Sylvester Stewart, later better known as Sly Stone. His band, the Viscaynes, had a minor hit in San Francisco back in 1961 with "Yellow Moon," thanks to Donahue and Mitchell's many spins of it on air. Soon after they'd started Autumn, they hired Stone to work with their bands.

That paid off. He'd produced Freeman's 1964 smash "C'mon and Swim" and the Beau Brummels' hits "Laugh, Laugh" and "Just a Little."

Whenever I tell people that Sly Stone produced us, I can tell they are envisioning superfly Sly, flamboyant and funky. He was *nothing* like that in 1965. His hair was straightened, a far cry from his trademark Afro. He almost always wore a suit and tie when we were with him. His shoes shone like black mirrors. He was more like a businessman than a musician.

Under Sly's direction, we recorded five originals. The two that Sly picked for the two sides of the single were "If I've Been Dreaming" backed with "Pay Attention to Me."

If you listen to the record today, our Beatles influences are everywhere. On "Dreaming," that's Eddie playing those great licks and that hot little solo. When I hear it, I cringe when my vocal begins. Listening to my own singing voice, for me, is akin to looking in the mirror and seeing an overweight, pimply kid with bad teeth. But I can hear shades of what became our trademark vocal sound with Harpers Bizarre.

One thing I notice about "Dreaming" is that the tempo is faster than we played it live. There are a couple of possibilities as to why it sounds so speedy. Sly might have had the engineer do what was called wrapping the capstan. The studio engineer took a length of tape and wrapped it around the capstan, the spindle that propels the tape through the machine. Adding tape to the capstan increased its diameter and thus the speed by which the tape traveled through the tape recorder. This raised the recording's pitch and tempo. To my ears, it sounds like the track is going faster than how we recorded it.

Of course, Sly might have had us play it faster than we normally did, or I was nervous and set too fast a tempo from behind the drums. Either way, if we'd done it more slowly, it might have been a lot better.

Scoppettone sang lead on "Pay Attention to Me." He's a great singer, though you can hear him straining a bit because he sang it several times before Sly liked his vocal. His voice has a little edge to it. His performance reminds me of Lennon's on "Twist and Shout." I'm certain that at the time, that is exactly what all four of us wanted to hear from him as a vocalist. I remember standing with him in the studio between takes. I was giving him advice, coaching him and encouraging him. I didn't realize it at the time, but by taking on that role, I was producing him.

Catching some rays at the Steamer Lane surf spot near Santa Cruz with Ed James while hitting the books for one of my Santa Clara University courses, spring 1965. GREG RENOFF COLLECTION.

In August, the single came out. KLIV in San Jose, a station that had been an early booster of the Tikis, played "If I've Been Dreaming" on the day of its release. I remember hearing from my family and friends back home after it was broadcast. "We heard you on the radio!" It had Santa Cruz abuzz — some local kids had made a record. Roberta and Kathi told us that everyone was calling KLIV and KMBY in Monterey, requesting it. That was a big deal, because our song got airplay on Top 40 radio stations. We felt like kings.

Even though *Billboard* gave the record a plug, and Mitchell and Donahue encouraged their former colleagues at KYA to play it, our single didn't chart nationally. Still, we'd logged a regional hit.

That summer we spent a lot of time in San Francisco. We'd hang out at Carl's place in Haight-Ashbury. This was about a year before that neighborhood became the epicenter of the Summer of Love, but it had already started to become quite the scene. There were tons of young people, hippies, who'd descended on San Francisco. Everything from the way people dressed to the way they loved was changing, and fast. You could see the culture changing, right before your eyes, week by week.

Drugs, as everyone knows, played a big role in this cultural revolution. I didn't drink at the time and wasn't a big drug guy, but I do remember one night someone showed up at Carl's place with some pot. We smoked it. I didn't feel very different afterwards. Then someone else pulled out a ball of opium. We smoked that too. Initially, I still didn't feel anything.

Then suddenly I started to feel numb, and everything got really strange. Somebody had the terrible idea to put on a Dionne Warwick record called "Don't Make Me Over." The song has this lilting tempo, and under the effects of opium, this three-minute song seemed to last half an hour. I never wanted to hear it again after hearing it while stoned.

Meanwhile, I remained a huge Beatles fan, and on the night of August 31, I took Kathi to see them at the Cow Palace. Our seats gave me a clear view of Ringo's hands while he played. I got to see how he held his sticks and hit his snare — he used lots of rim shots. I learned that without ever seeing him up close before, I had been holding my sticks and hitting my snare in a similar fashion. That was a cool moment for me as a drummer.

The other memorable thing for me was the audience's frenzy. The Beatles had to stop the performance multiple times because of all the girls climbing onto the stage. Once the police got their hands on these girls, they'd drag or carry them offstage. Then one guy who jumped onstage made it all the way to the drum riser. He tapped Ringo on the head. Three cops tackled the guy so hard I figured they'd broken his back. McCartney, who looked shaken, made an announcement between songs. He said, "You have to stop, or we have to go!" In fact, they had to leave the stage for a spell. They returned after order was restored.

By the seventies, I'd become very good friends with George Harrison after he signed a distribution deal for his Dark Horse record label with Warner Bros. Records. His perspective on their tours of the States was eye-opening. He said while they were flattered by the fan hysteria, it had downsides. Because the amplification equipment of the time wasn't particularly powerful, it didn't matter how well they sang or played, because no one could hear it. He also said that the fan enthusiasm was so intense that they were often very scared for their own safety.

Remarkably, Ed, Scap, Yount, and I got to perform at that very same venue just a few weeks later when Mitchell and Donahue put on their "Fall Spectacular." On October 2, we shared the stage with more than a dozen other acts, including stars like the Beau Brummels, Bobby Freeman, the Byrds, Sonny & Cher, and the Lovin' Spoonful.

Playing on this bill really shows how much we benefited from our association with Autumn Records. Sure, we had a record out, but it hadn't done much to transform our fortunes as a band. We were still playing the same places: San Jose, San Francisco, and Santa Cruz, and playing types of gigs we'd played before the record came out — the Grove, college campuses, small clubs, and even wedding receptions. But that night at the Cow Palace, we played our rock 'n' roll for a crowd of 13,000.

Just days after we played the gig at the Cow Palace, we received some unfortunate legal news. An attorney sent us a cease-and-desist letter on behalf of a Tennessee band called the Tikis. The letter laid out the case that this other band had legal possession of the name. Since nobody outside of Tennessee had heard of them, we had no idea there was another working band that had chosen the same appellation. After discussing it with Autumn's attorney, we decided it wasn't worth the money or effort to go to court over the issue, so we changed our name to the Other Tikis. It was kind of a dumb and lazy decision on our part, but I'm guessing we all decided that it made sense to keep the word "Tikis" in our band name even as we *changed* the band name.

In December, we went back into the studio to record another single: "Bye Bye Bye" b/w "Lost My Love Today." This time around, Sly didn't produce us. We started hearing whispers at the time that the label was in financial trouble, so maybe that's why he didn't work with us again. Instead, the label assigned Abe Kesh, later a popular KSAN DJ, to produce the record. That said, he didn't do much in the studio. His name ended up on the record label, but Scoppettone and I produced the sessions.

The results were less than stellar. Scap and I kind of liked "Bye Bye Bye," but hearing it now, it makes me shake my head. We were imitating the Beau Brummels, maybe even more overtly than we'd copped the Beatles on our earlier single. Our Autumn compatriots were all over the radio in 1965, so I understand why we took that tack. I think the chorus is catchy and our harmonies are tight, but the record doesn't hold up fifty years later.

The other very obvious thing is that I had a long way to go in terms of knowing my way around a studio. I didn't know how to use microphones to properly capture sounds or have a vision for how to get a vibrant soundstage on tape. It sounded good at the time, but in light of my future work as a producer, it's a good thing that Scap and I *didn't* get credited as producers.

About a month before our new single came out, Mitchell and Donahue informed us that they were preparing to sell the label. They spared us the details, but it was clear they'd mismanaged the company's finances, betting on hits that didn't materialize. By early March, they were feverishly looking for a buyer for the company's critical assets, meaning the bands Autumn had under contract.

Their saving grace came in the form of Warner Bros. Records. Joe Smith, a former DJ turned Warner A&R man, had his eye on the Bay Area music scene and spearheaded the acquisition, which cost Warner Bros. approximately $15,000 in March 1966. From what I learned later, Smith and his colleagues were understandably underwhelmed by almost every band on Autumn's roster, other than the Beau Brummels.

At almost the exact same time, "Bye Bye Bye," our last release on Autumn, came out. Just like our earlier singles, it saw minimal radio action. Of course, it didn't have a snowball's chance in hell since Autumn's offices were being cleaned out just as it hit record stores.

Another unimpressive chart performance meant there was no guarantee that we'd ever make a record for Warner Bros. But Carl Scott, who'd become our manager, made sure that Warner Bros. didn't act hastily. He argued that the Bunny should re-release "Bye Bye Bye" and give it the promotional push that Autumn had failed to deliver back in March. In May, Warner Bros. did just that. The record still stiffed. We figured, naturally, that we'd be dumped.

When all this was going on in the spring of 1966, I had my head buried in my textbooks. A couple of years back, I'd finished my two-year degree at Cabrillo; I then enrolled at Santa Clara University, where I majored in history. I'd wanted to get a music theory degree there as well, but Santa Clara didn't offer a music major. But I did take tutorials in counterpoint and harmony.

My last semester of college provided a welcome distraction from the uncertainty surrounding the band. To be honest, I suspected we'd reached the end of the line as a recording act, even though we still had a deal with Warner Bros.

I graduated in June. I remember taking off my cap and gown and wondering, *What the fuck am I going to do now?* My grades were pretty good, solid enough to enroll in graduate school or law school. As I mulled that over, I took a couple of summer courses so I could qualify to be an elementary school teacher. Other ideas also ran through my mind. I thought about starting a business, perhaps a music store in Santa Cruz, like my grandfather had done, since my parents had sold off John Anderson Music some years earlier.

When we weren't gigging, I fed my musical obsession by going to concerts. On July 2, I saw Herman's Hermits and the Animals at the San Jose Civic. They were both popular acts, but that night it was no contest. The Animals *kicked* ass and Eric Burdon was *amazing* live. He had such a powerful voice and such a magnetic stage presence — they were a deadly band. They were loud and raucous. Herman's Hermits had no chance.

The next month, Kathi and I got tickets to see the Beatles at Candlestick Park, a show that was billed as the Fab Four's final American performance. I wanted to surprise her with something special, so I finagled a press pass from the Warner Bros. publicity department so we could see them land at the airport. It's hard to believe, considering how tight airport security is these days, but we showed the pass to a guard and he let us drive right onto the tarmac. We parked, waited for a few minutes, and watched their plane land. As it taxied, I drove parallel to it on a service road. Kathi took pictures of their plane. We were close enough to see the Beatles peering out of the windows. John and Paul had cameras and were snapping pictures of the fans and reporters who'd gathered for their arrival. We parked a distance away and watched as John, Paul, George, and Ringo were whisked off the plane and put on a bus to be taken to their hotel.

That night we saw them perform. It was a thrill, of course, to see my musical heroes in concert, but you couldn't hear them at all. The PA system wasn't powerful enough.

Meanwhile, my band's fortunes were changing for the better, even though we didn't know it yet. Back in April, Warner Bros. had just hired a young, largely untested A&R man named Lenny Waronker. Lenny's father, the legendary Simon "Si" Waronker, had started and run a successful label called Liberty Records, so Lenny had grown up dissecting recordings and assessing songs. He'd gotten on Warner Bros. Records' radar after he delivered a demo to the label that executives there deemed worthy of release. Impressed, Mo Ostin, then head of the Warner Bros. subsidiary label Reprise Records, brought him into the Warner fold.

Ostin and Smith then handed Lenny the list of Autumn's recording artists and told him to separate the wheat from the chaff. The bands he liked, he could produce.

When my bandmates and I started meeting with Lenny, I didn't think we'd found our savior. He didn't seem very rock 'n' roll to me. He was a soft-spoken, dark-haired guy, about my age, who wore khakis and shirts with his initials monogrammed on the cuffs. Other times he wore a suit and tie. He drove a custom-made Italian sports car — with a specially installed automatic transmission. That offended my automotive sensibilities.

But he was bright and knowledgeable, and told us he was working on some ideas for us. He said he wanted to do something totally different with our sound. I didn't pick up on this at first, but he thought my voice, which I hated, had a unique quality. And he thought that when Scap and I sang together, our harmonies offered up a musical foundation for our band. In other words, he liked our singing, but he didn't think much of us as instrumentalists or, as we'd discover, as songwriters.

We all naturally responded positively to Lenny's ideas, but as a guy who wanted to play drums in a rock 'n' roll band, I wasn't thrilled with his take on our group.

Around the end of September, Lenny gathered us together again to more specifically discuss his plan.

We came to that meeting well prepared. Scap and I had put long hours into writing and demoing new songs. One that we thought had a lot of radio potential was a Beatles-influenced song called "Mad."

In the meeting, we told Lenny about our new tunes, including "Mad." When we asked if he was ready to hear them, Lenny politely said no.

He had his own blueprint for our success. He told us he'd heard a song on the radio called "The 59th Street Bridge Song (Feelin' Groovy)" by the folk duo Simon & Garfunkel. He had an advance copy of their new album and played the song for us. It was very short, and during the fade, their vocal parts repeated *ba da da da da da da*, like a leaf whirling in the wind. He envisioned an arrangement that featured our harmonies, something reminiscent of the way the Beach Boys stacked their vocals on songs like "Good Vibrations."

I didn't understand this at the time, but Lenny was doing A&R for us. He'd assessed our strengths and weaknesses as a commercial act and found what he considered to be the right song for us.

At this meeting, he told us that he had someone in mind to write an arrangement. It was Leon Russell, a piano player and member of the Wrecking Crew, the group of A-list Los Angeles session musicians who'd performed on dozens and dozens of hits.

He also told us that Russell's Wrecking Crew colleagues would work the session, so we wouldn't play our instruments on the song. In fact, only Scap and I would appear on the recording, because we were the vocalists in Harpers Bizarre.

Naturally, we were excited about the chance to make another record. But if it had been up to me, we would have never selected "Feelin' Groovy." I kept listening to this fingerpicked guitar part and precious vocal arrangement and thinking about the bands I loved. The Beatles. The Animals. Lately, I'd been getting into psychedelic bands like Buffalo Springfield, Moby Grape, and the Daily Flash. "Groovy" was just too cute and plush for my tastes.

Afterwards, Scap and I spoke about the song.

"I hate it, Scap."

"Me too."

So neither of us wanted to do the song, but all four of us had wisely kept our mouths shut while in his office. We got scheduled to go into the studio in late November.

In the meantime, I used my status as a Warner Bros. artist to start hanging around studios in Hollywood like Western Recorders and Sunset Sound. All of this happened before I'd ever sung in a Los Angeles studio, but I was eager to observe and learn about the recording process, especially since the Tikis had never made a great-sounding record. This was the start of my studio addiction.

On October 18, I was reading a magazine in the Western lobby, killing time. The front doors, which faced Sunset, saw occasional traffic. Deliverymen and studio employees filtered in and out, but otherwise I was alone.

Looking up from my reading, I saw him. Wearing a white shirt and dark suit, Frank Sinatra entered. He stood near me, waiting for someone.

I stared. He had a deep tan, like he'd been on vacation, but he didn't appear relaxed.

After a minute he felt my eyes on him.

"Hey kid. How ya doin'?"

"Um, just fine, Mr. Sinatra."

"I just got these new shoes. How do they look?"

I set my eyes on them. They gleamed.

"Ah, they look great."

"Thanks."

Soon after that, Sinatra's aide, Sarge Weiss, walked in from the street as well.

"Okay, I gotta go to work. See ya later, kid."

I stood there, dazed. I was so honored that Sinatra had spoken to me. He was a larger-than-life guy, a towering legend in my mind.

Then I thought: he said *work*. He was here to record.

I left the lobby, cruising hallways until I spotted activity around Western Studio 1. I loitered in the area until I saw Lee Herschberg, an engineer I'd met while hanging around Western.

I pulled him aside, asking if I could watch the session.

A few minutes later I was sitting in the back of the control room by the tape machines. Through the glass, I surveyed the scene in the big room. There was a full orchestra, strings and horns, with a conductor. Brass on one side of the room, strings on the other. There was a drummer, pianist, guitarist, and bassist. The female background vocalists huddled together before filing into the vocal booth. It was a huge session.

In the control room, Sinatra's entourage gathered. Soon after, Mo Ostin, and Sinatra's new wife, the actress Mia Farrow, showed up with some of her friends. Herschberg and producer Jimmy Bowen sat behind the board, getting ready.

Then Sinatra appeared. I saw him out in the studio, talking to the conductor, then behind the microphone.

The room quieted once Bowen said into the talkback, "'That's Life.' Take one."

When I heard him sing, I couldn't believe what was coming out of that guy. His huge, rich voice filled the room. His pitch was amazing. The whole three-hour session, he never *ever* sang off key. It was jaw-dropping.

I looked at the board, watching Lee. I'm thinking, all this music's in the air, and he's got to get it all on tape, in three minutes. When you've got a living legend like Sinatra in the studio, not to mention his wife and the label head, you don't want to miss a note.

The studio musicians also blew my mind. This was an era when everyone who performed in the studio could play. If you couldn't hack it, you didn't get calls from producers to play. Everyone's shared expectation was that every performer in the room would deliver when the red light was lit.

That premise got tested fast. During the first or second time they ran down the song, Sinatra waved his arm and stopped the proceedings. "Wait a second. The brass section's out of tune." The horn players studied their sheet music, and a discussion ensued among Bowen, Sinatra, and the conductor. He was right. There *was* a trumpet out of tune; there'd been an incorrect notation on the sheet music. I'm thinking, there are more than thirty musicians playing, and Sinatra could hear that? Amazing.

Sinatra sang it maybe one more time, and before long he was done and gone. Mia and the rest of the coterie in the control room left with him.

Then Lee and Bowen sat at the console and did a rough mix, mixing the multitrack down to two-track. In my mind I can see Lee's hands gliding from fader to fader as he listened to Bowen's directives. He was doing this incredibly complex dance across the controls, yet he looked no more stressed than if he had been enjoying an ice cream cone on a park bench on a summer day.

After they finished, I quietly thanked Lee, and left.

About three weeks later, I drove to Sausalito to see the hot new folk-rock band Buffalo Springfield. Soon after I met Lenny, we'd talked about them. He'd seen them live, at the Troubadour or the Whisky, during one of their early LA gigs. The band was three

Canadians, guitarist/vocalist Neil Young, bassist Bruce Palmer, and drummer Dewey Martin, and two Americans, guitarist/vocalist Richie Furay and guitarist/vocalist Stephen Stills. He thought they were the best live group he'd ever seen. They had three stupendous lead voices and a three-guitar attack. They took jazzy excursions onstage, improvising with abandon, and yet had written these remarkable pop songs. In fact, Lenny had been so taken by one, "Sit Down, I Think I Love You," that he would decide to cut it with another Autumn Records refugee, the Mojo Men.

Lenny went to Mo and urged him to sign Buffalo Springfield. Mo made an offer, but an Atlantic subsidiary, Atco Records, outbid Warner Bros., and Lenny didn't have enough influence with Mo then to persuade him to up his bid.

That night, at a club called the Ark, I saw them with another hot new band, Moby Grape. The Grape were excellent, no doubt, but the night belonged to Buffalo Springfield. Lenny was dead-on right. The whole band was *so* great, and the songwriting was extraordinary.

Musically, they were phenomenal. Furay played rhythm on a capoed Gibson twelve-string guitar. He held down these really nice chords while Stills played fingerpicked licks on a hollow-bodied Gretsch. Young played the more straight-ahead rock 'n' roll parts on his Gretsch. And their harmonies! They were perfect.

A week later, I went to see them at the Fillmore in San Francisco. Talk about a band that could play — Jesus God almighty, it was inspiring.

On November 17, I went back to Western after hearing that Sinatra had another session scheduled. Sitting in the control room of Studio 1, I focused my attention on Bowen, the producer, because at this point I was still learning about what a producer actually does in the studio. Bowen, like Frank, looked sharp. Instead of a tie, he wore this little cravat around his neck.

They recorded four songs that day. One of them was "Somewhere My Love (Lara's Theme)" from the film *Doctor Zhivago*.

After the first couple of takes of "Somewhere," Frank told the musicians, "Let's take it up a little bit." Frank started snapping his fingers to demonstrate the feel he desired. He thought the current tempo was too sluggish; he wanted it to swing. I was surprised, because they were doing it at a nice tempo, one that sounded good to me.

Meanwhile, he didn't even look at Bowen, much less check with him about the change. My eyes shifted to Bowen, expecting him, as the producer, to want to discuss everything. Instead Bowen just nodded, saying, "Okay, Frank."

Naturally, the quicker pace significantly altered the song's feel. Now, the change certainly didn't wreck things, but I kept thinking it was probably better at the original tempo. When I looked at Bowen's face, I thought that maybe that he was thinking what I was thinking, but Bowen, as far as I could tell, never said anything to Frank.

That's when it hit me: Sinatra pretty much produced himself.

That said, I'd learn later that Bowen was a hitmaker who'd picked landmark tracks like "Strangers in the Night" and "That's Life" for Frank, so he played a crucial role in the making of those albums. But from what I witnessed, Bowen deferred to Frank while recording.

It was a very surprising moment for me as an interested observer. I'm thinking, do big-time producers usually cede authority to their artists? I didn't know, but I also didn't think Bowen was doing Frank any favors. Now maybe Frank was right about the tempo, but to me, it wasn't even about right or wrong. Bowen was letting Frank make the decisions, instead of asserting his authority.

This was one of the first times I thought seriously about becoming a producer. Now at the time, I knew no more than the basics concerning the role of a producer. But I was envisioning myself standing on Bowen's side of the glass, because I knew in my gut that I wasn't truly cut out to be a performer.

As I watched, I thought, somebody should tell Frank — the artist — something other than what he wanted to hear. I had confidence I could do that with an artist in a studio. Maybe it came from my high school football experiences as a small guy who played defensive line. You know you're going to get steam-rolled by the offensive line, but you battle, clawing and fighting, to hold your ground. You have to stand fast in the face of seemingly overwhelming opposition. So if nothing else, I knew I could share my honest opinion. If the artist got mad, they got mad, and if my way's not right, I'll be the first one to say, "I messed up. Let's try it another way."

That said, I understood the dynamic at play in that room. A Sinatra session meant pressure for everyone, because he was such a musical giant, not to mention a professional who was on top of every detail. I'm sure Bowen felt like he had to walk on egg-shells around him. But still, Bowen was producing the record; he should've called the shots.

A week later, Scoppettone and I were in the same room, Western Recorders Studio 1, with Lenny, Lee Herschberg, Leon, guitarist Glen Campbell, and drummer Jim Gordon of the Wrecking Crew, to cut "Feelin' Groovy." (I can't recall who played bass, but it may have been the great Carol Kaye). That morning, Lenny ran down the song's arrangement one last time. Leon, brainstorming with Lenny, had come up with this Baroque-pop treatment. So in the studio that day would also be a woodwind quartet — flute, clarinet, bassoon, and oboe. Russell's idea was to dispense with a strings part, the kind that was all over the radio at the time, in favor of our harmonies. Lenny, who was a huge fan of the Beach Boys, immediately liked this idea. In keeping with the song's clas-sical arrangement, Russell would play harpsichord.

This arrangement would transform our sound as a group. We'd go from a British Invasion–influenced rock band to a soft-pop vocal group.

Scap and I stood back as Lenny and Lee recorded the instrumental tracks. The Wrecking Crew nailed their parts right away. All of them were unbelievably skilled and versatile. It wasn't hard to understand why budget-conscious record companies didn't think twice about using these pros to record instrumental tracks rather than the artists themselves.

When Scap and I sang, it was humbling. We're in a big Hollywood studio, doing these vocal parts, over and over and over again, trying to get it right.

"Take one."

"Take six."

"Take seven."

"Guys, can you come in right now? Let's talk for a few."

We'd talk to Lenny in the control room for a few minutes. We'd gulp a drink of water, trying to clear our throats.

Back out in the studio we'd go.

"Take eight."

Scap and I did something like thirty takes to get all the parts done. I'm sure somewhere in the Warner Bros. archives are tapes of all of these takes, collecting dust. Play them, and you'd hear Lenny stopping me, over and over, saying, "Okay, Ted. Let's do that part again." Now, we'd never done that many takes when we made our records up in San Francisco. As an artist in that situation, you feel like you're messing up. Years later, I'd learn that vocalists might need about seven wrongs in a session before they got a chorus or a bridge right, but at that moment, I'm thinking about how Sinatra had sung pretty much perfectly every time he cut a vocal. It was intimidating and yet an exciting experience.

After Scap and I finally got the job done, I was very relieved.

Mixing followed the next day. And at the end, to make us sound younger, Lenny asked Lee to wrap the capstan. Lenny was well aware of the technique, because Lenny's father's company, Liberty Records, had released the Chipmunks novelty records in the late fifties.

Personally, I hated it, but that was the sound that Lenny was after; he wanted us to sound like a cross between choirboys and the Beach Boys.

I walked out of the studio with mixed feelings. I was just knocked out by Lenny's abilities. He had a plan and he executed it. That didn't mean that he knew every move he was going to make along the way, or that he never made a misstep. He mulled things over sometimes, but he had a handle on how he wanted the record to sound. Most importantly from my perspective, Lenny kept Scoppettone and me feeling like we could get the job done, even when he and I felt Lenny should've thrown us out of the studio.

But if I'm honest, I never thought "Groovy" would get us anywhere. I finished the day thinking that while I was grateful to have participated in a big-time Hollywood recording session, Lenny and Leon's musical approach gave us no chance of charting.

Meanwhile, we had to come up with a new name. Clearly, the Other Tikis was a non-starter, and plus, Warner Bros. wanted us to have a fresh image and clean slate when we hit the market early in 1967.

Everyone around the band came up with ideas. Almost all of them were terrible. I remember one of the suggestions: Tom Donahue said we should call our band the Power Struggle. Then Lenny's secretary's friend came up with the idea for the name Harpers Bizarre — obviously it was a play on the famous fashion magazine's title, but the word bizarre gave it an ironic, unsettling feel.

The funny thing from our perspective as a band was that since "Groovy" was such a radical departure from our Tikis sound, we figured it was better that it come out under the new name, so our old name wouldn't be associated with such an appalling song.

Early draft of the Warner Bros. Records biographical sketches for
Harpers Bizarre, fall 1966. GREG RENOFF COLLECTION.

In the weeks leading up to the release of "Groovy," I remember I was actually more excited to get my hands on the
Buffalo Springfield album than our new single. When I heard
their album, I was shocked. It sounded terrible. The first two
songs on the album, "Go and Say Goodbye" and "Sit Down,
I Think I Love You," had sounded so resonant and full when
I'd heard them performed live. But on the vinyl I could barely
hear any drums. The bass was indistinct. Did they record it in a

cardboard box? I was so disappointed I wanted to throw it out the window. I looked to see where it was recorded: Gold Star — that was Phil Spector's studio, so the studio wasn't the problem. Then I looked at who produced it. My God, Stone and Greene, their managers, had produced it. They didn't have a real producer behind the board, and it sounded like it. I thought, this is a crime.

It was another key moment in my journey to becoming a producer. I'd seen these guys live, heard their magic coming off the stage. They had everything you'd need to make a great album, and the result sounded like garbage. Listening to that muddy mix was like watching a ballerina pirouetting in a fog bank.

In late 1966, the Vietnam War was underway, and the draft had become a harsh reality for military-age men. Because of the head injury I'd sustained during my car wreck, I'd been declared 4-F, or medically not qualified for military service, but Scoppettone had received a 1-A military classification from Selective Service, which made him eligible for conscription. To avoid being drafted, he joined the California National Guard. As a result, he'd have to depart the band for several months, starting in late March, when he'd begin his basic training at Fort Ord.

With Scap headed into the military, it became necessary for me to step out from behind the drums and serve as our vocalist. To be honest, it was for the best when it came to our vocals, because I was never able to adequately sing and play drums at the same time. When I fronted the band, I played a bit of trumpet, and guitar as well. To be sure, I wasn't much of a guitar player. I could mostly strum, but I'd learned a bit of fingerpicking too.

To fill my spot behind the drums, we first hired Bill Schoppe, formerly of the Grass Roots. But just a couple months later, in early 1967, Schoppe left us. I can't recall why he departed, but his replacement was John Petersen of the Beau Brummels. We'd known

John from our days on Autumn. That personal familiarity with him minimized the potential upheaval from our unsettled lineup.

Looking down the road, we decided that when Scap completed his military service, I'd continue to front the band with Scap. So while in his absence we'd be a four-piece, when he returned, we'd become a five-piece band. I hated the idea of permanently relinquishing my role as drummer, but I accepted it, because Scap and I singing together was the foundation of our band's sound. In addition, performing out in front would allow me to more directly interact with our audiences than would be possible if I was stuck singing behind the drums onstage.

At the same time we were sorting out our lineup, Warner Bros. released our single. Not wanting to sink a ton of money into an unproven, mostly unknown band, Warner Bros. undertook some initial, albeit limited, steps to promote us in January 1967. The label had us working in the Bay Area; we played a few gigs with the Mojo Men, whose song "Sit Down" had started to make waves on the radio.

I tried to enjoy performing as much as I could. I loved playing music, and knowing that it was unlikely that "Groovy" would become a hit, I figured I'd be back at home in Santa Cruz before long. So I certainly wasn't walking around picking up *Billboard*, wondering what was going on with our single. In my mind, our best-case scenario involved Lenny giving us another shot by producing a second Harpers Bizarre single.

Then the unexpected started happening. In early February, we got a call from Burbank. "Feeing Groovy" had debuted on the *Billboard* Hot 100 singles chart at No. 88. Now granted, having a song in the upper reaches of the *Billboard* chart didn't mean we had a huge hit, but the song had some significant momentum behind it. The Tikis, of course, had never even sniffed the national charts, so this was an exciting development.

Within days, Lenny called us. He told us the label wanted to capitalize on our newfound chart success by having Harpers

Bizarre return to the studio and record an album. At the time, this was standard operating procedure for record labels, even with their biggest stars. For instance, Sinatra returned to the studio to cut the *Strangers in the Night* album after the title track had become a big hit. Basically, if you had a hit single, labels considered it a worthwhile investment to make an album. He told us we'd start pre-production on our album at the beginning of March and would have the sessions, which would take place in Hollywood, wrapped up before the month was out.

Could I have been more wrong about Lenny's arrangement, and "Groovy" in general?

When pre-production for our album began, I got to see another side of Lenny's abilities. At that time, most producers who had a chance to rush-release an album after a hit single didn't worry about whether the other songs on the album had much merit. They knew the already-proven song — the band's hot single — would be the album's selling point. So they'd pack the rest of the album with throwaway songs — filler — oftentimes tunes that they owned the publishing for, thereby lining their own pockets.

But Lenny did something different. To give our debut some substance, he gathered together a handful of talented songwriters, all connected to Warner Bros., and asked them to write, arrange, and perform on it. Their talents would be supported by many of the same session players who'd performed on "Groovy."

The first person he tapped for this effort was his childhood friend, songwriter and piano player Randy Newman. Skinny and bespectacled, Randy looked more like an architect than a musician. While he'd penned a few minor hits for other artists, he wasn't a big-time songwriter. Still, Lenny had enormous confidence in his abilities.

On March 8, Scap and I went into United Recording — the sister studio to Western Recorders — with Randy, Lenny, and Lee and started work. (Since Scoppettone and I were the only two members of the band who were to sing on the album, and none of us would play instrumentally on it, Yount, John, and Ed didn't perform on the album at all.) We cut two of Randy's songs: "The Debutante's Ball" and "Happyland." Lenny was right. Randy was one hell of a writer. "Happyland" was a wistful meditation on carefree days at an amusement park; Lenny and Randy came up with the idea to use an accordion on the introduction of the song. For "The Debutante's Ball," Randy wrote us a waltz and paired it with humorous, ironic lyrics that poked fun at WASP culture. Lenny's production made us sound like choirboys, albeit misguided ones who sneak cigarettes and sip beers outside of church.

During our days off, we'd go back north. I'd visit my parents or Kathi in Santa Cruz, and then go hang out at our manager's place in Haight-Ashbury. At a gathering at Carl's, a William Morris agent named Marshall Berle reintroduced me to an actress and singer named Donna Loren. (Carl had first introduced me to her at a Harpers rehearsal some weeks earlier.) Dark-haired, she had a beautiful smile and a vivacious personality. At the time, Donna was a huge star. She'd been a Dr Pepper girl, so she'd been featured in the brand's national ad campaign. She was a regular on TV and in magazines. She appeared on a show called *Shindig* and was a teen magazine cover girl. I remember she had this brand-new cherry-red Corvette, courtesy of Dr Pepper.

When we talked, she told me she liked our hit, so our conversation turned to the topics of rapid fame and the nature of show business. She filled me in about her current career prospects, explaining how she juggled all of her different responsibilities. I was amazed how busy her schedule was from week to week. She had a million different things going on in her life, but I could tell she had kept herself centered. Like Sinatra, she was so proficient and so professional. I was very impressed.

Lenny, it turns out, also thought she was a remarkable person.

In fact, Lenny and Donna started dating soon after I met her, and they'd be married before the year ended.

We were also working with another songwriter and piano player, Van Dyke Parks. A transplanted southerner, Parks had been collaborating with Brian Wilson on the ill-fated Beach Boys SMiLE album. He had also previously worked with Lenny by arranging "Sit Down, I Think I Love You," for the Mojo Men.

Lenny selected a Parks song called "Come to the Sunshine" for us. We'd cut it in a couple of different rooms: Western Studio I and United Recording Studio A on March 13. That was a pretty damn good song, and a perfect choice for us. Our vocals floated above the strings and saxes; this one is an excellent example of the multi-layered harmonies that became our trademark. Scap and I sang take after take, which Lee would later painstakingly blend together in the mix. Van Dyke played piano on the track.

The next day, we went to Sunset Sound Recorders to work with Leon Russell on a couple of his songs, "Raspberry Rug" and "I Can Hear the Darkness." Leon, it turned out, loved to record at Sunset Sound. So that was my first introduction to the facility. I'll never forget, when Leon was recording his piano parts in Studio I, I could hear the "live-ness" of that room; it had this natural ambiance. And when you used Sunset Sound's live echo chamber, it sounded so phenomenally good.

By March 17, we'd finished recording. In the days that followed, I watched Lee and Lenny mixing our album in both stereo and mono. (The album would be released in both formats.) Watching them provided me with an invaluable education. One thing I learned was how important it was for an engineer to support his producer. Lenny might have a sound in his head — the way he wanted a tune to sound. Lenny would be biting his nails, head in his hands, and Lee would help him along. He was so quiet, but such a powerful advocate. He never made Lenny look bad, even if Lenny appeared lost at the moment. He just let Lenny find his way, gently offering a suggestion if Lenny asked for one. Lee's one of the best engineers ever to walk the Earth.

Because the studio only had four tracks, Lee had to bounce (or "ping-pong") multiple instrumental or vocal parts down to a single track of the four he had available, and repeat the procedure across the three remaining tracks. This is the same way the Beach Boys' *Pet Sounds* had been recorded and mixed; Lee had done the same for us on "Groovy." The trick was that this method had to be done judiciously, because bouncing tracks built up a lot of noise and hiss on tape. Lenny teased Lee about it by dubbing him Lee *Hiss*berg. Lee would smile and laugh. So even though these sessions were deadline-sensitive and stressful, we had fun.

As soon as the recording process wrapped, Dick, Ed, John, and I embarked on a short tour of the Midwest with the Beach Boys. At the time, "Groovy" was still climbing on the charts, so interest in our band was sky high.

These shows were a lot of fun, but generated two major bummers. First, Brian Wilson had stopped touring with the band. The five guys — Mike Love, Al Jardine, Bruce Johnston, and Carl and Dennis Wilson — put on excellent performances, but without Brian's voice in the mix, and his leadership of the band, something was missing.

Second, I had two prized guitars stolen at the Kiel Opera House in St. Louis. I had these gorgeous Rickenbacker twelve-string guitars, one red and one blond. At the time, they were scarce; there was a waitlist to purchase them, in fact. So I was thrilled that I'd received them for the tour.

After we finished, I put the guitars on their stands right behind the curtain. From there our stage manager should have secured them in preparation for the load-out. But he left them sitting

Heading to the stage with Ed James and Dick Yount while on tour with the Beach Boys, early 1967. I've got my trumpet in one hand and one of my prized Rickenbacker twelve-string guitars around my neck.

GREG RENOFF COLLECTION.

unattended, and somebody just walked away with them during the set change. I was sick when I discovered they were gone.

In April, "Groovy" peaked at No. 13 on the *Billboard* Hot 100. I've got to credit Warner Bros. here; at almost the exact moment our single had its maximum popularity, our debut album, *Feelin' Groovy*, reached record stores.

We toured to support the album. We went everywhere from Hawaii to England. All of these performances occurred without Scoppettone. We were close friends so I missed his presence on the road, but where I really missed him was on stage. Playing guitar and singing, I had to front the band by myself. The first issue with this arrangement was that I was a mediocre guitar player. I was a drummer and a trumpet player trying to strum my way through our songs.

The other issue was that I wasn't cut out to sing lead. Psychologically, it was tough for me. Your head understands that fans are here to hear you sing because you sang on a hit, but in your heart you know you can't deliver a great vocal performance. I had to stand up there and warble my way through stuff, without my vocal partner. It felt like I was faking it, all of the time.

On the morning of June 5, we flew to New York to perform an unusual gig. It turned out that our cheeky name choice had gotten us a plum booking: we'd appear that same day at the *Harper's Bazaar* Fall Fashion Preview show at the posh Hotel Pierre. We stayed a few blocks away from the Pierre, at the St. Moritz Hotel.

Because of the high-profile nature of the billing, a lot of Warner Bros. executives from the New York offices planned to attend. Lenny flew in from the west coast. Carl, our manager, who traveled with us, would be there too. We'd play two sets, and in between, models would show off the new fall fashions.

That night, things started out well. We shared a dressing room with a gaggle of scantily clad, gorgeous models. We did our first set and got a good response. We went offstage, the magazine's fashion show took place, and then we returned to the stage again.

Soon after we started our second set, the crowd started to thin, and fast. I could see Carl sitting at a table near the stage. He was turning white because all of these Warner Bros. suits had come, expecting to see us, a hot new Warner Bros. act, wow the crowd, and it was evaporating in front of his eyes. Carl, who was a big guy, looked ghastly. I'm thinking, *My God, he's going to have a heart attack*. Then he got up and left too.

When we finished and got changed, I left the dressing room to look for Carl. Lenny and the rest of the executives didn't know where he'd gone. Jesus. Lenny tried to reassure us by observing that the crowd had been comprised of fashion industry buyers and fashion journalists; once they'd seen the designers' new collections, they left. They hadn't come to see us.

Still, that didn't resolve the issue of Carl's whereabouts. We eventually found him wandering around Central Park near the hotel. He was getting drunk. We had to explain to Carl what had happened. He was devastated because the crowd walked out on us.

We stayed in the city for a few more days. In the spirit of our hit single, we did a fashion magazine photo shoot with a female model at the 59th Street Bridge.

That night at our hotel, I smoked a joint or two with some of the guys. We were hanging out, listening to music. Late in the evening, the phone rang. It was Carl. He was talking fast, saying that since it was a warm evening, he'd slept with the window open. When he rolled over in his sleep, he knocked a room service tray off the foot of his bed and out his open window. When a passing couple saw it smash into the sidewalk ten storeys down, they'd used a pay phone to call the cops, thinking that someone in the hotel had tossed the tray in preparation for a death plunge. The cops were in his room, on our floor, now! We all had to leap up, air out the room, and hide our pot, fast.

A few days later, we went to Philadelphia to make our first national TV appearance, on *The Mike Douglas Show*. It was a huge moment for us. We'd lip-sync "Feelin' Groovy" and our new single "Come to the Sunshine," which had just crept into the *Billboard* Top 40. But for me, to have to front the band, do these stupid dance steps, when I can't dance at all, was truly awful. I'm out there miming all by myself, camera on me. At least with Scoppettone at my side, it felt like I had a partner, and that we could get through it together. As a member of Harpers Bizarre I was happy for the success we'd had with our record, but I didn't enjoy my current role in the band.

Sometime in June, Carl conveyed some remarkable news. The label had gotten a call from Mia Farrow, Frank Sinatra's wife.

She, it turned out, was a big fan of Harpers Bizarre and wanted to hire us to play at the party for their first wedding anniversary. I was surprised to learn that she dug our music. I'd of course been in the same room with her when Frank did his sessions at Western, but at the time we didn't have a record out yet and, regardless, we hadn't exchanged more than a polite hello on those nights. Carl told us that the gathering would be held at Chasen's, a landmark eatery in Hollywood, on July 19. The place had a storied history; it was the hangout of Tinseltown royalty like Humphrey Bogart, Lauren Bacall, and the rest of the Rat Pack. You couldn't ask for a better crowd or venue, and we were all honored that she'd chosen us. We didn't hesitate to say yes.

The date of the party was fairly close to when Scoppettone would be finished with his full-time commitment to the army (even after he rejoined the band, he had to fulfill his "one weekend a month" National Guard service for years to come), so I called him at Fort Ord and told him about the Chasen's gig. "You gotta get out for one night, Scap," I said. Unfortunately, the base commander refused to give him leave, even for twelve hours. I felt terrible for him, because we both knew this was a once-in-a-lifetime opportunity.

That night, we were all nervous as hell, even though we'd been on TV and had gigged all over the States. Part of what made it stressful was that Chasen's wasn't really set up for live entertainment. We got dressed in the men's room. Since there was no stage, right before the party started, we did a quick soundcheck, sitting down on the floor of the restaurant, like we were playing a dance at Santa Cruz High School.

Soon after the guests started filing in, we saw Mia and Frank enter; they sat at a table with Yul Brynner, Henry Fonda, and all these heavy hitters. By the time everyone had arrived, there were probably no more than sixty or so guests. It was a relatively intimate gathering.

As soon as we started playing, I glanced at Frank. I'm singing, pondering the fact that I'd heard him sing magnificently in the studio and now he had to listen to me struggle through one tune after another. He's grimacing every time he looks our way. The truth was he didn't give a damn about Harpers Bizarre. He let his wife pick the band, but I knew from talking to Carl that she'd been hopeful that Frank would like our music. He didn't.

It was just an unbelievable night of stars. Usually, when you perform, you'll look at out at the audience, seeing one unfamiliar face after another. In this case, we played for the most famous entertainers in America. Jimmy Stewart was at a table right next to us. He was tapping his foot to the beat, smiling. He just exuded cool. Laurence Harvey was at another table. Gene Kelly was there. George Burns and Steve Allen were walking around. There were cast members from *Peyton Place*, the soap opera that had helped launch Mia's career.

In between songs, the actress Natalie Wood came up and whispered to me, "Will you play 'Elusive Butterfly'?" It had been a big hit for Bob Lind the prior year. She looked radiant. She was so beautiful it made me nervous. I stammered, "Sure, we can play that for you." She smiled and made a couple of other requests. We played them all. I looked over at her a couple of times; she was smiling.

When we finished our first set, Stewart approached us and said he had enjoyed the music. That was a great moment.

A bit later, as I walked through the restaurant, I passed two men chatting over a cocktail. They stopped me and complimented our performance. I said thank you, making small talk, and the whole time I'm trying to place them. They had both been in movies that I'd seen, but I didn't know their names. It was that kind of night.

I walked out into the front of the restaurant. I saw the actor Edward G. Robinson talking to his wife in a quiet corner by the coat-check stand. There was a bit of congestion in the area, so I got to overhear their conversation. He had this sheepish, embarrassed look on his face. "I don't want to dance. I can't dance." His wife was pleading with him to take her on the dance floor. It was a surreal moment. I thought about all of the tough-guy gangster roles he'd played, and there he was, begging his wife not to make him dance.

I went into the kitchen and joined the rest of the guys for our meal. It really hit me at that moment how modest our fame was as compared to the party guests. We had a big hit, but we didn't even get to eat at a table way in the back of Chasen's. We were the hired help.

After we finished eating, I sat on a stool by myself. All of sudden Natalie Wood came into the kitchen. She was holding a glass. She said, "You look like you could use some water." She sat down and we talked. She was so charming and beautiful.

After we did our second set, we were getting ready to leave. Mia came up to us and asked us if we'd do a third set, because the party was still going strong. So we stayed and played longer.

A few weeks later, we all got handwritten thank-you notes from Mia.

Sometime in August, Scoppettone completed his active-duty commitment. He returned to the band in time to participate in the in-progress recording sessions for our second album, which would be called *Anything Goes*. It would be our second album in a year, which was pretty much the contractual norm for successful artists in the sixties.

Lenny's concept for it was for us to pay tribute and update the musical styles of the past century. To bring that spirit to the album, Lenny came up with the idea to have the first track resemble an old-time radio show. We used the Warner Bros. Pictures "Fanfare" music as a prelude, and we had Joe Smith, who'd been a radio personality, imitate a DJ broadcasting in the 1930s.

That track segued into the album's title track — Cole Porter's 1934 show tune, "Anything Goes." Lenny had heard Van Dyke Parks play an arrangement of the song on piano. He loved it, and thought it would be perfect for us.

We cut it at Western. Along with some barrelhouse piano from Van Dyke, it featured a huge orchestra. It was a massive production. On the track, I sang with Van Dyke.

At Lenny's behest, we also did another classic, "Chattanooga Choo Choo." This one was a big-band staple. To my mind, it seemed way out of step with contemporary pop music, but Lenny felt like he had a handle on it. And so we recorded a song made famous by bandleader Glenn Miller back in 1941.

Randy contributed "The Biggest Night of Her Life." Lyrically, it told a story about the sixteenth birthday celebration of a girl named Suzy. Randy garbed her in a white dress and pink shoes, making it all sound very wholesome. If you listen carefully though, you'd begin to suspect that losing her virginity, rather than the party itself, is what made this evening momentous. It fit with Lenny's concept for us — subtle, wry, subversive lyrics sung in a soft-pop style.

This time around, two songs written by Scap and me made the cut. We came up with "Hey, You in the Crowd" while reflecting on our experiences as live performers. "Virginia City" was our tribute to the Gold Rush of the Old West. Scap and I also arranged that one. Lenny gave it a nineteenth-century feel with an accordion, fiddle, and banjo accompaniment.

The album closed with Van Dyke's masterpiece "High Coin." Along with playing piano, Van Dyke worked out all of the multi-layered vocal parts. When we rehearsed, he taught me my parts, and then we sang together in the studio. I remember it was a difficult track for me because it really stretched my limits as a singer. But Lenny did such a good job producing my vocals and getting me through it. The result was a gorgeous, ethereal recording. Along with "Feelin' Groovy," it was a landmark track for Harpers Bizarre.

When we finished recording in October, Lenny, and Lee to a lesser extent, continued to mentor me in the ways of studio recording. Lenny would have me stick around the studio when he and Lee were mixing. In fact, they let me get behind the board and mix. That's how I learned. You'd take a four-track or eight-track recording and mix it down to two-track stereo and mono. I never would have learned all that stuff without their willingness to share their knowledge.

This year was a bit of a blur. When we weren't recording or playing concerts, we'd appear on network television. Later in October, we appeared on NBC's *Kraft Music Hall* with Dick Cavett, Dionne Warwick, and George Burns. The show had a Tin Pan Alley theme, so we were booked to perform "Anything Goes." That was a fun experience because we spent a whole week rehearsing in a Manhattan ballroom with the other stars. I became really good friends with Dionne Warwick. We talked about our families and all of this stuff, but I didn't tell her about the bad experience I'd had when I smoked opium and listened to her hit at Carl's place.

The show came off well and since Scap was back, performing onstage was a lot more tolerable for me. Working with Burns, too, made it a pleasure. After we sang "Anything Goes," he joined us onstage and we did a medley of standards with him — he was so funny and talented.

In November, *Anything Goes* came out. Like our first album, it didn't chart well, running out of steam at No. 76 on the *Billboard* Top LPs chart. In contrast, our singles did quite well. "Chattanooga Choo Choo" and "Anything Goes" hit No. 1 and No. 6, respectively, on the *Billboard* Easy Listening chart. In addition, those two same songs cracked the top fifty on the *Billboard* Hot 100. Lenny had been right once again, especially about recording that Glenn Miller song . . .

In December, Carl Scott got us booked onto a musical comedy television special called *Romp*. In the late sixties, variety specials like this one were a staple of prime-time. The networks would book a wide range of stars, thinking that if you offer something for everyone, everyone in America will watch. That was the idea, anyway. We'd appear with the actors Ryan O'Neal, James Darren, Jimmy Durante, and Barbara Eden. The other musical acts on the show included Liberace and Cream.

The concept for our appearance called for us to share the screen with a small army of bikini-clad beauties, so the director decided to shoot some scenes on a cruise ship in the Bahamas. On a gray, blustery Manhattan day, Scap, Yount, Ed, John, Carl, and I boarded the SS *Oceanic* and sailed for Nassau.

When we left New York City, it had been freezing, and I was sick as a dog. I had a painful sore throat, a terrible cough, and a high fever. I was miserable and wanted nothing more than to climb into my bunk and sleep for a day.

Carl, our manager, saw my condition. Black pill in palm, he said, "Take this right now." I took it, thinking it was an antibiotic.

Enjoying some dinner on our Caribbean cruise, January 1968. While at sea we filmed skits for the *Romp* television special, which also featured Cream. (*from left to right*): Dick Scoppettone, Dick Yount, me, John Petersen, our manager Carl Scott, and Ed James. GREG RENOFF COLLECTION.

An hour later, I started feeling better. Two hours later, I felt cured. I said to Carl, "Whatever you gave me is working. I feel great." He laughed, "That's because I gave you a Black Beauty." It was an amphetamine. I was wired for five days, just so I could go out and shoot the show.

I didn't sleep much, but that worked out okay. While we were still moored in New York Harbor, the girls' handlers from the modeling agency told them not to fraternize with us. As soon as we left port, they were banging on our doors. It was a great trip.

In January, Ed James told us he was leaving the group because he wanted to return to school and finish college. He probably had a clearer view of things than the rest of us, and knew that our time in the spotlight would be short lived. There were no hard feelings among any of us; in fact, Ed would perform on some of our subsequent recordings for Warner Bros.

In February, we got word that we'd been nominated for a Grammy in the category of Best New Artist. The other groups that had gotten the nod were Jefferson Airplane, Bobbie Gentry, the 5th Dimension, and Lana Cantrell. Gentry ended up winning the award, but the nomination was a nice honor.

In 1968, we didn't have a hit on the charts. Without one, we couldn't get booked for long stretches of dates, so we ended up playing a lot of weekend gigs around the country. We'd fly all the time from Los Angeles to different cities to support *Anything Goes*. That wasn't a good trend for the band's popularity. On the other hand, 1967 had been a great year for us, so by early 1968, we'd all started making rock star money.

On March 9, we played a gig in San Diego with the 5th Dimension. The return flight was uneventful until we landed. The plane fishtailed on the runway. Everyone on board, all at once,

Dick Scoppettone and
I harmonize while on
tour, January 1968.
TED TEMPLEMAN
COLLECTION.

stopped breathing until the pilot corrected the skid. Then cheers
erupted in the cabin. That landing was unsettling to say the least.

Because I had business in town, that night I checked into
the Continental Hyatt House on Sunset Boulevard. This hotel is
better known as the infamous "Riot House" after Led Zeppelin
made it their Los Angeles home base.

The day after that scary flight, I popped into Western
Recorders. One of the employees whispered to me that Elvis had
booked an upcoming session. Right then I locked on to the idea
of seeing him record.

After I returned to the Hyatt, I called Lyle Burbridge, an engineer who worked at the studio. We'd become friends after he
worked on one of our albums. Subsequently I got in the habit of
coming to his sessions. I'd pick his brain about how he chose different microphones and pre-amps and how he set his headroom
for different frequencies when he recorded.

I asked him if he'd heard anything about an Elvis session.
"Yep, he's coming in late tomorrow night to do some vocals for

the soundtrack for an MGM movie, *Live a Little, Love a Little*, with producer Billy Strange. They've been working for a few days but tomorrow night after dinner it will just be him, no band members. Do you and Kathi want to come and watch the session?"

I couldn't say yes fast enough.

On the evening of March 11, Kathi and I called a taxi to take us eastbound on Sunset to the studio. While we waited for it on the corner, we saw a block-long caravan of limos rolling along Sunset in the direction we were headed. When we arrived at Western and saw the same limos parked out front, we knew that we'd seen Elvis and his crew going through town.

When Kathi and I got into Western Studio 1, Elvis was standing in the middle of the room, talking with a few people, while Lyle set up a Shure 545 microphone for him. He looked fit and healthy.

Colonel Parker, his manager, hovered nearby, wearing a Hawaiian shirt and chomping on a cigar. Chubby and balding, he struck quite a contrast to the preternaturally handsome Elvis.

I'd been around many superstars at this point, but seeing Elvis like this was surreal. In 1968, two acts possessed a kind of fame that made them seem utterly inaccessible: the Beatles and Elvis. If the former decided to venture out in public, they'd be instantly recognized and quickly mobbed. I'd witnessed that when the Fab Four flew into San Francisco a few years earlier. The girls would've ripped their clothes off if they'd walked beyond the police cordon and rubbed elbows with their frenzied fans. So seeing the latter in such an intimate setting, rather than onstage or onscreen, was a remarkable moment in my life.

After a minute or two, Lyle spotted us and waved us over. He introduced Elvis to Kathi first. Tanned and glowing, she was dressed in a preppy skirt and stylish blouse. Elvis flashed his electric smile. "Nice to meet you, ma'am." He shook my hand, and we all made small talk for a few minutes. What a thrill!

Lyle then ushered us into the vocal booth, since Elvis, wearing headphones, would cut his parts standing in the middle of the big room. From the booth, we'd have a front-row seat from which to watch the proceedings.

Elvis didn't disappoint. Hearing him sing, in this case a romantic ballad called "Almost in Love," gave me chills. Along with his vocal performance, his approach to studio work made an impression on me. Most of the artists I'd seen sing in the studio didn't move all that much while they recorded. Elvis moved — a lot. Eyes closed, he grasped the microphone in his right hand, holding it close to his face as he worked. For emphasis, he'd raise his left hand up in the air when he hit long notes. He was doing his concert moves as he sang.

Between takes, Billy Strange, the producer, spoke to Elvis through the talkback.

"Do you want to do one more?"

"Yessir."

He was such a gentleman, very respectful to everyone, even to the maintenance people and second engineers who worked at Western.

He only sang the song a couple, maybe three, times. He was right on from the start, just like Sinatra. Bang! He got his parts done and that was it. It was another important lesson for me as a guy who had dreams of producing records. When an artist can deliver a great performance right out of the gate, don't overthink things. Wrap the session, just like Billy Strange did.

It was just a remarkable, inspiring experience. I still don't know anybody who saw Elvis record other than the members of his inner circle and the people working the sessions. I would think I dreamed it if it weren't for Kathi being there too.

In early April, we did a two-week stand at the Basin Street West club in San Francisco. It was an intimate, classy venue, a jazz landmark. I'd seen Miles Davis there a few years earlier. But the highlight of the trip for me was that Scoppettone and I got to buy our dream cars. We went over to a performance car dealer on Van Ness Avenue. He bought a Maserati. I laid eyes on a red 1961 Ferrari 250 GT SWB California Spyder. The salesman told me that one of its prior owners was Nick Reynolds of the Kingston Trio. It was an unbelievably sexy automobile. There weren't too many of them in the States at the time; if I'd seen a Spyder before, it would've been at one of the Pebble Beach Concours d'Elegance shows I attended earlier in the decade.

I paid five thousand for it. It's a landmark moment for me, because it was my first Ferrari.

It was quite an expensive toy. The insurance alone on those Ferraris cost thousands a year back then, even if you didn't drive them many miles, because of their high replacement value. The actuaries who set those steep rates weren't stupid. As soon as Scap and I returned home from touring we road-tested our new

I sit behind the wheel of a Lamborghini Miura in a promotional shot for *Harpers Bizarre 4*, early 1969. My taste in vehicles had come a long way since my youthful beginnings as a driver, piloting my parents' trucks along dirt roads in Felton. ED THRASHER/RHINO ENTERTAINMENT COMPANY, A WARNER MUSIC GROUP COMPANY.

cars along the winding roads in the Santa Cruz Mountains. We even went so far as to buy special driving gloves down in Carmel and we both learned to "double-clutch" while pushing our little vehicles to their limits.

I had thrilling times behind the wheel of that Ferrari, and I'd sell it a decade or so later. I got a premium price for it at the time, but today this same car is worth many millions.

In the early summer, we started recording our next album, our third, in an approximately eighteen-month span. It was a rugged pace. We'd tour, do TV shows, photo sessions, and interviews, write songs, rehearse, and record. On the evening of May 17, Harpers Bizarre was working at United with Lenny and Lee Herschberg. Ron Elliott of the Beau Brummels and Randy Newman were both there with us, helping Lenny with the record. That night, Lenny received some difficult news. His mother's health had declined precipitously. She didn't have long to live, so Lenny departed to go to her deathbed. Trying to raise his spirits, we told him right before he left that we'd keep working while he was gone. In the middle of the night, we cut a version of Sonny Boy Williamson II's "The Goat," with Ron on bass, me on drums, and Randy on piano and vocals. It was one take, and my headphones fell off, so it wasn't my best drumming. But it did make Lenny smile when he finally heard it. It eventually came out decades later on Randy's career-spanning box set.

A week later, we appeared with Bob Hope and Raquel Welch at his USO Benefit Show, held in the brand-new San Diego Stadium. It was a radiant Southern California day, and there were thousands of soldiers, marines, and sailors present, including many recovering from wounds they received while serving in Vietnam. We were to appear in the round, on a stage situated in the middle of the field.

Because the script had me entering the stage from a different spot than the other guys in the band, I'd have to wait in the wings for fifteen or so minutes in this little alcove under the stage. It turned out that I'd be sharing that space with Welch. She wouldn't be performing with us, but would rejoin Hope onstage after our appearance.

During the show, we waited together, sitting so close that we were practically touching shoulders. I was trying to think of something to say, but my mind was blank. She was paying me no attention, and all that kept going through my head was "Wow, she's sexy" as I tried not to stare at her long, mini-skirted legs.

I'm not very gregarious by nature so I couldn't get up the confidence to start a conversation. Every minute of silence made me more nervous. Even worse, when Hope ducked into the enclosure to tell her something about their upcoming skit, she spoke to him immediately. He left, and she stopped speaking, never saying a word to me.

In September, Warner Bros. released our new album, *The Secret Life of Harpers Bizarre*. As with *Anything Goes*, Lenny used a couple of songs that Scoppettone and I had written. He credited us for vocal arrangements too. I remember well how good it felt to read the credits. Because I wanted to be a producer, receiving credit for work done on the making of the record other than just singing meant a lot to me.

The album's most successful single was "Battle of New Orleans," by Johnny Horton. It had been a big hit back in the late fifties. It crested at No. 95, a far cry from Horton's chart performance with the song.

That fall, we toured college campuses quite extensively. But the highlight for me happened in mid-August, when we played a week of shows with Louis Armstrong at the World's Fair in San Antonio. As a trumpet player, I idolized Satchmo, so to get the chance to trade solos with him was a thrill of a lifetime, one that helped me forget how much I disliked fronting the band.

Now even though *Secret Life* hadn't charted, and we didn't have a hit single, we still frequently appeared on television. We had a wholesome, family-friendly image and had a repertoire that included songs made popular by Glenn Miller and Rodgers and Hammerstein, so the networks loved booking us. In theory, an eighteen-year-old girl who loved "Groovy" and her grandmother who liked "Chattanooga Choo Choo" could sit on the couch together and watch us do our thing.

But the sunshine pop sound that we embraced had begun to falter as a popular genre, and we just didn't put out good enough songs to overcome that counter-current. We were swimming against the tide and, consequently, our fame dissipated. We didn't know it yet, but our days of performing in stadiums and arenas were over.

To keep us working during the Christmas season when colleges shut down, Carl Scott booked us into casinos on the west coast. We called the circuit we toured the "Triangle" — Reno–Tahoe–Vegas.

In December, we played a multi-week stand in Lake Tahoe at the Stateline Cabaret at Harrah's Casino. The Cabaret was a nice venue, a theater in fact. But the gig was a slog. Typically, when we headlined, we'd do a single evening show. At Harrah's we played three sets, alternating performances with Fats Domino. So a typical night of work had us onstage at nine p.m., one a.m., and four-thirty a.m. It was a test of endurance. The sun's coming up soon, your throat's raw, and all you want to do is collapse in bed. We're playing for thirty people, half of whom are blotto. We'd finish playing a song. No one claps. It was humbling.

It wasn't hard to see the writing on the wall. In a couple of years we'd gone from playing for sold-out crowds of screaming teenagers to small audiences comprised of people who generally didn't care who was performing for them. It was a big wake-up call.

One silver lining for me came after a few days of playing at Harrah's. One of the bands that we swapped sets with after

Domino's booking ended had a talented drummer named J.D. Souther. At the time, he was an unknown; this is a few years before he'd make a name for himself by penning hits for the Eagles and Linda Ronstadt.

We started hanging out together on our off-days. We'd smoke a few joints, and he'd play me records. He had a tremendous ear. I remember that he turned me onto the folk singer Tim Hardin. As we listened to Hardin's live album, he'd tell me what he liked and disliked about the material and performances. It was a real education for me, because he offered up insightful observations, things that I would've otherwise not picked up. I don't think I fully realized it at the time, but he was doing the same kind of analysis that an effective A&R executive might do when considering Hardin. I started looking at songs differently after I hung out with him.

Early the next year, we continued our casino run by appearing at the Blue Room at the Tropicana in Vegas. The Tropicana was a very swanky hotel, but we weren't making enough money to afford to stay there. Instead we stayed across the street at the Tropicana Golf Club Motel.

We soon discovered the real fringe benefit of the Trop gig: the ladies of the burlesque show Les Folies Bergère. Night after night, we'd catch their performances. I'd drink in the sight of the gorgeous, leggy showgirls, dancing in their feathered and beaded outfits. They were incredibly graceful and alluring. After a few days, we made a point to introduce ourselves to some of them and invited them to see our show. Intrigued, they did so a few times over the course of the week. We learned during those visits that almost all of them were also staying at the Tropicana Motel, because they too couldn't afford better accommodations.

By the spring of 1969, I was pretty disillusioned. My feelings didn't have anything to do with the guys in the band. We all got along well. The more we toured, though, the more I found performing live intolerable.

The thing that kept me going with Harpers Bizarre was the chance to make records with Lenny.

We went back into the studio in January 1969. It would be our fourth album session in about two years. It was grueling, but making records was what I lived for as a musician.

If nothing else, Lenny encouraged us to take on eclectic material. We could perform a song rooted in seemingly any musical tradition and make it our own. A good example is "Witchi Tai To." Written by Native American saxophonist Jim Pepper, the song's hypnotic chant had its origins in a tribal song Pepper had heard as a child.

This track was also significant for us as a band because Lenny let us record some instrumental tracks. Obviously, Lenny could've called in the Wrecking Crew to play every note on our album, and in fact, that would've made his life easier as a producer. So it felt like a sign of respect by Lenny to let me play drums and Scoppettone play bass on this song.

Scoppettone and I also played our instruments on another of our compositions, "Soft Soundin' Music." Lenny had the brilliant idea to bring in a young guitarist named Ry Cooder to play on it as well. Cooder, who'd go on to become a fixture at Warner Bros. Records, fingerpicked a swampy intro riff and laid down a slinky bottleneck solo. The track became the album's opener.

Considering our beginnings as a Beatles-inspired act, it made sense for us to finally cover a Beatles song. We did "Blackbird." We also cut John Denver's "Leaving on a Jet Plane," which was our typical set-closer.

After bending Lenny's ear for a few days during pre-production, Scap and I convinced him to let us record Eddie Floyd's 1967 smash "Knock on Wood." I'd sing, play acoustic guitar, and — if memory serves — drum on it as well. As we got close to finishing it, Lenny mentioned to us that he knew a young engineer that could give the track a unique mix.

That's how I came to meet Donn Landee. Lenny told me that Donn had worked as a second engineer on an Everly Brothers session that Lenny had produced at Hollywood's TTG Studios back in 1968. During their conversations, Donn had mentioned to Lenny that he'd recently worked on the single mix of the anti-war anthem "Sky Pilot," by Eric Burdon & the Animals. The song featured a sound effect called "phasing," which Donn, as the session's engineer, had gotten on tape. First heard on record in 1959 on Toni Fisher's "The Big Hurt," it produced a sweeping, whooshing sound. Lenny knew, like everyone else with trained ears, that Donn had done it masterfully on "Sky Pilot."

I got to watch Donn and Lenny work together when they mixed on "Knock on Wood" because as usual, I needed a studio fix. I was particularly interested to see Donn do the phasing, which he performed by using the tape machines and an oscillator.

That was the first time of many that Donn Landee wowed me in the studio.

We talked, and thus began our friendship.

In May, *Harpers Bizarre 4* came out to little fanfare and light sales. Still, we soldiered on as a touring act, playing college campuses everywhere from Alaska to Maryland. One highlight came in August when we appeared on a local TV show in Cincinnati with Muhammad Ali.

With demand for our services declining, we continued to do these fly-ins and fly-outs for these shows. If we were lucky, we could string together a few nights in a row in some part of the country before we'd head back to California. But we were home a lot more than we had been back in 1967.

Since we didn't have a very full schedule, I'd hang around with Lenny, watching his sessions at the United Western complex and Sunset Sound. After he finished, we'd go grab something to eat and then hang out at his place and listen to records.

During these hours I'd learn that Lenny was the ultimate song man. When you play trumpet for the kind of gigs I did as a kid,

ABOVE: Lenny Waronker, who produced Harpers Bizarre, listens to a playback at Sunwest Recording Studios, Hollywood, circa 1969. DONN LANDEE.

LEFT: Posing with an acoustic in a promotional shot for *Harpers Bizarre* 4, early 1969. ED THRASHER/ RHINO ENTERTAINMENT COMPANY, A WARNER MUSIC GROUP COMPANY.

everything from weddings to VFW talent shows, you need to know every old standard. Lenny knew them all. If I didn't recall the title of one of these songs that came to mind when I was talking to Lenny, all I'd have to do is hum the melody, and he'd know it. He had a masterful ear and, unlike me, he wasn't a musician. He'd play me country music, a genre I despised, to open my mind to the brilliance of Jimmie Rodgers and Hank Williams. He played me Woody Guthrie. He introduced me to the stand-up comedy of Lenny Bruce. He played me Elvis's Sun Sessions recordings. As a jazz musician, I'd never paid much attention to lyrics. He showed me the error of my ways in that area too. So he broadened my musical horizons.

And whether we were listening to albums or I was observing him in the studio, he was giving me a first-rate education in the art of producing. He taught me how to sequence an album and to find songs that suited an artist — the essence of A&R. He schooled me on how to recognize a great studio performance. And perhaps most importantly, he stressed the importance of identifiability when scouting for new talent. In other words, is the artist in question, when they sing or play, distinctive and special? You want to have your ears attuned to those attributes.

But here's the thing: Lenny wasn't a guy who was going to obsess over the technical intricacies of a recording, like Lee, Donn, or the other engineers. Lenny was way into the music and the songs. Period.

So if Lenny didn't have anything cooking, I'd call the engineers I knew, Lee or Lyle, and see if I could sit in the control room with them, either to observe or serve as their second engineer if they needed an extra set of hands. Spending time learning the technical side of making records from engineers, at the same time Lenny was coaching me, helped round me out as a producer in training.

I also used to go to Donn's sessions over at Hollywood's Sunwest Recording Studios, the facility where he worked, because I wanted to learn from him too. Now if Lenny and I bonded over songs, Donn and I connected over sounds. When everyone else had left for the night, we'd experiment at Sunwest. I'd ask, how do you make a kick drum sound full? What's the best way to get a good bass sound on an album? He'd show me. I was always interested into how recording was done: the sonic side of things, such as how to mike congas and acoustic guitars. I'd go crazy with that stuff.

Some days, when Donn had a day off, we'd hang out and listen to records. That's how we discovered that we'd outfitted our homes with nearly identical hi-fi systems. We had the same speakers, Altec Lansing Carmels. We also had the similar power amps. Almost nobody I'd met knew about how great McIntosh power amplifiers were. Donn and I had MC275s and MC240s, equipment that had a certain sound to our ears. Independently, Donn and I had both figured out that they were the best things on the market. Donn also liked Marantz power amps; he turned me on to them. We'd listen to albums on our systems, comparing the sound of the records and thinking about how our setups affected what we heard. So he and I studied mixes way before I ever began producing records.

My most memorable evening I spent with Donn during these years had nothing to do with stereo equipment, though. I popped in on this session Donn was working at Sunwest. It was Tina Turner, and Ike Turner, her husband, was the producer. I was excited to watch, because Ike was the guy responsible for "Rocket 88." It came out in 1951, and it's arguably the first rock 'n' roll song. In fact, I recall listening to the 78 in my grandfather's store when I was just little kid.

When I walked into the control room, Donn nodded hello as he sat next to Ike at the mixing desk. Ike stared me down before turning his eyes back to Tina, who was out in the studio. As my eyes adjusted to the darkness, I spotted a pile of blow on the console in front of him. His left hand hovered beside his coke while his right gripped a black revolver. I'm not sure if the gun was meant to intimidate everyone in the room or maybe just to keep everyone's noses out of his powder, but it got the message across either way. Ike was telling Tina what to do before she sang, his bony fingers caressing the pistol. I stood in in the control room, watching all of this go down, trying to stay off his radar.

In between takes, I wanted to get away from Ike, so I walked out into the studio. I introduced myself to Tina, but not a minute had gone by before Ike got on the talkback and started giving her orders about how he wanted her to sing the next song. He was really talking down to her, glaring at her through the glass, and I could see she was getting angry. While he was still barking at her, she smiled at me, and started to run her hand through my long blond hair. When she did that, she sang a few lines from "Black Boys/White Boys," a song from the Broadway musical *Hair*, about the silken feel of the hair of white boys. At that moment, it had gotten way too weird for me. I said goodbye to Donn and left, fast.

The day before Halloween, we were hired to play at the inauguration celebration of the new president of Caltech in Pasadena, California. It was an easy gig for us. After the show, Scap, John, and I went to LAX to take a TWA red-eye to San Francisco. I can't recall why, but Dick Yount stayed in Los Angeles. The three of us, along with one of our touring musicians, Ray Keller, were headed home to Santa Cruz. We had seats in economy on the Boeing 707. I remember I was spent from the show and just wanted to shut my eyes during the short flight. The plane had lots of empty seats — there were only a few dozen people on board.

The pilot dimmed the cabin lights after we left Los Angeles.

I dozed as we flew north, but awoke as the 707 began its descent. I caught sight of a flight attendant moving down the aisle, followed closely by a male passenger. What was happening didn't immediately register, but after a second my blood ran cold. A dark-haired, short man in an olive-drab army jacket had the business end of a carbine against the back of her neck. He jabbed, pressing her towards first class.

I remembered him from boarding. He'd lined up in front of me at LAX, carrying a long, thin nylon bag. I'd assumed it had fishing poles in it, but now I knew that's how he brought the rifle aboard.

He looked over his shoulder from time to time to ensure none of us had left our seats. Eyes set, he looked determined and agitated.

Everyone in my line of sight in economy sat there perfectly still, either petrified, like me, or choosing to remain in place, thinking that the gunman might pull the trigger and kill the woman if he felt threatened.

At that moment, I think my biggest fear was that somebody in first class was going to try to jump the guy. If such an attempt failed, and the gunman started shooting, I thought it likely that he had enough rounds in the rifle's magazine to cause a bloodbath.

Nobody stopped him. We all sat there, frozen, as they reached the cockpit.

He started yelling, "Open the door! Open the door!"

Soon after, the cockpit door opened and then quickly closed behind them.

We couldn't hear any talking or sounds of a struggle. But after a minute or so, the 707's engines revved and plane began to bank.

I started conjuring up our fate, thinking he'd killed or incapacitated the pilots and the plane would soon crash. At that moment, I thought we were all going to die.

Then a crackle from the intercom jolted me.

"This is the captain. If you've got any immediate plans in San Francisco, they've changed. There's a nervous young man in the cockpit with a gun to my head. He wants me to fly him to New York. We don't have the fuel to reach New York, but that's where he wants to go. So we're going up to 41,000 feet and heading east. Drinks are on the house. I'll keep you updated."

We'd been hijacked.

After we'd ascended and settled into our new eastward course, the cockpit door opened again. The flight attendant, a pretty girl, wore a vacant expression as she walked towards the rear of the plane. Bizarrely, she stopped at our seats and asked for our autographs. We signed the paper she handed us, and she moved along once again. She later returned to the cockpit, presumably because the hijacker said he'd kill a crew member if she didn't.

The flight towards New York was so quiet it was unnerving. No one was screaming or praying audibly. Dawn broke. Sunlight gradually angled into the cabin. To calm myself, I stared out the window. We cruised above the bed of clouds, with the brilliant azure sky above us fading into a washed-out blue at the horizon. The other flight attendants served drinks, which, understandably, a lot of passengers gulped down as fast as they could. I passed, because I didn't drink.

When I caught the eye of other passengers, we felt a connection, a sense of a shared fate. Other passengers had their eyes closed. I could see them mouthing prayers. I'm not a particularly religious person, so I didn't feel the desire to follow their lead. But at that moment I was glad that they were trying to get a message to God, because all I could think about was the inevitable moment when we'd run out of fuel.

It was wartime, so there were a few guys in uniform on board. None of them, or any other passengers, best I could tell, seemed to be thinking about rushing the cockpit. Everyone had surely come to the same conclusion: confronting the gunman could kill us all if the pilot and co-pilot perished during a struggle.

Some thirty or so minutes into our diverted course, the pilot came back on the intercom. He explained again that the plane didn't have enough fuel to reach New York, since we'd only been scheduled to fly from Los Angeles to San Francisco. He told us that he'd gotten the hijacker to agree to allow the plane to land in Denver to refuel, since that was about the limit of the plane's current range.

Faces around me relaxed a bit. Somebody near me said, "Thank God." Any relief I felt, unfortunately, was buried by my thought that if the hijacker changed his mind about landing in Denver, we'd probably do a nosedive into the Rockies when the plane ran out of fuel.

The next couple of hours were agonizing. The pilot popped on the intercom a few more times. When he updated us, he'd make these oddly lighthearted comments. In retrospect, I guess he was seeking to keep us, and the edgy hijacker, a bit relaxed. It didn't work for me.

When the plane descended again, the pilot announced that we'd been cleared to land in Denver. We touched down, which provided only minimal relief, as you might expect. When we started to taxi, the pilot told us that the hijacker had agreed to let the passengers disembark. The pilot, relaying the hijacker's orders, said that when the doors opened, we needed to exit quickly and quietly. He also told us that the hijacker had three members of the flight crew plus one flight attendant with him in the cockpit. They'd remain onboard for the next leg of the flight. The last thing he told us was that the hijacker had vowed that if anyone came near the cockpit door, he'd blow a hole in the flight attendant's pretty head.

Out the window, we could see two men wearing trenchcoats maneuvering the wheeled air stairs into place. We heard the doors creak open. Then, row by row, everyone stood and moved towards the exits.

When the guys and I got onto the air stairs, I could see we'd parked very far away from the terminal. It was cold, and we were all walking quickly towards the terminal, but it was taking forever to get there. I could see the police and FBI agents huddling near the doors into the terminal. When I elevated my gaze, I could see snipers crouched down on top of the terminal. I felt terrified once again, like I had when the hijacker had stood in the aisle, because I now knew that if he made the mistake of standing near a cockpit window or God forbid fired at the police, we might be caught in a crossfire.

As soon as we arrived at the terminal, police officers hustled us into the airport. We'd survived.

After such a terrifying experience, all you want to do is call your family, and tell yourself over and over that you're out of

danger so your hands will stop shaking. But instead, airline offi-
cials ushered us, one after another, into conference rooms at
the airport. Once the doors were closed, a pair of FBI agents,
freshly shaved and wearing tailored suits and ties, started asking
pointed questions about the flight. It was the classic good-cop,
bad-cop strategy. One agent empathized with my exhaustion and
shock after such a harrowing flight. The other probed, seeking to
discover if John, Scap, Ray, or I had assisted the hijacker either
before or during the flight. Between the two of them, they asked

When my bandmates and I were hijacked in October 1969, we were touring in
support of *Harpers Bizarre 4*. On it, we covered John Denver's "Leaving on a
Jet Plane." In light of my harrowing experience in the air, I can confirm it was
far more fun to sing about a jet plane than it was to be held hostage on one.
RHINO ENTERTAINMENT COMPANY, A WARNER MUSIC GROUP COMPANY.

all the questions that would trip us up if we were lying. It was ridiculous, but they were just doing their jobs.

Later that day, we got on another flight, taking us to our original destination of San Francisco. When we got off the plane at the terminal, I saw a couple of kids in costume. I remembered it was Halloween.

Naturally, we followed the news about the hijacking. The 707 departed Denver, headed to New York's Kennedy airport. After an aborted attempt by the FBI to storm the plane at Kennedy, it flew to Bangor, Maine, where it was refueled in preparation to fly, upon the hijacker's orders, to Rome. The 707's next stop was Shannon, Ireland, where it took on fuel once again, before traveling to the Italian capital. At Fiumicino airport, the hijacker released the flight crew in exchange for an Italian customs officer, whom he held hostage in order to facilitate his escape from the airport. Although, as we'd learn later, he hoped to make it to Naples, where he'd spent much of his childhood, he didn't make it that far. Italian police arrested him outside of Rome some twenty-three hours after we'd left Los Angeles, thus ending the longest hijacking in history.

A few days later, we got letters in the mail from TWA's president. He expressed deep "regret" for the air piracy that had "caused the diversion and termination" of our flight, and hoped we'd fly TWA again in the future. For our troubles, the airline blessed us with blankets, emblazoned with the TWA logo.

For me, this was the beginning of the end of Harpers Bizarre. It was also the beginning of a lifetime of intermittent nightmares about the hijacking. I dream scenes of terror from it, most often the chilling image of the black barrel of the carbine pressed against the neck of the flight attendant. I wake up gasping and sweating.

Chapter 4

THE OTHER SIDE
OF THE GLASS

By the end of 1969, Harpers was basically over. We'd run out of steam as a charting act and the other guys in the group had run out of patience with Lenny as our producer. From their perspective, Lenny was holding us back, in part because he felt strongly — and rightly, I think — that Harpers Bizarre as a musical entity was best served by having session musicians play almost every instrumental part on our albums. The guys thought that now that we'd made a few records, the time was right for Lenny to dispense with the Wrecking Crew and let us play our own parts. I didn't agree. Lenny was our producer and had been essential to our success. As much as I enjoyed playing drums on things like "Witchi Tai To," I couldn't convince myself that I could play drums better than Jim Gordon or Hal Blaine.

In end, these issues were deal-breakers. But before we went our separate ways, we cut a couple more singles.

Harry Nilsson, a songwriter who was tight with Lenny and Randy, penned a tune for us called "Poly High." The lyrics tell the story of a high school football game between a private and public school that ends in a tie because of a rainout. The subject matter was a bit loony for a pop song, but so was Harry.

We recorded it at Western in December, with Lee engineering. It's a classic Harpers Bizarre track; the instrumentation is subtle and the vocals are stacked. Harry came up with most of the vocal parts; he sings the low parts, with me on the rest. Later on, when I became a producer, I'd draw on these sessions when I worked out the intertwining vocal parts on songs like "Black Water" by the Doobie Brothers.

We then mixed the track at Sunwest, with Donn running the board. Lenny, Harry, Donn, and I all collaborated on the mix; I think Scap was there too. What I remember most about that all-night session was how stoned we were as we worked on the mix. After all we smoked, it was a major achievement just to get it finished and sounding so good.

As the band drifted apart, Kathi and I tied the knot. We were married on the morning of February 3, 1970, at Los Angeles City Hall. That afternoon, Donna, Lenny's wife, held a reception for us at their home. It was just Donna, Lenny, Carl Scott, Harry Nilsson, and Randy Newman. That was our big wedding day.

The band played a few scattered shows here and there during early 1970, but on May 24 we logged our final performance. It was like something straight out of *This Is Spinal Tap*. We performed at the sprawling Edwards Air Force Base, which was located north of Los Angeles. When we were there, the base commander gave us a tour of a military plane, the C-5 Galaxy air transport. The interior was monstrous and it was an impressive piece of technology. But the rest of the visit to the base was a stark reminder of how far we'd fallen. We had to set up and break down our own gear and the excitement and energy of 1967 seemed like an eternity ago.

A little more than two weeks later, we entered the studio a final time. We cut a single, "If We Ever Needed the Lord Before," at Sunset Sound. It was an old-time spiritual by Thomas A. Dorsey. I'm not sure who came up with the idea to record it, but it was a sensible choice, post-hijacking, for us. Scap and I both sang and played instruments on it. I played a number of different ones: piano, Hammond organ, and Wurlitzer electric piano. I added guitar too. Even though the song made zero impact on the charts, this recording represented a career milestone for me because Lenny let me share production credit on it with him. When I picked up the 45 and looked at the label, it said *Produced by Lenny Waronker and Ted Templeman.*

And that was the end for Harpers Bizarre.

I wasn't sure what to do next. I knew that as a musician, I didn't have the chops to sustain a serious professional career as a vocalist or a drummer. At the same time, while I did harbor a desire to be a producer, it was hard to imagine starting at the bottom once again, like I'd done with the Tikis, in the hopes that a label might give me a chance to work on the other side of the glass. So I wasn't sure I wanted to stay in the music business.

While I mulled things over, I drove down to LA from Santa Cruz and spent a few days with Lenny. I went to sessions with him and watched him work. In the car I'd tune into KHJ Boss Radio and KRLA to study the songs in the Top 40. I'd pick up the underground newspaper, the *Los Angeles Free Press*, to keep up on news about my favorite artists. I'd read the jazz and cultural critic Ralph J. Gleason's columns in *Rolling Stone* and the *San Francisco Chronicle*.

I had some time to think about what to do next because I had a bit of a financial cushion in terms of assets. I owned a house on King Street in Santa Cruz. I even had a Ferrari. But I didn't have any real income at all once we stopped gigging.

Part of me truly felt that the smart move was to divorce myself from the music industry altogether. I'd graduated from Santa Clara University with a degree in history and my teaching certification, so I thought maybe I should become a high school teacher. Or I could go to grad school and get an advanced degree in history so I could teach college. When I expressed my uncertainty to friends who weren't musicians, they'd almost always advise me to cut ties with the music scene. I do think they had my best interests at heart in saying that. From their standpoint, the music industry sure didn't look like a promising bet for someone in my position. It was hard for me to disagree.

Kathi and I even considered making a more complete break with the past. For a time, we considered moving to England and starting a whole new life. I loved English architecture and I knew we could buy a house there. So I started looking at properties for sale in England, along the coasts of Devon and Cornwall, in *Country Life* magazine. I also looked at properties in Nova Scotia. I thought we could relocate, and I could figure out what to do next once I got resettled. I just wanted to get away from everything and have a sane life after four years on the road.

Ultimately, we didn't leave the States. We did, however, buy a house on Grace Terrace in Pasadena. Meanwhile, I still didn't know what I was going to do with my life. As a matter of fact, after we started living in Pasadena I even considered applying to work as a salesman at Vroman's, this great bookstore located there. I just wanted to do something where I would feel good while doing it. After watching Harpers Bizarre flame out, I just didn't want to work in a business that didn't have much use for me.

When I was at my lowest, Lenny's wife, Donna, helped me a lot. She'd check in on me and encourage me not to leave the industry. She was a big star at that time, so when she'd tell me about how impressed she had always been when she'd seen me play drums and sing with Harpers Bizarre, that meant a lot, because she was a big music fan and had cut her own records for Reprise and Capitol. So her vote of confidence helped me to reenter the fray.

Even though I still harbored aspirations to become a producer, I knew that I'd have to get my foot in the door at a label and put in a lot of hard work before that even became a remote possibility. So I went to every record company in the city trying to get an entry-level A&R gig. Place after place, the verdicts were unanimous. Don't call us. We'll call you.

Some rejections stung more than others. At Columbia, I met with Terry Melcher. He was a very successful producer, so I wasn't necessarily shocked that he didn't want to hire me. But because he'd had a lot of hits with acts like the Byrds, I asked him for career advice before he rushed me out of his office.

I said, "What do I need to do to get an A&R job at Columbia?"

He said, "Go cut some hits and come back, and I'll decide if you're good enough to work here."

As the rejections mounted, I considered giving up and falling back on grad school. But Donna didn't lose faith, even as I was losing it myself. She was in Lenny's ear, reminding him to talk to Warner Bros. about hiring me. She'd say, "Teddy, don't give up. Just keep going. Just keep trying. Just call Lenny up again. Tell him that he's got to hire you." Even though Lenny and I were great friends, it felt awkward to call him, because it felt like I was practically begging. So then Donna would drive over and see me and say, "You've got talent. You're good at what you do. Hang in there." I was going to fold the tent, but she was really supportive.

None of these companies offered me a job, except for Motown. The person I met with there said, "Okay, yeah, we'll start you off as a tape listener, but we're not going to pay you more than twenty bucks a week." In other words, I'd spend my days culling through demos and submissions to Motown and write memos about the artists I thought had potential. That sounded good to me. Somehow, though, that didn't pan out either. I can't remember what happened, but in the end Motown didn't actually hire me.

Eventually, though, in September 1970, Warner Bros. Records offered me a tape listener position. Naturally, I'd been in to the Warner Bros. offices looking for work before that, but along the way, Lenny had been helping me from the inside. He kept saying to people, "Give Ted a chance." He even had to convince Mo to give me a shot. Mo apparently didn't think I was right for the job; he said to Lenny, "Ted's too quiet. He never says anything." Lenny did, in time, convince him that I was up for the task and I got the job.

Once I got hired, I'm sure Lenny figured I didn't really understand what I was getting myself into by starting at the bottom. Lenny was probably thinking, *Hey, Ted's been on television.* He's had *Billboard* hits. He's taking on one of the least glamorous jobs in the company. He's going to tire quickly of doing grunt work at Warner Bros.

So for my first job at Warner Bros. Records, I'd go to the offices and pick up boxes of demos by artists looking for the label to sign them. I'd take tapes home and listen to them, for fifty dollars a week.

By this time, our cash flow was quite tight. I think most people have been in that position, worrying about paying their bills, but when you're moving in those same Hollywood circles after enjoying success as a pop star, it's really hard to be broke. Kathi was doing what she could to keep us afloat; she was working in a doctor's office to help us make ends meet. It was an anxious time for both of us.

Eventually, though, with the bills going unpaid, I swallowed my pride and decided to ask Lenny for a loan. I actually broached the topic with Donna first.

"I'm going to ask Lenny to loan me five hundred dollars," I said.

She said, "Ted, he won't remember to give you such a small amount. Ask him for five thousand instead."

So that's what I did, and Lenny did in fact loan me the money.

Soon after, Lenny helped me out again. He got me a desk in the Warner Bros. offices so I didn't have work out of my house any longer.

Still, this didn't mean that I'd gotten a promotion; it wasn't easy to forget that I was at the very bottom of the corporate food chain. In fact, one day I was talking with some secretaries in the offices. One of them remarked that when she'd first met me back in 1967, I'd been a star. I grimaced and said, "Well, now I make fifty dollars a week. I wish I could make more."

One of the other girls flashed a cruel smile. "Well, hey, beggars can't be choosers." They all laughed.

That exchange made me feel terrible. I'd been a pop star a few years before; now I was just some schmuck with an entry-level office job. I've never forgotten the humiliation I felt that day.

I knew the only way out of my predicament was to prove myself. So hour after hour, I listened to demos. Listening to tapes all day long is like panning for gold. You become a prospector. You cue up reel after reel, hoping that something will resonate. After ten or twelve bad demos in a row, you have to get up, take a break, and clear your mind. During those breaks you're also reviving your hope that something will jump out at you before long. Then later that day, something does, and you're elated, thinking that you've found an act worth pitching to the A&R team. But it's an illusion driven by comparison. The recorded performances you think are stellar are, in actuality, just okay. They only seem to have potential at the time because you've listened to so many weak songs that day.

Meanwhile, Lenny helped get me some opportunities to work as a second engineer on some sessions and projects.

In fact, since I happened to have been hired around the same time that Jimi Hendrix died, my first studio job for the label was reviewing Hendrix live recordings. Working with an engineer named Rudy Hill at Amigo Studios in North Hollywood, which was Warner Bros.' new recording facility, we edited his solos together for the label to release on posthumous Hendrix albums. In the years that followed, Amigo would become as familiar to me as my own home.

I also, on occasion, worked alongside Lee Herschberg and Lyle Burbridge over at the United Western complex. They were great guys and I always felt like I was taking a masterclass in engineering anytime I got to assist them.

Lenny offered me a chance to work as a session musician at the end of 1970. While producing a Nancy Sinatra single ("Hook and Ladder" b/w "Is Anybody Goin' to San Antone") for Reprise, he asked me to come in and play shakers, tambourine, and a marching bass drum. Ry Cooder worked on the same session, playing mandolin and a slide guitar. Ry and I also sang on those songs. We sang the low background parts together and I sang the middle and high backgrounds. Nancy couldn't have been nicer; she was easy to work with and reserved.

Lenny gave me another boost by allowing me to arrange the musical components of "Hook and Ladder." I had been credited as an arranger on a couple of Harpers Bizarre songs, but in this case I was working on a record by a well-established artist. Back in those days, getting an arranger credit also meant that when the single came out, the record label had my name on it. That gesture was good for my aspirations as a producer, and my work on Nancy's single didn't go unnoticed by higher-ups at Warner

Bros. Once again, Lenny had helped me out in a big way: both by giving me the arrangement credit and by booking me as a studio musician.

Lenny and I also sometimes helped Ry Cooder when he was gigging on the west coast. His band at the time was packed with talent. He had former Flying Burrito Brother Chris Ethridge on bass; I'd met him previously when he'd worked sessions for Harpers. Richie Hayward, whom I'd later work with when he was in Little Feat, played drums for Ry.

In November, Ry opened for Elton John at the Santa Monica Civic Auditorium. At soundcheck, I went onstage to test Ry's microphone. Elton was over at his piano at the same time, doing his own preparations for the gig. When he saw me, he started playing and singing "Feelin' Groovy." That was a funny moment.

The next month we went up to San Francisco for Ry's show at the Fillmore West. Backstage, we bumped into the great piano player Spooner Oldham. He, Ry, and Lenny were all friends. Spooner's credits, even at that point in time, were unbelievable. He'd played on Wilson Pickett's "Mustang Sally" and Aretha's "I Never Loved a Man (The Way I Love You)" before he'd moved from Alabama to Los Angeles to work as a session player. I was thrilled to meet him and he was so nice to me.

Later on that evening, Lenny and I were looking for Spooner. We asked around; nobody had seen him. We went upstairs, into one of the dressing rooms, and called his name.

"Spooner?"

"Yeah?"

We heard him answer, but couldn't see him.

"Spooner?"

"Yeah!"

We walked towards his voice and were running out of real estate when we reached an open window. Lenny and I looked out and saw a pair of hands hanging from the sill. He was hanging outside the building! We were terrified, especially as he grasped for handholds as he clambered back into the room.

Lenny shrieked, "What the hell are you doing?!"

"Aw, man. Nuthin'. Just getting over my fear of heights."

He was so funny. He's this one-of-a-kind sweetheart of a guy.

That reminds me of another Spooner story from later years. Lenny and I were over at Amigo. Spooner was working the session. He'd played piano, and now Lenny wanted him to play accordion on the track. Lenny asked, "Do you have an accordion?"

"Yeah man, I have an accordion. Do you want me to go home and get it?"

"Yeah."

"Okay, I'll be back."

One hour goes by. Two hours go by. After five hours, Lenny sent the other musicians home and then we left too.

Two days passed. We hadn't heard a thing from him. Meanwhile, we were still working at Amigo on the record, wondering if he'd been kidnapped or killed.

Then on the third day, he walked into the control room, carrying his accordion.

"Spooner! Where the hell have you been?"

"Home. I flew to New Orleans to get my accordion, at my house there. Told you I'd be back."

During my time as a listener at Warner Bros., I tried to keep my ear to the ground regarding unsigned acts in the Hollywood clubs. One night, I went to see a comedy duo at the Troubadour called Cheech & Chong. They were outrageously funny, edgy, and raw. The crowd just ate up their act. Thinking I'd struck gold, I went to the label's big A&R meeting the next day and told everybody about their skits, especially the one about driving loaded on weed, which was my favorite.

Mo Ostin, who was now president of Warner Bros., thought it over for a beat from his perch at the head of the table. Then he said, "Okay, Ted. Clyde will go see them." Clyde Bakkemo, the label's general manager, was one of Mo's most trusted fellow executives. As much as I'd wished that Mo had been willing to pull the trigger based on my recommendation, I knew I had no credibility as an A&R guy at that point in time, so it made sense he'd want Clyde's take before he committed. Clyde also could, unlike me, sign Cheech & Chong on the spot if he liked their act.

Mo did throw me a bone though right after the meeting. He told me to call Cheech & Chong and tell them that Warner Bros. was interested. Later that day, I got a hold of Tommy Chong's number and called him up. I introduced myself, telling him that I worked for Warner Bros., and that I loved their act. I told him that as a result, Clyde would be at their next show, pen in hand.

Tommy cut me off mid-sentence. He said, "Hey man, listen. If Warner Bros. wants to see us, tell Clyde to fucking come down to A&M Studios and watch us recording our new album with Lou Adler."

Then he hung up.

Ugh. I didn't know that they'd just signed a deal with Adler's Ode Records. At the time, showing up a few days late to sign them felt like a big swing and a miss for me.

In the late summer of 1970, a Bay Area engineer by the name of Marty Cohn, and the owner of San Mateo's Pacific Recording Studios, Paul Curcio, delivered a demo tape to Warner Bros. Records. The name on the tape box said *The Doobie Brothers*. When I listened, I really liked the first song on the tape, "Nobody." The rest of the songs weren't as good, but that first tune had really grabbed me. I loved the lead singer's voice and the song's driving, percussive acoustic rhythms. One of the other songs on the reel had a different vocalist. He was also a good singer. Since I'd been a member of a band with two vocalists, I was particularly intrigued by their potential. They kind of sounded like a cross between CSNY and Moby Grape. They did some great harmonies, and I thought the songs, on the whole, had promise. Most importantly, they sounded identifiable: they had ear-catching guitar interplay and their lead singer had a distinctive voice.

I played it for Lenny, and he liked it too. We rang Paul, and told him we were interested. He filled in the holes for us about the band. He told us they were a quartet: Tommy Johnston on guitar and lead vocals, Pat Simmons on guitar and vocals, John Hartman on drums, and Dave Shogren on bass.

Lenny and I went up north a couple times to scout them. They had a regular gig at a mountain roadhouse north of Santa Cruz called the Chateau Liberté. It was in the middle of the redwood forest, miles and miles outside of town. When we ducked inside, we immediately felt uneasy, because we definitely didn't fit with their typical clientele. Long-haired, leather-clad bikers and their old ladies grasped their beer bottles and stared. There we were, two guys dressed like we'd just stepped off a college campus, standing in a sticky-floor dive with an army of bikers to see the Doobies. In retrospect, it's funny, but at the time we were both nervous.

I really liked what I heard and saw that first night. Visually and sonically, they presented an interesting contrast; like their audience, they were long-haired and leather-garbed, and yet they did these angelic harmonies. Their blend of acoustic and electric sounds, along with their vocal approach, also reminded me of Buffalo Springfield, a band I loved.

In between sets, we talked to them. At this point — maybe with the exception of Pat — it didn't seem to us like there was a lot of difference between the band members and their biker friends. Everyone except us was in engineer boots, battered denim, and black leather. There were all these guys with their chains clanking around — these were the one-percenter outlaw biker types: Gypsy

Jokers and Hells Angels. John and Tommy, especially, fit right in with them.

Lenny and I struck up a conversation with Tommy and Pat. We told them that we liked their live act and thought their demo material showed promise. Despite their tough image, Tommy and Pat were both affable and intelligent. It turned out that both of them had attended college.

Before they went back onstage, one of the Doobies pulled out this little box. He opened it up and started crushing up some tablets. Some of the guys then snorted the powder. I didn't even know what they were taking; Lenny had to explain it to me. They were inhaling time-release amphetamines. These guys really were bad boys.

After Lenny and I did our due diligence, we pitched them to Mo for Reprise. (Even after his promotion to president of Warner Bros., Mo remained the head of Reprise.) He wasn't against signing them, but he thought they weren't going to be worth the investment that Reprise would need to make to get the deal done since Columbia had already offered them more money than Mo was willing to pay.

Lenny and I then turned to Joe Smith, one of Warner Bros. Records' executive vice presidents. We told Joe about the band, explaining that Reprise had passed. He said, "Well, if you guys like them, go ahead. Let's sign them. You guys know what this band's all about; you two should produce the record."

Joe also told me that he'd be giving me a promotion in preparation for my new role. In September, I became a staff A&R producer for the company. It was an incredible moment. I'll always be grateful to Joe — he really helped me out by giving me a chance.

It felt great to pass the word to those guys that we'd be signing them. The band at the time was living and rehearsing in this absolute dump on Twelfth Street in San Jose. When Lenny and I visited the house, Tommy and Pat were literally sharing a can of beans for a meal. If I remember correctly, they were on public assistance just so they could eat. For an advance, Warner Bros. gave them something like twenty thousand dollars, which in those days was a lot of money. I think they partied away half of it, and the other half went for equipment, but hey, they were dirt-poor before we signed them and deserved to celebrate their deal.

After Lenny and I listened to all their material and figured out which songs we'd record, we took the Doobie Brothers into Pacific Recording. In theory, it made good sense to do the record there; Paul owned it, and that's where they'd recorded their demos with Marty. Accordingly, we'd use him as an engineer.

In practice, none of this worked well.

Right off the bat, Lenny and I made a mistake by not keeping outsiders out of the sessions. The Hells Angels guys would come and park their bikes in front of the studio; they were hanging around in the control room because they were friends with Tommy. One of them came and sat right next to me in the studio with a quart of Jack Daniel's. He was just knocking back shots of that stuff. I'm sitting next to him in my pressed trousers and oxford shirts, trying not to look nervous.

Of course, Tommy didn't mean any harm. These were his friends and they'd been big supporters of the band from their earliest gigs. But their presence was disruptive.

Even when the bikers didn't show up, that vibe was still present. John, the drummer, wore a gun in a holster in the studio. I'd grown up around guns, but I was still really uneasy about this. We're trying to make an album and the drummer's walking around with a revolver. People are drinking and doing drugs. Meanwhile, John had his issues nailing his parts, and I'm supposed to tell him, while he's armed, that he's screwing up his parts? But John's a good guy and he did have a well-developed sense of humor. Because I had to act like an authority figure — despite the fact that all these guys could've kicked my ass in ten seconds flat if they'd wanted to — he gave me this great big wooden club he'd made on a lathe. On it, he'd carved *Ted Templeman's Equalizer*. So we had our good times.

One thing I discovered during these sessions is that even if you've observed recording sessions, worked as a second engineer, and even sung on hits, you're not suddenly qualified to produce a record. I made a lot of mistakes.

First of all, Lenny and I were using a facility and an engineer that we'd never used before. Marty deserves credit for getting the Doobies' demo into our hands, but he wasn't a very good engineer. In fact, Lenny and I called up Donn and had him come to the studio to help us out for a day. Donn improved things, but there was only so much he could do to fix tracks that were recorded in a substandard fashion, in a studio he'd didn't know either. As a result of all of this, Lenny and I never got the sonics right for this record.

Second, I didn't quite grasp the psychological aspects of working with a group. For example, I'd learn that if you're hard on one guy, it can affect the morale of the others. Bands have inner workings that can be delicate and a producer has to think at least two steps ahead before opening his mouth in the studio. So, for example, when John's timing was off, I'd blurt out through the talkback, "Hey, you're speeding. You're rushing." That just blows the vibe for everyone. If the band hears you singling out one member for criticism, it causes tension and makes everyone nervous.

Third, I had to learn to appreciate studio performances from a comprehensive perspective. For instance, if you're tracking live, and the bass player flubs a note, you need to consider that the whole might be greater than the sum of the parts. Listen to "All My Loving" by the Beatles — McCartney misses a note after the guitar break, but George Martin put that take on their record, because the overall band performance was so special. I got too hung up on trying to make everything perfect. That kind of micro-management and perfectionism don't magically make an album great.

So I blew it — I didn't know what I was doing.

Even small things I had to learn the hard way. As a producer, you can't ever look like you're unsatisfied with a take or a performance. I knew that rule, on some level, because when I was on the other side of the glass, if I looked in and Lenny looked like he was the least bit displeased, I'd think, *Oh man, I am fucking up.* You *never* want to give an artist that impression, especially a group of guys who'd never cut an album before. But in the heat of the moment, it takes discipline not to react when you become frustrated. I didn't always display that discipline. Same thing goes for when you're loving what you're hearing while a musician's playing a part: if you're digging the music, you don't ever let your head go from side to side, because they'll read that as "no, no, no!" These were all things I still needed to learn.

Another thing, one that became even more apparent to me in later years, is that I don't thrive in co-production situations. Lenny's my best friend and a great producer. But we hear things differently, and when it came to putting the material on tape, that became a stumbling block. For instance, Lenny isn't a guy who loves loud, amplified guitar rock. He prefers acoustic-based material and, inarguably, he's had enormous success with that sound. When we were doing that first album, he wanted to soften everything up, which led to some tough compromises for me.

Despite these problems, I thought Lenny and I had picked some great material to showcase their talents. "Nobody," for instance, captures the genius of Tommy Johnston. It's about sailing down the Mendocino coastline to the little Northern California town of Jenner. He was inspired to write the lyrics while he was driving Route 1, looking out at the ocean. It's one of my favorite Doobie tunes.

I also liked "Slippery St. Paul." Pat had written this guitar riff, but there was no melody, no lyric. But right in the studio, Tommy came up with the melody. He played it on guitar and *bang*, he got the lyrics together, and we recorded it. On the second take, they nailed it. That was something they just came up with in the studio. That was a great moment; Lenny and I were thrilled.

In April 1971, the album came out. We picked "Nobody" as the first single.

To help promote the band, I met with Carl Scott, who'd managed Harpers Bizarre and now worked as an executive for Warner Bros. He put the Doobies on the road with a new addition to the Reprise roster, Mother Earth. The Warner Bros. publicity department dubbed it the "The Mother/Brothers Show" tour. Unlike many labels, Warner Bros. gave our artists tour support by subsidizing their expenses in the hopes that the band's following would grow after fans got a chance to see them live. With a new act like the Doobies, the company underwrote the entire tour, everything from transportation to advertising.

Despite all the company's efforts, their single stiffed, and the album didn't sell well either. As a producer, it's crushing to have a record do as poorly as that one did, and it's even worse for the artist. Because beyond your own sense of failure, you feel like you've let your artist down, and that feels rotten. Those guys looked to us to get it right, and, for a whole host of reasons, we didn't.

The other reality is that while Warner Bros. was a label that stressed artistic merit over crass commercial considerations, the label was way in the red now with the Doobies, and I'd been the person banging the drum most loudly for them. I still believed in them even after the first record didn't connect, but that didn't mean other people in the label saw things the same way. In the end, I was the guy who pushed for an investment that had at this point only produced a loss for the company.

For me, the saving grace was the fact that Lenny and I had done the record together. Lenny had a track record of success, and to be honest, if I'd produced it alone, I might've never had another chance to produce a record. Since Lenny had cred with Joe and Mo, he could vouch for me in explaining why we'd not gotten things right. That was huge.

Chapter 5

WILD NIGHT

Despite the Doobie Brothers debacle, I didn't have time to feel sorry for myself. By the middle of 1971, I had a few other irons in the fire, and I'd certainly tell anyone who'd listen that the Doobies had a tremendous amount of talent that didn't properly get showcased on their debut.

Joe Smith, thank God, didn't lose faith in me.

In the beginning of 1971, Joe took me up to the Bay Area to meet with some of the label's artists. Our first appointment was with Mickey Hart of the Grateful Dead. Joe had signed the Dead, so he and Mickey knew each other well.

Before we walked into Mickey's home, Joe said, "Don't touch *anything*. If he puts something out, don't eat it — don't put anything in your mouth." Hart, Joe told me later, had dosed him by putting LSD on potato chips. Joe introduced me to people; he was trying kickstart my career. Needless to say, I didn't eat or drink anything at Mickey's place.

Later that day, Joe took me to meet the Northern Irish singer-songwriter Van Morrison. Morrison and his wife, Janet, had just recently relocated from Woodstock, New York, to Marin County. In the late sixties, Joe had bought Van out of his prior recording contract and brought him into the Warner Bros. fold, so he was the ideal person to introduce me to Van. At that time, he was already a star in America and seemed poised for even greater success. I'd long admired Van's artistry, so naturally I took Joe up on his offer.

Van and Janet lived in a funky, rustic house nestled in the woods in the town of Fairfax. When we arrived, Joe introduced me to Van and his wife, and suggested to Van that I'd be a good person to get to know at the label.

Van and I sat down and talked. Solidly built, he had flowing red hair, a fair complexion, and a commanding, albeit quiet, presence. I mentioned that I'd been to Woodstock a few months earlier, upon the urging of Dylan's manager, Albert Grossman, whom I'd met at the Warner Bros. offices right after I got promoted to staff producer. Grossman had then summoned me to New York to collaborate on a recording project, one that in the end never fully materialized. I worked at Grossman's Bearsville Studio with Robbie Robertson of the Band to produce a session for a young musician named Todd Rundgren. The fact that I knew some of the guys Van had hung around with during his time in New York helped build a rapport between us.

Van and I also talked jazz. When we started naming our favorite albums, it turned out that he and I owned many of the same records. I know he cut his teeth on Lead Belly and the blues, but we clicked over our love for jazz.

That night, or soon after, Van turned me on to a soul singer from Philadelphia named Lorraine Ellison. She'd been on Warner Bros. since the sixties, but she wasn't someone who was on my A&R radar. She'd worked with producer Jerry Ragovoy, first releasing the outstanding single "Stay with Me" in 1966, and then an album built around that same track in 1969. Van was a really big fan of hers and encouraged me to see about working with her.

Upon his recommendation, I sought her out. She was a dark-skinned woman in her early forties with a kind disposition. In fact, she'd put her recording career on the shelf for the previous couple of years because she'd gone home to care for her ailing mother.

When I rehearsed her, I thought she was a massive talent. She had a beautiful, soaring voice that sounded straight out of the Baptist church. In a general sense, she reminded me of Aretha Franklin. To be sure, Aretha had more vocal control, but they both had awe-inspiring power. She also took my suggestions seriously and seemed to sincerely appreciate my insights into her performances.

Meeting her at that point was a real gift. When I revisited "Stay with Me," I was struck by its raw emotion. I was so knocked out by her chops, her religious dedication, and her interest in collaborating with me that I felt reinspired to pursue production work, especially after the Doobies record hadn't turned out the way I'd hoped. So we agreed to work together.

In the Warner Bros. system, producers also served as A&R advisors for their artists. So my first task was to find a song for her before we got near a studio. This process is not wholly different from constructing a home. A&R involves securing the raw material needed to build a house. Production involves utilizing that raw material to construct the house.

At that time, Carole King's *Tapestry* record had just come out. I thought one of its tracks, "You've Got a Friend," would be good fit for Lorraine. It sounded like a hit to me, and in point of fact, singer-songwriter James Taylor hadn't yet released his version of the song, which would go to No. 1 later in 1971.

If memory serves, Lorraine and I first went to New York and recorded "You've Got a Friend," and then we cut it again at Sunset Sound in April. In retrospect, the song choice was fine and the arrangement is solid. But when I listen to her vocal, I can hear my inexperience. She over-sang in a couple of spots because I didn't do a good enough job of reining in her performance.

I'm not sure why, but this song didn't get released until decades later, on her career-spanning box set. Still, these sessions were a milestone in my career, because "You've Got a Friend" was the first track I ever produced on my own.

In the weeks that followed, Van and I spoke regularly. He asked me to co-produce his next album for Warner Bros. — what became *Tupelo Honey* — with him. Needless to say, I was very excited about the opportunity to collaborate with such a unique and exceptional talent.

So beginning the late spring, I went to San Francisco to work with Van and his band. I stayed at the Fairmont over on Nob Hill. The hotel was beautiful and I love the city, but it was tough being away from Los Angeles for long stretches. Kathi was expecting and I had wanted to be there with her during the pregnancy.

We'd end up working at three different facilities, including Wally Heider Studios, where we began the project.

Van and I soon settled into a general routine for our workdays, albeit one that was subject to change depending on his moods. First thing in the morning I'd drive to Heider's and meet with head engineer Steve Barncard and Van's band members to go over the day's material.

Then I'd jump back in my car to fetch Van. (Along with being his producer, I was his personal driver.) On the nights he'd stay in the city, we had a short commute, but at other times I'd drive the twenty or so miles up to Fairfax and get him at his home.

He was definitely cut from a different cloth. I'd knock on his front door. He'd open it. I'd say, "Hey, how ya doin', Van?" Sometimes, he wouldn't answer; he might not say a word for the first few minutes I was with him. But then during the ride to San Francisco, we'd have these long conversations on everything from California's redwood trees to a certain aspect of a song we planned to record that day. Once I got used to his quirks, I realized it wasn't personal; he'd do the same to other people as well. There was a certain social disconnect with him, but what a talented motherfucker.

This carried over to our sessions. When we'd arrive at Heider, he'd walk into the studio and I'd head into the control room. Often, before I even had time to get my bearings, check levels, or run things down with Steve, he'd pick up his acoustic guitar, look around and go "one-two-three-four . . ." and we'd be off and running. He wanted the band to follow him right then into the song. In retrospect, I think this habit was, in part, his way of breaking the ice in the studio. It began the day's work, and yet he didn't need to say a word to anyone.

Luckily, I had Steve running the board at Heider. He seemed to understand Van's habits intuitively, and was a tremendous help to me as I tried to find my sea legs as a young producer.

At the end of the day, I'd drive Van back and drop him off at his place, or, if he had a gig, take him to someplace like San Jose. I'd hang out with him before he went on, because he got nervous and wanted someone to talk to keep his mind off the stage. Then I'd head back to my hotel in preparation for the same drill the next day. Needless to say, we spent a lot of time together, just the two of us, during the making of this record.

After I got back to my room, what I'd do typically is call Kathi and check in, and then ring up Lenny. We'd talk for a few minutes, then I'd then lay the phone near the tape player and let him hear, say, that day's recording.

When a song ended, I'd pick up the handset and ask what he thought.

A typical conversation went like this:

"So what do you think?"

"Well, I think it's good."

"Yeah, but Len — what about the guitar part? Too busy?"

"Don't touch it."

This went on, night after night. I'd be indecisive and unsure. He'd say, "Oh, relax," and then make a suggestion for improving "Moonshine Whiskey" or some other song. At the end of most conversations, Lenny said, *"Ted, just get it done."* He didn't want me to lose sight of the big picture.

I can't overstate how crucial his help was during these times. He was my sounding board, my coach, and my friend as I tried to make it as a producer. The truth is, if Lenny hadn't walked me through those rough patches and kept me on the right path, I would have *never* had a successful career as a producer.

Even with Lenny's mentoring, though, Van's way of working made me anxious as hell. It was almost impossible to predict where he'd go with a song while it was in the process of being recorded. Van was a truly great arranger, but his arrangements lived in his head. They could evolve and he expected the band to follow him on the fly. A lot of times this got magic down on tape, although not always. Ideas I'd hoped to implement got lost in the shuffle because frequently Van couldn't be persuaded by me or anyone else to try something a different way. That frustrated me.

To try to keep up with him, I started taking detailed notes whenever he'd step out of the studio. I'd write down my thoughts at night too, so I could stay organized. When we recorded, I'd pull out my notebook and furiously scribble down my observations about which takes and individual performances I liked best, so I'd have this information at my fingertips when we mixed. I kept this habit up for my whole career.

Even though I found it unsettling, Van's methods would teach me one of the most significant lessons I ever learned: a producer needs to be prepared to not only capture spontaneous and inspired performances on tape but also to value them appropriately, even if on their face they seem to be at odds with your plan for a track.

Van, invariably, wanted to nail things down on the first take and be *done*. I quickly learned that if I opened my mouth too much, thinking that I could persuade him to do another take or sing something differently, I risked unmooring him creatively and wrecking the day's session. If he reacted poorly to my input, he'd brood, or just walk out the door. I never quite struck the right balance with him, but the bottom line was that he was *so* spontaneous and creative in the studio. I learned that in some cases, less is more when it comes to production.

To be sure, I'd be reminded in the years to come that most artists, unlike Van, are unable to deliver quality on a first take. The truth was, as I learned, that Van was exceptional: he was just so great in the studio. His singing was always spot on and full of soul. We *never* had to patch up his vocals. Never. That said, sometimes I thought his band could play something better a second time around, but thanks to Van's impatience and tempestuousness, I'd bite my tongue unless there was something egregious on the take. So Van, in his own way, taught me to think differently about studio performances, and in doing so, taught me the most valuable lesson when it came to making records: first takes can be magical, and some imperfections can be beneficial.

I don't remember why we decamped from Heider's for a spell, but at some point we decided to do some recording at a small facility in Haight-Ashbury called Funky Jack's. It was kind of a weird setup: a professional studio located a converted turn-of-the-century Victorian house.

Late one evening Van and I drove over there to work. I eased into a space a few blocks away from the studio, on a street that wasn't the safest in the city.

On our way, I asked Van what he thought about a saxophone part we planned to record that evening. As always, he didn't say much and let me do most of the talking.

While we walked we came upon two streetwise Black guys leaning against a building. They laughed, heckling us about the thought process that led two short, long-haired white guys to venture into their neighborhood at that time of night.

As we passed, one of them stepped towards Van and said something disrespectful, right to his face. Without a word, Van pivoted and smashed his fists into the guy's chest, pinning him against the building.

Van might have been short, but he was barrel-chested and blue-collar strong. He'd grown up in a tough Belfast neighborhood and was no stranger to these kinds of confrontations. Unlike me, he knew how to handle himself in a street fight.

At that instant, I was certain that one of these guys was going to pull a knife or gun. I'm backing away, thinking, *Oh Jesus we're going to die*. Tomorrow's above-the-fold headline in the *San Francisco Chronicle*: SINGER VAN MORRISON AND HIS PRODUCER KILLED IN BLOODY STREET SKIRMISH. It was the second time in less than two years that I felt certain that I might be killed.

The thing is, once Van attacked, those two guys were more afraid of him than I was of them. They were terrified. Van had stunned his tormentor, putting him on his heels in a flash. His friend stood slack-jawed.

At that instant those two guys decided they wanted nothing more to do with Van Morrison.

As they ran off, I struggled to compose myself. My hands were shaking, because thirty seconds earlier my life had flashed before my eyes.

For Van, best I could tell, it was business as usual.

After a moment, we resumed walking. Van then turned to me, and said in his halting fashion, "So, Ted. Wut are we gonna do about the saxophone solo?"

My head was swimming, day and night. I worried about getting him to and from the studio, about which engineer I'd have working at which session, and what we'd be cutting where. I knew I was making rookie mistakes, or I had failed in my responsibility to catch mistakes made by one of the assistant engineers. We'd record using the wrong mics, or on one of the "edge tracks," the outermost tracks on a multitrack, which by their very nature were the least stable and desirable place to record on a reel.

For the most part, though, Van was a cool customer. He rarely complained, or if he did, he did so in a gentle manner.

Let me give you an example.

In those days, there were no counters on the tape machines, so we'd put a slate tone — a beep — on the reel so you could find the beginning of each take. As you rewound or advanced the tape, the music would audibly chirp along at high speed. Once you heard the tone, you knew you'd found the spot on the tape where a take started.

When we were recording at Wally Heider, blues guitarist Mike Bloomfield and Grace Slick of Jefferson Airplane were there, watching from the control room. When Van Morrison was doing something, people came around. As much as I'd struggled to deal with the Doobies and their biker friends, I found I couldn't easily turn away Van's famous friends. He was co-producing, after all.

So after Van finished, he wanted to hear what we'd just recorded. He came back into the control room as the engineer was running back the tape. After a minute, my engineer was looking nervous. Mike and Grace were staring at us. Van was too. The engineer whispered, "I forgot to put on the slate." He was frantically starting and stopping, fast-forwarding and rewinding. Van impatiently fingered a cigarette, while I felt embarrassed.

After another awkward minute, Van announced in his brogue, "So Ted. You shuda put a slate on it. I mean, y'know, if you're going to drive the bus, you've got to get a handle on the driving, from soup to nuts. Y'know?"

I remember listening to him, thinking, *What the hell does that even mean?* It was a peculiarity of his speech; he'd often combine idioms in a nonsensical manner. But I knew *exactly* what he was *trying* to say: "Ted, why don't you know what the *fuck* you're doing?"

The person in the studio who most helped me get through it all was Van's guitarist Ronnie Montrose. I first met him when he came in to work on the record. Ronnie was a wiry, raw-boned kid with straight brown hair that barely reached his shoulders. Van had hired a then-unknown Ronnie, and once he started playing his Les Paul in the studio, I knew he was special.

But Ronnie's value to me soon ranged beyond his musicianship. He became a friend and an ally; I felt like he and I were in the trenches together when things got dicey during the sessions. Anytime I was losing my bearings, Ronnie would help me get dialed in to what we needed at that moment.

He also got along great with Van. He could make Van laugh and cheer him up if he was in a bad mood. He also knew how to deftly cover for his mistakes, without missing a beat, knowing that when Van was rolling, we didn't want to do anything to disrupt his creative flow. That was key.

After a tough day's work, Ronnie knew how to keep me from ruminating about what had gone wrong in the studio. One night, when I was back in my hotel room, the phone rang.

"Hello."

"Ted? Ah, it's Van."

"Hi."

"Ah, I need to cancel."

"What?"

"For tomorroah. I mean, I can't be at the studio."

"What? Well, Van, I'm not sure we can reschedule easily —"

Stifled laughter, growing louder, came from other end of the line.

"Ted, Ted, Ted. It's Ronnie."

He could do spot-on imitations of Van, and he fooled me more than once. That was great for keeping things light.

Pranks aside, Ronnie was phenomenal. As we worked on arrangements in the studio, he'd come up with these perfect parts. Listen, for instance, to "(Straight to Your Heart) Like a Cannonball." On it, Van is singing and chugging away on his acoustic, and Ronnie's playing electric. Ronnie added this two-note hook right after the "doodle-oodle-doodle-ooh" vocal part, which Ronnie and I sang together. It was a simple lick that any guitarist could have played, but the way he played was special. It brightened the tune right up and gave it this pop sheen. Even though Ronnie became famous later for his heavy-metal riffs and solos, if you hear Ronnie's playing with Van, it's so commercial. His instincts as a session player and a writer were fabulous.

Another of my favorite tracks, "Tupelo Honey," particularly benefited from Ronnie's talents. He was the person who suggested that I play Hammond organ on it. When we did the take, I was out in the studio playing the B-3. Then later Ronnie and I sang the song's background vocals together.

That track is also a particular highlight for me because one of my favorite drummers, Connie Kay, performed on it, and three other tracks on the record. He'd played with Chet Baker, was the drummer for the Modern Jazz Quartet, and was an in-demand session cat. Van and I were both huge fans of MJQ. To get him to do the session, he had a list of requests that the label needed to fulfill. He always wanted a driver in a certain type of car — a new Pontiac — to pick him up. He wanted to stay in a certain room in this certain hotel on the wharf. But jumping through those kinds of hoops was well worth it. He was brilliant.

By early summer, we'd finished tracking and overdubs, so Van and I set out to mix the album. With the engineer, we'd put together a board, or preliminary mix, of the different songs. Van would listen as the engineer and I worked, chiming in on what he liked and didn't like.

This process became a challenge too.

What happened, often times, was that after we finished a rough mix, and had things sounding good, Van would play it for some of the guys in his band. They'd bend his ear, so when we got together to mix again, he'd want to start from scratch on that same track again. While this was aggravating, we'd eventually get it the way he liked, and then we'd then move on to another song.

Incidentally, I learned from this experience, and in the future I'd almost always bar artists from my mixing sessions with my engineers.

But mixing the title track presented another whole degree of frustration for me.

On the multi-track of "Tupelo Honey," I'd ended up with a lot of leakage. In other words, the recording had guitar bleeding into the drum tracks, which made it difficult to mix properly since the individual instruments weren't well isolated. Since Van liked to cut live — with everyone playing together in the same room — and didn't always provide the assistant engineers time to properly baffle the room, we'd often get a bit of leakage. But this was a particularly bad case of it. After some long hours of work, the engineer and I had made improvements, but I didn't think it would ever sound satisfactory until I did something to better address the problem.

Van, however, thought the rough mix sounded good enough to release. I told him I was going to keep working on it over the next few days to try to improve it.

So I took the reel down to Los Angeles and went into the studio with Donn to mix the song again. Donn suggested we use a Kepex, a noise gate unit that could reduce the leakage. At the time, it was a fairly new and uncommon piece of rack gear, but he had gotten his hands on one. Donn and I sequestered ourselves for several hours, and when we'd finished, our new mix sounded fantastic. Donn, as usual, had worked wonders.

When I played it for Van, I was certain that he'd immediately hear the difference. He did, but for some inexplicable reason he *still* wanted to use the rough mix for "Tupelo Honey." I couldn't believe it, because to my ears, there was no comparison about which one was superior. I really lobbied him. I said, "Van, let's go with Donn's mix. The original mix is flawed."

He said, "No, no, no."

I was beyond frustrated. I pleaded with him, knowing he was wrong. But he was co-producing with me, and after he refused to bend, I eventually let him have his way. It was his record, after all.

In the meantime, we finished the other mixes and delivered *Tupelo Honey*. In September, Warner Bros. released "Wild Night" as the advance single for the album, which was due out in October.

It was a great song and captured what was special about Van and his band. Van's vocal delivery was wonderful, but I think the secret to its success was his lyric. It celebrated the anticipation of getting ready for a night on the town and the excitement of an evening spent dancing and drinking. That experience, of being young and looking for love, was easy for people to relate to.

The guitar playing, too, is superlative. Ronnie's guitar part, which he wrote, is another sterling example of his great pop sensibility. When the song plays, Ronnie's guitar is the first thing you hear. John McFee, who played pedal steel, sweetened up the choruses with gorgeous, soaring licks. Van had heard about John and his band Clover and asked him to come in and play on "Wild Night." In later years, John and I would work together again after he joined the Doobies.

"Wild Night" entered the *Billboard* Hot 100 on October 9, and had ascended to No. 28 by early December.

After all of the struggles, it felt great to see this song do so well. Van had enjoyed previous success on the singles charts with "Brown Eyed Girl" and "Domino," but this was my first hit as a producer. I remember the first time I heard it on the radio. I was driving. As soon as Ronnie's guitar intro came cutting through the speakers, I pulled off the road and listened, whispering my thanks to Van, Joe Smith, and Warner Bros. Records.

The album itself did well too. It peaked at No. 27 on the *Billboard* Top 200, spending twenty-four weeks on the chart. It wasn't a runaway hit, but it did respectable numbers — and I was relieved.

Van didn't love touring, but he played a number of dates around California in support of the album. On October 16, he performed at Pauley Pavilion at UCLA with a young singer named Linda Ronstadt as support. I went to the show with Joe Smith. We found Van backstage after the show and started talking to him. Joe saw Linda passing by and grabbed her so she could meet us. After she and I met, Joe introduced her to Van. She smiled and said to Van, "Hello, nice to meet you!" He just stared at her, turned, and walked away. She looked confused, wondering what she'd done to offend him. But it wasn't her fault — that was just the way Van was, even though he didn't mean any harm. He probably didn't know what to say to her, so he just bailed. In any event, that was the night I first met Linda; I'd get to know her well a few years later when she came in to sing backgrounds on a Carly Simon album I'd produce.

Even though *Tupelo Honey* had just arrived in stores, Van called me because he wanted to lay down a track called "Almost Independence Day" for his next album. Inspiration had struck and he said he was ready to go.

Donn Landee and I went up to San Francisco and met Van and his band at Pacific High Recording.

In preparation for the session, Van and I had hired the superlative jazz bassist Leroy Vinnegar. It was a thrill to work with him. He'd played on one of my favorite records by drummer Shelly Manne, *My Fair Lady*, which also featured André Previn on piano. It was a foundational recording for me as a young musician when it appeared in 1956. It documents an unbelievable performance by that trio.

This time around, I tried to stay mindful of the lessons I'd learned. Van had his arrangement of this moody, ten-minute ballad ready to go. The minor-key song opened with him humming along with a melody he played on his twelve-string acoustic; we supported his sparse guitar part with tones from a Moog synthesizer and Vinnegar's somber bass lines. He sang about watching fireworks illuminate the darkened skies above San Francisco Bay. It was a lyric that painted a picture. When I listened, I thought, what was I going to do to make the song better? His creativity was spilling forth, flowing like a mountain spring after the snows had melted away. So I left him alone.

Now on the *Tupelo Honey* sessions, I'd thought I needed to chime in during lulls, to spark his creativity and keep him on track, when in fact backing off and remaining quiet was more effective. I never knew for certain what a track was going to end up becoming, but that was far preferable to confusing or frustrating him while he was in a creative headspace.

I remember that fall was a stressful time for me. I had a lot going on in my personal life, as Kathi and I prepared for the birth of our first child. Meanwhile I was trying to make sure I kept my employer happy. I had A&R responsibilities, so I'd spend time in my office, reviewing songs and meeting with artists. I'd also keep on top of sales and promotion issues for Van, since he didn't like dealing with that stuff. So it was a time of uncertainty and struggle, most importantly because I was still trying to prove myself worthy of my staff producer position.

My harried work life actually allowed me to bring my sister, Roberta, into the business. Because I couldn't keep up with all of the demo tapes I was receiving, I got her a job at Warner Bros. as a tape listener. Like me, she'd always had an ear for great songs and musicians, and so she excelled at the position. In fact, before the decade ended, she'd play a major role in the signings of Devo and Dire Straits, and become the general manager of West Coast A&R for Warner Bros.

On December 1, Kathi started having contractions. After we got to the hospital, we received the difficult news that there were complications with the birth, so things were touch and go right from the outset.

Van had asked me to call him at his home in Fairfax when the baby was due. He was a new father himself, so he'd been through the same experience. When I got him on the phone and explained what was happening, he said he was going to go right to the airport. A couple of hours later, he showed up at the hospital in Los Angeles to be by my side as I sweated things out.

That was a touching gesture of friendship I will never forget.

Soon after he arrived, I talked to the doctor. He said that Kathi's labor had stalled. She needed to rest for a few hours, so Van and I had a long, stressful wait ahead of us outside her hospital room.

Van could sense my worry. To get my mind off my fears, he suggested we go say hello to a friend of his, guitarist Doug Messenger, who was playing at a San Fernando Valley nightclub that evening. (Doug, as it turned out, would join Van's band in the coming weeks.)

On our way to the Valley, we stopped at my house in Pasadena for a few minutes. I was a terrible host, because my mind was elsewhere. Van had a bunch of drinks while I took care of a couple of things for Kathi before we went to the club. Van helped himself to some frozen cheese out of my freezer, telling me how good it tasted, in an effort to make me laugh. When that didn't do the trick, he started doing some James Brown imitations, which did make me smile. I know now that he was trying to express his affection for me in an indirect manner. It meant so much to me that he was there to help me get through the experience.

We then drove to the Valley and visited with Doug for a bit, but before long, Van had to catch his red-eye back to San Francisco. I drove him to the airport, where he hugged me and flew back home. On December 2, my son, Teddy Junior, was born, and both he and Kathi were healthy, thank God.

Soon after Teddy was born, Van asked me to record his upcoming performances at a blues-and-jazz club called the Lion's Share in San Anselmo. I called Donn and enlisted him to engineer the recordings. If I remember correctly, Van wanted them professionally documented because he'd invited so many guests to play with him. He performed with an acoustic and a harmonica. Those who joined him onstage during that week of shows included Rick Danko of the Band, John Lee Hooker, and folk singers Bob Neuwirth and Ramblin' Jack Elliott. Donn recalls that on the last night, Levon Helm of the Band played with Van too. I don't know whatever happened to the tapes, but Van was on and they were hot performances.

At that point, Warner Bros. had released "Tupelo Honey" as a single. It didn't do great on the charts, stalling outside the *Billboard* Top 40. I tried not to think about it, but I couldn't help but wonder if the flawed mix contributed to its struggles.

Soon after, I was working in my office. I got a phone call.

"Hello."

"Ted, it's Van."

"Oh hi."

"Ted, y'know, you were right. About 'Tupelo Honey.'"

All the frustration, the fruitless pleading with Van, came rushing back. I felt angry. Angry with him for his bullheaded stubbornness, and at myself, for allowing him to convince me to do something that I knew wasn't the right thing to do.

As I thought about something constructive to say, he said something even more infuriating.

"So let's go with the other mix. Let's put it out."

I went *nuts!* That drove me crazy, it really did. He was wrong, and then he called up and wanted to go back to the other mix after the album had been released, the single had been pressed, and it had gone to radio . . . In effect, he wanted to put the toothpaste back in the tube. It was another reminder that I didn't like co-producing.

Meanwhile, I had a couple new and exciting projects come my way. At the tail end of 1971, Lenny, now head of A&R at Warner Bros., had told me that the Doobies had inquired if I'd be interested in producing their next record. When I'd last checked in with those guys, they'd been producing their own recording sessions up at Wally Heider. The results, I learned from Lenny, had not been stellar. They'd booked marathon sessions at the studio, which had decimated their budget. Even worse, when Lenny had taken a listen to their work in progress, he hadn't liked a lot of what they'd put on tape, and thus they stood perilously close to being dropped by Warner Bros. When Lenny and I talked, though, I told him that I thought I could right the ship. He agreed, and so I'd be producing their sophomore effort.

Lenny also suggested that I consider producing another of the label's young acts, Little Feat. Comprised of bassist Roy Estrada, guitarist and vocalist Lowell George, keyboardist and vocalist Billy Payne, and drummer Richie Hayward, the band had put out *Little Feat*, one of my favorite rock records of 1971. All four guys, I'd find out, had been in the business for a few years.

During the sixties, Lowell and Richie had been in a band called the Factory. Then in 1968 Lowell joined Frank Zappa's Mothers of Invention, a band that Estrada had started with Zappa a few years earlier.

When I first saw Little Feat perform that year, I thought they were one of the greatest live bands I'd ever seen. But, like the Doobies, their debut hadn't sold a lick, and Lowell and my colleague, staff producer Russ Titelman, had been at loggerheads by the time the sessions had wrapped. I eagerly agreed to take them on as well.

In both cases, I enlisted Donn to be my engineer. We planned to record the Doobies and Little Feat at Amigo and Sunset Sound, with recording sessions that would fill a good stretch of weeks on our calendars.

Taking on these two records, both of which we were to record in Hollywood, made it impossible for Donn and me to be in San Francisco at the same time to participate fully in the making of Van's next record.

So we largely left Van to his own devices when it came to cutting *St. Dominic's Preview*, other than a few overdub sessions, which we logged in April.

One of the songs Donn and I did work on was the title track. When I heard the lyric for "St. Dominic's Preview," I chuckled, because I saw myself in the lyrics. Van sang a line about my frantic note-taking during his sessions. That was his commentary on my efforts to keep track of everything he was doing when we were recording.

When it was all said and done, and the album emerged in July 1972, "Gypsy," "Almost Independence Day," "St. Dominic's Preview," and "Listen to the Lion," which we'd put on tape back in the summer of 1971, but hadn't made the cut for *Tupelo Honey*, appeared on it. I co-produced all of them with Van.

The next summer, Donn and I got the chance to work with Van again as he and his then-current band, the Caledonia Soul Orchestra, prepared to record a live album, entitled *It's Too Late to Stop Now*. We rolled tape at the Troubadour in Hollywood, and at the Santa Monica Civic Auditorium, where Van graciously invited Lorraine Ellison to open his show. Donn and I also traveled to England to record him at the Rainbow Theatre in London.

The London shows left the most vivid memories.

I spent time with Jo Bergman, who'd worked for the Beatles and was now working for the Stones, while I was in the UK in July 1973. She brought me to Mick Jagger's mansion, Stargroves, in Hampshire. I don't recall why Jo needed to go there, because Jagger wasn't at home at the time. But I met Mick's parents; they were lovely, and Jagger's adorable daughter Jade, who was there too, charmed us.

As an aficionado of British architecture, I loved seeing the place. It stood on dozens of well-landscaped acres. When I walked into the two-storey entrance hall, it blew my mind. It was twenty feet long and fifty feet wide and had an imposing stone fireplace. It reminded me of the aristocratic spaces you see in old movies, except it was filled with amps, guitars, and Anvil cases rather than suits of armor and tapestries.

Soon after, Donn and I retrieved the Pye Mobile truck to tape the shows. It had a remarkable number of hit albums to its credit and had been used to record performances at the Isle of Wight Festival as well as the Who's *Live at Leeds*.

To record the shows, Donn and I worked in the back of the truck, which we parked outside the Rainbow. Even though we weren't in the hall, every note and cheer we heard through our headphones sent electricity coursing through my body. Van's one of the most soulful cats on the planet; the performance he put on was *incredible*. The place pulsed with energy, and when he did "Gloria," the room exploded. The ambiance was unparalleled.

Recording Van Morrison in London was one of the most exciting things I've ever done in the music business. Period.

After Donn and I got things dialed in, I'd leave Donn in the truck for a spell and go into the hall to watch Van perform. Because Van knew that the Pye Mobile had just one tape machine on board, and that Donn and I had to swap reels quickly to avoid missing a note, he felt compelled to check in on us from the stage. He'd be out there onstage at the Rainbow, finishing a song. The crowd would be cheering him, but he'd be talking just to me. Looking out over the audience, he'd whisper into the mic, "Hey, Ted? Didja get that, Ted?" It was funny.

After the shows, Van came to the truck to hear what we'd gotten on tape. He'd knock on the door, and he'd enter, sweat coursing down his bare chest. Van looked like a bare-knuckle fighter stripped to the waist. It reminded me of the scuffle in back in San Francisco. I smiled to myself, thinking of the mistake those two guys made in mocking Van. He wasn't a man to be trifled with, under any circumstances.

After one of the shows, Van and I went to get a drink. He'd torn the Rainbow apart, leaving his fans spellbound, but none of that seemed to register with him. I really think he had no idea how much people loved him and his music. To his credit, he just wasn't on an ego trip when it came to his celebrity.

Chapter 6

LISTEN TO
THE MUSIC

At the close of 1971, I had my hands full. I was working with Van Morrison and the Doobies, and I was in talks to produce the eccentric blues-shouter Captain Beefheart. But I didn't hesitate to say yes when the opportunity to produce Little Feat presented itself. As a unit, I thought they were right there with the Band, Robbie Robertson's group, in terms of creativity and musicianship. I'd worn the grooves out on Little Feat's debut.

Although they'd failed commercially thus far, they had a lot of support in-house. People believed in the band. It was one of those acts that demonstrated that Warner Bros. was an artist-centric label. We could point to them and credibly say we are committed to talent, even if consumers and radio programmers didn't seem to get the group.

In the fall of '71, I started attending their rehearsals. They worked at one of the Warner Bros. sound stages; that's where we did pre-production.

The more I watched, the more impressed I was by their talent and potential.

A drummer myself, I locked in on Richie. There are lots of drummers who are great live performers, but a lot fewer who can also play precisely enough to shine in the studio. Richie did both well. His drumming was one of the initial reasons I wanted to work with them. He sang great too, and more importantly, he had a unique voice. You could hear it when we rehearsed "Easy to Slip" — Lowell and Richie harmonized beautifully. Plus, when we talked on breaks, Richie and I got on well.

Billy Payne, too, was an excellent keyboardist. Piano or Hammond B-3, he was a master at both. Roy Estrada, the bassist, was a solid player.

Out of all the guys, I hit it off best with Lowell. He had a sawed-off frame and dark hair. Charming and charismatic, he was soft-spoken, headstrong, and had a wicked sense of humor. Lowell was a phenomenal, multitalented individual. A natural leader, he was a great guitarist, singer, and writer. In fact, he wrote or co-wrote most of the songs that we'd record for *Sailin' Shoes*.

One thing that almost immediately struck me was his smarts. He was a deep, original thinker, creative, and unconventional. Read his lyrics for "A Apolitical Blues." They're clever and funny, especially when you realize that he took his political principles seriously and always worried about the problems of the world.

Needless to say, as a producer, it was a dream to have a band packed with this much talent and with such a unique individual as a band leader. I loved Little Feat.

We booked studio time for late 1971, at both Amigo and Sunset. Lowell, in particular, was eager to start recording. He'd badly cut his fretting hand during the making of their debut. As a result, he'd had to cede a lot of guitar work on the record to Ry Cooder. Bizarrely, he'd injured himself in his house while trying to grab a model airplane engine while it was running. He caught hold of it by the propeller and it sliced deeply into his flesh.

When I heard what had happened, I'd asked Lowell why he spent so much time tinkering with model planes. I was curious, because Lenny built them too. I figured he'd give me some spiel about the beauty of aircraft design. Nope. He told me he wanted to fly drugs in from Mexico on his model airplane. Maybe he was bullshitting me, but I swear to God — that's what he told me was his main motivation.

This Little Feat record would be the first time that Donn and I recorded an entire album together. But I will tell you that from the very beginning we had the most comfortable rapport. For instance, we discovered we shared the same philosophy when it came setting up the studio for recording. Many other engineers, I'd found, began by miking all the instruments and then started trying to get sounds and levels set for them.

Donn and I both thought this was the wrong approach. We'd go after the sound of the kick drum and the bass before anything else. Once we'd got the kick drum going *dumm*, and the electric bass going *dooooom*, and they sounded good at the same time, we'd move on to the other instruments, because now we'd nailed down what we considered the heartbeat of an album. We built the rest of the sound of an album out from there. When you've got those two sonic components in sync, it sounded great.

During the sessions, Donn and Lowell became sonic partners. When Lowell had an idea, Donn knew how to bring it to life. Over time, I swear, Donn knew what Lowell wanted before Lowell even asked him. At those moments, I'd hang back and let them work. Donn was absolutely instrumental in the recording of this album.

One of the reasons why Lowell and Donn worked so well together is that Lowell had a good handle on the technical aspects of recording. That wasn't a given when it came to musicians, even those who'd been in the studio many times. For instance, Van didn't concern himself with the intricacies of the recording process. So to have a songwriter and guitarist who could think like Donn and I did about making records was a real blessing. Lowell had been in the studio a lot by this point, even before Little Feat started, so he had good ideas and knew what he was doing when we recorded.

In fact, if his life had turned out differently, he could've become a staff producer at Warner Bros. He had the mind for it, great ears, and the studio bug. I'd forgotten this, but Donn reminds me that the day when Donn and I mixed "Jesus Is Just Alright" by the Doobie Brothers during the *Toulouse Street* sessions, Lowell showed up at Amigo. He sat in the control room, staring at us while we worked. Eventually Donn and I gave him something to do. We let him run a phaser on the cymbal track. Like me, he couldn't stay away from the studio.

A great example of his creativity appears on the title track for *Sailin' Shoes*. On it, Lowell played shuffle brushes on a snare drum. Now, as a drummer, I'm allergic to bad meter. So here's a guitarist playing drums, and he's not on the beat. So I said, "Lowell, your timing's off." He said he wanted it that way, because it would make the track sound off-kilter. That was counterintuitive to me, but it worked great on record, especially on a song that Van Dyke Parks had inspired by saying to Lowell, "If you're gonna get loaded, you better put on your sailing shoes."

Although we recorded the bulk of the album at Amigo, I wanted to cut one particular song, "Cold, Cold, Cold," at Sunset Sound. I'd done a lot of work in Studio 1 with Harpers, even before I'd met Donn, so I was very familiar with it and its sonic characteristics.

Even though we could work cheaply at Amigo, since Warner Bros. owned it, I had good reason for booking Studio 1 for this song.

Studios, you see, have different sonic fingerprints. Amigo was flat, level, and dead. The designers had apparently EQ'd the rooms to be sonically perfect; when we recorded there, there weren't a lot of surprises, in terms of room sound, when we played back our takes.

Sunset's Studio 1, in contrast, often delivered the unexpected. Recording there was like walking on ice. You'd record something, not knowing exactly where you were going to end up sonically, but it was always weird, great, and sometimes even dark. That was part of the excitement of Studio 1. Listen to the first two records by the Doors. You can hear how working in such a live room colored their sound. Anything I ever did in that space turned out interesting, so I was always eager to work there.

Donn, Richie, and I wanted to get a massive drum sound on tape for "Cold, Cold, Cold." What we started with for a drumbeat, actually, was a tape Lowell had made of a pattern he'd gotten on his Doncamatic, a primitive, first-generation drum machine.

When you hear the song fade in, the first thing you hear is the drum machine plodding away. We used it because the Doncamatic's electronic beats sounded so mechanical and sterile that they would contrast sharply with the ambiance of Richie's live drums when they entered.

Donn and I put Richie's drums on a riser against the wall of Studio 1. We close-miked his kit, but also placed microphones way up in the corner of that room. We then compressed the hell out of his drum sound.

As a result, every time Richie played it sounded like a dinosaur stomping around the room. That was part of the magic of Sunset 1; it has a relatively low clearance, which helped produce vibrant drum sounds. It also had another peculiar architectural feature. Because the building that housed Sunset Sound had been an auto repair garage, the floor sloped towards one corner, where a drain had been installed to remove oil and other fluids that ended up on the floor. That meant that the walls and ceiling all slanted that way too. Those asymmetrical surfaces generated a room sound that was "alive" and loud.

We built the track up from there. Lowell's guitar, Roy's bass, and Billy's Wurlitzer and piano entered next, followed by Lowell's sax, harmonica, and guitar in unison. Guitar and sax together were something I'd loved ever since I'd heard "Rocket 88" in my grandfather's music store in the fifties, so I loved pairing those on "Cold, Cold, Cold." Incidentally, we got Lowell's harmonica sound by having him play through a little Fender amp, which Donn had placed in a bathroom in the studio. Donn then miked the amp so we could get his harmonica parts on tape. Donn and I had a field day with that stuff.

Lowell's vocal performance was a standout. When I listen, he sounds like he's shivering, chilled to the bone. The lyrics, too, evoke dark alienation. Lowell wrote about ending up alone, desperate and fucked up in a hotel room in the middle of the country after your woman's dumped you. That was, at some point, a chapter in the life of every musician I knew. Even though the subject matter was depressing, I thought the lyric was a hopeful one, because if you've survived that kind of despair, you've come out of the experience a stronger person.

Because their debut didn't sell, I really wanted a hit single for them. Lowell wanted the same thing too, because he'd co-written a song called "Easy to Slip" with his friend Martin Kibbee, with radio in mind. I thought Lowell had it dialed in — it sounded like a surefire hit to me.

We layered that one with a range of instruments. I'm a percussion *freak*, so we put tabla, these Indian drums, on it. I brought in Milt Holland from the Wrecking Crew, who'd played in the studio for Harpers Bizarre, to play on the track. Actually, using tabla might have been Donn's idea. And I should mention it is not easy to record that instrument, but Donn captured it so well. We added shakers, Lowell's acoustic and electric guitars, and some driving B-3 organ courtesy of Billy too.

But what I thought was going to connect with the public was Richie and Lowell's harmonies. Richie's voice was great and provided a wonderful counterpoint to Lowell's. In fact, I wanted to make Richie a lead singer on a track or two, but Lowell wasn't up for it. I really thought Richie's voice was an underutilized resource: it was identifiable and commercial.

The other song I thought might make a good single was "Willin'." They'd recorded it for *Little Feat*, but Lowell wanted to cut it again since Ry Cooder had played a lot of the guitar on it after Lowell had torn up his hand. Our re-recorded version came out very well. Billy's piano solo is so pretty and recorded so well by Donn that it damn near brings a tear to the eye. To give it a country flavor, we had "Sneaky" Pete Kleinow of the Flying Burrito Brothers play steel guitar. And once again you had Richie and Lowell's gorgeous harmonies.

We finished tracking and overdubs in early January 1972. Donn and I then mixed the record. I was optimistic that we had a hit on our hands.

Before I'd started working with Little Feat, I attended a martial arts demonstration for the forthcoming Warner Bros. film *Billy Jack*. It starred Tom Laughlin as a Native American Vietnam vet who was an expert in a Korean martial art, hapkido. That day, the movie's martial arts consultant, Bong Soo Han, showed off his sparring techniques. He was a true master of his craft; I was really impressed with Han's abilities. Before I left, I asked a couple of the production people how I could get in touch with him; they told me he taught classes not far from my Pasadena home.

The next time I saw Lowell I told him about what I'd seen at the demonstration. He'd been studying kung fu since he was a teenager and he took it seriously, so I asked his advice. I told him that I wanted to learn how to defend myself. No one in those days that I knew carried a gun, but situations like the one that happened to Van and me in the Haight still could get you killed. Lowell encouraged me to sign up for the classes, so I did.

The classes met early each morning in this small studio. We started with about thirty-five people. Han had us do nothing but intense calisthenics, every day. The people who wanted to learn fighting techniques right away, naturally, got frustrated and stopped attending. Every day the group got smaller, which was Han's goal. He wanted to see who would quit. The class eventually dropped down to eight or nine people.

Sometime in the third week, he said to the class, "Everyone come out front of the building with me, please." We gathered on the sidewalk. He said, "I want to show you something." Right then he bent his knees and jumped. Tucking his legs towards his chin, he rotated his trunk to a horizontal position, eyes to the sky, about four feet from the ground. He landed with a sickening thud on his back. I'm thinking he was hurt. Bad. But he popped right up off the sidewalk. Dusting himself off, he said, "If you stay with the program, I can show you how to do things like that with your body and mind." Wow. Holy shit.

Over the next months, he taught us how to spar, to kick and punch, and to execute throwing and blocking techniques. The learning curve was steep and it was physically demanding. But I loved it, because it was a good release for my workaholic schedule.

So by the time we were finishing up *Sailin' Shoes*, I'd been taking hapkido classes for several months. Lowell and I were sitting at the board, listening to a playback. He slid a cigarette from a pack, lit it, and asked if I was still taking hapkido.

"Yeah."

"Did Han teach you three good moves yet?"

"Yeah."

"Which one do you like?"

"The side kick."

He stood up, motioning for me to follow him out of the control room.

He led me into Amigo's office area. He pushed a table and chair out of the way, shuffled back a step, and said, "Okay, well, try it on me."

"The side kick?"

"Yeah."

"I don't want to hurt you."

"You won't," he said, body coiled. "Do it full force."

I shifted my weight to my left so I could kick with my right foot.

"Are you sure?"

"Yeah. I'm ready."

I threw my hardest kick at him, right at his sternum.

Lightning quick, he caught my foot in his hand. He held it and didn't let go.

From there he could have tossed me into the file cabinets. Or broken my leg. He looked me in the eye and said, "See what I mean? I was ready."

The record came out in February 1972. I thought my instincts had been right. *Billboard*, *Cash Box*, and the *Washington Post* gave it good reviews. "Easy to Slip" started getting added to radio playlists, but never charted. The album, too, toyed with the *Billboard* Top 200 in late May, but never built any real momentum.

I was devastated. When you pour your heart into something that you think is great and the public doesn't seem to give a shit, it hurts.

I was most upset that "Easy to Slip" did nothing. I really thought that could be a hit. I still don't know why it wasn't. It just wasn't in the grooves. But it was a good lesson for me to learn. Usually, when I attempted to manufacture a hit single, it didn't happen.

In the end, it just felt like unfinished business for me. They had the songs and the players, and still I produced an album that stiffed.

Now, when "Easy to Slip" came out as a single, I didn't get many calls from our promo guys telling me that it had been added to radio playlists. But I did get a few calls from some disgruntled producers.

At the time, engineers didn't get a lot of respect. More often than not, they didn't get credited in album liner notes. And to the best of my knowledge at the time, engineers rarely got credited on the record label itself. You'd typically have the name of the artist, songwriter, arranger, and producer who worked on the recording. But almost never the name of the engineer.

Meanwhile, the engineer is contributing something special to the record too. The engineer's capturing the sounds, mixing the songs, and holding the fort when the producer can't be at the studio. My point is that an engineer's role in the making of great records is often quite significant and yet they frequently became an afterthought when the champagne corks got popped.

So I decided that I wanted Donn's name on the record label for the "Easy to Slip" single. In fact, I insisted that it appear there, because I wanted to do for Donn what Lenny had done for me by crediting me as an arranger or co-producer.

When his name appeared, it caused a stir with some producers around town. They didn't seem as happy to share credit with their engineers. My thought was, hey, a gold record at the time was a very big deal. If I get one, I wanted Donn's name to be on the label so it would appear on the gold record award, so people knew who'd been the sonic magician behind it all. And, just to be clear, this had nothing to do with royalties; putting an engineer's name on a record label didn't grant that person a single penny more in income, so the producers who were calling me weren't mad because of money. It was about who got to stand in the spotlight. I got a lot of pushback about that from my peers, but I was happy to suffer the slings and arrows for Donn.

Soon after Donn and I finished *Little Feat*, we turned our attentions to the Doobie Brothers. Since their first album, they'd added a couple of new members. Their bassist, Shogren, had quit; they replaced him with Tiran Porter, who'd played with Pat in the past.

They also added a second drummer, Mike Hossack. The drummer in me loved this idea. At the time, the highly successful Allman Brothers Band showcased the rhythmic potential of a two-drummer lineup, but as I recall they added Hossack because John, the band's primary drummer, wanted to produce a louder, more powerful drum sound.

Once I started rehearsing the band with Mike and Tiran, I knew they were going to make a major contribution. Mike was a metronome, so precise and yet powerful. I'd often compare him to Jimmy Gordon from the Wrecking Crew. He was that good. Tiran's bass lines grooved and yet were so clean. He's a killer. Even before those guys joined, the Doobies were already a rhythm-centric band. Even Tommy's guitar playing was very percussive. So I was excited about the potential for more complex rhythm ideas.

Their songwriting, too, had taken a step forward. Here's a good story on that front.

I was in bed at home, asleep, and the phone rang. I look at the clock. It's two a.m.

I picked up the phone.

"Yeah?"

"Ted, it's Tommy. Sorry to wake you. Check this out. It's called 'Listen to the Music.'"

He started strumming his acoustic and singing it. It was a classic Tommy Johnston tune; it had his signature relentless train rhythm and a sing-along chorus. Now, the song would evolve a bit once we got in the studio, but he had the lyrics, chords, and melody written. The song was, in effect, complete. When he finished, he said, "Ted, it's a hit. *I know it.*"

I wasn't convinced. I liked the song, but it didn't sound like a single to me. But he had a demo of it on tape, ready to go.

Before we went into Amigo, I assessed what they'd recorded at Heider. Although the way they'd worked was wildly inefficient — they had hours of material on tape, but most of the songs weren't good enough to release — they did have a few diamonds in the rough. For *Toulouse Street*, in fact, we'd end up using some of the the performances they'd tracked with Steve Barncard for "Snake Man," "White Sun," and the album's title track.

Building on that starting point, we worked up and arranged their best tunes, including "Listen to the Music." Because a lot of their original material wasn't quite polished enough, I suggested "Cotton Mouth" by Seals & Crofts. The guys weren't familiar with the song, but once they heard it, they loved it and decided to cover it. We'd record two other covers as well: "Jesus Is Just Alright," which had been made popular by the Byrds, and Sonny Boy Williamson's "Don't Start Me to Talkin'."

When I thought about how I wanted this album to sound, I resolved to stay true to their identity while broadening their sonic horizons. For instance, I wanted to continue to showcase their harmonies. That was one of the original aspects of their sound that really appealed to me when I heard their demo tape in 1970. In addition, their layered two-guitar attack, warm acoustics jangling alongside clean electrics, would remain. Lenny and I, for better or worse, had pushed that to the forefront on their debut.

Nonetheless, I wanted to make sure we made a record that better reflected their full range. When the Doobies played live on the Mother/Brothers Show tour, they had a more muscular approach to their material than the way Lenny and I had presented their songs on *The Doobie Brothers*. I wanted Pat and Tommy's electric guitars to *crunch* on certain tracks, while still capturing the contrast between Tommy's power-chording and Pat's finger-picked parts. That counterpoint was a cornerstone of the Doobies sonic identity.

I had a couple of other ingredients in mind to spice up the Doobies' stew.

I wanted to add horns to some of their songs. I hired a New Orleans sax player, Jerry Jumonville, to do session work. He'd perform on the record and do the horn arrangements on "Cotton Mouth" and on "Don't Start Me to Talkin'." He'd appeared on Ry Cooder's *Into the Purple Valley* — which Lenny produced — and Delaney & Bonnie and Friends' *To Bonnie from Delaney*.

Keyboards, too, would broaden out their sound. I immediately thought of Billy Payne from Little Feat. He'd play some swirl-ing, churning Hammond on "Jesus Is Just Alright" and "Cotton Mouth," some rollicking barrelhouse piano on "Rocking Down the Highway" and "Don't Start Me to Talkin'." Bringing Billy on board was, I believe, the first time I hired an artist I'd already produced to perform on an album I was producing with another one of my acts. I can't tell you how many different projects the guys in the Doobies and Little Feat would appear on as session players for me in the years that followed.

My most distinct memories of recording *Toulouse Street* involve the making of "Listen to the Music." When we recorded it, I had an idea for how to dial in an unorthodox guitar sound. I brought my father's hollow-body Epiphone electric guitar into the studio. I had Donn place microphones on the F-holes and the strings, miking it as you would an acoustic. We didn't use an amp. Instead, we used a DI, or direct input, meaning we ran the signal from the microphone out in the studio directly into the mixing desk in the control room. That approach captured the attack of the pick on the strings really well. I'm not sure if anyone else had done this previously, but it sounded cool.

Then we doubled that same track with an acoustic and an electric guitar to brighten it all up. I liked the way it sounded on the record. And it turned out that the Epiphone track added a sparkle to the guitar parts that cut through on AM radio.

The guys in the band thought up some great ideas in the studio too. Someone — I think either Pat or John — suggested that Mike Hossack play steel drums on the song. Starting with the second verse, you'll hear that unmistakable Caribbean sound. Pat came up with a banjo part and some electric guitar licks for the song's outro. I called Pat's guitar lines on "Listen to the Music" his "Layla" moment, because to me his playing is reminiscent of Clapton's work on that classic. All of these elements made an already great song better.

When we worked on the vocals, I suggested that Pat sing the bridge for "Listen to the Music." I loved it, not only because it gave the song room to breathe in the middle, but also because it allowed us to spotlight both of the band's talented vocalists.

This song, too, showcases a Doobie Brothers signature: Pat and Tommy's unison vocals. On this track, and all the others that featured their two-part harmonies, I first had them sing the lower part, twice, so Donn could double it. Next, they'd do the same on the upper part. That was the way Donn and I got their pretty backgrounds on tape.

When we were mixing "Listen to the Music," Donn had the idea to use phasing on the track. Donn, of course, had been the engineer who'd created the same effect when Harpers Bizarre cut "Knock on Wood." We added the effect to Pat's vocal during the song's bridge.

Needless to say, if I hadn't had Donn, I couldn't have done all of this intricate work on the second Doobies album. Not only was he a fantastic engineer, he could practically read my mind, which made my job so much easier. I'd throw him a certain look when we were sitting together at the mixing desk, and he'd know what I wanted done. Or, if a guitar lick was out of tune, he'd give me a subtle glance but not say a word, knowing that I might not even use that part on the final mix. With Donn as my co-pilot, I never had to worry about the technical aspects of making records. I could focus on working with the musicians and on crafting their songs.

That summer was a big moment for me as a producer. Warner Bros. released Van Morrison's *St. Dominic's Preview* and the Doobie Brothers' *Toulouse Street* in July 1972. Van's record reached the Top 20 of the *Billboard* Top 200 in September.

By this time, the guys had long convinced me that "Listen to the Music" was single material. I'd sequenced the record with it as the opening track, but still, credit goes to Tommy Johnston for immediately recognizing its potential. He said it was a hit from the first time he played it for me, and he was dead right. It started moving up the *Billboard* chart almost immediately after its release and became a pop hit on AM radio.

In November, the song would top out at No. 11 of the *Billboard* Hot 100. I was so happy for those guys; they'd labored in obscurity, playing keg parties and biker bars. Now they were stars.

The album had real legs too. "Jesus Is Just Alright" hit the Top 40, and the LP itself would ultimately spend more than one hundred weeks on the *Billboard* Top 200, selling more than half a million copies a little more than a year after its release.

As a result of these successes, Warner Bros. promoted me to A&R executive producer. I'd thus join the label's A&R executive team, which was headed by Lenny. I'd also be working alongside Russ Titelman, Velvet Underground founding member John Cale, and Andy Wickham, an Englishman who'd worked closely with Mo for years, helping to land Jethro Tull and Joni Mitchell for

The A&R Staff of Warner Bros Records, 1972 (*from left to right*):
Lenny Waronker, Andy Wickham, me, Russ Titlelman, and John Cale.
RHINO ENTERTAINMENT COMPANY, A WARNER MUSIC GROUP COMPANY.

Reprise. Before the year was out, Warner Bros. ran a full-page ad in *Billboard* calling the five of us the architects of "The Burbank Sound." (Warner Bros. Records was headquartered in Burbank.) It was an exhilarating period in my life.

By this time, I'd turned my attentions to Captain Beefheart and his Magic Band. Don Van Vliet, whose stage name was Captain Beefheart, was an utterly unique talent. His musical approach paired the avant-garde zaniness of Zappa with his blues bellow, which was reminiscent of Howlin' Wolf. He was wildly creative and incredibly tempestuous. His prior albums had been uncommercial — jazzy and noisy, bluesy and atonal — almost to the point of parody. But that made no difference in many ways because his artistic talents were undeniable.

Beefheart had a broad, imperious face framed by dark curls, often enveloped by a top hat. Even before I agreed to produce him, I went to some band practices. He rehearsed the hell out of his musicians (who all had stage names of their own): guitarists Bill Harkleroad (Zoot Horn Rollo) and Mark Boston (Rockette Morton), former Little Feat bassist Roy Estrada (Orejón) and drummer Art Tripp (Ed Marimba). His band was outstanding, and his drummer was funky and yet technically great. He'd played with a symphony in the past.

When I watched his rehearsals, I became very impressed with his songwriting. Along with writing lyrics, he'd written all of the different instrumental parts to his songs. He'd arrange the songs: the drum parts, guitar lines, and bass fills. I really liked his material. One song that I couldn't get out of my head was the shuffling "Nowadays a Woman's Gotta Hit a Man." Another one, which I thought might get AM airplay (something that would have been inconceivable for Beefheart before this album) was a Stax-like tune called "Too Much Time."

So my goal for the record was make his music more accessible without losing the off-the-wall, raucous elements that made him so magnetic as an artist.

Even though the music was compelling and his Magic Band was tight, it wasn't a fun record to make. Beefheart was a tyrant. While I tried to keep things calm, he and I often butted heads, because I had to assert my authority over him and his band, which he didn't like at all.

Since he couldn't hold sway over me, he'd bully the guys in his band, keeping them in a constant state of unease. He'd do these nutty things that made everyone feel like they had to walk on eggshells around him. For instance, he made Estrada *dance* in the studio. He'd say, "You've gotta dance!" You have to understand — this is while he's trying to play the bass and get the take!

Sometimes he'd get violent. I remember one time I was out in the studio in Amigo with all the guys, including Beefheart. Donn was behind the board, waiting to record the next part. We'd been at it for a while, working on a certain song.

Apropos of nothing, he snarled at Harkleroad. "Hey! What did you eat today?"

"Huh?"

"Tell me! What did you eat!"

"Tacos."

"Tacos?"

Boom. Beefheart struck him square in the face. Harkleroad tumbled over his chair and sprawled onto the floor.

I was speechless.

Harkleroad proceeded to dust himself off, climb back in his seat, and put his guitar back around his neck.

Cutting vocals with him was a challenge too.

Amigo Studios, along with its recording facilities, had offices for the staff who ran the place. One of the staff members was a secretary named JoAnne. Like every secretary in America during those days, she did a lot of typing.

Donn, Beefheart, and I were all in the studio — the one the farthest away from the offices. Sound-dampened doors, windows, and walls all stood between us and the offices.

After another bad take, Beefheart ripped off his headphones.

"Goddammit! I can hear her."

Donn and I were puzzled.

Through the talkback, I said, "You can hear who?"

"I can hear her typing. Right now! Right now! *Listen*!"

Now she may have been typing, but he couldn't have heard a typewriter from where he was sitting.

"I don't hear it."

"Go tell her to stop typing, or *I'll tell her!*"

So I walked down the hall. She wasn't typing, but I asked her not to type again until we left.

This type of stuff became a pattern with him. Sure, some of it stemmed from his eccentricity, but most of all, he just wanted to take out his frustrations. Whenever he got bogged down creatively

Donn and me sitting behind the board at Amigo Studios, circa 1972.
TYLER THORNTON/RHINO ENTERTAINMENT COMPANY, A WARNER MUSIC GROUP
COMPANY.

Another shot of Donn and me at work at Amigo Studios, circa 1972.
Rolling tape, we concentrate, trying to get the take. TYLER THORNTON/
RHINO ENTERTAINMENT COMPANY, A WARNER MUSIC GROUP COMPANY.

or struggled to get a take right, he'd blame it on whomever he could. In this instance, it was easier to scream, "I can hear her typing!" than say, "Hey Ted, I can't get this part right. Can we take a break?"

When we were working on a song called "Circumstances," another crazy episode happened with Beefheart.

There's a short breakdown in the middle of the tune where all the instruments drop out and Beefheart sings *a cappella*.

We'd given it a few tries and he hadn't gotten it right. I didn't want him to blow up, so I prepared to tell him we'd come back to the part later and try again.

But right before I did that he announced, "Okay, I'm taking the headphones off. Ted, point at me when the track starts and I'll sing."

In other words, he wanted to sing along to a recording while not listening to it. To me, it made as much sense as trying to run a football play while blindfolded. It wasn't going to work.

Donn shot me a sideways glance. He was apparently thinking the same thing. It will not work.

After going back and forth with him, it was just easier to let him try, even though I thought it would be a waste of time.

The funny thing is this: Donn recalls that Beefheart *did* in fact get that vocal right without listening to the instrumental track, and that very vocal performance is the one on the record. My memory differs, but Donn could very well be right. It was just one of those moments that was, in my mind, unnecessarily filled with drama and difficulty.

But this pales in comparison to what happened subsequently.

At a day or so later, Donn and I were back in the studio recording Beefheart. We'd been through a number of vocal takes with him, and he started to lose his cool. He was in front of the microphone in the studio, getting frustrated. Donn and I were behind the glass, sitting at the board in the control room.

The band wasn't there. His wife was sitting in the corner, like she always did.

Suddenly, he ripped off his headphones, slamming them down. In his gravelly bark, he growled into the microphone, "I know why I'm not getting anywhere tonight. It's because of *you, Donn!*"

He stabbed his finger right at Donn. I watched, appalled and amazed, as he leapt off his stool and headed toward the control room.

Donn was understandably upset and scared. He just got out of his chair and zip — he split. Getting into a fistfight with an artist wasn't in his job description.

After all of his bullshit, I was pissed.

To me, fucking with Donn like that was like fucking with one of my kids. Here's Donn, one of the planet's most creative engineers, busting his ass and doing a great job. He's got to get all of the technical minutiae right, from cords to faders. He's the first to arrive and the last to leave the studio. Plus in this case, he's got to endure all of Beefheart's insane excuses and loony ideas while trying to make me, the producer, happy.

And now this guy decides to take a run at him?

Fuck that.

It's funny to think about this now, but I was trying to think through my best hapkido moves so I could defend myself. I decided that if he attacked me, I'd kick him right in the throat.

Once he'd bulldozed his way into the control room, he started ranting about Donn.

I told him, as calmly as I could, that I'd had enough of his bullshit.

He had a choice. Either he worked with my engineer and me and we finish the album, or the label would bring in another producer and engineer, and he wouldn't have any say in the matter.

That's the only time I had to make that kind of speech to an artist.

At this point, I knew he was only trying to deflect attention away from his own failings. In this case he targeted Donn instead of me, because I was the person who signed off on Beefheart's budgets and had control over his album.

Despite these difficulties, Donn and I saw things through. In fact, he and I appeared on the album cover photo. It was taken at the Griffith Observatory. We're sitting behind the telescope console, while Beefheart and Carl Scott peer over the panel at us. In the liner notes, Beefheart paid tribute to Donn. He gave him the nickname "Mit," because, as Beefheart explained to me later, "Donn caught everything I threw at him." He was a strange cat.

When *Clear Spot* came out in late 1972, it didn't do much commercially, in part because "Too Much Time" didn't chart. But I am very proud of the record. The rhythms are infectious, the lyrics make you smile, and the songs are strong. I'm biased, but I think it's the most accessible album of Beefheart's career.

In early 1973, Ronnie Montrose called and said he wanted to meet with me about a new hard rock band he was putting together. I invited him to come stay at my house in Pasadena. Beyond the fact that Ronnie was such a positive guy and a good friend, I was excited to hear about his current project. Even before he parted ways with Van Morrison, I knew Ronnie was going to end up doing something on his own. He was too talented to remain a sideman forever.

When we sat down and talked, he filled me in on what he'd been up to since he left Van's band. He'd joined the Edgar Winter Group, performing on the hit album *They Only Come Out at Night* and touring with the band. After that tour wrapped, he left Edgar's band and started putting together a new group, which he called Montrose. He started by pairing up with bassist Bill Church, who'd worked with Ronnie and me on Van's *Tupelo Honey*. Ronnie then recruited two young, raw Bay Area players to round out the group: singer Sammy Hagar and drummer Denny Carmassi. I was immediately interested in this project because I knew that Ronnie and Bill made a great team, and of course because I loved Ronnie as a musician and friend.

Soon after, I heard a demo. It had a number of tunes that ended up on their debut, like "Rock Candy," "I Don't Want It," and "One Thing on My Mind." The demo also let me evaluate Hagar and Carmassi. Sammy had a bit of a Robert Plant feel to him, without imitating Plant, and Denny was a monster. So the whole goddamned band was great. I was sold. I signed them in the spring.

For me, hearing Ronnie's new band took me back to 1968 or so, when I first heard Cream. Harpers Bizarre did a TV show with them, in Philly I think. I was in a band that specialized in airy sunshine pop, while Eric Clapton, Ginger Baker, and Jack Bruce were playing incendiary hard rock.

At the time, too, Harpers Bizarre performed one song, "Fire" by the Jimi Hendrix Experience, in our live set like a power trio. I played drums, Scap played bass (he was a guitarist by training, but played *great* electric bass), and Eddie played guitar. That was, by far, my favorite song to do live with Harpers Bizarre. When I heard Ronnie's material, I thought back to watching Cream and playing the Hendrix song with my band as reference points for what kind of album I'd like to make with Montrose.

Despite my enthusiasm, there was some skepticism inside Warner Bros. about this band. Ronnie had only been a sideman to this point. The same went for Bill Church. The other two guys were untested and unknown. There were no clear signs that this band was destined to break big. In fact, some of my peers at the label warned me against taking on this project. They thought I was nuts because I seemed to be pinning my hopes on a long shot like Montrose rather than playing it safe by producing acts with more commercial potential.

But here's the thing. Ronnie and I talked about the fact that Warner Bros. Records had some big-time heavy metal outfits on its roster, including Alice Cooper, Deep Purple, and Black Sabbath. They sold a lot of records, and even sometimes wrote hit singles ("Smoke on the Water" and "School's Out" come to mind). But these groups were all so dark, strident, and serious.

With Montrose, Ronnie was trying to make heavy metal that was both commercial and fun. I loved the idea. My way of phrasing it was to say we needed to make a heavy metal album with a sense of humor, one that would make you tap your toes and smile. Sammy's lyrics worked in that context. He didn't write poetry, but his subject matter emphasized the positive side of life rather than overdoses and nuclear war, topics that were the stock-in-trade of the heavy metal acts of the time. So Ronnie, Sammy, and I were on the same page.

In my mind, I had this monster guitar player who wrote these aggressive riffs paired with this powerful singer, backed by a supercharged rhythm section. But I also knew that Sammy had cut his teeth on Top 40 as a working musician and that Ronnie

Listening to a playback at Wally Heider Studios in San Francisco, most likely while working on the Montrose debut album, summer 1973. DONN LANDEE.

had an innate feel for pop music. So in this weird way, I was trying to draw a line from Ronnie's work on Van Morrison's "(Straight to Your Heart) Like a Cannonball" to a song like Montrose's "I Don't Want It." I know it's anathema to say this about a song that Van wrote and sang, but I believe Ronnie's infectious strumming and catchy fills made "Cannonball" worthy of release as a single. Listen to it with an ear for Ronnie's playing, and then follow it up with "I Don't Want It." On the latter song, Ronnie trades off with Sammy and adds these little hooks at end of every verse. So he knew how, as a guitarist, to make his playing fit in a pop context. Ronnie was a fantastic talent.

In the summer of 1973, we tracked *Montrose* at Amigo and Sunset. If memory serves, we did overdubs at Heider. Once we got to work, Ronnie proved himself to be a lot more than just a great guitarist and songwriter. He had this amazing technical mind when it came to guitars, pickups, amps, and how to get great sounds in the studio.

As a producer, I saw that one key to the album's success would be making sure that Donn and I, just like we'd done while working with Lowell, got what Ronnie was hearing in his head on tape. My experiences with Little Feat and Lowell taught me that Donn and Ronnie needed to become collaborators. And that's exactly what happened. They both had a tech-minded bent to them; they were both gear-heads. But they were also both very creative. In the studio, Ronnie had multiple ways of approaching sounds. He brought in his own limiter to the studio, and we did in fact use it on the album. He'd always think outside the box. He'd fool around with his amplifiers all the time; he'd put in different tubes. I didn't always understand what he was doing. But Donn did.

The one track I insisted we record at Sunset Sound, in Studio 1, was "Rock Candy." I wanted to get a big drum sound on tape, one similar to the one that Donn and I had dialed up on "Cold, Cold, Cold" for Little Feat. We put Denny's drums up on a riser, miking it the same way that we'd miked Richie's kit. When Denny tracked his drums, we got a booming, thumping sound that moved a hell of a lot of air.

The other thing I'm particularly proud of in regards to "Rock Candy" is its tempo. We got it just right. If you listen back to the demo, it moves at a bit of a brisker pace. I had them slow it down so it could sound mean and heavy.

Lastly, I have a soft spot for it because Ronnie asked me to play B-3 Hammond organ on the song. Listen to it in headphones and you'll hear it mixed into the background. I played some dark chords underneath Ronnie's guitar, just to help thicken everything up.

By now, Donn and I had become a well-oiled machine. Let me give you an example. We'd lay down a drum track. We'd play it back in the control room with Denny and Ronnie. We'd listen once, twice. At the end of the second one, Donn would eyeball me. I'd think, *Oh shit, I missed something.* Maybe I had one of the toms tuned differently than I should have? He'd roll the tape back, give me a subtle indication of what was amiss, and sure enough, he'd be right. He'd do it in such a way that Denny didn't feel like he'd made a mistake, and also gave me the chance to look good in front of the musicians so they wouldn't think I was asleep at the wheel. We'd redo the take, after I'd had a chance to couch things in a way that didn't erode anyone's confidence. It's hard for me to overstate how important it was to have an engineer who's knowledgeable about both the technical and psychological aspects of making an album at my side as a young producer.

Montrose hit record stores in December 1973. I had such high hopes for them. I thought we'd made a tremendous record.

So I was truly flabbergasted when *Montrose* didn't sell well or get much radio attention. The playing, the songs, the sound, they were all there in the grooves. In that sense, the Montrose record felt like a repeat of what had happened with Little Feat. As a producer, you then have to do some soul searching when records you think are special don't sell. You feel terrible because you feel like you've let your artist down. In this case, it stung more acutely because Ronnie was my close friend.

Of course, the guys wanted a hit single. We put out "Rock the Nation" and "Space Station #5" as singles, but they were too heavy for AM radio, which drove the singles chart. When Montrose songs did get airplay, it was on what was called underground radio, on FM stations that didn't follow trends or formats. For instance, Tom Donahue, who'd returned to radio and at the time was managing just such a station, KSAN, loved the album. So the DJs at that Bay Area station played it a lot.

The fact that Montrose didn't become a big band, despite all of its strengths, was a big wake-up call for me. We couldn't get the album played on a pop station, because we didn't have a song that was a natural fit on AM radio. I never forgot that, and would try to make sure never to make that same mistake again.

Because Donn and I worked as a team, we spent an enormous amount of time together. That made work fun, because we were tight. We traveled together on projects, and when we worked long hours at Sunset, we played one-on-one basketball when we had an hour to kill. We'd worked a lot of weekends at Amigo Studios. Since the label owned it, we had keys to the building. We'd go in there at night so we could have the place to ourselves.

Naturally, because of our friendship, I wanted to do right by him. I'd already made sure his name and engineering credit started appearing alongside mine on record labels. But I felt that wasn't enough, because he'd demonstrated that he was a creative contributor to these albums. So I offered him co-production on *Clear*

Spot and a couple of other records we made together around that time. But he turned me down, saying, "No, I'm an engineer, not a producer."

Even though he didn't want to be a producer, the one thing he really wanted was a Warner Bros. Records business card with his name on it. Like me, he was proud that he worked for such an amazing company.

When he and I first talked about it, I told him I'd be happy to make the request for him, thinking that would be a snap to get done for him. I went to Lenny, then to Mo, and even talked to the company lawyers, but none of them would okay it. I don't recall what the exact stumbling block was when it came to the label, but it had something to do with the fact that Donn, technically speaking, was employed by Amigo Studios rather than Warner Bros. Records. It was really frustrating, because I could not get them to bend. The whole thing was a drag, because it was the one thing he asked me to do for him. I felt I'd let him down.

Around this time, Mo, Lenny, and the rest of the label leadership decided to invest more resources into Black artists. Warner Bros. had recently released albums that did well on Black radio stations by Ashford & Simpson, an R&B act; Tower of Power, a jazzy-funk group; and Graham Central Station, a funk band. There was a sense that we'd been underserving that market, so this gave me my opportunity to do work with a couple of Black female singers.

In early 1973, I produced some sessions with a successful background singer named Claudia Lennear, in an effort to establish her as a solo artist. I'd met her and saw her sing over at A&M's soundstage in 1970 when Joe Cocker's Mad Dogs & Englishmen — the supergroup that featured Leon Russell and Cocker — rehearsed there. That was an amazing experience, and she stuck out for her beauty and her voice. Later on, I'd bump into her over at Sunset Sound when she was doing session work.

The more I got to know her, the more I liked her. She was sweet, and knew all the hip English rock stars like Jagger and Bowie. In fact, at that time guitarist Marc Bolan was on Reprise, and she was the one who introduced me to him at the label offices.

After Warner Bros. signed her, Claudia, her manager, and I met in my office to talk about the recording sessions with her that I was planning. I remember she'd been very ill with the flu, but her manager thought she was on the mend, so we held the meeting. While we were talking, though, she suddenly collapsed.

We rushed her from my office to the emergency room. By the time she saw the doctor, she was semi-conscious. The doctor ordered an injection for her. The nurse swabbed her arm before picking up the needle.

When she saw the syringe, her eyes got huge and she screamed. I'm talking shrieks of terror like she was about to be murdered. She had a horrible phobia about needles. I can't overemphasize how loud her screams sounded in the examination room. Here's a woman with an incredibly powerful set of lungs experiencing a full-blown fight-or-flight panic attack. Needless to say, the doctor decided to administer her medication orally.

I cut a few tracks with her, but in the end only one was released. It came out as a single in the spring of 1973, a cover of Little Feat's "Two Trains." That was Lowell's song, so I had him play on it. Nick DeCaro, who'd worked on sessions with everyone from Randy Newman to Harpers Bizarre, did the horn and string arrangements. One funny memory I have of the sessions with Claudia is that a major challenge for Donn and me was to keep her "on" the microphone while we were recording her vocals. When the music started to play, she'd start dancing, and she'd intermittently sway away from the mic, which made for bad takes. Donn, naturally, knew just how to solve this issue. He took gobos, or portable acoustic barriers, and caged her into a tight space around the microphone. It worked like a charm.

That same year, Van and I discussed co-producing an album with Lorraine Ellison. His interest in the project was sincere, but he had so much going on with his own career that he'd bow out before Donn and I went into the studio with her in Los Angeles.

For these sessions, I brought in a lot of the guys from bands I'd already produced. For instance, I used Mark Jordan, who'd played on *Tupelo Honey* and *St. Dominic's Preview*, on keyboards. From Little Feat, I recruited the group's two new members: bassist Kenny Gradney and guitarist Paul Barrere. The Doobies' John Hartman played percussion.

When I tried to think about how to present her on this album, I kept coming back to an inescapable truth: she was a gospel singer who'd had one huge pop hit. What I mean by that is that she was truly a vocalist who came straight out of the church to find success in the music business. To stay true to that identity, we recorded a late-sixties gospel song by Cassietta George called "Walk Around Heaven." She actually suggested that song to me. It's so affecting — it reminds me of an old-time spiritual. She sings her ass off on it with her incredible church-gospel voice. It's one of those songs that at the time, I felt like I'd done as good a job as I could as a producer. It's almost like the perfect record in my mind. Mark played a piano part like you might hear at Sunday services in the South, and I drew up a swelling string arrangement with Nick DeCaro.

She also wrote a bit. She came up with this heart-rending tune called "Country Woman's Prayer." It's a lament by a wife and mother, a plea to a home-wrecker to leave her husband alone.

I picked Jimmy Cliff's "Many Rivers to Cross" for her. It's such a great song. She sang it like she was in church, and I didn't have my act together enough to be able to dial her in properly, because when I listen now, it's clear she over-sang it. But here's the thing, as the producer, I'm the one who signed off on the performance. I didn't get it right.

"Rivers" was the album's main single, and the song that I thought might really resonate with the public. But in the end, "Rivers" was not good enough, and neither that song, nor the album, made any noise on the chart. So it was another record, like the Doobies debut, that left me feeling like I'd not done right by my artist. My concept of trying to fuse gospel and pop, to make spiritual music commercially successful, didn't quite work. I can look back now and see I was still cutting my teeth. As a producer, it takes a while for you to find your way.

Chapter 7

TAKIN' IT TO THE STREETS

In late 1972, the Doobies train was rolling. *Toulouse Street* had been a smash, but on the flip side, we needed to capitalize on its success by getting started on their third album, *The Captain and Me*, right away. In fact, we'd begin work on it less than six months after *Toulouse Street*'s release.

But we could only move so fast. Because of their busy touring schedule, I couldn't sequester all of us in Amigo for several consecutive weeks so we could cut the album from beginning to end. Instead, we recorded for a few days, and then they'd travel across the country to perform. Sometimes, Donn and I flew to them so we could keep working. For instance, we'd book time in a studio in Washington, DC, so we could to do overdubs.

We probably could have sped up the process by making a formulaic album that replicated their last album, but none of us wanted to do that. To broaden their sound, I brought in two synthesizer pioneers, Malcolm Cecil and Robert Margouleff, to program the sounds we'd use on one of Tommy's songs, "Natural Thing." I enlisted Nick DeCaro, who'd worked on the

Lorraine Ellison and Harpers Bizarre albums, to arrange strings on a B.B. King–style blues that Tommy had written, "Dark Eyed Cajun Woman," and a wistful ballad written by Pat, "South City Midnight Lady." On keyboards, I relied on the talents of Billy Payne of Little Feat once again.

The core of the album would remain Tommy's ballsy rockers, though. Because we needed to get the songs together fairly quickly, Tommy and I revisited some of his old ideas, including a song that had originally been called "Osborne." I'd actually heard them perform it live at the Chateau back in 1970; I remember thinking it had potential, even though in their live set it was more or less a just a vehicle for Pat and Tommy to trade leads. Tommy scatted more than sang lyrics. Lenny and I had considered recording it for their debut, but because it wasn't well developed, we decided not to cut it.

When we got into the studio for *Toulouse Street* in the spring of 1972, Tommy had played me the song's riff while singing variations on the same lines about love and trains, over and over. In fact, they'd cut a rough version of it with Steve Barncard at Heider before I took over production duties on *Toulouse Street*. The more I listened to Tommy play it, and the Heider demo, the more and more I liked it. I loved the sparkling minor seventh chords, moving back and forth on the neck, that he used. I told him, "This could be a good song. Finish the lyric. We'll arrange the musical parts and record it." Tommy, for whatever reason, still didn't love the song, so he didn't finish it.

So for their third album, I pulled it out of hibernation again. Tommy had actually forgotten about the song, but I hadn't. I had kept their original demo tape they'd submitted back in 1970 in my desk. Whenever I'd open the drawer it inhabited, I'd see the reel box, with the song titles on it, including "Osborne."

After I jarred his memory about "Osborne," he agreed to work on it some more. I pressed him hard about the lyrics. He already had the locomotive imagery, so I said, how about making the whole song about a train? We talked about wheels and rails. What had come to mind, actually, was Swiss classical composer Arthur Honegger's "Pacific 231," which was inspired by the movement of a locomotive, when I was suggesting lyrical content to Tommy.

That sparked his creativity. He locked in on the train idea. He sat down and worked out the lyrics, adding line after line. I kept feeding him ideas as he wrote. He called it "Long Train Runnin'."

Before he finished the lyrics, the song's musical parts got fully fleshed out. Tommy wrote a harmonica solo, which seemed fitting considering the song's train lyrics. Pat, too, right in the studio, had come up with his own corresponding guitar part that supported Tommy's riff. In effect, Pat had the counter-melody. He'd write these amazing, spidery, fingerpicked licks that contrasted beautifully with Tommy's dense chording. He did this all the time. Pat was so integral to the Doobie Brothers' hits — all of them.

Tommy came up with some new ideas too. Before we got into the studio, he called me at home from San Jose and played, on acoustic guitar, a power-chord riff. Even though it was just an idea, it was a great hook and sounded well suited for the radio, so we all wanted to try to develop it.

Now I know Tommy recollects this story a bit differently, but here's how I remember "China Grove" coming to life. When we got into Amigo, we'd laid his riff down as basic track. But it had no lyrics or melody, and no real title. It was listed on the tape boxes as "4/4 Rocker." Tommy often had trouble coming up with lyrics until the very last minute. So we brainstormed.

We had a few false starts and nothing seemed to work. We kept working on the music, though. Billy Payne of Little Feat, who was in the studio with us, came up with this piano run for the song that sounded vaguely Asian, maybe Chinese.

Now when I was a kid, my friends and I used to go to the beach at a place near Santa Cruz called China Ladder. We'd tie a rope to the top of the cliff and climb down and go surfing or fishing for sea bass and perch. So when I heard this Asian-sounding piano lick, I said, "How about China Ladder?" I stopped myself right there, and said to Tommy, "No, that sounds stupid. No one's going to know what a China Ladder is. How about we find another place in the States named after China?"

Tommy said okay, and it started from there.

I went and got an atlas of the United States for him. He looked through the index and settled on a place in Texas called China Grove. He scribbled down more ideas. He'd say to me, "How about this?" I helped him edit his lines and encouraged him along the way. He wrote the lyric in one afternoon.

He later told me that when the Doobies had toured Texas they probably passed a sign with that town's name on it, so I'm sure "China Grove" stuck out to him when he saw it in the atlas.

This writing process with Tommy offers another example of how Donn and I made a great team. Because Tommy tended to write lyrics in the studio, right up to the last minute, I used to spend a lot of one-on-one time with him. So I didn't have the time to fully think through the sonics on a lot of these songs. We couldn't have been in better hands, though. There was nothing he couldn't handle behind the board. I never would have made it through those days without Donn.

To hear the magic of Donn Landee, listen to "China Grove." Start with the bass. To be sure, Tiran's a *great* bass player. His dynamics were perfect. He'd done some session work before he joined the Doobies. Truth be told, if he hadn't gotten hired by the Doobies, he could've had a long career as a session player. He's the secret weapon that made the Doobie Brothers *groove*. But plenty of great bass players don't end up with great bass sounds on record. Donn typically took a DI of his bass, straight into the mixing board, and miked his bass speaker cabinet, so we could blend those two tracks when we mixed. Donn knew how to record electric bass maybe better than any engineer that ever lived.

Donn's equally responsible for how great Tommy's guitar sounded on record. Instead of having him play through Marshalls, we almost always had Tommy play through a Fender Bandmaster bottom with stock speakers and a Fender Bassman top. That's why when you listen to "China Grove" the distortion sounds different than a lot of the guitar sounds of that era.

Meanwhile, Pat remained a steady and solid writer. He contributed a couple of songs, including "South City Midnight Lady." Pat suggested that we bring in guitarist Jeff "Skunk" Baxter, who was working with Steely Dan at the time, to play pedal-steel guitar on it. Baxter added some beautiful, lyrical parts that blended smoothly with the track's strings and synths.

A nice contrast to the gentle "South City Midnight Lady" was the churning riff-rocker "Without You," co-written by all the band members. I loved that one, because it crossed into the same heavy rock territory favored by Montrose. We paired Tommy's rock 'n' roll rhythm guitar with some Hammond organ from Billy, which gave it a nice thick crunch. With its big, loud power chords, it was perfect for their live show.

This track also showcases the double-drum sound that became a Doobie signature. This was something I was obsessive about getting right on the records. With John and Mike, I took this general approach: since Mike was the more skilled drummer, I'd have him perform the more challenging songs, and then have John play on the tunes with the more straightforward drum parts. They both got to participate in a way that set them both up for success in the studio.

But at the same time, we'd usually have one or two songs per album that featured *both* guys playing at the same time. The way Donn and I handled this when we mixed was by placing John Hartman's drums in one channel and Mike Hossack's drums in the other channel.

This was a time-consuming and challenging undertaking, but as a drummer myself, I knew it was worth the time and effort. When they played together, it sounded absolutely thunderous, a wall of sound that exploded out of the speakers.

But here's the thing: you couldn't have them playing the same patterns and beats. You see, when two drummers, trying to mirror each other's patterns, hit notes *nearly* at the same time, on the snare or the kick drums, the drums sound muddy with these elongated notes — *bummmph*. This happens even if the guys were almost always perfectly in sync. It's an ugly sound — a flam. So we worked out those parts, note by note, to avoid flams.

Here's how we did it: before Donn and I recorded the Doobies we'd rehearse for a few days in a room at Amigo with Donn behind the board. During that time I'd have Donn record scratch, or preliminary, tracks of the instrumental parts that Pat, Tommy, and Tiran had written for the double-drum tunes. That step allowed Donn to start dialing in his levels in preparation for when we'd record in earnest a few days later.

Then I'd have those three guys stay home and have just the two drummers come into Amigo. I worked with them, showing them my ideas for how to marry the two drum parts. Donn would roll tape on the guitar and bass tracks. While the tracks played back through the speakers, we'd experiment and test different fills and beats.

When we'd quit for the day, Donn or I would photograph the mixing desk, just in case someone came in when we weren't there and moved the faders. I'd also make sure Donn would put tape over the board so the faders couldn't be moved. We didn't have automated consoles in the studio yet, so if someone screwed with your faders and you didn't keep track of where things were, you'd have to start working out your levels again.

After a couple of days, we'd be getting close. When I thought we had the two-drum parts right, I'd signal to Donn. He'd play Tiran, Pat, and Tommy's parts while those guys drummed along.

I'd be looking at Donn through the glass. He was my second set of ears, making certain that I didn't miss something. Eventually, Donn and I nodded together, giving a thumbs-up, because we had it nailed down and could now record the song.

Donn, to his credit, never complained about the fact that I wanted to do the drum parts this way. Some engineers would've gotten grumpy and impatient, wondering why the hell I didn't just use one drummer. Same thing goes for Mike and John. They endured all of my crazy ideas, trusting that we'd eventually get it all right. I don't think other producers ever did it that way, because it was so time-consuming, but I loved the results.

I don't have vivid memories of the day we cut "Without You," but Donn recalls that what's on the record is in fact two separate live takes of all the guys playing together, joined together at around the three minute and fifteen second mark. During that first segment, I made a contribution to the song's vocal parts. On the breakdown, I sing backgrounds as part of a call and response with Tommy. My voice sounds disembodied in the echo return, but you can hear me.

I was so pleased with how the song came out. And as much as it kicked ass on record, it was a barnburner in concert. Because the end of the track had a bit of a "Won't Get Fooled Again" by the Who vibe, it became their encore song. In fact, they set off their smoke bombs and pyro during the song's final verses during their live shows.

The album came out in March, which kicked off a magical 1973 for the Doobies. Tommy's two standout tunes, "China Grove" and "Long Train Runnin'" both became huge AM radio hits. The former reached *Billboard*'s Top 20, while "Long Train Runnin'" peaked at No. 8 on *Billboard*'s Hot 100, making it my first Top 10 hit. Then in the late summer, I got my first gold record award. It was for *Toulouse Street*. My parents were so proud; I had my mom take a picture of me holding it.

By September, Donn and I started gearing up for the next Doobies album, which would be entitled *What Were Once Vices Are Now Habits*. Building on what we'd done with *Captain*, we'd further expand the band's instrumentation by bringing in some extraordinarily talented musicians to guest on the album. Folk singer Arlo Guthrie, whom Lenny produced for Reprise, agreed to play autoharp on an airy acoustic tune written by Pat, "Tell Me What You Want (And I'll Give You What You Need)." We also recruited New Orleans pianist James Booker to play some boogie-woogie piano on a Tommy riff-rocker, "Down in the Track." Incidentally, Booker was incarcerated when I went looking for him. The label had to bail him out so he could come to the studio.

This album also really let me go to town with percussion. That impulse grew out of my childhood love of Latin-influenced percussion. I first got a taste of it as a teenager by listening to Stan Kenton's *Cuban Fire!* and *Kenton in Hi Fi*, especially its standout track, "The Peanut Vendor." Those two albums really inspired me;

Laying down a percussion track at Amigo with drummer Michael Hossack of the Doobies, summer 1973. DONN LANDEE.

Cuban Fire! has some great stuff on it. Kenton's *New Concepts of Artistry in Rhythm* also was a favorite; I was very influenced by the Cuban-influenced "23 Degrees North, 82 Degrees West."

When I dug deeper during my teen years, I discovered percussionist Tito Puente. Puente was *it* for me. He's the best player you'll ever hear in your life. He just kills. I loved his orchestra, which was a big band with timbales, vibraphones, and marimba. He'd put drums, congas, and timbales together for his mambos. Likewise, I devoured recordings by the Cuban bandleader Pérez Prado. I'd find out later that Kenton was influenced by all of these Cuban musicians who'd paved the way for Prado by playing in New York and Los Angeles after World War Two. Their music is just the most unbelievable shit.

This is why on many of the albums I did after *Toulouse Street* you'll hear layer upon layer of percussion. While Mike Hossack had ably played congas and timbales on *Captain and Me*, I took things to the next level on *Vices*. I brought in Eddie Guzman from Rare Earth, who was an especially great percussionist, to play the same instruments on "Road Angel," "You Just Can't Stop It," and "Daughters of the Sea." I again hired Milt Holland from the Wrecking Crew. (He'd done session work on *Anything Goes*.) Among other instruments, he played marimba on "Another Park, Another Sunday" and tabla on "Tell Me What You Want."

Along with Latin music, this album drew inspiration from the R&B of the sixties. All the guys, especially Tommy, dug the same Stax/Volt, Atlantic, and Motown records I devoured as a kid. I'm talking about performers like Otis Redding, Carla Thomas, Aretha Franklin, Sam & Dave, and Wilson Pickett. On a lot of those records, one common denominator was the soulful brass of Wayne Jackson and Andrew Love, the Memphis Horns.

When I was doing pre-production for the album, I thought, shit, I should get these guys to play on some of the songs. I called them, and they were eager to do it. So I flew them out to LA. I was so excited when the Memphis Horns came out and worked with us for the first time. They played on "Eyes of Silver," the album opener, "Song to See You Through," and the funky "You Just Can't Stop It."

But when I think back on the album, the story of "Black Water" is what comes to mind.

Like some of Tommy's biggest tunes, this song, written by Pat, had taken shape over the course of a couple of years. I'd forgotten this nugget, but in a recent interview Pat recollected that he'd played the riff for "Black Water" in the studio on a break during the *Captain and Me* sessions. I'd overheard him noodling around with it and told him he needed to use that riff for a song.

Pat took my advice. Before we got in the studio to record *Vices*, he called me and said he had turned the riff into a song, which he'd come up with after spending time in New Orleans watching the riverboats churning their way up and down the Mississippi.

When I heard it, I thought it was a good tune, a nice album track by Pat, but that it didn't sound like a single.

When we arranged it, we came up with the idea to add either a violin or a viola to the mix. It turned out I knew a viola player named Novi Novog. She was in a group called Chunky, Novi & Ernie that I'd signed to Warner Bros. She traded licks with Pat in the song's solo section. As an instrumental counterpoint, it gave the song a down-home feel.

In my production of "Black Water," I drew inspiration from a couple hits from the past. First, I borrowed an idea Lenny had used on "Feelin' Groovy" for Harpers Bizarre. To make our vocals stand out at the end of "Groovy," Lenny had Lee do an instrumental fade until only our vocals remained. After a few seconds, the music then reappeared in the mix.

I did the exact same thing on "Black Water." But it took some skillful work to get right. In the mid-seventies, we recorded on a sixteen-track tape machine. On "Black Water," we'd recorded something like a couple of guitar tracks, a percussion track, a few drum tracks, a viola track, a bass track, three background vocal tracks, and a lead vocal track.

To create the *a cappella* section, Donn and I had to fade out all of the non-vocal tracks on "Black Water" manually. (In later years, the development of programmable mixing desks allowed engineers to automate this process.) As the tape rolled, Donn and I dropped twelve of the sixteen faders, or sliding volume controls for each track, together. It was like running a play in football. It took four hands and great timing, because if one of us mistimed something, we'd have to redo the entire mix. The extra effort was well worth it, because that part became the tune's biggest hook.

On "Black Water" I also wanted to showcase Tommy and Pat's vocal mesh. I remember Tommy didn't love my idea. He didn't want to sing on "Black Water" because he felt it was Pat's tune — he didn't play a single guitar note on it — and so he didn't want to hog the spotlight. Pat and I had to drag Tommy into the studio and have him sing his vocal part, which appeared at the song's end. In it, he improvises some vocal lines. Like I'd done for the *a cappella* section, I borrowed an idea from another hit tune for this part. The melody that Tommy sings is pretty damn close to what Bruce Channel sang on his 1962 hit, "Hey Baby." Take a listen and you'll hear the similarity.

Everybody borrows ideas from everybody else.

When *Vices* came out in March 1974, *Toulouse Street* and *Captain and Me* were still going strong in the *Billboard* Top 200. In fact, all three of them charted together in the Top 200 before the month was out.

At this juncture, the Doobies had built up a big fan base and a lot of support with radio programmers, so I had every confidence that this album, which I loved, would spawn a couple of hits.

As the producer, I made the call on the singles. I started off in March with a song that was a bit of a departure from the Doobies' other hits. Rather than releasing a high-energy rocker, I put out "Another Park, Another Sunday," a tranquil, introspective acoustic tune reminiscent of Crosby, Stills, Nash & Young.

Back in those days, we'd put out singles on 45s, with one song on each side of the record. The A-side had the "single" — the tune the label thought had hit potential. On the B-side was a song that seemed unlikely to make a splash on the radio, because if the album took off and you had the opportunity to release multiple singles, you'd want the chance to release all of the songs that had chart potential on the A-side of another 45.

So for the B-side of "Another Park," I placed "Black Water," which I viewed as an album track unsuitable for radio.

"Another Park" crept into the *Billboard* Top 40 in June, but flamed out at No. 32.

We followed up "Another Park" with "Eyes of Silver" that same month. With its funky riffs, smoking horns, and catchy chorus, I thought it would do brisk business at radio. But it staggered to No. 52 in August, going no higher.

This all came on the heels of "China Grove" and "Long Train" becoming AM radio staples all through 1973. The fact that the two singles from *Vices* hadn't connected with the public was both disappointing and troubling.

After these two misses, I came up with an unorthodox idea. In the summer, Donn and I remixed the first single from their debut album, "Nobody." The guys and I all loved the song, and I didn't think it had been given the best opportunity to succeed back in 1971, in part because Lenny and I hadn't mixed the song in a way that showcased its intricate and infectious rhythms. I was sure that once Donn worked his magic, "Nobody" would be a hit. Released in October, it did even worse than the other two songs. Frustrated, I felt like I had let the guys down.

Meanwhile, the guys were running themselves ragged on tour, playing everywhere from Macon to Morgantown, but getting very little traction at radio. *Vices* actually dropped completely out of the *Billboard* Top 200 by November 2. Poof, *gone*.

Unbeknownst to me, however, our luck had begun to change. In September, WROV-AM, a little station in Roanoke, Virginia, began playing "Black Water." The request calls lit up the station's switchboard. That was back in the days when a record could break organically like that; the DJs at the station liked the song, and turned out that their listeners did too. It started spreading, like a virus, to radio playlists across the country.

Looking to capitalize on this good fortune, Warner Bros. rushed a "Black Water" single to market.

On December 21, "Black Water" debuted at No. 75 on the *Billboard* Hot 100. In the following weeks, it climbed higher.

As the single rose, it pulled *Vices* along for the ride. The LP re-charted in January 1975 and would go into the Top 10 again, reaching No. 4 in March. In fact, this was its peak, about a year after its release. Talk about a slow burn! All of this Doobie chart action drew *Toulouse Street* and *The Captain and Me* back into the Top 200 as well that same month.

The culmination of this Doobie resurgence came on March 15, 1975, when "Black Water" hit No. 1 in *Billboard*. It was an unbelievable feeling; it was the first No. 1 hit that any of us had experienced.

The story of "Black Water" reminds me of three things.

First, I was generally lousy at picking singles.

Second, I think that I'd been subconsciously following a lesson impressed on me when I started apprenticing under Lenny at the very end of my days in Harpers Bizarre. He told me that back in the fifties, when his father owned and operated Liberty Records, most producers didn't worry much about the other songs on an album as long as they had an obvious hit single in place. But Lenny stressed never to do that; instead, when you're making an album, try to make *everything* good enough to be a single, because it's difficult to pick hits with a high degree of certainty. As our experience with "Black Water" showed, Lenny was dead right.

Finally, the overwhelming success of "Black Water" demonstrated to the rock world that Pat Simmons was the Doobies' secret weapon. Now, I'd known this from the beginning. Before Warner Bros. signed them, I loved the way he added these finger-picked guitar parts, ones that contrasted with Tommy's churning *chugga-chugga* rhythms. You can hear that very juxtaposition, for example, during the intro of "Long Train Runnin'." That blend of Tommy's and Pat's styles made the Doobies' hits stand out on the radio. Now the rock world knew how well he could both sing and write.

The Doobies had a monster 1974. With great fanfare, the band announced in a full-page *Billboard* ad in January 1975 that *Toulouse Street, Captain,* and *Vices* all went platinum during the past year. And their hit singles had become AM-radio staples.

On a personal level, their success did wonders for my confidence. I'd discovered this band, and despite the fact that I'd made missteps during the making of their first album, I'd now produced a series of albums that had helped them reach new heights of success.

But the biggest thing was that those guys had *made it.* I was so happy for everyone in the band, but especially for Tommy, Pat, and John, guys I'd met in San Jose back in 1970. I'd think about how when I met them they were on food stamps, eating cold beans out of tin cans, and playing for a few bucks a night at the Chateau.

Of course, I'd financially benefited from the Doobies' achievements. At Warner Bros., staff producers earned a salary, plus a percentage, between 3 to 5 percent (or points), of the sales of a record they produced. So like all of the company's staff producers, I had a shared stake in the success of my artists.

One thing I did with my increased income was to invest in real estate. I purchased a few homes in the Pasadena area, including one showcase property on Los Altos Drive. Designed by the pioneering California architect Wallace Neff, the 14,000-square foot home was built on a hill. It was so big inside that my son used to get lost going from his bedroom to the kitchen. The rooms surrounded a gorgeous courtyard garden with a fountain and flora. The rear of the house had a lovely terrace that provided spectacular views of the Arroyo Seco. We lived in it for a few years until we found a home we liked better in town.

By the end 1974, the Doobies had already had a few lineup changes. Tiran had replaced Dave Shogren right before I took over the reins for *Toulouse Street*. Mike Hossack, who'd become disenchanted with the band's musical direction, quit soon after he'd finished his drum tracks for *Vices*. He'd be replaced by former Lee Michaels drummer Keith Knudsen. Another album, another lineup change. This inconstancy would prove to be a constant throughout their long career.

In December, the band expanded their brotherhood by making guitarist Jeff Baxter a Doobie. After playing on *Vices*, Jeff had been sitting in with them on the road, and after Steely Dan cut ties with him, he joined.

From my perspective, Jeff's addition was an exciting proposition. Like Moby Grape, a band Tom, Pat, and I all loved, the Doobies now had three guitarists, all possessed of very different styles. Along with the Grape, I loved another three-guitar band, Buffalo Springfield, so bringing together a trio of different guitar voices under the Doobies umbrella offered up a world of sonic potential.

Soon after Baxter joined, we started pre-production on a new record, the Doobies' fifth, with a feeling of freedom. With their chart success established, we had the opportunity to be even more adventurous on *Stampede*.

The guys had worked up some great songs. One new development was that Pat, perhaps inspired by the success of "Black Water," was coming up with more material. He'd co-write half of the original songs on the record. To his credit, he wasn't playing it safe. He could've just tried to write another "Black Water." Instead, he wrote two breakneck, hard-rocking numbers, "Double Dealin' Four Flusher" and "Neal's Fandango." Tommy, too, played his part in this role reversal. He wrote a Pat-like, mellow ballad, "Texas Lullaby."

In orchestrating the record, I wanted to push their sonic boundaries beyond what we'd done on *Vices*. Once again, I'd ask Nick DeCaro to write string arrangements and Billy Payne to play keyboards. But I'd also recruit Maria Muldaur, who was riding high on the success of her smash "Midnight at the Oasis," to sing backgrounds.

This record also gave me the opportunity to hire some of my jazz idols. I was ecstatic when Conte and Pete Candoli, the trumpet-playing brothers who'd starred in the Stan Kenton big band, agreed to contribute. Percussionist Victor Feldman, a dual threat who'd also played piano for Miles Davis, signed on to play marimba and percussion.

The album ended up featuring two R&B/soul tracks. Tommy suggested the Doobies cover Holland–Dozier–Holland's "Take Me in Your Arms (Rock Me)," which had been a minor hit for Motown singer Kim Weston back in 1965. That was a great idea.

The guys really delivered. Tommy sang his ass off on that one and unleashed a gutty, cutting solo. Tiran laid down a sinewy groove. To nail down that Motown sound, we brought in some of the girls from the Blackberries, a vocal group that had worked on a lot of rock and R&B records, to sing backgrounds. Donn and I brought the tambourine and handclaps up front in the mix, giving it that Motown vibe. And of course, I got some congas on the track. When you listen to it all together, you can't help but tap your feet.

This song is a great example of how Motown records — Berry Gordy's production style, in particular — influenced me. For instance, if you listen to my records, especially the Doobies records, you'll hear how when I used strings, I almost always used *high* strings — viola and violin as opposed to cello and double bass. That was borrowed from Gordy. He's a genius record man and producer. I'd love to shake his hand. If I could have the chance to meet anyone, it would be him.

That's why I hired Motown arranger Paul Riser to write the horn and string charts for "Sweet Maxine," the album opener, and "Take Me in Your Arms." His track record was unparalleled. He'd arranged the Temptations' "My Girl" and "Papa Was a Rollin' Stone," for which he'd won a Grammy. Shit, he'd worked on Smokey's "Tears of a Clown" and Marvin Gaye's "I Heard It Through the Grapevine." There was nobody better.

We recorded the big string section on a soundstage on the Warner Bros. movie lot. Paul flew to Los Angeles and met me on the lot. He went to work, sipping his drink and finalizing his charts.

It was eye-opening to watch him do his thing. In the midst of this session he even let me in on one of his secrets. He explained that when he recorded strings for Motown, he had the different instruments ever-so-slightly detuned from one another. That's why they don't sound slick. They have a rich ambiance about them when their pitch is not uniformly perfect. That's how he got that distinctive Motown string sound.

If "Take Me" represented the sixties side of the Doobies' Black inheritance, "Music Man" was a more contemporary take. So I asked Curtis Mayfield, who was still riding high after his monster success with the soundtrack to *Super Fly*, to chart the horns and strings.

When we talked, I found out that he *loved* the Doobie Brothers. So I flew to his studio in Chicago and played him the basic tracks. He proceeded to write the arrangements for "Music Man." He didn't charge me a dime to use his studio or for the charts he wrote. After we finished for the day, he took me out for a fabulous dinner.

Between the contributions of Curtis and the rest of the guys, "Music Man" was a notable achievement for the band and for me as a producer. Curtis's string and horn parts gave the song a gritty, urban feel, which contrasted nicely with some of the album's more pastoral material. Donn recorded a Baxter solo and then ran it backwards. He soloed overtop of some wah-pedal rhythm guitar, sounding like Hendrix playing on a Blaxploitation movie soundtrack. Billy made things even more soulful by adding some impassioned gospel organ. As a vocalist, Tommy never sounded Blacker.

I also wanted to find a way to showcase the versatility of the band's guitar players on *Stampede*. When Lenny produced Harpers Bizarre, he added brief interludes in between some of the songs on our albums. Following his lead, I did the same here by including two short acoustic pieces. On "Précis," Jeff played some elegant Spanish-sounding classical guitar. Pat added "Slack Key Soquel Rag," a beautiful acoustic instrumental. It sounded like you were sitting with him on a front porch, late on a summer day, listening to him play as the horizon swallowed the sun. Those short instrumentals helped pace the album — it was something I'd do later on the Van Halen records.

In something of a follow-up to "Black Water," Pat contributed "I Cheat the Hangman." It's a moody ballad about a condemned man who escapes the gallows. It opens with a flanged, fingerpicked guitar figure supported by ghostly piano lines. Pat sings a plaintive, lonely vocal, accompanied by Maria Muldaur on a couple of verses. We stacked harmony vocals, ones that would have fit on a Harpers Bizarre record. Nick wrote a string arrangement that unfolded beautifully, eerie and haunt-ing. The second part of the song featured some strident strings and a repeating open-string guitar riff that galloped alongside Victor Feldman's chiming orchestra bell runs. The song ends in unsettled fashion, with the impassioned horn solos of the Candoli brothers building tension throughout the song's fade. It was another landmark for the band — particularly for Pat, who came up with the song's different movements — and for me as a producer.

But maybe the song that best demonstrated the Doobies' musi-cal evolution was Tommy's "Rainy Day Crossroad Blues." The song commences with Tommy's patented foot-stomping acoustic strumming. Soon joining him in the mix is Ry Cooder, his slithering bottleneck guitar dancing with Tommy's galloping rhythms. To that point, the tune sounded like something off of *Vices* or *Toulouse Street*, very much part and parcel of the Doobies' rock-and-blues roots. Halfway through, though, the song takes a left turn by seg-ueing into a cinematic, Eagles-like ballad, complete with some shimmering strings courtesy of Nick DeCaro and melodic pedal-steel lines from Jeff Baxter.

Even the album closer, "Double Dealin' Four Flusher," a Doobies boogie, revealed their growth. Pat and Tommy shared lead vocals with Keith, the band's triple-guitar attack churning along as Billy's piano pounds away. The song's middle section, however, takes an unexpected detour. It has a jazz-fusion meets Allman Brothers Band feel, propelled by a skittering bass line from Tiran and soft chording from Pat, Tommy, and Jeff. It all showed a real commitment to stretch things out and not play it safe. I couldn't have been prouder of the guys. We wrapped the sessions in March.

From what I recall, in early April 1975, before their album had even been released, I got an ominous call from a very worried

Bruce Cohn, the Doobies' manager. He told me that Tommy had been so violently ill that he collapsed backstage in Baton Rouge, just minutes before they were scheduled to go onstage. Needless to say, they had to cancel their show.

I remember from my own years on the road that illness is a harsh reality — you're living hard, indulging, getting bad sleep, and eating bad food. You're meeting tons of people and there are germs everywhere. You get sick and yet you have to keep moving to the next city, the next hotel room. Meanwhile, you're feverish and dizzy, and you feel like you'll collapse if you don't sleep for a day straight. But what was most concerning to me was that Tommy shouldn't have been running on fumes already, because the tour had just started. Even worse, Bruce told me that Tommy had been bleeding from the mouth when he hit the ground. Bruce said it was ulcers, and that he'd be out of action for the foreseeable future.

Tommy had lost a lot of weight and looked unwell at times when we did the record, but I had no inkling that he'd end up hospitalized.

Tommy was their heart and soul, the guy who sang most of their hits, and in many ways the face of the Doobies. He was not replaceable.

Still, the tour needed to continue. In the midst of this crisis, Jeff suggested that they call on Mike McDonald, a session musician originally from St. Louis, who, like Baxter, had played on some Steely Dan records. Mike, who was playing clubs in Los Angeles at the time, flew to Louisiana, rehearsed for a couple of days, and appeared with the band, playing organ and singing. He'd remain for the rest of the tour, with the expectation that he'd play with the Doobies until Tommy's health improved.

Even though Tommy's illness had everyone in the Doobies camp extremely worried, the band's success continued unabated, which I always thought must have provided him with some peace of mind as he recovered. When the album came out in May, "Take Me in Your Arms" got added to radio playlists all over the country, entering the *Billboard* Hot 100 at No. 77. By June, the band had an incredible *four* albums in the *Billboard* Top 200, spearheaded by *Stampede*, which had settled into the Top 10. So even though Tommy was laid up, the Doobies were selling records hand over fist.

Sometime during the tour, Pat called me from the road. He told me that Mike wasn't your typical backing musician. He said that when the Doobies got back to Los Angeles, I needed to meet Mike and hear him sing. His words went in one ear and out the other. When we talked the next time, he said it again, more emphatically: "Ted, you *need* to listen to this guy play." He raved about Mike's abilities as a keyboardist and vocalist. The implication was that Pat thought Mike might be a good fit as a full member of the band, even if Tommy made a speedy and full recovery. To be honest, even though I respected Pat's opinion, I wasn't all that interested. I wanted things to return to the status quo with Tommy at the helm. So I wrote Mike off as a fill-in guy, before I'd met or heard him.

Of course, my initial response to Pat's suggestion had a lot do with my focus on getting Tommy back on his feet. Tommy lived up in the Bay Area. I'd call him and see how he was doing. I flew up there a couple of times to visit him. When I saw him, I didn't think he was healing up all that quickly. I was concerned about him, but at the same time I secretly feared that he wasn't going to come back to the band, even though that was everyone's working assumption.

The longer Tommy was out of action, the more I worried about him. Bruce wasn't able to give me any sort of definitive answers about Tommy's prognosis either. When I spoke to Pat, I could tell the whole situation was eating at him; he had to bear a bigger burden now, because the Doobies' leadership had been in many ways a partnership between Pat and Tommy. Now it was all on Pat.

Pat, too, I think, was feeling more pressure because I was trying to convince him that if Tommy couldn't participate in the making of the next record, that Pat should become the band's focal point. He could write, play, and sing. It would take the band in a different direction, but Pat was already a big part of the Doobies' sound, so there would be continuity too. Pat wasn't enthusiastic about that idea.

It was frustrating. I knew the clock was ticking. Those guys would come home from the road by the end of the year and we'd need to start a new record.

This, I believe, is what shifted my thinking about the possibility of Mike staying in the band. It just became an inescapable fact — Tommy almost certainly wasn't going to be in shape to fully participate in the recording of the next record. That meant we'd be minus our main vocalist and songwriter.

So when those guys came off the road, I called Pat, looking to get a hold of Mike. I don't think I could even call Mike, because he'd been thrown out of his apartment and was living in a garage in Los Angeles. As I recall, he'd gotten evicted from his apartment because he'd insisted on playing his electric piano at all hours of the night. So I drove to this garage and met him. It was a pretty bare-bones situation, as you'd expect. He had a hot plate to heat up food and coffee. There was a mattress on the concrete floor, and he was living out of a suitcase. The most valuable thing he had in the place was his Fender Rhodes.

After we'd gotten acquainted, I asked him if he had any songs. He told me he did. As it turns out, he and Tiran had recently worked on and demoed one of Mike's songs, "Losin' End." Mike sat down at his little electric piano and sang and played it for me.

I was impressed. He had a very distinctive voice, kind of like Joe Cocker meets Marvin Gaye. It didn't sound like it should be coming out of his body. Along with having an identifiable voice — one that sticks in your head — he had great pitch and control. I also loved the song; it was catchy, with an earnest lyric.

So my mind was opened.

I think the next time we got together I had him come into the studio with Pat. I asked, "Do you have any other songs?"

He said, "Yeah. Here's one, but it's not very good."

He sat down at the piano. I stood behind Mike, because I wanted to watch his hands as he played. Pat was standing in front of Mike, by the piano's soundboard.

He started playing. Its first line was about brotherhood. I remember he didn't have a second verse yet, so he sang the first verse twice, but that didn't matter at all. Then he went into the chorus of this song, which was "Takin' It to the Streets."

My jaw dropped. I looked at Pat. He was smiling. I could read his mind; he was thinking, *I told you so, Ted!* That voice, paired with the gospel-like song, was just electrifying.

That said, his lyrics for the song did give me pause. Here was this white guy, singing about the brotherhood of man and about social protest in the wake of the civil rights movement. Coming from Mike and the Doobies, would that message resonate with the public, or would it come off as preachy? I wasn't sure.

Still, Mike's delivery was heartfelt; you could *feel* what he was singing. So in the end, I kept my reservations about the lyrics to myself.

Next, he played me "It Keeps You Runnin'." That would be the third great song I'd heard out of this guy, and I'd just met him.

That day, I think he showed me a couple of other song ideas. While we worked on them, I made a couple of arrangement suggestions. I may have suggested he change a chord or two in a turnaround, or something minor like that. Before we were done, he said, "Ted, if they ever end up on an album, you should get writer's credit." I thanked him but said that wasn't necessary. I didn't write a lyric. I didn't write a melody. I wrote nothing, and he wanted to give me writer's credit. But that's the kind of genuine, sweet guy he is.

The other endearing thing about Mike was his almost complete inability to recognize his own talents. It was charming to see such humility in a musician, and he'd preface each song by telling me, "Oh, this one's nothing special." He was leading me to believe these tunes were mediocre throwaways, when in fact they were *great*. In fact, the first three he showed me all ended up on *Takin' It to the Streets*.

So we hit it off right away.

Later I told Pat that never, ever in my life was I happier to be wrong about something.

Still, I felt uneasy. When Mike came along, I was thrilled because such a talent had fallen into all of our laps. It was singular greatness. But it all turned my stomach in knots. I couldn't shake my fear that once Tommy heard Mike's voice and songs, Tommy might think that Mike was a guy who could permanently replace him in the Doobies. So I'm imagining Tommy, the guy who sang and wrote the band's biggest hits, feeling like he could be cast aside, relegated to the past.

So paradoxically, I was personally troubled that I *knew* how good Mike sounded, because I feared that it was going to bother Tommy. And of course, like all the guys, I wanted Tommy in the group. I loved the guy. We all did. That was the only time I personally felt horrible while working with an act I loved. I felt conflicted, because I recognized Mike's talents.

Despite my unsettled personal feelings, the recording sessions for *Takin' It to the Streets* weren't difficult. The Doobies were always great to work with in terms of cooperation and talent. We always had fun making the records.

For this album, the band brought conga player Bobby LaKind into the studio. He'd been a longtime member of the band's road crew. If I recall correctly, he used to jam with them at soundchecks. It didn't take long for the guys to recognize his talents, so Pat asked him to start playing with them onstage, even though he wasn't made an official member of the band until a few years later. I was thrilled to have him on board, because it gave me the chance to further integrate percussion into the band's sound.

Going forward, I used him as much as possible on the Doobies' records, alongside Hartman and Knudsen. I don't think the casual music fan grasps how a good conga player can draw together an array of percussion parts. Listen to "Takin' It to the Streets." Along with drums, we added handclaps and tambourine. But the glue, especially on the verses and instrumental sections, was Bobby. His contributions to the Doobies' later hits haven't been fully appreciated. Out of all the percussionists I used as a producer, he's my favorite.

One thing that cheered us all was when Tommy participated in the making of the record, albeit to a limited degree. Tommy contributed a couple of songs and sang lead on "Turn It Loose." It was a classic Tommy tune, and it was wonderful to have him back in the fold. But with his future in the band still up in the air, Mike would serve as a focal point for the record.

Another song that stands out in my mind is one of Pat's, "Rio." I ended up writing an arrangement that was highly orchestrated. We used two drummers on the track, along with Bobby's congas, and string and horn parts, plus bass, guitar, and Mike's keyboards. Then I had Pat and Mike sing together. Listen closely and you'll hear Maria Muldaur's sexy and sweet voice singing a line as well. It was one of the most challenging arrangements of my career. I love the way it came out, but it was a real bear to get on tape.

In the meantime, I was hearing doubts from my fellow label executives about the band's future. That all stemmed from the fact that Tommy wasn't a major contributor to the album. At the time, the Doobies were one of Warner Bros. Records' biggest-selling acts. They were a cash cow that paid for a lot of the less commercially successful acts, the ones that Warner Bros. prided itself on keeping on the label. The sense around the offices was that this forthcoming album was unlikely to sell many copies.

In response, I purposely didn't let people at the label — especially the promotion department and sales guys — hear the in-progress tracks that featured Mike. At times, in the past, I might have played an in-progress song at the weekly A&R meeting so I could get feedback from everyone at the table. Because the band had taken a few musical left turns, I feared this might just further the narrative that the Doobies had drifted off course. In particular, the promo team could be influenced negatively by those kinds of perceptions, and if they thought the Doobies were a sinking ship, they might not push the record as aggressively as they'd done in the past when Tommy's voice and songs were all over the radio. So I didn't let anyone preview the new material. I wanted it to be as good as possible before anyone outside the band's immediate orbit heard it.

The bigger picture here was trying to bridge the gap between the albums that featured Tommy and *Streets*, which would feature Mike. In the meantime, I had to sell the idea that bringing Mike into the fold had the potential to be great news, because the Warner bean counters always wanted hits, and, perhaps understandably, had misgivings about any changes to a winning formula. So anytime anyone at the label asked how things were going in the studio, I expressed my honest opinion that the new record would hold up well against the earlier releases.

In the midst of making *Takin' It to the Streets*, I flew to New York to meet with Carly Simon about producing her next record. She was coming off a string of very successful albums for Elektra, a label that was part of the WEA (Warner-Elektra-Atlantic) conglomerate. In fact, her last three albums, which had all been produced by the talented Richard Perry, had hit the Top 10. At the time, she was married to James Taylor. They were the music industry's *it* couple — two super-successful singer-songwriters.

That day, I went to her Manhattan brownstone. Over coffee, we talked about her influences, her records, and the albums she admired. She couldn't have been nicer — a total sweetheart. During this conversation I pitched my ideas for her next album to her.

It was a productive meeting. Soon after, I signed on to produce her next album for Elektra Records, one that would be entitled *Another Passenger*.

In the months that followed, we became good friends. Because she and James, who was a Warner Bros. Records artist, were both signed to WEA deals, Lenny and I hung out with them quite a bit. (At the time, Lenny and Russ Titelman were producing James.) I remember, in fact, that in 1976 Lenny and I flew on a small plane from Boston to Martha's Vineyard to visit them at their home. That wasn't even on business. We went to hang out with them. She was such a down-home girl, and they had such an idyllic life together. It was like a fairy tale.

The more I got to know her, the more I learned about what made her tick. Most of all, I sensed that she was a sensitive person, who probably didn't have sharp enough elbows and thick enough skin to deal with a lot of the unsavory aspects of the industry. For instance, she told me a story that broke my heart on her behalf. Some years before, she'd been invited to a party at Groucho Marx's house. Marx, who was then in the twilight of his career, liked to hold court and socialize with celebrities. That night, he organized an activity for his famous guests. He asked every person at the party to come prepared to entertain the other guests with a skill. People, including talk show host and comedian Dick Cavett, took their turns. When Carly was up, she sang a song. After the applause died down, Marx leered at her and said, "That's great, honey. *But how do you fuck?*" Carly said she wanted to die, but Cavett came to her rescue by defusing the situation. When she recounted the story, I could see and feel her pain about the way Groucho had humiliated her in front of a room full of people. Just hearing that story made me angry, but it also was a concrete reminder of her fragile, gentle nature.

This record would only be the second I'd done that didn't feature a self-contained group, the first since Lorraine Ellison. So I started making lists of people I'd like to play on it. Donn would engineer and we'd record at Sunset Sound.

By the time I'd finished brainstorming with Carly, we ended up with an all-star roster of session players and guest performers. James and Carly were huge stars at the time, so people were eager to contribute. For instance, Linda Ronstadt sang backgrounds. I'd met her previously when she opened for Van Morrison, but she and I became friends during the making of Carly's record. Glenn Frey of the Eagles played guitar on "Libby." Dr. John, the New Orleans singer-songwriter, played guitar on "Dishonest Modesty." Naturally, James helped out on it as well. He played acoustic on "Fairweather Father," a wife's lament about a selfish husband. Jackson Browne sang on that one with James and Carly. Drummer Jim Keltner, who'd been a member of Joe Cocker's Mad Dogs & Englishmen and had played on some of Carly's earlier albums, performed on a couple of cuts as well. He was one of my favorite drummers, so I loved watching him lay down his parts. From my perspective, it was all a big zoo trying to keep track of who was coming and going through the doors of Sunset Sound on any given day, but Carly was extremely happy that so many of her very talented friends got to contribute.

This project gave me a good opportunity to produce the biggest stars in town. But that also gave me pause. I thought back on the sessions I'd seen with Sinatra and Bowen, and wanted to make sure I didn't fall into the trap of deferring to the whims of the record's contributors just because they were so famous. At the time, James and Carly had sterling careers; the same could be said for everyone else who guested on the record. But I couldn't let that affect my approach. If you're overwhelmed — or intimidated — by an artist's presence in the studio, it can make you ineffective as a producer.

I also called on some of the artists that I produced to work on the record. A few months before we started recording her album, Carly and James had watched a session at Amigo when Donn and I had recorded the Doobies cutting a track Mike had written called "It Keeps You Runnin'" for *Takin' It to the Streets*. She met the guys and hit it off with them.

So she was enthusiastic when I suggested we get the Doobies to play on *Another Passenger*. She had co-written this wonderful piano ballad called "Riverboat Gambler." When she played it for me, her chord changes reminded me of a Cole Porter tune. The lyric was so evocative and engaging and clever, and her melody was so seductive. Soon after I heard it, I paired her up with Mike McDonald. Mike, who was a veteran studio musician himself thanks to his session work for Steely Dan, played electric piano on it. I added a dense string arrangement, which gave the song a romantic, dreamlike feel. It came out very well.

Carly and I also decided she should cut her own version of "It Keeps You Runnin'." I brought in all the Doobies, minus Tommy, to back her. The arrangement all of us came up with gave the track a funky feel. Mike played Fender Rhodes, and Donn engineered a swampy, phased bass sound for Tiran. The rhythm parts featured what's called second-line drumming: a style that features a marching beat with a shuffle feel that New Orleans musicians favored during funeral processions. Although

Allen Toussaint had used this beat quite a bit in the seventies, I was more directly influenced by Richie Hayward and Little Feat's use of second-line drumming. Take a listen to "Fat Man in the Bathtub" and you'll hear it.

I also had the Little Feat guys do one of their songs with her. We recorded "One Love Stand," which the Feat had released on their 1975 LP *The Last Record Album*. On Carly's version the Little Feat guys played greasy-slick yet tight as a drum. Lowell and Paul especially sound great swapping licks. And with this one, I once again had Mike McDonald sing with Carly. They sounded wonderful together.

Carly was an absolute dream in the studio; she sang like an angel and was so skilled as a singer. I've worked with vocalists where I'd have to put them through days of takes in the hopes that later we could comp their good moments together to finish a vocal for a song. Not Carly. When it came to singing, she was right on, all the time. Pitch, phrasing, vibrato, whatever attribute you'd want in a singer, she had it. So it was never a slog to record her. I even sang a few backgrounds on the record, when we needed to finish a part and there was no one else at the studio to do it.

But she had a lot of pressures coming down on her, especially because of the celebrity nature of her marriage to James. That caused them both stress. And they were living at the Beverly Wilshire — if you're living in a hotel for too long, it's never good. When you're that famous, it's like living in a fishbowl when you walk through the lobby every day. There are photographers and gossip columnists hanging around, digging for dirt, and everyone's watching your every move.

Eventually, they moved out of the hotel. They rented, believe it or not, the house that O.J. Simpson later owned on North Rockingham Avenue in Brentwood, the infamous murder house.

Like most couples, they had some heated arguments. When I'd get into the studio with Carly in the morning, she'd sit with me and vent about what had gone down. At the same time, Lenny and Russ Titelman were cutting a record with James. Lenny and James talked too, and so Lenny would hear James's version of what happened. When Lenny and I would go to dinner, we'd compare notes. Even though they fought, they loved each other passionately; it was simply an intense relationship.

Other days, Carly got emotional for reasons that had nothing to do with James. For instance, a couple of times I had to fire studio musicians who just didn't deliver what I needed. She'd ask me to give them another chance. When I told her that I had to get someone else, she would get so upset that she'd get under the recording desk and cry.

All this time, Carly was so wonderful with my family. I was gone from home a lot, and Carly understood how hard it is to strike a balance between the demands of work and family when you are involved in the music industry. She sent my children gifts on their birthdays and was always kind to them.

For example, I remember Carly called my Pasadena home when my wife was eight months pregnant with my daughter, McCormick. Kathi was lying on the couch, resting, so she asked my son, Teddy, who was about five, to answer the phone.

"Hello?"

Kathi couldn't hear the voice on the other end, but could tell it was a woman.

"This is Teddy."

He struck up a conversation. Kathi, quite logically, assumed it was my mother, Teddy's grandmother, since the conversation had so engrossed him.

After a while, Kathi asked, "Does she want to talk to me?"

"Excuse me, miss, do you want to talk to my mom?"

"Teddy, who is it?"

"Who is this?"

"She says her name's Carly."

He'd been talking to her for like twenty minutes! She'd asked for me — Teddy — but she just carried on the conversation with my young son.

That's exactly the type of person she was.

I remember the worst day we had together. She came into Sunset Sound one day, eyes red, makeup smeared.

We went into a storage closet, and I closed the door.

She started sobbing.

"Carly, what's wrong?"

She opened up to me about her relationship with James. They were going through a very rough patch in their marriage; she was distraught. All of the pressure of being one of industry's most famous couples, along with both of them trying to write and record new albums while living far away from their home, was taking a toll on them. As she shared her feelings, I thought back to the days that Lenny, Carly, James, and I spent at Martha's Vineyard, and how their tranquil home life so differed from what they were dealing with at the moment. I really felt for her.

I comforted her the best I knew how. After a few minutes, she pulled it together and we went to work.

They managed to weather these types of incidents, both personally and professionally. Along with "Fairweather Father," James also played on a lovely ballad she'd co-written called "Be With Me."

When we were cutting this track, they were working on their parts. She wanted him to play the guitar line a certain way. To refresh his memory about the way they'd practiced the part, she said, "Play that chunky part."

James, who'd struggled with substance abuse, smiled as he made a not-so-subtle drug reference. "That junkie part?"

The room got ice cold.

From there things got a bit dicey, but they were both civil and kept their cool. Eventually they got back on track, and we got back to work.

In early 1976, Donn and I had two sessions going at the same time. While we were finishing the recording sessions for the Carly record, we mixed and mastered *Takin' It to the Streets*. It came out in late March 1976.

Despite the whispers inside Warner Bros. about the Doobies' new direction, their album sold well right out of the gate. It hit the Top 10 and went gold by May; it was their fifth gold record in a row.

We released "Takin' It to the Streets" as the lead single. It did well, topping out in June at No. 13 on the *Billboard* Hot 100. Thanks to Mike's smooth R&B vocal and its socially conscious lyric, the song also crossed over onto the *Billboard* Hot Soul Singles charts. And despite the fact that I'd not previewed the album's tracks for the promotion department, once the album came out, Russ Thyret, the label's brand new vice president of promotion, did great work in making sure it got a big push, which kept it doing big numbers for months.

I was so relieved and happy for the Doobies. To be frank, if Mike hadn't come along, I don't think the band could have continued, because I don't think Pat wanted to front the band. And even with Mike in the mix, it wasn't a sure thing that the public was going to embrace their evolution. It's very difficult to sustain success when you change a lead singer. Tommy was the person that fans most identified with the Doobies, since he'd sung most of their hits. The fact that Mike stepped in and filled the void was a remarkable thing, but it's a tribute to his talent and the talent of the other guys, who didn't miss a beat.

Right around the moment that *Streets* was peaking on the charts, Carly's record was released.

At the time, Carly was coming off a big streak of radio hits; she'd done all those great albums with Richard Perry, and I wanted to do the same for her. I thought we had two solid singles.

The first, "It Keeps You Runnin'," spent a couple months on the charts but went no higher than No. 46. That was disappointing.

I thought I had an ace in the hole, though. She'd co-written a song called "Half a Chance" that I thought would connect because the chorus was really catchy.

It featured the Doobies guys, Mike, Tiran, Jeff, Pat, John, and Keith. Linda Ronstadt sang backgrounds on it. Andrew from the Memphis Horns did the sax solo. We all thought it had significant chart potential.

I remember, when we mixed, that I wanted to explicitly tailor it for AM radio. So it came out maybe a bit softer than it should have. When I listen to "Half a Chance," it's crafted to *sound* like a hit. But it just didn't connect like that, so I had overestimated its commercial appeal. While it did make the *Billboard* Easy Listening Chart, it didn't do anything on the pop chart. So I didn't end up with a hit single on the album. In the final analysis, that's on me, and no one else. I didn't hold up my end of the bargain.

When I look back on why Carly's album didn't become a big hit, I know now that I took my eye off the ball. I didn't focus enough on the songs as we worked on the record. Carly's a great writer, period. The songs *I* picked for her, though, like "It Keeps You Runnin'" and "One Love Stand," didn't have enough radio appeal. I should've recognized that, but I didn't. In some ways, it was such an all-star affair that I became more focused on the players and the performances — which were great — than I was on doing everything I could to make sure the songs were the best they could be. I lost focus, and that's why the album didn't sell like her previous efforts.

In the end, the album did sell a few hundred thousand copies. It was a good record, but it missed the mark, commercially. As a producer, you feel terrible for your artist when that happens, because they've put their trust in you. It's like you're a pilot flying through a thunderstorm. The artist and all the musicians are your passengers. You're saying, don't worry. In the end, I didn't crash the plane, but we had a very bumpy and uncomfortable landing. I felt like I'd let down the sweetest person in the world, Carly. But she never said a cross word to me. In the years that followed, she'd write me letters and postcards from New York or Europe. I have a beautiful Gucci portfolio folder she gave me. Carly was so warm and kind. She's such a loving person.

Because I had a personal and professional relationship with Carly, I got dragged into a nasty corporate dispute involving James Taylor in December 1976. James's contract with Warner Bros. Records was up for renewal that fall, but Mo hadn't closed the deal yet. Sensing an opening, Columbia Records head Walter Yetnikoff made James a *very* lucrative contract offer. Walter and Mo hated each other, and at the time, James was one of our marquee artists, so Walter's move sparked a heated bidding war.

James, who was caught in the middle, felt pulled in both directions and couldn't make up his mind about whether to stay with us or move to Columbia. He and Carly had both been WEA artists for some time, but now they faced the possibility of being under contract to different, competing corporations. Their phone rang incessantly. When Mo spoke to James, he put a lot of personal pressure on him. He'd tell James, "We *need* you at Warner Bros." Meanwhile, Walter was telling him similar things.

Carly was so distraught over the effect it was having on James that she called me. She told me that she'd find James on the floor crying. She asked me to intervene with Mo and ask him to stop making counter-offers, so the negotiations could end. The bidding war was putting enormous strain on their marriage. Of course, I couldn't tell Mo that — even though, seeing how it was affecting them, I would've let James walk if it had been my call — because then I wouldn't be acting in the best interest of the company. James was a star and we didn't want to see him leave the company. But the negotiations never should have gotten so personally intense for James and Carly.

During the final days of the negotiations, Mo, Lenny, and I flew to New York so we could sit down with James and Carly at their apartment. It was a heavy, emotional evening. Mo made his pitch again, and James just seemed paralyzed with indecision. I could now see on James's and Carly's faces the distress it was causing them. That night, I tried to be Carly's friend and record executive at the same time. I'd almost always been able to balance my dual roles with my artists: I could act as a house producer for Warner Bros. and act in the best interest of my artists, who in almost all cases were my friends. This night was tough for me, because I knew the best thing for Carly and James wasn't necessarily the best thing for WEA's bottom line. In the end, James did leave Warner Bros. for Columbia.

After *Takin' It to the Streets* ran its course, the band and the label decided to give the guys — particularly Tommy — some breathing room. In the fall of 1976 Warner Bros. released a greatest hits album, *Best of the Doobies*. At this point, the Doobies had a great back catalog. The compilation rocketed into the Top 10 and was certified platinum before the year was out.

Early the next year, it was time to get back to work on a new album.

By the time we entered the studio in the beginning of 1977 for *Livin' on the Fault Line*, the Doobies had begun to become Mike's band. That wasn't the result of some sort of hostile takeover by Mike. He had a voice that was immediately identifiable on the radio, so he became the embodiment of their new sound. He'd also written, or co-written, the band's last round of hits.

When Mike started writing new songs, he came up with a ballad. He played it for me and asked if I thought if Carly might want to write lyrics for it. I wasn't sure, but I sent her a tape.

She sent him back a lyric: "You Belong to Me." She wrote it, as you might expect, from a female perspective, so Mike made a couple of minor changes and he sang her lyrics when we recorded it for *Fault Line*.

It's in the running as my favorite Doobies track of all time. In fact, it's on my short list of favorite songs I've ever produced. Jeff played some wonderful lines on it, and the orchestration, the strings, the female backing vocals, the horn solo, nestled in beautifully together.

But Mike's performance on "You Belong to Me" is what made that song *great*. Listen to the middle of the song; the way he cries out as if his heart is breaking gives me chills because his angst is so palpable.

During the sessions, Tommy began showing up, which heartened us all. We *all* wanted Tommy to rejoin the band, and I know Pat really worked to get him back in the fold.

When people ask me about that moment in the band's history, they expect to hear that there was tension between Mike and Tommy. Their assumption is that Mike didn't want Tommy back in the Doobies. Nothing could be further from the truth. They got along great, because they're two good guys.

There was an odd dynamic though, based on mutual admiration. Tommy held Mike in such high regard, especially as a songwriter. But Mike felt the same way about Tommy. In the studio, he'd say to me, "Oh man, that Tommy's really something." Mike admires Tommy more than most people even know. He looked up to Tommy as the guy who'd blazed the trail for him. To Mike, Tommy was the ultimate Doobie. Because of that, he always felt that he was the wrong guy in there to front the band. He almost felt like an interloper. He thought he was this schlubby piano-playing guy who had to replace this alpha-male, rock 'n' roll guitarist who'd written and sung stone-cold hits like "Long Train Runnin'," "Listen to the Music," and "China Grove." He'd say to me, "It's Tommy's thing, man. The Doobies are his band." So it was almost like they were intimidated by each other's ability. But

A sketch by Mike McDonald of the Doobies on Sunset Sound stationery, done around the time we recorded *Fault Line*. Note that I'd written "Call Tommy" on the paper. Even after he'd left the band and Mike had become the musical leader of the Doobies, Tommy was never far from my mind, and in fact I always tried to involve him in the band's recording sessions. TED TEMPLEMAN COLLECTION.

when they did play together in the studio, it was cool, because they had this shared respect.

Ultimately, though, Tommy decided to bow out when we were working on *Fault Line*. I can't speak for Tommy, but my sense was that the band's new sound didn't get him excited. It was smooth and subdued, with a jazzy feel. Tommy's a rock 'n' roll, R&B guy at heart, which didn't fit with the thrust of the band's current direction.

At the time, I kept a poker face about Tommy's exit in front of the guys, so everyone would stay optimistic, but it was an incredibly deflating experience for me. I loved Tommy as a person, and as a musician: his playing, his vocals, and his writing. He wrote the hits that put the band on the map. And now he was gone.

Maybe more to the point, I'd signed the band because I'd loved the musical interplay between Tommy *and* Pat. There's a certain magical sound produced when Tommy and Pat sing those *oooohs* together, like on "Long Train Runnin'." Listen to their background vocals. It's an identifiable sound, one that's almost as unique as the Eagles. The two of them together, in the Doobies, just created something that was different. Without Tommy, that partnership had been dissolved.

So I was heartbroken when he walked away. I never told anybody this, but some part of me didn't want to continue producing the Doobie records. I stayed on, though, because I didn't want to let down the remaining guys or the company. But if I'm being completely honest, I was gutted that Tommy had quit. I don't think I slept well for three weeks. Tommy's the nicest guy in the world and a great human being. So it depressed me, because I'd convinced myself that he'd come back.

A few weeks later, Mike and I were sitting in his apartment in Hollywood, stoned on weed. We were going into the studio the next day. We were listening to *Moods of Marvin Gaye*, and "Little Darling (I Need You)" started playing.

Mike said, "Ted, let's try to work up that song tomorrow."

"That's a great idea!"

Like Mike, I'd fallen in love with the song when it was a hit back in 1966. It was another of those Holland–Dozier–Holland tunes that felt upbeat despite its lyrical focus on heartbreak.

So the next day, we laid it down; Mike came up with this perfect intro. I played tambourine to open the song. I think I laid down a drum track too, but I'm not sure if any of my playing appeared on the record. When we listened to the basic tracks it all sounded so good on tape, and it got better and better when we did our overdubs. I was so happy with everyone's work. That night, we went out for a celebratory sushi dinner, toasting our success with sake.

But after we finished recording it, I made a series of mistakes that I regret to this day. I had this plan to put a saxophone solo on it, and on the second verse, I wanted to bring in some horns and strings. I hired David Paich of Toto to write the horn and string arrangements. He came up with incredible parts, which we recorded, along with a sax solo.

Now during the sessions, Baxter had pressured me to put a guitar solo on the song. To humor him, Donn and I recorded a dual solo by him and Pat, which I didn't plan to use, since I intended to use the saxophone part.

When Donn and I mixed, I broke my own rule about allowing artists to attend mixing sessions, and let Pat and Jeff, and maybe a couple of the other guys, sit in with us.

When we did that, as you might expect, they started voicing their opinions. Jeff, in particular, started lobbying me about the solo. He kept saying, "We've got to make this tune about the guitar, man." A couple of the other guys chimed in with, "Yeah, we're a guitar band, *man!*" The truth was that Jeff was a contrarian. And when he got that way, with Pat in the mix, he could often sway Pat into seeing things his way. So that day, Pat, who also liked their solo, backed Jeff. The other thing the guys wanted was for me not to use the strings and horns.

I started to waver. The thing is, I wanted the song to represent where the Doobies were musically. Baxter wasn't wrong — the Doobies were a guitar-based band. Still, I wanted it to be as good as possible as a single, which I knew meant that I should use the sax, strings, and horns. But I got caught up in what they were saying, and said, what the hell, let's use their guitar solo. While we're at it, let's leave the strings and horns off of it. They were all excited,

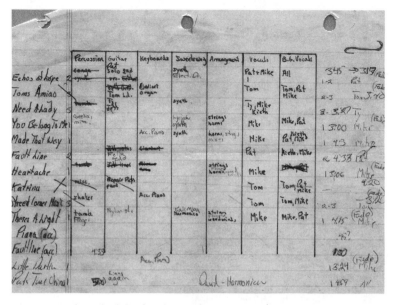

My personal track sheet for the *Fault Line* record, summer 1977.
Keeping detailed notes on everything I did and planned to do during
the making of an album was a habit I'd picked up during my 1971
sessions with Van Morrison. TED TEMPLEMAN COLLECTION.

because they'd convinced me. And at that moment, I *had* been convinced. All of this would soon come back to bite me in the ass.

The *Fault Line* sessions also generated one of my most embar-
rassing studio incidents. I was in Amigo one morning with a
second engineer; I was getting ready for the day's work. A nicely
dressed Black woman and an older gentleman came in and sat
down on one of the couches in the lounge area. She said to me,
"I'm Martha." I said, "Hello, I'm Ted."

I went back into the control room, figuring maybe she was
there to meet another producer or musician. About forty minutes
went by, and I'd forgotten she was around. Suddenly, she walked
into the control room and confronted me. "I'm not going to sit
around here anymore. I'm leaving!" The guy yelled, "Who the

hell are you to insult my artist like that?" He was very angry. They both stormed out.

I was totally baffled, thinking, *She's got to have me confused with someone else.*

Soon afterwards, Mike came into the studio. I told him that this woman named Martha sat here, yelled at me, and stormed out.

He said, "Oh shit! Martha Reeves!"

Mike had been at a party a couple of nights before and met her. He was so thrilled to make her acquaintance — the *Martha* of the group Martha and the Vandellas — that he invited her to sing on the session. The thing is, he got so drunk that night that he'd forgotten the conversation the next morning, so he didn't tell anyone, much less me. I had no idea she was coming in with her manager, and I had no idea who she was when I met her. We both loved her records, so we were both embarrassed and disappointed that we missed our chance to get her to sing on a Doobie Brothers album.

This period was an intense one for Donn and me. We worked for hours and hours, recording or mixing. Donn had an incredible ability to concentrate. He'd sometimes get angry if something didn't go right — but I understood that, because on our side of the glass at times it feels like you've got a million factors working against you in your efforts to get sounds and performances on tape for a record that people may be listening to a hundred years in the future.

Once we were done recording and mixing, Donn and I still had a ton of work to do. For example, when we got ready to master the records, Donn would run a short-distance radio signal from the studio to the parking lot, where we had a '57 Ford. Even though everyone recorded albums exclusively in stereo by the late seventies, lots of cars only had an AM radio with mono playback, so we needed to ensure that the stereo mix, when it folded down to a mono signal, sounded good.

So I'd go out to the car and listen while Donn played it back. I'm pretty sure that the short-distance radio method of testing our tracks in this manner was all Donn's idea. So because of Donn, the records I produced would always sound good, even on an AM radio. That mattered a lot when AM play drove the charts.

In these final days before we finished a project, I used to keep Donn very busy, because I'd re-sequence the records constantly before we mastered them. Take a look at the back of the dust jackets of the original vinyl releases of albums like the Doobies' *Fault Line* and *Minute by Minute* or Van Halen's *Fair Warning* and *Diver Down*. The sequence on the art doesn't match the actual running order on the record. That's because I'd change the running order over and over, even after the art department had finalized the dust jacket layout. Donn would patiently re-cut another reference lacquer, or test version of the album, for me with my newest sequence. He'd be working over the holidays while all the musicians had packed it in for the year. He was the MVP who made all of these records sound great.

But once he and I finished working, we knew how to have fun. After marathon sessions, we'd shoot hoops. There was a basketball court inside of Amgio; we'd play one on one. Other times we let loose in a more rock 'n' roll way. After a marathon session while we were recording *Stampede*, we had a fire extinguisher fight at Amigo. I recall that Lee Herschberg, who was the label's chief engineer, wasn't amused that we'd trashed the studio he managed.

When the album came out in the summer of 1977, we released "Little Darling" as a single. At the time, I hadn't thought much about the fact that I'd deviated from my original plan for the song. I had all the confidence in the world that it was going to be a huge hit.

I was wrong, once again. It stalled at No. 48 on the *Billboard* chart. That's when I had to admit to myself I'd gotten the arrangement wrong. To be sure, Jeff and Pat had played a good solo, but it didn't belong on that song. Even worse, I left off the strings and horns. Those were big mistakes. As a producer, you've got to do what you think is right, no matter what. I should have gone with my instincts. I *hate* hearing the song now, because it reminds me of how I didn't do the right thing for it. When Donn and I had it all laid out with the strings, horns, and sax, it was a beautiful little tune, one that could have been perfect. In the end, it wasn't all that different from what had happened with Van Morrison and the "Tupelo Honey" mix: once the horse is out of the barn, there's nothing you can do as a producer.

Even though *Fault Line* didn't sell as well as the previous four Doobies albums, it's one of my favorite albums. I like the jazz-fusion material, a lot of which came from the input of Baxter. He was a special talent — his playing, in fact, reminded me of jazz guitarist Barney Kessel of the Wrecking Crew — but he was a musical pedant, which made working with him difficult from my perspective as a producer. His role in the band, and his personality quirks, would become a bigger issue when we worked on the next album.

Chapter 8

AIN'T TALKIN' 'BOUT LOVE

In January 1977, I was working in my Burbank office. My secretary came in and said, "It's Marshall Berle for you on line one. He says he has an unsigned band for you to see in Hollywood."

To be honest, I rarely bothered to take or return calls concerning unknown local bands. But he was an old friend. I'd met him during my Harpers Bizarre days when he was an agent for William Morris; he'd booked the Beach Boys, so I knew he had an eye and ear for young musical talent. He'd also been instrumental in introducing me to Donna Loren. That's how he and I had become friends.

So I picked up his call. He proceeded to tell me that he was managing the recently reopened Whisky a Go Go and was booking a lot of young acts. Then he said, "Ted, I've got a band for you. Their name is Van Halen. They're from Pasadena, and next month they're going to be playing two shows on back-to-back nights at the Starwood."

I didn't know anything about this band. The first time I ever heard the name Van Halen was when Marshall said it to me.

This wasn't some sort of oversight on my part. At the beginning of my career at Warner Bros., I'd gone to clubs like the Troubadour to hear acts like Cheech & Chong and to scout talent. But by 1977, that kind of street work was no longer part of my portfolio. My typical days included two studio sessions, financial, promotional, or A&R staff meetings, and meetings with label artists like Neil Young or George Harrison.

Still, based on Marshall's recommendation, I was intrigued. I put the dates on my calendar and told him I'd be there.

So on February 2, I went down to the Starwood. Once inside, I didn't go looking for Marshall. In fact, I didn't speak to anyone. I spotted an empty table with a candle and a card with my name on it, but I didn't sit down at it. I bounded up the stairs to the balcony, so I could watch the show from the shadows, thinking that if this band wasn't any good, I could exit without any drama from anyone in their camp.

One thing hit me before the show even started. They hadn't drawn a crowd; the Starwood was almost empty.

When Van Halen came onstage, it was like they were shot out of a cannon. Their energy wowed me, especially because they performed like they were playing an arena and not a small Hollywood club. So my interest was piqued, even though their singer didn't impress me. At that moment, that didn't matter much, because their guitar player blew my mind.

Right out of the gate, I was just knocked out by Ed Van Halen. It's weird to say this, but encountering him was almost like falling head-over-heels in love with a girl on a first date. I was so dazzled. I had never been as impressed with a musician as I was with him that night. I'd seen Miles Davis, Dave Brubeck, Dizzy Gillespie, all of these transcendent artists, but Ed was one of the best musicians I'd ever seen live. His choice of notes — the way he approached his instrument — reminded me of saxophonist Charlie Parker. In fact, as I watched I was thinking there are two musicians in my mind who are the absolute best of the best: Parker, jazz pianist Art Tatum, and now here's the third game-changer, Ed Van Halen. So right away, I knew I wanted him on Warner Bros.

When I think back on that night, it wasn't just one thing about him that grabbed me. It was his whole persona. This guy, when he played, looked completely natural and unaffected; he was so nonchalant in his greatness. Here he was, playing the most incredible shit, acting as if it were no more challenging than snapping his fingers. For instance, that night he did some two-handed finger tapping. He only did it in one song at that time, I think. But the way he did it was fresh — I'd never seen someone play that way in person.

By the time their first set ended, I was sold. I slipped out of the club and hustled back to my car. Driving home in the rain, I was so amped about what I had seen from Van Halen that I stopped at two different pay phones, one on Santa Monica Boulevard, trying to get Donn on the line.

I finally got him on the phone after I got home. I said, "I just heard this band called Van Halen at the Starwood. We've got to go after these guys. You're not going to fucking believe it when you hear them. This kid guitar player is amazing!" I was so excited. In fact, I was so electrified by what I'd seen that I hardly slept a wink that night.

At daybreak, I called Mo Ostin, asking him to clear his calendar for that evening because there was an unsigned act he needed to see with me in Hollywood. He said, "If you're that excited about this act, I'm there."

By approaching Mo I was being strategic. I could have just as easily gone to Lenny, but I knew Mo, unlike Lenny, was a heavy metal fan. Mo listened to the Who. He'd signed the Kinks and the Jimi Hendrix Experience to Reprise. So in my mind I had Mo pegged as the executive most likely to respond to Van Halen the way I had.

Now I knew that even without Mo or Lenny's endorsement, I had enough juice inside the company to get them signed. But I'd have to make my case to the other top executives and jump through some hoops to get a deal done. I wanted it to happen *fast*, before any other labels got wind of our interest in them. And I knew Mo, as the company chairman/CEO, could sign them on the spot if he dug them.

That evening the two of us, along with my colleague Russ Titelman, went to the club. We met Marshall, and the four of us sat in the balcony and watched. Once again, Ed's performance moved me. His sound! The low-end thump from his cabinets — it just didn't seem like those kinds of seismic tones should be coming out of those speakers. The other thing that sticks out in my mind is that they played "You Really Got Me." I knew that Kinks song would resonate with Mo.

On this second night, I thought I should pay more attention to the band's singer. As a performer and vocalist, he underwhelmed me. His stage presence was awkward and his singing wasn't great. I didn't know it at the time, but David Lee Roth had definitely patterned himself as a performer after Jim "Dandy" Mangrum of Black Oak Arkansas. Sitting there in the darkness watching Roth, I was actually a bit nervous that Mo was going to be turned off by the singer's antics and perhaps might pass on Van Halen.

Truthfully, the singer made me nervous too. I thought, *What am I going to do with this group if we sign them and the singer can't hold up his end of the bargain?* A few things ran through my mind. I could make the guitar player a solo artist, if the worst came to pass and things didn't work with the singer or the rest of the band. The other thing that I found myself mulling over was dumping the singer for a stronger vocalist, like Sammy Hagar. I thought, *Hell, he might be the perfect singer for Van Halen.*

When the lights came up, the three of us shared our impressions with each other. As it turned out, Russ didn't really like Van Halen all that much, but Mo wanted to sign them. We told Marshall we'd like to meet them, so he took us backstage. The four guys were all really nice, and when I talked to Ed about perhaps making a Van Halen record, it was refreshing to discover that he was so unaffected by his talent.

During our backstage visit, Mo pulled Marshall and me aside. Mo said to Marshall, "Do they have a manager?"

"No. I'm just kind of looking after them."

"Well, they do now. You're their manager."

Right there, we made the deal. I was ecstatic.

Now that we'd landed them, my next order of business was to schedule a demo session at Sunset Sound. Giddy with excitement, I must have called Donn thirty times in two days, telling him how great they were, saying, "Donn, you're going to love this band." That said, I did concede to him then that I had doubts about Dave as a singer and may have mentioned to him that I'd been mulling over the possibility of replacing Roth with Hagar.

During this same general period, someone gave me the demo tape that Van Halen had done with Gene Simmons of KISS. When I got a hold of it, it was the first I'd heard that Gene had worked with them. I don't think Mo had any knowledge of Gene's involvement either before we went to the Starwood. But Gene, who's a visionary when it comes to spotting talent and setting trends, deserves a lot of credit here. He knew the band had potential, but for whatever reason, he couldn't get them a recording contract.

A few weeks later, Dave; bassist Mike Anthony; Ed's brother, drummer Alex Van Halen; and Ed came to Warner Bros. headquarters in Burbank to finalize Van Halen's deal with the label. Before they headed upstairs to sign the contracts, I wanted to talk about a couple of things with them. So I grabbed them and got them in my office and shut the door.

First, I warned them that no matter what, they shouldn't give up the publishing rights to the songs they had written if the label offered to purchase them. I was actually acting against the company's best interest in giving them this advice, but I wanted to help them avoid a decision they'd likely regret in the future. I explained that even if their record sold modestly, their publishing would provide them with some long-term income. I gave them concrete examples, and probably talked about Berry Gordy and Motown. Gordy, back in 1959, had set up his own publishing company called Jobete Music. Songwriters, like Holland–Dozier–Holland, and others who wrote hits for everyone from Martha and the Vandellas and Marvin Gaye to the Supremes and the Four Tops, *had* to use Jobete when their songs were recorded for Gordy's label, Motown. That's huge money, millions and millions, that went straight into Gordy's pocket. He wasn't the only producer and record man in the business to take that kind of cut. For my part, I thought it was a move that could only poison a producer's relationship with an artist. If someone wrote a song, that person deserved to get paid for it. This is the same reason I rarely took a songwriting credit on an album I produced, even when I helped one of my artists during the songwriting process.

Second, I brought up the related issue of writing credits. A few days earlier, they'd told me about their plan to split their songwriting four ways. I thought this was a potential pitfall, because not all the guys in the group contributed equally in that area. I'd worked with enough groups at this point to know that this was exactly the kind of decision that had the long-term potential to fracture relationships among band members.

So I told them, flat out, that they should make changes to that arrangement. I said, "Don't do the split this way. You guys would be crazy to do it. It will cause bad blood among the four of you down the road. Trust me."

They all disagreed. Dave spoke for them, saying, "Oh no, man. We're brothers. We're in this together."

I tried again to convince them otherwise. I brought up bands like the Beatles and the Stones, noting that Richards and Jagger didn't share credits with Charlie Watts for songs the drummer didn't write. The same followed for Lennon and McCartney; they didn't just give George and Ringo an equal cut on songs like "Love Me Do."

Once again, they brushed me off. So I said, well, okay, good luck, and off they went to meet with the attorneys. Soon after I found out that while they had smartly decided to hold onto their publishing, they had in fact kept their four-way songwriting split in place.

In the meantime, I frequently discussed Van Halen with Donn before we first got them into Sunset Sound. He knew how passionate I felt about them, particularly when it came to Ed. I insisted, "Above all else, we *have* to get his guitar sound on tape and not try to do anything to it. We've got to capture it." Donn understood. Truth be told, without his involvement, I don't think Van Halen would have happened.

For their demo session, my goal was to run through their best originals and a couple of their covers. In the spirit of the sessions I'd done with Van Morrison, I wanted to capture their sound and their songs on tape in as raw and live a fashion as possible, so I planned to get all the basic tracks laid down in a few hours. In this way I'd have a reference tape that documented the band's repertoire and thus could assess the strengths and weaknesses of the different tracks. Our time in Sunset would also give me a good sense of how the band members handled the studio environment. I certainly knew well that some musicians who were phenomenal live performers crumbled under pressure once the red record light illuminated.

For the session, I booked Studio 2 in Sunset. To be sure, I preferred the dark sound of Studio 1 to Studio 2's more conventional sound. But Studio 2's layout had certain advantages when it came to engendering a live feel and sense of cohesiveness among a group of musicians. Donn and I put Dave in the vocal booth so he could sing along while the other guys played together in the big room. From that vantage point, he and Ed could eyeball each other. I put Al's kit in a corner, near the control room. That way, not only could Donn and I make eye contact with Al and signal to him as we worked behind the glass, but Al could lock in with Ed as well. Mike was right there next to the brothers too. This arrangement fostered communication and built connections among all of us, and was an important reason why Donn and I were able to so accurately capture the band's live energy on tape.

The control room for Sunset Sound Studio 2, circa 1978. During this era, Donn and I worked behind this board to record hits for Van Halen, the Doobie Brothers, Nicolette Larson, and Little Feat. DONN LANDEE.

On the day of the session, the guys came into Sunset with their roadies and started preparing. Now I'd seen a million guitar players lay out their amps and effects in a studio, but I'd never seen a rig quite like Ed's. His pedal board consisted of a little piece of plywood with his effects and cables duct-taped to it. It looked like it was held together with spit and baling wire, all jerry-rigged together. But of course when he plugged in, turned up, and stepped on these different pedals, it all sounded fantastic. He was a little genius on guitar.

As he tuned up, Ed asked me if I'd ask Ronnie Montrose to loan him the amp that Ronnie had used on *Montrose* so Ed could use it on Van Halen's debut. He said, "Could you see if Ronnie would let me use his Marshall head?" Ed obviously knew that there were certain Marshall heads that just had a little bit more crunch than others, and he loved Ronnie's guitar sound. Ultimately, we never used Ronnie's amps on a Van Halen record, and honestly, I think his guitar would have sounded the same regardless of what amp Ed used. Ed sounded great whatever he played through.

Once we started tracking, we worked right down their song list. We knocked something like twenty-five tunes down in about three hours. They were well rehearsed and powerful, and Donn did a remarkable job of getting the band's sound on tape, even though this was the first time he and I had recorded Van Halen. Some days later, Donn and I did some vocal fixes with Dave, but on the whole, the demo was recorded live.

When I listen back to the tape, it's as obvious now as it was then that they had a bunch of excellent songs: "Runnin' with the Devil," "Feel Your Love Tonight," "Somebody Get Me a Doctor," just to name a few. At that point they were like gemstones that needed cutting and polishing before they really shined.

Still, it's clear to me why I chose not to put some of these songs on their first album. For example, they had a song called "Voodoo Queen," which later became "Mean Street" on *Fair Warning*. On the demo the riff and groove are fantastic, and the breakdown

— especially Roth's bloodcurdling screams — are great. But his lead vocal, in part because he couldn't vocally pull off the melody he'd written, sounds strained. Another example of a song that I didn't think was their strongest is "Let's Get Rocking." The solo section, with all of the interplay between Ed and Al, is good, but the b-section that followed the solo is terrible.

Rehearsal and pre-production, in my experience, can cure a lot of ills that bands faced before they entered the studio. But Van Halen's biggest issue was one that as a producer, I feared I couldn't fix. The truth was that Dave's performance in Sunset Sound only raised my anxieties about his abilities. Some of his vocal performances, to be frank, just weren't acceptable. To be sure, he had a whiskey-soaked, throaty, almost Black sound to his voice. He was distinctive as a singer. His train-whistle screams, too, were identifiable in a good way. But every time I heard him get pitchy or completely miss a note, I worried that the public was just going to be turned off by this band because of his limitations.

Donn picked up on the same things. He didn't think Van Halen would work with Roth at the helm. Since I'd confided in him my thoughts on Sammy, he'd turn to me when we were both at the board and whisper, *"You've gotta call Sam."* I'd nod and say under my breath, "You're right." He knew that Dave scared the shit out of me. Thinking back on that first go-around with Dave in the studio, I started wondering if I should stop talking about it and actually see about firing him. While he had his moments, he mostly just croaked along while the other guys played the most amazing shit.

Still, I didn't want to do anything rash. I knew that before Donn and I would make an album with Van Halen, we'd be preoccupied in the studio with other artists, including the Doobies, for the next few months. So in the meantime I could spend time listening to their demo, puzzling over what I approaches I could take to producing Dave's vocals that would deliver better results.

That process wasn't easy. At first, Van Halen was like a really terrible algebraic formula that you *need* to solve but don't know *how* to solve. On the one hand, I had a great band with an incredible guitar player and a singer who did these screams that were different than anything else I'd ever heard. I still don't know how he did them. He also had this engaging personality and looked great onstage. But the fact remained that he really couldn't sing well. Could I find a way to pull better performances out of him? I honestly didn't know.

On the other hand, I knew that Sammy, who's a great singer, might be a good fit for the band. If Sammy was game, I could tell the other three guys that it wasn't going to work with Roth, and if they agreed, make Sammy the singer of Van Halen.

But Sammy wasn't necessarily a cure-all, either. His lyrical ability wasn't stellar. In addition, there was no guarantee that the chemistry between Sammy and the other guys would materialize if he joined Van Halen.

As I mulled things over, I tried to attend as many Van Halen rehearsals as possible. They practiced in the basement of Dave's father's house, which was in Pasadena. I lived nearby, so I popped in on a regular basis. The weird thing for me was the first time I met with the guys there, I realized that I'd taken notice of the house a few years earlier, when it was for sale. At that time I'd been looking to move to a different house in Pasadena, so I'd discussed the listing with my realtor. Ultimately, I didn't make an offer on it, and in the end Dr. Nathan Roth, Dave's father, bought it.

Down in the basement, I listened to their new songs and gave them feedback as they crafted them. I also made suggestions on how to tweak their standards, like "On Fire" and "Feel Your Love Tonight." I spent hours with them down there. It was a lot of work. They had a great big blackboard, like you'd have in a classroom, and we'd write these ideas down. I'd take my own notes in a little notebook so I could keep on top of things as we worked through their songs. A lot of times, too, the names of songs would change as we went along, so taking notes helped me keep track of how their songs evolved.

They were so great to work with. Ed might play some new parts he'd written. I'd hear something I liked so I'd stop him and say, "Hey, wait a second." I'd dig into my notebook and say something like, "Remember that descending riff from that shuffle tune? Let's put it right after this part you're working on now. What do you guys think?" Those guys almost always knew exactly what I was referencing. If Ed didn't remember, Al knew just how to jar his memory. Then we'd work on re-arranging the song in question. After we'd get the new arrangement worked up, Dave would write an improved melody and often times update his lyrics. They had this ability to be modular with their songwriting, but they didn't even realize how well they did it. During that time, the songs came together just like *that*.

And Ed, in particular, was the guy who led the way. I'd make a suggestion for a song, and say, "How about we try this?" He'd listen to me explain what I wanted. He'd smoke his cigarette, furrow his brow, and go, "Oh, okay." Then he'd play a few things on his guitar as he worked with my idea. Then he'd go, "Oh, how about this?" *Boom*. He knew exactly what I wanted. He was *so quick* to understand, more so than anybody else in the band.

Again, Al was helpful, but Ed *really* got it. In terms of musical communication, he made things easy for me. He'd almost immediately be able to express my ideas through his fingers on guitar. It was uncanny. Of course, he also came up with all of these great ideas of his own for improving the songs. When I pointed to something that I saw as a weakness in a tune, he'd say, "Well, how about if we did this?" He'd play something incredibly brilliant, something better than what I had in mind.

They were also so flexible and open-minded. They weren't married to anything, and readily took my advice. When I made a suggestion, I'd hear, "Sure, Ted, anything you want." Dave was great. Al was great. Mike was great. The thing I remember about Ed is that he was the most vocal supporter of my ideas. He'd say, "Whatever you want, Ted."

At these rehearsals, Dave would show me his lyrical ideas, things that became classics like "Atomic Punk" and "Ain't Talkin' 'Bout Love." I loved how the latter song came together. Ed played that killer riff — the very beginning of the song — and I was sold. "Satisfaction" by the Stones is probably the best riff of all time, but Ed's riff on this one is probably my favorite, by any guitarist, ever. As they smoothed out the song's rough edges, they worked out how to punctuate the musical parts that accentuated Roth's lyrics. It all sounded so thunderous within that confined concrete space.

When we took breaks, I'd talk at length with Roth. That's when I came to appreciate his astounding intellect. To be sure, he was not possessed of a conventional mind. Conversing with him definitely had its off-the-wall aspects. A lot of people, I'm sure, thought he was just acting wacky when he'd quote a line from *Tom Sawyer* and then a comic book, but that's really how his mind works. He'd talk a blue streak for thirty minutes without missing a beat, and the whole time you're smiling because it's so clever and on point. Then at the end you realize he's covered all these seemingly disparate topics, and yet they'd all fit together in the way he presented them. I still don't know anybody else who can keep those kinds of stream-of-consciousness raps going like he can. Captain Beefheart used to try to do that; all the guys around Frank Zappa thought they could do that. They'd all *try* to be clever. But Dave naturally *is* that way. You're actually dealing with genius.

His intelligence came through in his writing, too. The more I read his lyrics, especially "Ain't Talkin' 'Bout Love," the more impressed I became. His line in that song about bleeding for something you really desire just stuck with me. That's how I came to realize that despite his vocal shortcomings, there was something unique about the way he put words together. He was extremely well read and smart, and that showed up in his whole approach to fronting Van Halen.

He also had a tremendous sense of humor and dead-on comic timing. I thought that aspect of his personality, in particular, made for something unique within the heavy metal realm. For me this harkened back to what Ronnie and I had talked about when we were making *Montrose*. Most bands of that genre were so strident and serious to the point of cliché. Dave had a unique way of seeing the world, and a way of laughing through the daily events of life that was infectious.

His smarts and humor, to be honest, didn't shine through during my first lengthy interactions with him at the Starwood and in Sunset because his singing was such an issue. So for me, solving the puzzle of how to make Roth work within the confines of Van Halen came down to this: Roth wasn't a conventional singer, to be sure. But he had a certain array of gifts that were rare in the rock world, and those assets outweighed his flaws. In the end, I hung in there with Roth, thinking that I'd find a way in the studio to accentuate his strengths and minimize his weaknesses. That's why I decided against calling Sammy. I love Sammy as a person and as a singer, but if I'd tried to put him in Van Halen in 1977, I'd have made the biggest mistake in rock history, because Van Halen never would have made it without Dave fronting the band.

When we went into the studio in August, I had a good handle on how I wanted them to sound on their record.

I wanted *Van Halen*, sonically, to have its heavy and dark aspects, but at the same time, I wanted the band's pop sensibilities to shine through. When people listened to the album, I hoped they'd smile rather than grit their teeth. Their harmonies, I thought, would be their secret weapon in this area. When Mike and Ed sang together, they sounded youthful, like the teenage sound of the early Beach Boys. It reminded me of what Lenny had been after when he had Lee wrap the capstan for our first Harpers Bizarre single: he wanted us to sound young. In fact, I think the guys and I talked about putting "Happy Trails," which showcased their harmonies, on their debut. Ed was really high on doing that one, and in retrospect, it would have fit perfectly on the first record. So with Van Halen, I wanted to have this pop, fun, Southern California sun-kissed vibe.

Roth's wonderful sense of humor also fed that upbeat feeling. Roth was more like a smartass talk-show host with great comic timing than a gifted singer. Yes, he had an identifiable sound as a vocalist — which is something that shouldn't be underappreciated — but he didn't have great vocal chops. When he sang songs like "Little Dreamer," "Feel Your Love Tonight," and "I'm the One," he made me smile, though, because his lyrics were clever. How he sang would be less of an issue, I thought, if people picked up on his smarts and wit.

Ultimately, though, Ed's guitar playing would be the x factor in helping to determine the success or failure of their album. His fretwork was unbelievable; that was a given. If Donn and I showcased it properly, it could cover up a whole host of sins related to Roth's vocals.

Even though we could have recorded at Amigo, there was never a question about us going back into Sunset. When we set up for the album, Donn and I followed the same formula we had for the demo. Sunset 1 had a phenomenal, dark sound to it. Studio 2 couldn't compare, sonically.

But as a producer who was trying to coach and interact with musicians, I felt especially comfortable in Studio 2. When I stood up in the control room in Studio 2, I could make eye contact with Mike, Dave inside the vocal booth, *and* Al, who was positioned in a corner right by the control room, behind his drums. Al could look through the glass and see me. Ed was right in the middle of the room, behind his baffles, He had his back to the control room, but he could make eye contact with Al and Mike from where he stood. Dave could see Ed, Mike, and Al too. So all of us, including Donn, who sat to my left in the control room, could lock in with each other. There was this great communication in the studio, especially on the first album.

The vibe during the session was upbeat and loose, which I think came through on the record. Dave was instrumental here; his enthusiasm was infectious. For instance, when we cut "Runnin' with the Devil," he started goofing around with this English bobby whistle that he wore on a chain around his neck while he was in the vocal booth. He made all kinds of noise with it and we ended up using a bit of it on the record. I recall having a good time tracking that song. I always tried to keep things fun, and Dave did as well.

If there was any overt tension when we made the first record, it was between Ed and Al. They played off each other to a significant degree, so if one of them made a mistake, they'd turn on each other. Ed and Al had worked out these parts — these little synchronized parts for the bass, drums, and guitar — that came from playing off each other so closely. Alex was Ed and Mike's guide in the room. Ed would sometimes forget a fill, and he and Al would yell at each other, but they'd work it out after blowing off some steam. The brothers certainly had their own way of communicating.

Truth be told, it was Al who struggled more in the studio than Ed. Listen to the drum fill right before the second verse on "Feel Your Love." It's a bit floppy and imprecise. As a drummer, that made me *crazy*. Now compare it to Ed's rhythm playing right after the solo. Ed's like a fucking metronome. He was always so locked in terms of timing.

But also notice that I left Al's fill on the record, because the rest of the take was good. I'm not sure I ever mentioned to Al that I had a problem with it. It was more important to keep those guys at ease and confident that the record was coming together than try to rework a basic track that, apart from a minor flaw, was excellent.

When we were recording, Ed was always so serious. He'd get nervous. As an artist myself — one who didn't have a fraction of the musical talent that Ed possesses — I remembered what it felt like for me when I was recording with Harpers Bizarre to have someone from the control room breathing down my neck when I was trying my best to nail a part. So I tried not to interrupt takes because when I was performing a part myself, I would get gun-shy from having the talkback in my headphones. After he was done, Ed was always pulling me aside when we were listening to the playback of what he had just cut, asking if I thought his performance was okay. I couldn't tell if he was politely asking to do it again or just getting my opinion, but we worked great together.

Working with Ed also gave me a chance to really draw on my bebop jazz influences. I thought of Ed's solos as similar to saxophonist Charlie Parker and trumpeter Dizzy Gillespie's solos. When I watched and listened to Ed within the confines of Van Halen, I had a visual of those two jazz legends playing with a piano or bass accompaniment. When they soloed, the piano and bass dropped down in the mix and played a supporting role. I thought of Ed's solos in the context of Van Halen's instrumental attack the same way; that's why I wanted to feature his parts so prominently on the record. My bebop chops allowed me to understand Ed's playing and how to make Van Halen work on record in a way that a lot of record executives — the guys who passed on signing the band — didn't.

I'd be remiss if I didn't point out what is in some ways obvious: Mike's bass was an important part of the Van Halen sound. Forget the vocals. The root of the chord was always so solid with Mike, you never had to think about anything else when working with Van Halen. He knew, almost intuitively, how to stay a simple course when we recorded so Ed's guitar parts could shine. I didn't need to work all that much with Mike on the first album because I knew he was right on top of things.

When we cut the basic tracks, I wanted to be sure to get performances on tape that felt fresh and energetic, especially with a great live band like Van Halen. So we'd record a few takes and then pick the best one as the master.

That still meant, though, that we had work to do with Dave. When we cut the tracks, he always sang along with them and we'd coach him through it. As a producer, I then needed to do triage — and decide which aspects of Roth's performances we'd later fix. If he hit a sour note, and I didn't seem to react, Donn would throw me a look.

He'd whisper, "Are you going to keep that [take]?"

I'd feel guilty, but I'd say, "I gotta, Donn." He'd whisper, "That's terrible." Donn, as I mentioned, was very low key and discreet. But you can't work that closely with an engineer and expect him not to have any opinions about the performances.

To get things right on the record with Dave, we had to patch things up. After we'd laid down the basic tracks, Donn and I would work alone with Dave. Along with the second engineers, I'd cut Ed, Al, and Mike loose for the day and keep working with Dave. To be honest, I did that because I didn't want anyone, especially the other three guys in Van Halen, to see how much we had to struggle to get Dave's vocals on tape. It took forever, sometimes, to get Dave on point. He'd be straining, and we'd work on getting him to hit certain notes. I did my best to keep Dave's confidence up, knowing from experience as a vocalist how shitty it feels to feel like you're not pleasing the producer. But it was a tedious process, one that I know was draining and frustrating to Donn. Unlike the three other guys, he had to be there for every second that Dave was in the vocal booth.

Even though Dave wasn't a natural studio vocalist, he was great when it came to tweaking lyrics and melodies. If I thought something wasn't working, I'd toss him an idea. Almost always, he came up with something better. Dave was such an integral part of that band, in no small part because he's so bright.

When I think about those long sessions with Dave, I am reminded of the multifaceted nature of a producer's role in the studio. You're trying to coax the best performance you can out of an artist. To do that, the producer needs to be a part-time psychologist, coach, cheerleader, and musical director. I had a good handle on that because I'd been a recording artist, and a not very good one to boot. Actually, the best analogy I can give is to the famed director/producer Cecil B. DeMille. He'd been a mediocre stage performer early in his career, but once he began coaching actors about their on-camera performances, his particular talents really came to the fore, because he'd walked in their shoes. I felt the same way about my career and abilities when it came to working with musicians.

Accordingly, I knew that, as a producer, I had to constantly assess the artist's state of mind. Maybe the artist is tired or hung over, or maybe he's scared to death because he's thinking about how this song might make or break his career. At that point, maybe it's time to take a break, or maybe it's time for me to sit with them in the room and help them get their head right.

Conversely, maybe a part isn't coming together because the artist is nearing a breakthrough. Maybe they are sitting out in the studio, in the zone, inspired and working to improve a part of a song. Or they are thinking about how to explain what they want to do on a song to you, the producer. At that moment, my best move might be just to shut up, grab a cup of coffee, and let the artist work it out for a spell.

On breaks from recording those guys, we did have time for some fun. Donn and I used to shoot hoops on the court outside of

Sunset Sound. Dave and the other guys, when we had an hour to kill, would tell their roadie to call Krellman. At first, I didn't know what they were talking about. But I quickly figured out that Krell was their slang word for coke. To push through and finish a day's work, some of the guys and I did a few maintenance bumps every few hours. I just did enough to keep my focus when I was at the point of utter exhaustion.

Even though recording this album was less time-consuming and onerous than some of the other bands I produced, I'd walk out of the sessions totally drained, because I was *obsessed* with getting everything right on *Van Halen*. I don't know how else to explain it other than using that word. In fact, I started to feel guilty that summer, thinking that I was spending more waking hours thinking about Van Halen than I was about the other projects I had committed to for the label. In my head, between things like Al's fills and Dave straining to hit notes, I was crazed. But eventually I realized those imperfections weren't really flaws — that's why it's Van Halen. So I wanted it to be perfect, but you know what? The humor came across. Ed's virtuosity came across. Al's power came across. Dave's smarts came across. It didn't need to be a pristine performance.

Probably my favorite song I ever worked on with any artist is "Ain't Talkin' 'Bout Love." It's like the perfect rock song, in a way. The guitar part is timeless. You can't get a better riff. One thing that people often miss is the way Ed constructed it. He spilled that final part of the riff into the next bar. That made the whole thing groove.

Roth's lyrics about disease and standing on the edge are so good too. Roth really conveyed that sense of darkness in those lyrics. And the three other guys did such a great job with the music. As I mentioned, they'd worked out ways to the punctuate Roth's lines. Yet when they recorded it, it sounded like they'd spontaneously come up with those accents. That's the greatness of Van Halen and an example of the album sounding live.

Donn added a lot to that song. He got Ed's massive rhythm guitar sound on tape, and I'm almost positive it was Donn's idea for Ed to double his solo with a Coral electric sitar. Ed's solo really sparkles as a result.

Roth's vocal on this one turned out very well. But when we did overdubs, I struggled to get Dave to hit the notes during the outro; it was difficult for him. He was straining. But his brains, personality, and swagger are all at the forefront and that's what makes it a special performance. With Dave, it was a matter of finding out what notes he could sing or couldn't sing and working accordingly. But overall he did a great job on this song.

Mike's vocals here, too, are so good. Everyone who's a Van Halen fan needs to ask themselves, where would they have been without his voice? There's no one better when it comes to doing background parts.

One of the last things we worked on was "Jamie's Cryin'." When we first got into the studio at the end of August, the guys had most of the song together, but it wasn't finished. The bridge wasn't done, so we didn't have a full melody. Dave didn't have the lyrics yet; he scatted his vocal when we initially ran through it. I really dug Ed's riff, though.

Dave told me he had an idea for the lyrics. He wanted to write about a high school romance gone bad, about a girl who was heartbroken. I think that came from the two-note lick that Ed played in the song, *wha-ha*, that sounded like someone crying. So *sad!*

The song came together after Ed wrote the bridge. In it Ed played these minor chords, just like the Animals with Eric Burdon used to do.

Dave wrote the lyric with almost no time left on the clock. He basically did it right on the spot in Sunset. At first, I was worried that the lyrics were too reminiscent of a fifties white pop breakup song, but eventually I realized Dave's lyric was a lot like those wonderful Holland–Dozier–Holland Motown tracks like "Where Did Our Love Go?" Those songs sounded happy, but were about heart-rending breakups. The way it came off was in keeping with that heavy-metal-with-a-smile, upbeat sound, this teenage thing. It ended up being one of the singles off the record.

During our last sessions for the album, something serendipitous happened. We'd moved from Studio 2 to Studio 1. I'm still not sure why. One of the days we worked in Studio 1, Donn and I were preparing to track something in the next few minutes. Ed was by himself in the studio. I remember he was kind of noodling around on his guitar.

I was out in the little side room getting coffee. I headed back and walked out in the studio. Ed was playing what became "Eruption."

My ears perked up.

I stopped him and asked, "What's *that*?"

"Ah, nothing. It's just something I warm up on."

"Well, let's hear it again. We gotta record it."

"Are you kidding?"

"No, we have to record it. Right away."

"Okay, I'll play it for you."

He really didn't think it was anything. But it was astounding.

I walked up into the booth, through these two doors, thinking Donn hadn't been listening to what Ed was doing.

I said, "You've got to hear this. Turn on the monitors."

Donn turned on the speakers and we listened for a minute.

I said, "We've got to record this. Let's roll tape."

Donn looked at me and said, "I'm already rolling."

So it turned out that he had in fact heard Ed playing and had turned on the tape machine. Donn was always ready to go, no matter what.

We got Al and Mike in the room. I don't think more than ten minutes went by from the moment I first heard "Eruption" to the time we recorded it.

I don't remember if he did it twice — all I know is we got it. Probably we did one as a backup, so I could splice it if he made a mistake on one of the takes.

I remember — and this makes me chuckle — after we'd gotten it on tape, Ed looked uneasy.

"What's wrong, Ed?"

"Ah, I dunno. I think I can do it better."

I said, "No. No. That's good."

I didn't let him do it one more time. Sometimes I regretted that, because, I swear to God, three, four years later he'd remind me that he "could've played it better" than the version that ended up on *Van Halen*. Even more mind-boggling to me is that Ed wasn't even going to show this piece to me or to Donn. If I hadn't walked by at that moment, it wouldn't have ended up on the album. Now it's pretty much universally recognized as the greatest guitar solo of all time.

Donn deserves a tremendous amount of credit for how massive it sounded on the record. Now to be sure, if you sat in front of Ed's amp that day and heard him play "Eruption," dead-ass dry with no reverb, you'd go, "Wow, that's really something." The musicality

Ed Van Halen, Alex Van Halen and Michael Anthony recording in Sunset 1 during the making of their debut record, September 1977. Not pictured is David Lee Roth, who was likely singing along in an adjacent vocal booth while his three bandmates played. DONN LANDEE.

of the piece itself, without any effects from the board, that's what sold me on it. It's super impressive as a composition, obviously.

But the way that Donn engineered it, by using the right amount of delay, made it sound like a Bach organ played in an old stone church. Donn's skill at being able to hear things and translate that onto tape is genius.

After the record was in the can, the guys invited me to see their farewell show in Pasadena at the Civic. I stood out in the middle of the audience and soaked up the scene. They put on a great performance; Ed sounded exactly like he did on the record. At that show, I noticed too how Dave put the spotlight on Ed every time he went onstage: when Ed played "Eruption," Dave hit everyone with all of this *"Edward Van Halen!"* hyperbole. He made their performances a showcase for Ed. Dave was savvy that way.

The other thing I remember about that show at the Civic is how incredible "Ain't Talkin' 'Bout Love" came off live. The whole crowd was pumping their fists. It was like I was at a Beatles concert in the middle of Pasadena, and they didn't even have a record out yet. That was great to see and a confidence booster for me as their producer. The game changer — I'm telling you, maybe the most emotional moment in music, for me, ever, in anything — was when I heard them play that song that night.

I believed in Van Halen and wanted them to break through. But what was a bit weird for me was that most people at the record company weren't high on their music. When I'd play the record, nobody there was enthused. That was upsetting, because, honestly, that meant that nobody at the label was really interested in Van Halen as one of the promising new acts for 1978. Meanwhile, I was sold 100% on these four guys. It was like dating a girl in high school that you thought was the biggest catch, and all of your friends thought she was nothing special. So it was frustrating, because I knew these guys had limitless talent.

I knew breaking Van Halen was going to be an uphill battle at the label and in the marketplace in general. You couldn't easily get Warner Bros. people to put a lot of money behind a heavy metal act like Van Halen in those days. Just think about it: Montrose didn't pay off for the label, so why was Van Halen suddenly going to be a cash cow for Warner Bros. Records? Van Halen, on paper, seemed too niche and too out of step with the times.

So it was up to me to really push them behind the scenes. Along with signing and producing them, I'm the one who got the promotional and tour support train rolling for them at the label. Promotion matters. You can't manufacture a hit out of a terrible song, but you also can't very well sell a great song that nobody hears. So I did my best to "work" the system to prioritize things for them at Warner Bros. Otherwise, I feared they'd never get the financial support they needed to break through.

I'm sure they didn't know it then, and I'm not sure they know it now. For example, they didn't know I would regularly reach out to Carl Scott, who was then vice president for artist development, regarding Van Halen. I'd known Carl since 1965, during my Autumn Records days, even before he became Harpers Bizarre's manager. He owed me a couple of favors, so I called them in for Van Halen. I don't mean to sound like the Godfather, but that's the way it was. I also had good relationships with Russ Thyret, who was vice president for promotion, and Bob Regehr, who was the head of artist development. Carl worked for him.

At that point, in 1978, the Doobies already had a few monster hits, so they didn't need me to put my finger on the scales. Little Feat, likewise, was an established act. Van Halen, in contrast, *did* need an extra push behind the scenes. "You Really Got Me" was a good tune for them, but my gut told me it wasn't a stone-cold, Top 10 hit and, in the end, it wasn't. We had to juice it. How does that happen? In part by making sure that Warner Bros. properly took care of the DJs and radio people to let them know that Warner Bros. was very high on the record. In the end, the song topped out in the *Billboard* Top 40, which was enough to get Van Halen, a brand-new act, on the radar of rock fans and industry types.

That's not to take anything away from those guys. They made a great album and were killers in concert, so they made their own breaks. "You Really Got Me" was all testosterone and raw energy. It got people excited when they heard it and, beyond the tunes, they had the looks, charisma, talent, and drive that it took to become stars. But my point is there's a lot that goes on behind the curtain when it comes to breaking a new act. Until you've established a band, a label can't just sit back, expecting that a single or an album is going to organically run up the charts. You have to build a hit.

See, along with being their producer, I was also a vice president. That was part of what those guys got from working with me. I could go into a meeting and the promotion guys had to listen to what I had to say because I was a vice president. Every Thursday we'd have a priority meeting regarding promotions. I'd help allocate funds. Everybody in the room fights for his or her budget, and the label has to dedicate a certain amount of money to each act. Are we going to spend more on the Doobie Brothers or on Fleetwood Mac? When Van Halen came up, there'd be hemming and hawing. I'd be in those meetings — talking about millions of dollars — pumping up money for them.

Still, I had to be careful. Van Halen was seen as "my" band, and as an executive you have to seem objective. So I'd have to do it on the sly. I'd have lunch with Carl. I'd tell him to juice these things that I believed in, like Van Halen. If I got word from Marshall Berle, who was managing them in 1978, that their record wasn't getting a good push in certain markets they'd toured through, as a vice president, I could address that and try to fix it for them.

I also helped with tour support. An unknown band like Van Halen, one that doesn't have a huge group of believers at the label, wasn't just magically going to have the kind of funds they needed to put on a great show. In fact, when it came time for Van

Halen to first go on the road, Carl, Marshall and I had trouble finding a big tour for them. I had to flex my muscles to get them onto a tour with Journey and Ronnie Montrose. They might have never gotten that kind of live exposure otherwise. The amount of money we'd put out in 1978 for publicity and promotion for them — it was a small fortune. If I hadn't been a vice president, if it was just Marshall calling up and making these requests to another executive who didn't give a shit about Van Halen, Warner Bros. never would have invested that kind of money. It cost tens of thousands to send them to Europe and Japan. Carl, Marshall, and I worked hard to get them all those shows with Black Sabbath, too. Those tours paid off big and had a lot to do with them getting recognized internationally.

The tour support they received was another advantage that came from being a Warner Bros. act. Other labels weren't as sophisticated in their artist relations tour support. I'd been through this process to one degree or another with the Doobies, Little Feat, and Montrose. We built up the Doobie Brothers' name a lot through those early tours, like the Mother/Brothers Show tour with Mother Earth and Long John Baldry. I tried to do the same thing for the Doobies that I'd later do for Van Halen, asking the promotion team to put extra money behind the Doobies. Of course, the big difference was that in 1971 I was a junior producer with little pull; by 1978 I was a powerful executive.

Again, when it came to live performances, the band made it all happen. I'd seen it in Pasadena; they were incredible in concert. I spearheaded tour assistance from the label, but really, what I was trying to do was invest corporate resources in something that I believed was going to pay off for everyone and, in the end, it turned out I was right. By October, their album had sold over a million copies and we'd released four singles from it. Those guys became superstars, Warner Bros. made a lot of dough, and I did well too.

I guess I want to share a bit more about my behind-the-scenes role because I want it known how much I wanted to see those guys make it. I poured my heart and soul into Van Halen, because I saw how hard they'd worked and how little they had to show for their years of effort when I signed them in 1977. They were so broke it was ridiculous. Ed had his car door tied closed with guitar string. Ed and Al hauled their gear in this battered, ragtag Ford Econoline van that looked like they'd driven it straight out of a junkyard. Sure, Dave's dad had money, but Dave wasn't living high on the hog. Dave's car was in such bad shape that when he couldn't start it one day after a session at Sunset, he left it and never came back for it. I swear, it was still sitting there, tires flattening and covered in pollen and bird shit, months after we finished the record. I know Mike was in hock to his parents. It's so great and fulfilling when you see someone coming from nowhere, and suddenly put out a record. It's even better when you see guys like that finally be able to make money from their music. That's what really makes you feel good as a producer.

The thing is, years later a lot of artists don't remember that hungry feeling. If I'd said to them, down at the Starwood, "So here's the deal, we're going to lay out a million and a half bucks to put you on the road around the world to build your name, but you'll have to pay us back," they would have said, "Great! Where do we sign?" Any unsigned, unknown artist, whether it was 1967, 1977, or 1987, would have given *anything* for a deal like that from Warner Bros. But instead, decades later, it became a point of contention with Van Halen. They seem to resent the way Warner Bros. treated them. But I think if they'd reflect back on how badly they wanted a record deal, they might see things differently.

Chapter 9

LOTTA LOVE

At the end of 1976, Billy Payne and Paul Barrere of Little Feat asked to meet with Lenny and me. When we all sat down, they confided that Lowell's health was poor, and as a result, he wasn't going to be able to handle the rigors of producing their next album. This wasn't some sort of band revolt against Lowell; even he, from what I recall, had conceded that he wasn't up to the task.

Lowell, of course, was the band's main creative force, so this wasn't good news. But Billy and Paul seemed to have a good handle on things and felt confident that they had the pieces in place to make a great album. They asked if Donn and I would be willing to work with them. I was excited to get another shot with them and said yes.

That said, I knew there were going to be challenges. Lowell, I was betting, wasn't just going to bow out completely, which was a good thing, obviously. But he often clashed with the other five guys in the band. One day, Lowell might not want to work with Billy, or whatever. There was always bullshit band drama that, considering the personalities involved, made for a combustible mix. Lowell, under the surface, was a nice, gentle person, but he didn't get on with people a lot of the time. So getting the Little Feat guys together and focused, without a bunch of static, could be a problem.

We started pre-production work with the guys coming into my office. Billy would get on the piano and the other guys joined in on their instruments, giving me a chance to get up to speed on their new material. We'd kick ideas around, getting the songs into shape.

Eventually, we moved into a rehearsal space in Hollywood as the tunes began to come together. As a jazz guy, I was particularly drawn to an idea that became an up-tempo fusion-influenced song called "Day at the Dog Races." I also dug "Red Streamliner." Lowell, as I recall, didn't show up for many of these meetings or rehearsals.

We then moved into Amigo and Sunset Sound to start tracking. One welcome development was that Billy worked to fill the

Richie Hayward of Little Feat working in Sunset Sound Studio 2 during the *Time Loves a Hero* sessions, early 1977. I liked to place the drummers in the bands I recorded in Sunset 2 in that same corner so Donn and I could maintain good eye contact with them from the control room while they worked. DONN LANDEE.

Little Feat's guitarist Paul Barrere and me standing behind the board in Sunset 2 during the *Time Loves a Hero* sessions. The trippy photo effect comes courtesy of Donn Landee, who is a talented photographer as well as engineer. DONN LANDEE.

void left by Lowell. He was so helpful to me on that record. He should have been credited as a co-producer, to be honest.

I could say the same thing about Donn; *Time Loves a Hero* was as much Donn's record as mine. He was really instrumental in its making. One area where Donn really was invaluable to me, as a producer, was through his work with Lowell. Donn had this knack of getting in tune with guitar players, whether Ronnie, Lowell, or Ed.

Donn's patience with Lowell was extraordinary. Lowell had a gift for studio innovations; he'd come up with an unusual guitar sound by miking the room in an unorthodox way, for instance. But a lot of times Lowell would take us on fishing expeditions. He'd want Donn to try something out, but in the process, we'd often waste three or four hours, or three or four days. Even when Lowell should have cut bait, he'd want to keep at it. Now to be sure, Ed Van Halen, too, could get obsessive over something he was hearing in his head, but it never took *anywhere* near that long with him because Ed always had a great sound, period. But Lowell, just for the sake of experimenting, would want to move the amp or mic here, there, and everywhere. It was just a big pain in the ass for a producer who was trying to make a hit record.

More often than not, though, Lowell didn't show up to work. I had no idea where he was from day to day. Then one day he'd waltz in, listen to what we had on tape, and start picking things apart. Lowell didn't like the direction of the material. That was his prerogative, and naturally I had enormous respect for his musical input. But here's the thing: it's what came out of rehearsals and from the writing efforts of the other guys while Lowell stood on the sidelines. As a producer, that's what I had to work with in terms of songs. He particularly hated "Day at the Dog Races" and "Red Streamliner." He'd bitch about them all the time, which pissed me off, because I thought they were good tunes.

Trust me, it would have been easier for all of us if Lowell had shown up, tunes in hand, ready to work. But he was unwell. I tried to cut him some slack, but finally lost patience. I said, "Well, you need to come around to the studio more often if you really want to be part of this process." It was frustrating for me and the other guys, not knowing if he'd show up. He was just MIA for long stretches of time.

As I liked to do, I brought in some friends — in this case, the Doobie guys, Pat, Jeff, and Mike — to act as session players. I particularly remember the day Mike came in to sing backgrounds on "Red Streamliner." After Mike finished, he and I were talking. Lowell wandered over and joined our conversation. A few minutes later, Lowell pulled a big vial of blow out of his pocket and dumped it on a nearby Anvil case. He offered us some. We declined. He divided it into two huge lines and quickly snorted it all. Mike looked shocked. Mike was expecting him to do a bump or two, then offer it to some of the other guys, not hoover up every last bit. I was more used to Lowell's habits, but stuff like that did scare me. He then jumped back into the conversation with us like he'd just finished eating a candy bar. Eventually he wandered off. Mike whispered, "Jesus, Ted, this guy's not going to live long." Unfortunately, he was right.

As a producer, you have to be very attentive to deadlines. I was trying to finish *Time Loves a Hero,* and Lowell literally would not get out of bed to do a slide solo on a song he'd written, "Rocket in My Pocket." I'd call, and he'd say he was sick and couldn't — or wouldn't — come in and record. I told him it was now or never, but he wouldn't leave his bedroom. I was sorry to hear he wasn't feeling well, but we were out of time.

So I called blues guitarist Bonnie Raitt and asked her to lay down the solo. She came in and nailed it.

Once Lowell got wind of that, he got moving. In the heat of the moment, I'd called Bonnie because I figured Lowell wasn't going to show up, but the news that she'd played on the record apparently was a cure for what ailed him. He jumped out of bed and raced down to the studio the same day she'd cut her solo. He barreled into the studio, wearing his pajamas under a London Fog overcoat, looking completely disheveled. He was so pissed off, yelling, "I'll play the fucking thing. I'm here. Let's go!" He wasn't quite firing on all cylinders, but he recorded a hell of a solo. We kept his take.

Another time he came down, I couldn't get him to sing the lead vocal for "Rocket" with any balls. I had to badger him to get him in the right frame of mind — I told him he was singing like a pussy — which made him mad. He literally jumped off the ground when he sang the chorus of the song. A producer's sometimes got to reach into his bag of tricks to get a performance out of an artist.

The record came out in April 1977. It sold respectably, staying in the *Billboard* Top 200 for eighteen weeks, peaking at No. 34 in June. Critics, not surprisingly, remarked on the fact that Lowell had made only limited contributions.

Listening to a Little Feat mix during the *Time Loves a Hero* sessions.
DONN LANDEE.

In the summer of 1978, I got a call from Linda Ronstadt. She told me that she and Jackson Browne were in the studio with Lowell working on background vocals for Lowell's forthcoming solo record, *Thanks, I'll Eat It Here*, which he was self-producing. They'd been at it for hours, bogged down and getting nowhere. "Lowell's flailing around, Teddy," she said. "He's going nuts trying to get our vocals done. Can you come and help him out?"

I said sure, knowing that as an artist, it's so easy to lose perspective on the strengths and weaknesses of your own material. After I arrived, I offered to take over the session, and Lowell, looking relieved, said sure. I just calmed everybody down, got everyone organized, and got things going again.

The song they were cutting was called "Easy Money." It just floored me. I couldn't believe it. I just went *holy shit*, because you don't hear a song like that very often. It was great and clever.

I said, "Lowell, that's an incredible song. Who wrote it?"

I expected him to name of one of the top songwriters in town. Instead, he said, "Oh, just some girl who plays at the Troubadour."

I asked more questions about this girl, and he started getting more and more cagey with me.

I figured out later that Lowell was holding back her name because he was angling for a piece of her publishing when she got a deal.

Eventually, I wore him down. He told me that she didn't have a record deal, and that her name was Rickie Lee Jones.

When the session wrapped I drove right to Burbank. I went to Lenny's office, and I told him about this unsigned talent who wrote this unbelievable tune.

"Lenny, we've got to find this girl. *Now*. You've got to hear this song."

Lenny made some calls, tracked her down, and got the wheels in motion at the label.

Soon after, she auditioned in Lenny's office for the two of us. She played her guitar and sang "Easy Money" and another of her songs, "Last Chance Texaco."

She didn't disappoint; she was a rare talent and, as we'd learn, had an edge to her as well.

After she finished, she stepped out so Lenny and I could talk. I asked Lenny what he thought. He'd gotten lost in the moment and had gone on autopilot. He said, "Well, we need to think about this. Let's kick it around at this week's A&R meeting."

I said, "Come on. Let's do it. *Now*. You're not going to find anyone else like that. She's amazing." I insisted we had to try to make a deal right then and there.

Once he talked about her songs and performance with me, it was obvious to both of us that another label was bound to snap her up imminently, especially once word got out that we'd had her in for an audition.

We called her back into the office and Lenny told her the good news that we were interested in signing her. She took the deal.

Incidentally, Lenny later told me that when he first got her on the phone he had to use his best persuasion skills to convince her to even come into the offices.

"So, Rickie, what would you think about auditioning for me and Ted Templeman?"

She got quiet for a spell, and then sighed, "Uh, why would I audition for you two? I bet you guys at Warner Bros. are gonna try to make me sound like the Doobie Brothers!"

Hey, at least she was talented *and* direct. Her 1979 debut album, produced by Lenny and Russ Titelman, was a critical and commercial success. She'd appear on the cover of *Rolling Stone* and her album would sell over a million copies in less than a year.

After I worked with Linda Ronstadt on the Carly Simon record, she and I became good friends. A couple of times, we swapped cars late at night when we were both working sessions at Sunset Sound, when her car was on empty and she didn't want to stop for gas on her way back to her house in the Malibu Colony. She and I both loved to talk music, and I loved the water, so I'd go visit her at her beach place. The sunsets there were spectacular, and she always had the coolest people around.

One of my visits to her place that year got unexpectedly awkward. Linda called me up one night and asked me to come over and hang out with her. When I got there, we sat down in her living room. She got me a glass of wine and put on a record. We were catching up on each other's careers when I heard a car pull up in front of her place. She went to the door, and in walked the governor of California, Jerry Brown. She'd been dating him for a while, but I'd never met him. He eyeballed me. "So what's going on here?" She introduced me, but he looked a little pissed off, in part because they had a date that she had forgotten about. She left the governor and me alone for several uncomfortable minutes while she got ready to leave with him.

She soon bounced back into the room. "Teddy, we'll be back in a couple of hours. Just make yourself comfortable." So here I am, left sitting in her house, holding a glass of wine, alone. I was gone before they got back.

The next time the three of us got together, things were more relaxed. Jerry and I, over the months that followed, became friends. I'd come to hang out with him and Linda quite a bit, sometimes at Jerry's place in Laurel Canyon.

I have a lot of good memories of her beach place, which was really just a small cottage. But my worst memories are of the March 1978 days when a massive storm battered Malibu. The Colony was a spectacular place to live, but you were right on the water. It poured rain for days and the surf rose higher and higher. I drove down late one night to help Linda get her belongings out. By the time I arrived the tide had already reached her back door. Torrents of rain kept falling and monster waves just kept coming and slamming into the structure until, inevitably, the part of the house she called her tearoom tore off its foundations. Helpless, we stood there in the rain under slate-gray skies at two in the morning, watching half of her house wash out to sea. My heart broke for her because she loved her home so much.

With and without Jerry, Linda and I spent a ton of time talking songs. She'd call and ask if I'd heard a new album by a favorite artist. She'd pick me up and we'd drive out to her place, or she'd come over to my house. She'd sit down with me and we'd listen to things like sixties Sinatra records or older jazz albums she'd find in my collection. She was an insatiable song searcher.

It was then that I learned about her great ear. At the time, she was recording all of these hits like Warren Zevon's "Poor Poor Pitiful Me." That song was perfect for her — and she could hear that long before she recorded it. One thing that I remember about her was that she really zeroed in on a song's lyric when trying to decide if it was right for her. And her instincts were great. Not all artists have the ability to select material that they can perform successfully. She has *great* A&R sensibility, and at the time she had the perfect partner in producer Peter Asher.

Along with an ear for songs, she knew talent. Hell, she had Glenn Frey and Don Henley of the Eagles in her backing band in the beginning of the seventies. She'd worked with J.D. Souther too.

I tell you all this to explain why I was so excited and curious when she gave me a tip that year about a friend of hers, singer Nicolette Larson. I remember she called me up. She said, "I've got just the ticket for you. I'm out to lunch with a girl you've got to meet. She's a singer and you're going to love her."

Linda told me that Nicolette was living with Neil Young in Malibu at the time. A day or so later, I picked up Linda and drove to Neil Young's cottage on Zuma Beach to hear Nicolette sing. When we arrived, Neil greeted us at the door. I'd known Neil for years; we'd become friends in the years that followed his stint with Buffalo Springfield because he'd signed to Reprise. He introduced me to Nicolette, and in the process he told me that the writer F. Scott Fitzgerald had owned this very house some decades past. At that moment I was more excited to tour the house than to hear her sing. As a Fitzgerald fanatic, that gave me a real thrill.

At the time, Nicolette and Neil were in a relationship. She'd sung on a couple of his records and toured with him, and somehow that had transitioned into a romance. She appeared to be totally in love with him. Everyplace Neil would be, Nicky would be right next to him.

I remember he played an acoustic tune called "Lotta Love" for me at his house. She sang it. I thought, *Well, Linda's right. This girl's got talent.* She had a husky quality to her voice and had good pitch control. But to be honest, her voice wasn't as distinctive as I'd hoped it would be. It's a hard fact about the radio. You can have the best technical singer in the world sing a great song, but if that person's voice isn't unique, the song isn't going to stick in the head of the listener as well as it would if the singer has identifiability. The perfect example here is Linda. When she sings, people know it's her. She's identifiable.

Nicolette and I talked for a long while before Linda and I left. She was a petite girl, with long, wavy brown hair that flowed down her to her ass. She was from the Midwest and spoke with a bit of a twang. I liked her personality; she had a fun energy about her, a silly sense of humor, and a lack of pretense that was refreshing. I also liked the fact that, like Linda, she had great song sense. She had concrete ideas about tunes she'd like to record if she ever made an album.

We talked again a few more times in the weeks that followed, and she told me she'd be thrilled if I'd produce an album for her. Soon after, I decided to take a chance on her. I signed her to Warner Bros. Records.

Not long after we did the deal, something went on between her and Neil and the relationship went south. Rather than deal with their differences head on, he just walked away and left her in the house. Literally, he just got on a plane and left town rather than actually having that final conversation and breaking it off. She took it really hard.

Not wanting to live in a house with the ghost of Neil, Nicolette moved in with Linda and then into a hotel in Universal City. I used to visit her there at both places. She'd come stay with Kathi, the kids, and me at our place in Pasadena. She'd drive over in her little blue Honda Civic and spend a few days staying with us, eating meals with us, and playing with my kids. At night she and I would talk songs and do pre-production.

Now Nicolette and Linda, unlike Carly, aren't songwriters. To me, that wasn't a problem at all and in fact had its own advantages. It meant we had a bare canvas on which to bring her artistic vision into focus.

As I mentioned, she, like her friend Linda, had great instincts when it came picking tunes that would work for her as a vocalist.

In other words, she had A&R skills. That made pre-production go smoothly.

Let me give you an example. Because she ran in the same circles as Linda, she had gotten to hear a mournful ballad called "Last in Love," which was written by Glenn Frey and J.D. Souther. She turned me on to it; man, it was a tearjerker, with a gorgeous melody. I couldn't wait to cut it with her.

The rest of the song list slowly came together. I had an idea to do an R&B song with her, so I picked soul singer Sam Cooke's 1957 hit "You Send Me." Linda handed us a song too. She gave me a tip about a talented songwriter who was living in her guest-house named Adam Mitchell. He had this tune called "French Waltz." He played it for me and I loved it. So we had that song too. Billy Payne of Little Feat and his wife, Fran, co-wrote a soft ballad with a hooky chorus called "Give a Little." I asked Lauren "Chunky" Wood of Chunky, Novi & Ernie if she had any songs. She offered up "Can't Get Away from You."

When we were kicking ideas around, Nicolette brought up "Lotta Love" again. She said, "I really like that song. I like the lyric." She told me that while Neil intended to release his own version of it, he hadn't done so yet.

Now it was a *great* song, but I didn't think it would be right for her. It was a folk song. We weren't doing a folk album. But she wanted to record it, so I called up Neil, and he agreed to give us "Lotta Love."

The album, as it turned out, really reflected that late-seventies, soft-rock California sound and scene: Neil Young, Linda Ronstadt, Glenn Frey, J.D. Souther, and Billy Payne all contributed to it.

In June and July we went into Sunset and Amigo to make the record. I called in the guys that I liked for sessions: Bob Glaub, a first-call session player, on bass, Billy Payne on keys, Rick Shlosser, whom I'd worked with when I produced Van Morrison, on drums. Bobby LaKind played congas, Andrew Love of the Memphis Horns played sax, and Linda and I, along with Chunky

Nicolette and I talk between takes for her debut album in the control room of Amigo's Studio A while a friend of hers, who'd come to the studio to watch the session, stands nearby. DONN LANDEE.

and Mike McDonald, sang backups on a few songs. It was more like a little band that I'd put together to back her onstage, rather than the typical studio situation of a bunch of different session cats I'd pick to play on different songs.

When we worked up the arrangement of "Can't Get Away From You," it ended up as more of a riff-rocker than the way Chunky had demoed it. Once we went in that direction, I wanted the guitar on that track to really jump out of the grooves, so I asked Ed Van Halen if he'd play the solo on it. He agreed, but after consulting with the other Van Halen guys he asked to be uncredited so as not to dilute his identity as the guitarist of Van Halen. When he was home on a break from Van Halen's tour, Ed came down to the studio and played a melodic part that was perfect for the track.

Some of my most vivid memories about the making of this album involve Nicolette on roller-skates. At the time, Nicky and

Linda were obsessed with skating. It was the big fad then; everyone had those leather skates that laced up, with the polyurethane wheels. At some point that summer, I bought them both new pairs. Linda was so into it that when her *Living in the USA* album came out later in '78, she posed in her skates for the jacket photography — the ones I'd bought her.

Likewise, Nicky was skating everywhere she could. I swear to God, she'd wear them during Amigo sessions. On breaks, she'd skate in the halls or in the parking lot. Then when I needed her to sing a vocal she'd roll up to the mic to sing. She'd twirl around and skate backwards up to the microphone. Then she'd go right out to the office areas. Everyone who was working would stare at her like she was crazy. She was a lot of fun.

One of the last songs we worked on for the album was "Lotta Love." I'd scheduled it for the end of the sessions because I was still uneasy about it. The arrangement I had in my head was still that same sparse, guitar-based template that Neil had laid down when he wrote it, which I didn't feel great about. That morning, I'd listened to Neil's version a few times, trying to think outside the box. No luck. I was still stuck.

So I left my house in Pasadena and headed for Amigo in North Hollywood. Donn was already there, setting up, and the session guys were there too. They were waiting for me to run down the day's schedule with them before we'd start recording. Nicolette would be arriving later.

So as I was driving on the freeway I heard this song on FM radio by Ace, "How Long." I liked the groove. I thought, *That's it! I've got to change my arrangement and use those chords.* I floored it all the way to Hollywood.

I flew into the parking lot and ran into the studio. They were playing, rehearsing the Neil arrangement. I said, "Stop, stop. I've got to remember these chords." Billy let me sit down at his piano.

After a minute, I recreated the chords that I'd heard. Those changes became the intro to "Lotta Love."

After Billy heard what I played, he sat down next to me on the bench. He said, "How about we also do this?" He played around with the chords, working with the other musicians in the room, especially bassist Bob Glaub, to write the rest of the arrangement. They picked up on Billy's lead and helped to flesh the rest of the song out.

The result was the complete opposite of what I had planned. It came to me like someone had dropped it right on top of me. If I hadn't been driving at that time on the 134 Freeway and flipped on the radio at that moment, her version would've been folky, just like Neil had demoed it. So I took the acoustic guitar arrangement away. The sax line became the hook. And because disco was big at the time, we added a little disco bass run.

When Nicolette arrived, she was surprised by the changes but loved the arrangement. She understood what I was after, and she sang it great. I think, actually, one reason why her vocal is so moving is that she was still in love with Neil at the time. You could see it in her eyes; she'd get spells of melancholy that gripped her. I think in her head she sang the song to Neil.

Looking back, it was just a remarkable, fortuitous series of events. If I hadn't heard the Ace song, Nicolette's version wouldn't have been a single, or a hit, period.

Looking to blow off some steam after I finished her record, I performed with Randy Newman's band when he gigged in August on the west coast. Randy was an old friend and thought it would be fun to play some shows together. His band was stellar. It consisted of Fred Tackett on guitar, Willie Weeks on bass, Billy Payne on synth, Mike McDonald on Fender Rhodes, Bobby LaKind on congas, Andy Newmark on drums, and me on percussion and timbales. When I was out with Randy, Mike, Bobby, and I all got to know Willie, whom we'd later recruit for the Doobies. We played Berkeley, San Diego, Monterey, and Los Angeles.

Those shows generated a lot of good memories. You're playing with your friends and, of course, I was backing Randy, who's a musical genius. The most enjoyable parts of the shows for me were, of all things, Randy's band introductions. He has this dry, sardonic sense of humor, and he'd always come up with a line that was dead-on accurate and yet lighthearted to describe me. He'd say, "On percussion and vocals, the last remaining rock 'n' roll Republican, Mr. Ted Templeman." Then the next night he'd poke fun at my blond hair and surfer haircut and say, "Ladies and gentlemen, we have the aging Beach Boy Ted Templeman performing with us here tonight." Those were some funny times.

In September, I worked closely with Nicolette to help launch her career. Kathi and I had an impromptu listening party at our Pasadena home for her debut. Jerry Brown and Linda, along with some of Brown's staff and Nicolette, came to hear Nicky's new record. As we played it, Jerry got a big smile on his face. "That's great!" He called over his chief of staff, Gray Davis, who'd later be governor as well. Jerry said, "Go get the seal."

Kathi, Nicky, Linda, and I had no idea what Jerry was talking about, but Davis went out to the car and came back with a California state seal sticker. He gave it to Jerry, and he made a big show of affixing it to the album cover. It was tongue-in-cheek, but in effect he was signifying that the state approved of her work. It was emblematic of who Jerry is — a good guy. It made Nicky feel great.

In December, Nicky played the Roxy, and Donn and I recorded a live album. The guys who'd recorded the studio album with her backed her onstage. Her parents and siblings came in from the Midwest for the gig and there were a ton of journalists and industry types in the audience too, hoping to hear what the buzz was about.

Nicolette and I had a mutual friend, the television actress Mary Kay Place. Before the show started, Mary Kay came out and introduced Nicky as her dippy southern belle character,

Performing onstage with Nicolette at Hollywood's Roxy Theater, December 20, 1978. I loved playing with her and her band so much that I'd accompany them on a short tour of the states in early 1979.
ANDREA BERNSTEIN/RHINO ENTERTAINMENT COMPANY, A WARNER MUSIC GROUP COMPANY.

Loretta Haggers, from the *Mary Hartman, Mary Hartman* television show. She was so funny.

Even though the Roxy show was only the second gig that Nicky and her band played, it went well. Linda came down for the performance and the two of us sang backgrounds for Nicky. Ed Van Halen was in the audience too, and hung out with us backstage after the show. It was a great night.

Linda and Nicky were inseparable during those days; if you hung out with one, you'd hang out with both. I remember one time Linda and Nicolette had spent the day at Warner Bros. headquarters in Burbank on business. When the workday ended, they took me up on my offer to take them out to dinner. I walked to the parking lot, fired up my red Ferrari, and pulled up to the entrance to pick them up. Linda and Nicolette climbed in and we took off.

I came into work the next day and went to a big meeting of the Warner Bros. leadership team. We were all sitting around a conference table. When Russ Thyret took the floor, he said, "Before I give my report, I just want to offer up a wish. I saw Linda Ronstadt and Nicolette Larson climb into a red Italian sports car with this man right here." He pointed to me. "So with God as my witness, I want to say that in my next life, I want to be Ted." Everyone had a good laugh about that line.

By the end of December, Nicolette's career was really taking off. Warner Bros. had released "Lotta Love" and it just blew up, eventually peaking at No. 8 on the *Billboard* Hot 100. When the first single from a new artist has a song that does that well, it's a godsend, because it means your unknown artist isn't going to be unknown any longer. Not only does it deliver the all-important name recognition, it also drives sales of the album. Critics showered her with praise; *Rolling Stone* would name her best female vocalist. I was so happy for her. She had been a background singer, a girl who never dreamed that she'd ever have that kind of success, and when it happens to someone as nice as she was, it's particularly satisfying.

At the beginning of 1979, Nicolette was dating the writer Cameron Crowe. I'd known him from *Rolling Stone* but the three of us got to spend a lot of time together, especially on weekends. During the week, he wasn't in town, he was living down in San Diego. When I asked him what he was doing down south, he explained to me that he'd enrolled in a high school there, even though he'd long since finished that chapter of his life. His plan was to research and write a book based on his experiences, which became *Fast Times at Ridgemont High*.

Over the course of a few months, I'd see him with Nicolette at social events. I'd ask him about his day-to-day life as an undercover student. Needless to say, he had a ton of memorable stories. One time, he said, "Ted, you're not going to believe what I saw this week. Inside a bathroom stall, some kid had scrawled *Van Halen Rules!*" He'd seen Van Halen's logo carved into desks. He said, "Ted, when kids risk in-school suspension to write a band name on school property, you know that band's getting huge."

In February, Nicolette's album went gold. Warner Bros. did something special for her; the label threw her a big BBQ on the grounds of the Burbank headquarters. All the staff, along with Mo, came out for it. Everyone celebrated with champagne and cake, which had been decorated with a pair of roller-skates. She was really popular around the label, in no small part because "Lotta Love" was a really big hit.

In the spring of 1979, I decided to go on the road with her and her band. It was an all-star group, made up mostly of the musicians I used on her record. We had Bob Glaub on bass, Billy Payne on keyboards, Rick Shlosser on drums, and Paul Barrere on guitar. We had Bobby LaKind from the Doobies on congas. Billy's wife, Fran, sang backgrounds. Lee Thornburg was on trumpet and Jerry Jumonville on sax. I played percussion and drums on a couple of tunes and sang backgrounds.

Warner Bros. Records CEO Mo Ostin and I, along with the entire staff of the label, help Nicolette celebrate her first gold record at a barbecue held outside the label's Burbank headquarters, circa February 1979.
ANDREA BERNSTEIN/RHINO ENTERTAINMENT COMPANY, A WARNER MUSIC GROUP COMPANY.

I'd always gravitated towards a support role in band situations, so backing her up felt very comfortable and enjoyable. I also knew that playing shows with her would pay dividends down the road; since I'd be in the thick of things, I could identify songs and musical ideas we could use when we went into the studio in a few months to make her next album.

We toured by bus together all over the United States. As a label vice president, I was plugged in across the industry, so I could make calls to help promote her. I'd say I was coming to town to perform with her, and lots of people with the company or in the business would come and see us.

The shows came off well. She was still learning how to front a band, but she'd rise to the occasion. We played "Oh, Atlanta" and "Old Folks Boogie" by Little Feat, almost her whole debut, and "Breaking Too Many Hearts," which was written by my old friend Lauren "Chunky" Wood. We'd cut that one on her next record.

I remember the time on the road with her and her band so fondly in no small part because she was so much fun. She put out good vibes all the time. She was always up, always joking. You know, as a girl in that situation, it can be hard to keep everybody happy and never cross the line into flirting. She was a master at that. We were on the bus and she was like this cheerleader, keeping the mood light. Everybody had a good time. I loved playing those shows.

As the tour rolled on, she garnered lots of positive press. The *Washington Post* and the *New York Times* wrote glowing profiles of her.

Our tour stop in New York City was particularly memorable. We had two days, with two shows each, scheduled at the Bottom Line in March. It was an intimate space with a postage-stamp-size stage. We'd play before a full house, with lots of luminaries in the audience; some cast members from *Saturday Night Live* were coming down and a reporter from *Rolling Stone* would be there too.

Backstage before one of the shows, though, a difficult situation developed.

Now, the Bottom Line was seemingly always overcrowded. I'd been there with Linda for other shows when we'd ended up in New York City at the same time, so I was prepared for the wall-to-wall people. But for Nicolette's show it was *packed*, as in way oversold.

The crazy thing about the club was that there were not enough fire exits. When you were in the dressing room, which was behind the stage, you were very far away from the front door. I had already remarked about the door to Nicolette earlier in the day, saying that somebody must've paid off a fire inspector so the club could remain open without having more exits. That night, one of the band members, whom I won't name, noticed the same thing we did. He had a full-blown panic attack out of the fear that a fire might break out and we'd be trapped. He was terrified. Needless to say, when you're about to go on stage for one of the biggest shows of the tour, that's not an ideal situation.

Nicolette's response really impressed me. Instead of worrying about the crowd or the show, she sat down and comforted him. Her empathy and kindness helped him get through his fears so we could make it to the stage.

Despite those troubles, the shows were excellent. David Sanborn, the great sax player, sat in with us. Carly Simon came down and watched. The crowd loved the shows, and I got a nice telegram from Carly a few days later saying how much she'd enjoyed the performance.

Soon after we got off the road, we started pre-production for Nicky's next album. In putting together a song list, I drew on the work of artists I'd produced in the past. For instance, we selected Little Feat's "Trouble," a song written by Lowell from the *Sailin' Shoes* album. I loved that song from the first minute I heard it; he wrote it about his wife. Lauren Wood gave us "Fallen," "Breaking

Too Many Hearts," and a song idea that Nicolette and I would bring to fruition as "Just in the Nick of Time." Mike McDonald contributed a song he'd co-written called "Let Me Go, Love."

We also reached back into past decades for a few songs. We picked "Back in My Arms Again," a Holland–Dozier–Holland tune, for her. It had been a No. 1 hit for the Supremes. As I've mentioned, I'd loved their songs from the time I first heard them in the mid-sixties. We also worked up "Daddy," a big band song from the 1940s.

We went into Amigo in June and worked for the next two months. I used the same band we'd had on the road, so they were tight and ready to go. I'd also call on my favorite session players and friends, including Van Dyke Parks, Ronnie Montrose, and the Memphis Horns. I played piano, percussion, and sang backgrounds.

Since we were going to record Mike's song, "Let Me Go, Love," Nicolette really wanted him to duet with her. He was at home on a break from a Doobies tour and was working another session at Amigo at the same time we were in there, so it was easy to get him on the track. He just came in and sang it. Once. He was that good.

She was good too. Intonation-wise, Nicolette was always on the money. She'd sing right through a song and her pitch would be perfect. She'd sometimes want to repair — patch — her vocal if she thought she could sing a line better. But she'd listen to me if I said it was all right because I thought the performance on the whole was strong. She was great about it. Some singers, like Mike, would go crazy if they had a flat note. He'd want to change it. If I didn't let him, he'd start sulking.

When we'd finish at the studio on a Friday, I'd invite folks to gather back at my house. We'd have dinner with Kathi and talk and laugh and play with my kids. Nicolette and Linda would come over quite a bit. Other times they'd come over on a Saturday, and Kathi, Linda, and Nicolette would all lace up their roller-skates and skate by the tennis court or even around the pool. When they skated by the pool, it used to make me nuts. I felt like an overprotective parent. I'd go outside and yell at them, saying if one of them fell in they'd drown because you couldn't swim with skates on your feet. They'd laugh and keep doing laps around my pool. In the summertime, we'd all jump in the car and drive up to my house on Lake Arrowhead and take the boat out on the water.

Nicky was really sweet with my kids. When little Teddy's bedtime rolled around, she used to sit up on his bed, cross-legged, and play her guitar for him. His favorite was "Mexican Divorce."

Looking back, I really loved a couple of the album tracks. In fact, one of my favorite songs that I ever recorded is "Rio de Janeiro Blue." It between the verses it sounds like a little mariachi band playing in a club. I played Agogo bells on it. What I really like about it is that it transports you when you listen. If you close your eyes and let it carry you away, you are somewhere in South America.

I love its lyric. It's about a girl who gets stranded in Rio. I dig the feel of the track, the melody, and the string arrangement. Jerry Hey, who was a first-call session musician, played a forlorn flugelhorn solo that perfectly captures the song's lyrical vibe. The night before he came into the studio, I had pulled out my trumpet and wrote the solo I wanted Jerry to play on his flugelhorn. He played the part I'd written beautifully. After the solo, I added strings and electric piano, and during the last verse, we sang backgrounds together. For me, everything works *together* on that track.

I also sang harmonies with her on "Daddy." I had so much fun doing vocals with her, because I was doing the kind of singing I excelled at. You see, when I sang on the Van Halen records all I was doing was supporting another vocal. If Ed's voice needed to be boosted, it was just a matter of doubling it. And with Nicolette, it was about making the harmonies work. I can carry a tune. But if I'm singing by myself, it's lame. I need somebody else

ABOVE: Nicolette and I cruising the waters of Lake Arrowhead in my boat, summer 1979. DONN LANDEE.

LEFT: My son, Teddy, wearing Nicolette's mirrored shades at my home on Lake Arrowhead, summer 1979. DONN LANDEE.

to sing with. I'm like mortar in between bricks. I fill in and make things come together.

In the midst of making her record, I left town early one Thursday for a long weekend at my house on Lake Arrowhead. The next day, June 29, I got a call from Lowell's wife, Liz. She told me that Lowell had died in an Arlington, Virginia, hotel room. It was a terrible moment. I was shattered. In my life, Lowell was more than a musician I produced. He was one of my closest friends. My nightly ritual involved talking to Lenny and Lowell on the phone. I spoke to him nearly every night. A lot of times our conversations didn't even involve music. For example, he was interested in Zen Buddhism, so we talked about that all the time. Or his favorite film, the Japanese epic *Seven Samurai*. Or about the ecological damage that cars did to the planet. It was a crushing loss for me, and for everyone who loved him.

In early August, I participated in his memorial concert at the Forum. The constellation of stars that came together to pay tribute to him was remarkable, but honestly, what sticks out about the gathering was that we were all his friends. Those onstage that night included his Little Feat bandmates, Linda, Nicolette, Emmylou Harris, Mike and Pat of the Doobies, Jackson Browne, Rosemary Butler, Bonnie Raitt, J.D. Souther, and the Tower of Power horn section. I'd play percussion: cowbell, timbales, and tambourine, right alongside Bobby LaKind, who played congas. It was like a big family reunion, or a maybe an Irish wake filled with tears and laughter. Linda and Nicky sang "Rhumba Girl" from Nicky's album. Mike and Bonnie sang together on Del Shannon's "Runaway," and as the set built to a climax, Linda led everyone through "Willin'."

In September, a number of us who had participated in Lowell's memorial concert gathered together for a star-studded five-day run of concerts on the opposite coast. The Doobie Brothers, along with Jackson Browne, Bonnie Raitt, Carly and James, Ry Cooder, Nicolette, and Bruce Springsteen performed at Madison Square Garden under the umbrella of MUSE (Musicians United for Safe Energy) to raise money for anti-nuclear causes. This all came in the aftermath of the Three Mile Island nuclear accident, which was a big wake-up call for the world regarding the safety of nuclear energy. It wasn't a cause I felt passionate about, but I wanted to help put on the show.

Lowell George working at the console in Sunset 2 during the *Time Loves a Hero* sessions. He was a great friend, possessed of a brilliant and creative musical mind. DONN LANDEE.

I joined the Doobies onstage during the first two nights. Nicolette and I sang backgrounds, and I contributed percussion when they played songs like "Depending on You," "Long Train Runnin'" and "Takin' It to the Streets."

Since I'd played drums in the studio for "What a Fool Believes" (I'll explain how that all came about in the next chapter), I jumped on new Doobies drummer Chet McCracken's kit and played alongside Keith Knudsen.

There's footage of this performance on YouTube. When I watched it recently, I remembered that Mike and I had a funny exchange. During the end of the song, he can't keep a straight face. That's because I was flipping him off from behind from behind the drums. We were both cracking up as the song ended.

As I walked offstage, I grabbed my bottle of Emerald Dry and headed backstage.

What happened next was a huge moment in my life. Jim Keltner, who at the time was playing with Ry Cooder, approached me right after I got offstage. He said, "Wow, Ted, you're my new favorite drummer, man. I had no idea you could play like that!"

Keltner, you have to understand, was one of the *cats*. He was one of the world's most in-demand session drummers. I got to know him well when he played on Carly's record. But before that he'd played on *Mad Dogs & Englishmen* with Leon Russell and Joe Cocker. He'd played with Dylan, Randy Newman, Ry Cooder, and three of the four Beatles. Jim Gordon and Hal Blaine were the other big players in town doing sessions but, to me, Keltner was *the* man.

He gave me a hug and proceeded to just go on and on and on, praising my playing. "I'm so moved when you play. You're such a soulful drummer." It made me feel so great. He was emotional; it was one of those instances when you could see, as a musician, that your performance had deeply affected someone. He said, "I was getting tears in my eyes watching you play."

Looking back, I think it hit him so hard because that song had been such a huge hit, and the Doobies were one of the biggest bands in the world that year, but I have to tell you that I was totally blown away by his praise. It was one of the best compliments I'd ever received in my life. Jim's one of the sweetest guys in the world and that was *the* absolute highlight of my musical career as a live performer.

The following month, in late October, *Nick of Time* was released. Nicky and I, and the label's whole A&R team, had really high hopes for the album. The songs showcased her talents beautifully and the packaging was gorgeous. In fact, the label flew the two of us, and a photographer, to Kona to take photos together on the volcanic sand beaches for the album art. (Those were the high-flying days when expensing that kind of trip didn't even raise eyebrows among the label's accountants.) She'd had me appear in a photo with her on the first record — I held a clipboard, standing next to her in her skates — so for good luck she wanted to include another picture of us for her sophomore effort.

The album got a decent push from Warner Bros., but ultimately it didn't match the debut in terms of sales. When you have a single that ascends into the *Billboard* Top 10, like "Lotta Love" did, an LP will run up the charts almost in lockstep with the single. In this case, lightning didn't strike twice.

The big single from *Nick of Time*, "Let Me Go, Love," made the *Billboard* Top 10 on the Adult Contemporary chart, but didn't break out as a pop hit. And ultimately that song wasn't enough to drive huge sales. *Nick of Time* crept into the Top 50 albums for just two weeks before slipping back down the charts.

It was a tough reminder for me, and for her, that it's really hard to find and deliver a hit single. She just didn't have one on the second record.

Some acts, regardless of their greatness, never have one. Look at Little Feat. I was *sure* "Easy to Slip" was a Top 40 hit, but it didn't connect. None of their songs ever became big singles, and Lowell was among the best songwriters I ever worked with.

Even if you do end up with a pop hit, like Nicolette did in 1978, and you have thus made a name for yourself, it's still difficult if you don't deliver another hit on your second album. Take Van Halen, for instance, and what happened to them during the same period. They followed up "You Really Got Me" from their debut with "Dance the Night Away" from *Van Halen II*, which hit the Top 20 in 1979. Having those two hit singles really helped their prospects going forward, because even though their next two releases didn't have similar hit songs, that pair of albums still went platinum.

What eased my disappointment with the muted reception that *Nick of Time* received was Nicky's genuine appreciation for my efforts. She had this well-maintained scrapbook, and from page to page to page you could follow her career. She showed it to me soon after we first started working together. A couple years later, she showed it to me again. It traced all of her successes, and on the last page, she'd written *And I owe it all to* with an arrow pointing to a picture of me. That's another reason why, I think, she always wanted my picture on the dust sleeve.

The year ended with more politics for me. Jerry Brown and I had gotten pretty tight. In fact, we'd hang out when Linda was busy recording or whatever. When I think back, I'm reminded of how different he was than most of the other politicians — or music industry figures — of the era. Rather than making the rounds in a limo, he rode around in an early-seventies sky-blue Plymouth sedan. Dirty and dinged, it had one incongruity. Because he was governor, Brown had a car phone, a very expensive and uncommon auto accessory at the time. You could tell the Plymouth had one because it had a huge antenna swaying from its fender. Even though it handled like a dump truck, he loved it. I'd have my Ferrari in the parking lot in Burbank, but he'd insist we take his car to grab lunch. Needless to say, he wasn't a guy who'd be flying from Sacramento to Palm Springs on a Lear jet and billing it all to the taxpayers.

I supported him politically because he was a liberal's liberal. Jerry was talented and honest — the real deal. I'm not a registered Democrat, but I respect him a lot.

In the late summer of 1979, Jerry approached me and said he planned to run for president in 1980. He wanted to raise money for his campaign, so a bunch of us in the industry worked together to put on two benefit concerts. On December 21 in San Diego, and the next night in Las Vegas, Linda Ronstadt, Chicago, and the Eagles all performed. During Linda's set in both cities, she invited Nicolette to join her onstage. They sang "Lotta Love" together. Incidentally, I'd asked Van Halen to play these gigs but David Lee Roth told me that Van Halen didn't want to get involved in politics. Considering their image, that was the right move for them. They never took themselves seriously enough to think about supporting a political candidate.

In the meantime, I dealt with a health scare involving my young son, Teddy. He'd developed a bad allergy to pollen and smog, which eventually developed into severe asthma. He was hospitalized twice. After the second time, when he was so sick that doctors placed him in an oxygen tent, Kathi and I decided to sell our Pasadena home. We loved our home and had a lot of friends nearby, but we both agreed that we wouldn't be able to live with ourselves unless we did everything we could to improve Teddy's heath. We had to get him in an environment that had better air quality.

Over the past decade, I'd made a bunch of good real estate investments. I owned a house on Lake Arrowhead. I also owned a couple of nice places on the coast, one in Malibu and one in Montecito, so we had good options when we moved out of Pasadena.

Initially, we went to the beachfront house in Malibu. It was stunning, three storeys, on Broad Beach Road. Our neighbors were all celebrities. Goldie Hawn owned a home on one side of my property; I'd met her back in my Harpers Bizarre days when she was a cast member on NBC's *Laugh-In*. Carroll O'Connor, of *All in the Family* fame, lived on the other side of me. Robert Duvall lived a few houses away.

There are not many places in California better to live than on the water in Malibu. I used to sit with Goldie Hawn on the sand. She'd tell me about how much she'd loved working with Lenny when she'd cut a single for Reprise under his supervision back in 1972. McCormick and Teddy made friends with Goldie's daughter, Kate, who was just a toddler at the time. They nicknamed her "Water Baby" because she kept delivering tiny buckets of water to them as they played together on the beach. Goldie, Kathi, and I would watch the sunset as the kids made sandcastles.

Unfortunately, Malibu had limited options for schools for the kids, so eventually Kathi and the kids moved to Montecito.

The Montecito property was particularly beautiful. Architecture is one of my passions, and my real estate brokers had a good sense of my likes and dislikes. So when this place went on the market at a bottom-of-the-barrel price I got a call. I loved it as soon as I saw it, in part because the floor plan resembled the house we'd had in Pasadena. I always had this thing, like Yuri in *Doctor Zhivago*, about owning an estate that could serve as an escape from the city. This place fit the bill. It had a six-car garage, complete with its own gas tank and gas pump, and a guesthouse. So even if the world was ending, you could invite your friends over and keep your cars fueled.

It was a Reginald Johnson–designed Italianate mansion with oceanfront views. When you turned onto the five-acre property, you drove up a quarter-mile-long driveway lined with palm trees and guava hedges. The property's grounds were exquisite. It had big lawns, dotted with avocado and citrus trees. It was a great property for the kids and their friends to explore while they played. The place was so big that we used golf carts to go to the pool and tennis court.

The commute would've been impossible from the beach to Burbank, so I got myself a condo in West Hollywood. Since I kept my cars up at the new house, I also got myself a driver and a limo to ferry me back and forth from the city to Montecito. Although there was no question that this living arrangement was the right thing to do for Teddy's sake, it was tough on all of us. I only got to see my family on the weekends, and even then, there were weekends I was tied up in the studio and couldn't get home.

I think I dealt with the loneliness and tremendous guilt about not being able to spend time with my kids and wife by drinking more frequently. Drinking dulled that sadness. On the rides back and forth to LA in the limo, I took to drinking Emerald Dry. When I reflect on it all, I think the separation from my family was one of the events that most contributed to my substance abuse. It was a way to blunt the pain of separation and my feelings of guilt for not being more present in the lives of my loved ones.

Chapter 10

WHAT A FOOL BELIEVES

Because this was the busiest period of my career, I've got to circle back here and talk more about what was going on with the Doobies during this time period. In the summer of 1978, while I was working on Nicolette's record, I also had to get the Doobies cranked up for their next album, which would be called *Minute by Minute*. When we started pre-production, I was well aware that this was a crucial moment in the band's existence. We'd all successfully navigated the Johnston-to-McDonald transition with the platinum-selling *Takin' It to the Streets*, but their last album, *Livin' on the Fault Line*, had barely cracked the *Billboard* Top 10 and spent only twenty-one weeks on the *Billboard* Top 200. We all loved the record, but it didn't connect with the public in the way that their prior five albums had, mostly because the singles from *Fault Line* hadn't broken out on AM radio. "Little Darling (I Need You)" didn't reach *Billboard*'s Top 40, and the follow-up, the Motown-flavored "Echoes of Love," had done even worse. In the end, *Fault Line* "only" went gold. As far as my colleagues at Warner Bros. were concerned, the album, by one of its biggest sellers, had stiffed, which seemed to signal that the McDonald-fronted Doobies were beginning to lose their luster.

Corroborating evidence of this trend seemed to appear when I'd get the financials on *Best of the Doobies*. Nearly two years after its release, it was still selling like crazy. But out of its eleven tracks, only two featured Mike. The public, it seemed, preferred the Doobies with Tommy as its focal point.

Without a radio hit, the band's box-office draw suffered in 1978. One unfortunate consequence for the band was that Bruce Cohn, their manager, needed to book longer tours to cover the overhead for their large touring operation. As a result, the guys were burning out after years of heavy roadwork, which wasn't going to do much to foster the creative spark we'd need to put together a hit album.

Despite their difficulties, they rarely complained to me about their troubles. But as I kept abreast of things from my perch in Burbank, I knew they were in a tough spot. Pat, especially, remained resolute though. When I talked to him, it was clear he was the cornerstone of the whole Doobie edifice. He was the guy holding the band together.

When we started working, I asked Mike to let me hear his demos. He seemed hesitant, uncertain whether what he'd written was up to snuff. He'd say, "Oh, Ted, I don't feel good about any of these tunes."

I'd say to him, "Mike, this is good. Why are you so down on it?" My read on it was that the rough patch the band was experiencing was sapping his confidence.

When Donn and I took them into Amigo, things started off well and we made good initial progress. But it soon became clear that we were facing a test of endurance. We'd record for a stretch, and then those guys would have to go back out on the road, which is never an ideal way to write and record an album. When we worked, some of the guys struggled to come to grips with the band's sonic evolution. Over the course of the past five years, the Doobies had gone from a hang-tough rock group to a sophisticated R&B-and-jazz-influenced act. I think a guy like John, who, like Pat, had been in the band since before they had a record deal, felt like he'd been dragged into a musical landscape he had no interest in inhabiting.

As always, I was their sounding board, but Jeff, Mike, Pat, and I most acutely felt the effects of these changes. We often differed on the band's musical direction. We clashed over which drummer or guitarist should play which part, and how things should sound. Things remained civil, but they were tense.

As the sessions wore on, I tried to balance the band dynamics. For instance, I knew from our one-on-one conversations, and from observing the sessions, that Mike was struggling to get his songs on tape the way he was hearing them in his head. Naturally, that involved conveying his vision to the other guys in the band, which made Mike behave in a more territorial fashion about his songs than he had on prior records. So oftentimes when one of the guys crafted a part to fit within the musical template that Mike had sketched out, Mike rejected their approach, because it didn't fit with what he envisioned for a track. It was a frustrating process.

The most strident disagreements developed between Mike and Jeff. Mike was writing soulful, moody R&B songs that didn't mesh with Baxter's experimental, jazz-minded approach. They didn't fight it out in front of me, but I knew there was a *lot* of tension.

I'd get frustrated too. Jeff would stir the pot in the studio, knowing the finger wouldn't be pointed at him, since he was trying to be creative, even though in my view his ideas didn't fit with the kind of record we were trying to make.

Let me give you an example of the dynamic. Donn and I would be in the control room, hunched over the board, and the guys would be in the studio. I'd be sketching out an arrangement, explaining to the guys how all the parts would fit together.

With everyone seemingly in agreement, we'd be ready to do another take.

Right then, Jeff would say, "How about this?"

He'd play some loony lick.

I'd gently shake my head. "I think we need something less busy there."

He'd proceed to play another line, once again way outside of what the song needed. "How about that?"

And so on.

I eventually lost my temper. I asked him why he kept playing like we were recording a Miles Davis record. Mike had written R&B-influenced pop songs; you couldn't have some sort of chromatic bebop line in the middle of them. It just wasn't going to work.

The thing about Jeff was that his musical ideas, in a vacuum, were good. It's just that everything he played sounded like jazz guitarists like Howard Roberts or Barney Kessel. He wanted to play these jazzed-out licks, which you didn't need on something bluesy like "Minute by Minute."

I get it. He'd come out of Steely Dan. He'd played on some of their biggest tracks; he'd done the solo on "My Old School," a song I love. I'm a massive fan of Walter Becker and Donald Fagen. I wore out those Steely Dan albums, and even more so Fagen's solo release, *The Nightfly*. But the Doobies weren't Steely Dan.

So it was difficult at times to make this album.

That fact, however, made it incumbent on me to try to keep things moving forward in a constructive fashion and to try to keep things on an even keel. You see, one key part of producing groups is to make sure that that the interpersonal relationships among the members continue to function reasonably well despite the stresses of trying to make a record. You want everyone to feel like they are contributing and are appreciated. Even if you're a guy who has written hits, that doesn't mean that you don't have insecurities. And just because the drummer isn't loudly bitching, that doesn't mean that he's happy with the way things are going. So it's important to have your finger on the pulse of the band and make sure everyone's okay. It's almost like being the leader of a group therapy session at times.

In my experience, a shared sense of humor and fun can go far in helping keep everyone loose. Mike, who has a great wit, helped with that when nerves got raw. I remember in one instance, we'd been working for a long while, but I wanted to rehearse this certain section of a song yet another time. I went down my checklist, offering directions to Pat, Mike, Tiran, John, Keith, and Jeff.

"You guys cool with that?"

Mike raised his hand slightly. "Ted, can I make one suggestion?"

"Sure."

"Ted, I think I speak for the entire band when I say: go fuck yourself."

The whole room exploded with laughter.

But the truth is that the tensions between Mike and Jeff did have a negative effect on the sessions. Things weren't coming together as well as they had on *Fault Line*, because those two guys didn't see eye to eye about the band's new music. We'd work for a few days straight, just spinning our wheels. Pat had this shell-shocked look on his face every time we left the studio, just amazed and deflated that things were taking so long to finish. Equally demoralizing was the fact that we'd have unproductive sessions and *then* those guys would have to head out for yet another leg of their 1978 tour. They'd leave town feeling as if we'd made no meaningful progress on the album.

At one point, it really felt like I was the last one in the room who had any confidence that we'd finish the album. I'd keep saying, "Guys, don't worry, we'll figure it out." I kept the faith because I didn't want to let them down. But in the midst of the process, it must have appeared like there was no light at the end of the tunnel. We'd work on tracks and fix arrangements. We'd do rough mixes, assess, and then recut things that didn't translate on tape the way I expected they would. When we were making *Minute by Minute*, Donn and I were in Amigo *constantly* with some or all of the guys, fixing parts. Mike would listen and say, "Ted, I don't know. I hate this fucking song." I'd go, "No, no, it's going to work. Let's keep going. Let's try this instead." And we'd just keep plugging away.

I have fonder memories of working on a ballad called "Sweet Feelin'." I wrote it with Pat. It begins with a lovely acoustic guitar figure supported, naturally, by Bobby's congas. Pat and Nicolette sang a gorgeous harmony vocal, and Mike sang backgrounds on the chorus. It was wonderful to blend those three voices together in such a sensuously rich fashion as part of my collaborative style as a producer. I was blessed to work with such amazingly talented artists, all of them my good friends.

By far the most difficult part of making the record was "What a Fool Believes." Mike had this piano riff for the verse back in 1977 when we were making *Fault Line*. He played it for me. Before I could open my mouth, he gave me a sour look and said, "I don't know. I don't think it's got potential."

"Yes it does. Come on, finish it."

"Yeah. Yeah. Okay."

I kept asking him about it. He'd say, "I'm still working on it."

I'd see him again a few weeks later when he was home from the road.

"Are you getting anywhere with that tune?"

"Not really. You really think it's good?"

"It's a great thing. Just keep on going with it."

Then in 1978, he and Kenny Loggins got together at Mike's house in Santa Barbara and wrote the bridge and chorus. Mike already had the lyric; I believe he'd written most of it on an airplane flight. But when Mike played it for Kenny, things just clicked musically. It had gone from being a song idea to a song.

Mike demoed it with his keyboard and his drum machine. The melody was there and the lyric was about the same as what he'd sing on *Minute by Minute*. He had the b-part, and the arrangement was close to what would end up on the album. The tempo, however, the feel, felt stiff. It sounded promising, but it was a bit uneasy and didn't quite groove the way I thought it could. But the song was whole, and as compared to some of the other songs we were trying to paste together, there didn't seem to be any reason why we'd struggle to record it.

I know it's hard to believe, but Mike didn't think we should record it. Even after he had his demo complete, Mike still wasn't convinced that the song had merit.

We'd listen to it, and he'd say, "You really want to put this on the record?"

"Yeah, we're gonna work on it."

Work on it we did. We recorded "What a Fool" on three separate occasions, all at Amigo. Pat later estimated that in the process of trying to get it together during those three marathon sessions, we'd done as many as seventy takes. On principle, I'd never dream of asking musicians to do that many takes, because at some point, it will start to degrade their confidence. But I thought these guys, who'd been working together for years, could handle it and I knew how not to make them feel bad about not getting it right. They were troopers.

It was, for whatever reason, a very tricky song to nail. It had a certain kind of simplicity to it, but it was unconventional; it wandered around. The song itself puzzled me, because it didn't have the typical structure for a pop tune. I felt like we had a vision for what it *should* be, but it remained just out of our grasp. Even though we kept missing the mark, I wanted to keep trying to hit the target. I recall in the midst of all of this, Mike said after a take, "I hate this fucking song!" I think Donn got that on tape. I refused to throw in the towel, but at times I'd think, *He's right. This is a piece of junk.*

One special thing about working at Warner Bros. was that we had an amazing in-house A&R staff. We'd all work together to give feedback on each other's projects, make suggestions, call in favors for each other as we worked to finish records.

We'd meet every week and discuss potential signings and work in progress. I took a cassette copy of the rough version Donn and I had put together of "What a Fool Believes" over to our A&R meeting. All of these hitmakers — Michael Omartian, Steve Barri, Lenny, Gary Katz, Russ Titelman — were sitting there.

Soon after I sat down, someone said, "Hey, does anyone want to play something?"

I said, "I've got this thing, but it's a *mess*. I don't know where I am with it."

So I played it. Mike's syncopated keyboard lines and soulful, smooth voice flowed from the speakers.

When it finished, I said, "I don't know what I should do with it. I may toss it. It wanders all over."

Lenny looked at me like I had two heads.

"Are you crazy? That's incredible!"

I don't recall who else said what, but the general consensus was that it was great record.

"Really?"

More compliments and suggestions came from around the table.

I realized at that moment that I'd come to take on Mike's sense of doubt about the song.

The truth is that up to that point, it still hadn't locked in for me. I still wasn't happy with it, because I knew it still wasn't right; the drum part didn't *feel* right to me.

At the same time, it's also true that I'd lost perspective. I didn't know what I had in terms of potential. But all the positive feedback I'd gotten from the A&R team bolstered my confidence. Feeling reenergized, I couldn't wait to try to finish the track.

When we got back in Amigo, it *still* didn't come easy.

Fuck!

At this point, I was almost ready to admit defeat. We were running out of time, and I remained dissatisfied.

As takes continued to mount, we ended up with a stack of two-inch tape, in boxes, piled up nearly to the ceiling inside the control room at Amigo. It was insane. And it still didn't feel right to me. I just couldn't get the groove right. That was probably hardest on the late Keith Knudsen. He was a great drummer who always nailed his parts. To have me sitting in the booth, telling him we still didn't have it on tape, was demoralizing for him, especially in light of the fact that this was not a technically difficult song. There's not even a tom-roll on it! He was a sophisticated drummer who could play anything. But it wasn't easy for me to articulate what I wanted. It was an almost ineffable aspect of the song; it just didn't sit right, tempo- and feel-wise.

By now we'd done dozens of takes over three marathon sessions at Amigo. It was now or never if the song was going to make it onto the album.

I hadn't slept for two days.

I remember Donn being behind the board, surrounded by 24-track tape boxes. I'd been out in the studio, talking to John and Keith, and was ready to end the session, knowing that once I did that, we'd likely have to wave the white flag on "What a Fool Believes." I'd hopped on John's drum kit and played with all the other Doobies. But I'd done that before with them. The groove just wouldn't sit; it wouldn't work when we'd track the drums. I was so frustrated.

I came back in the booth, sat down, and laid my head on the console. I whispered to Donn, "I don't know what the fuck to do."

He said, "Go play it. You'll get it right."

I said, "I don't know if I can."

"You've got to do it. I heard you playing it. You can do it."

So on Donn's urging, I went out into the studio again. I said, "Okay, let's just do it one more time." Keith and I played together with the other guys. I just slammed it along like I was killing snakes or something. We'd found the pocket!

Through the glass, I could see Donn listening, nodding his head. He gave me a thumbs-up and a big smile.

We all listened back in the control room. Donn had known. We did indeed have the drums right. Finally.

That moment of celebration passed quickly. When the guys glanced around the room, they got despondent. The reels were everywhere. Some of the stuff on tape was good and some of it wasn't. Even though we had the drum part down, we still had to put the song together.

The idea of having to review so much material turned all of their stomachs. We *still* weren't done with this damn song.

I said, "Listen, guys, we've got it all here." I pulled out my notebook. I'd written down comments and notations regarding every take we'd done.

I told Donn which reels we needed and how we'd need to splice things together with the new drum track that Keith and I had just laid down.

Mike didn't believe me. I showed him my notes. It didn't seem to make him feel better.

Donn and I grabbed the tapes and got to work.

Once we found the proper parts, Donn wisely suggested we create safety copies of what we'd recorded. Like me, he knew that it was a dicey proposition to cut two-inch tape. An errant razor blade slice could spell disaster.

I said no. None of the guys, me included, could stand to wait any longer. And because Donn was such a good engineer, I trusted him to get it done without a backup.

"Donn, let's slice it now."

Donn pulled out his blade and began to cut.

And this is another example of how Donn was so essential to our success, because what he spliced together is what we put on the record.

When we played back what we had, I knew we'd gotten it as together as it was ever going to be. It still felt a bit floppy to me, but we were done.

When I listen to it today, I'm struck by the greatness of Mike's vocal. He did the lead and background vocals, all those parts. It's difficult to believe now, but before the album came out, Mike wasn't thinking he'd gotten a great performance on tape. Just like Ed Van Halen, he had his moments of self-doubt. It's something that people who lack that kind of talent have a hard time understanding, but you learn as a producer. Supremely gifted people don't have supreme confidence.

Something else that I believe flew under the radar, because it's a piano-and-synth song, is Pat's contribution. His guitar part, even though it's understated and back in the mix, is one of the reasons the record was a hit. Give another listen to the tail end of the first verse and the pre-chorus and you'll see what I mean. Pat's guitar part makes that record sing.

For me, one of the more disheartening parts of the process was by the time we'd finished *Minute by Minute* in the late fall, none of the guys seemed to like the album. I know Pat and Mike weren't really satisfied with it. John, because of its pop sheen, wasn't a big fan. For my part, I thought *Minute by Minute* was a good album but not as strong as *Fault Line*. There were whispers around the building too that while certain tracks, like "Minute by Minute" and "What a Fool," were good, the album as a whole lacked depth.

At the same time, there was serious unrest in the band. I'd hear whispers from Pat and Bruce that Mike was considering leaving the band. And as I'd learn later, he wasn't the only one. It was almost like the album had wrecked the band's sense of camaraderie.

The album came out in early December. I didn't have much time to think about the release, after we picked "What a Fool Believes" as the first single. Donn and I were, as always, in the midst of our next projects. We'd booked Van Halen into Sunset Sound for their second LP and were working on Tom Johnston's first solo album, which we'd record up at Wally Heider's in San Francisco. Donn and I were also getting ready to record Nicolette at the Roxy on December 20 for a live album.

Meanwhile, the Doobies toured the States, ending the year with a New Year's show at the Forum on the same night Kathi and I hosted Ed and Al at our house — the night that Ed first played "Spanish Fly" for me.

When I checked the *Billboard* charts, the album was doing better than I'd expected. In fact, it hit No. 30 on the *Billboard* Top 200 by early January and climbed into the Top 20 by February. So at that point I felt like we'd at least made a record good enough to keep the band going for another year.

In late February, I was up at my house at Montecito. The phone rang, and it was someone from the Doobies camp. I can't remember who it was; it was probably Mike or Pat. Whoever it was told me that the Doobies were done.

"Excuse me?"

"We've split up."

I immediately knew it had something to do with Baxter and Mike, but the details I heard didn't make a lot of sense to me at the time. It was crazy.

When I hung up, I was mostly angry, but from what I'd heard, I didn't think it had the air of finality, because the Doobie Brothers were the Doobie *Brothers*. To be honest, with Jeff and Mike at odds with each other, it was just a matter of time before something like this happened.

Still, beyond the internal disputes, there was a larger problem. They'd broken up at *exactly* the wrong time. We'd just killed ourselves and spent a fortune finishing an album that the band thought was going to flop, and lo and behold, it was continuing to move up the *Billboard* Top 200. Moreover, "What a Fool," had cracked the Top 30 after just six weeks on the charts.

When I got off the phone, I vented to Kathi for a few minutes, then I called the Doobie offices, looking for Bruce.

When I got him on the phone, I said things I normally don't say. I think I just reamed him. As an officer of the company, I felt compelled to inform him that because Warner Bros. had poured significant resources into the making of the album, there's a certain amount of promotion that the band owed the label. I told Bruce, that contractually speaking, these guys couldn't dissolve the group right now without significant financial consequences.

Soon after, I spoke to Pat, and he indicated that even he was done with the band. Pat had been the heart and soul of things since the beginning, even more so after Tommy quit. Without Pat, there were no Doobies. I told him to reconsider, but he was non-committal. He and some of the guys were hanging out in Hawaii, trying to get their heads right after years of grinding.

In the meantime, I went on the road with Nicolette and her band. We had a great time, but the Doobies mess was never far from my mind, since their song and album were all over the radio. ·

Sometime in March, when we were touring on the east coast, I got word that Pat, Mike, Tiran, and Keith were going to reform the Doobie Brothers with some new members. Jeff was leaving the group. John, who'd been behind the drums since we signed them, was also calling it quits. To fill Jeff's spot, they asked guitarist John McFee to come aboard. Like me, he was from Santa Cruz, and we'd worked together when he played guitar on *Tupelo Honey* and *St. Dominic's Preview*. They hired Chet McCracken, a well-respected session drummer, to replace John. The final recruit was my old childhood friend Cornelius Bumpus. He was such a great guy. I was all in on the idea of hiring him. He was a wonderful singer, saxophonist, and keyboardist. Indeed this latter talent would come in particularly handy when playing new material live like "What a Fool," which featured multiple keyboard parts.

This time, their timing was better. On March 24, "What a Fool Believes" hit No. 3. On April 7, it crept one notch higher.

That same week, the album hit No. 1 on the *Billboard* Top 200 chart. It would spend five out of the next six weeks in the top spot. Then on April 14, "What a Fool Believes" topped the *Billboard* Hot 100. The Doobies had a No. 1 album and a No. 1 single on their hands.

The rest of their year was just magical. One highlight for me was watching as they sold out a week of July shows at LA's Universal Amphitheater. Knowing that a year prior they were struggling to fill small venues in some markets, it was great to see them revive their drawing power in such a high-profile manner. By this time, the album had sold three million copies and they had followed up "What a Fool Believes" with "Minute by Minute," which had reached No. 14 on the *Billboard* Hot 100.

While those guys toured, Donn and I were finishing up Tommy's first solo record. We'd been working on it for the better part of a year, with pauses when I had to turn my attention to records by Nicolette and Van Halen. Tommy had written a bunch of songs that were sixties R&B flavored, funky and raw, and some straight-up Doobie-style rockers. I brought in an all-star cast to support him: Nicolette, Bob Glaub, Jim Keltner, Billy and Paul of Little Feat, drummer David Garibaldi and the horn section from Tower of Power. Even Mike and Keith of the Doobies did some session work for us.

There were lots of flavors on the record. The first single, "Savannah Nights," was a disco anthem powered by the Memphis Horns. On Joe Tex's "Show Me," Tommy channeled James Brown. "Small Time Talk" captured the classic Doobie Brothers/Tommy Johnston sound. One of my favorites was a Tower of Power–inspired track called "I Can Count on You." Tommy sang his ass off on it. Nicolette sang with Tommy on the breakdown right before the fade. The whole track smoked. I had both Tower's drummer David Garibaldi and the band's horn section on the track. Nobody plays drums like Garibaldi — what a *funky* groove.

Tommy's album, *Everything You've Heard Is True*, finally came out in September 1979, while Doobie fever was still at its peak. "Savannah Nights," the first single, made a bit of noise at radio but didn't get beyond No. 34 on the *Billboard* Hot 100.

The Christmas holiday gave me a chance to reflect on the success I'd experienced with my artists in 1979. I'd produced three chart-topping albums, selling millions of records in the process. I'd been behind the board for two Top 10 hits, including a No. 1. I'd been so busy that I don't think it fully dawned on me until Lenny said something to me at dinner a few weeks earlier, noting that I'd produced huge hits for the Doobie Brothers, Nicolette, and Van Halen all in the space of a year.

Since I was one of six or seven Warner Bros. Records vice presidents, I'd go to these year-end financial meetings in Hawaii. Mo, the chairman/CEO of the label, headed them up. Warner executives from all over the country flew in for these sessions. They made for long days. You'd be indoors from morning until night, looking at budget documents and spreadsheets, stealing a glance here and there to watch the palm trees sway in the tropical breezes.

These meetings were always serious business, but of course when the company did well, the vibe in the room was upbeat.

But in the years when the company struggled, faces around the table would be grim. The accountants would point fingers at certain individuals, noting that a record by one of our key artists had flopped. There'd be multi-million-dollar shortfalls. These were unsettling conversations, because jobs hung in the balance. You'd have to debate whether ten percent of all the promotions people should get fired to make up a shortfall. I remember one year Mo and Lenny actually floated the idea that the label should consider selling its headquarters in Burbank to get us out of the red.

I also went to a couple of the annual meetings of our parent company, Warner Communications, in New York City. At those meetings, Steve Ross, the head of Warner Communications, got reports from Mo, along with the CEOs of Elektra and Atlantic Records. In late 1979, Mo asked me to come along with him to Manhattan.

In the meeting, I remember when our label's sales came up for discussion, Ross said, "Good bottom line this year, Mo. These are strong numbers." Mo pointed to me and said, "Thanks to this guy." That gesture by Mo made me feel great.

When the executive team flew back to Los Angeles, we traveled on the company jet. The flight was crowded, but I got the chance to sit next to Ross. I'd had a number of conversations with him over the years, and I loved talking to him. He was one of the brightest, most charming men I'd ever met. Even in the air, he'd be reading files, taking notes, and working on a deal with an attorney or agent he'd invited on the flight. Before we landed, he shaved and changed into a freshly pressed shirt in preparation for his next meeting. He was an unusually gifted executive and a great leader.

At the dawn of the eighties, my schedule was packed. I had five projects in the queue, including Van Halen's *Women and Children First*, Mike McDonald's first solo album, the Doobie Brothers' follow-up to *Minute by Minute*, and a new Tower of Power album.

In the case of the latter act, I'd just signed them. I'd made the deal in a San Francisco garage with their manager. He and I did a few bumps to celebrate. As a vice president riding a long hot streak, I could make that deal on the spot. They'd been on Warner Bros. but had left the label in the mid-seventies. I loved their groove and sound and was excited to get them back on the Bunny and to produce them. Just listen to "Oakland Stroke" and you'll be a believer. As a drummer, I was especially ecstatic to work with Garibaldi. Some months later, however, the deal fell apart after Garibaldi left the band.

Before January was out, the National Academy of Recording Arts and Sciences announced its Grammy nominations. I was nominated for three awards: Producer of the Year, Album of the Year (for *Minute by Minute*), and Record of the Year (for "What a Fool Believes"). To be sure, it felt great to garner the plaudits of my peers and to have a chance at winning a Grammy, but this was not the first time I'd been nominated. Back in 1968, I'd received a Best New Artist nomination as a member of Harpers Bizarre, but our band hadn't won the award.

The nominees in the Producer of the Year category were all superstars: my friend Quincy Jones (Michael Jackson's *Off the Wall*), Larry Butler (Kenny Rogers' *The Gambler*), Mike Chapman (the Knack's *Get the Knack*), and Maurice White (Earth, Wind & Fire's *I Am*). Still, I felt like I had a good shot at winning because of the hits I'd had with the Doobies and Van Halen. But I had thought we had a shot back in 1968, and we didn't win then either. To be honest, you have to be a bit delusional to go to the Grammy Awards evening *expecting* to win, especially when you size up the competition.

The guys in the Doobies kind of felt the same way I did. The band had been nominated for six Grammys. To say the Grammy nominations had been a surprise to them, and to all of us, would be an understatement; we were all shocked. None of us in the Doobies orbit were the perennial darlings of the Recording Academy. In fact, despite all of the Doobies' success — platinum records, No. 1 hits — the band had never been previously nominated by the Academy. So they didn't think we had much of a chance.

One big reason why was that in 1980, disco was still *huge*. (Hell, Warner Bros. had even issued a disco remix of "What a Fool Believes.") Media and industry observers believed that the genre would win big at the Grammys. Donna Summer and Earth, Wind & Fire were up for a ton of awards. Pundits expected country to likewise sway the voters. Kenny Rogers, who was hosting, was nominated for five Grammys. We'd had a big year, but *Minute by Minute* didn't seem to be the right album at the right time for a Grammy win.

The awards were held at the Shrine Auditorium in Los Angeles on February 27, 1980. It's the industry's biggest night of the year. Every major star and power player attends, and it was broadcast live on CBS.

One vivid memory I have of the evening was seeing all four members of Van Halen dressed in tuxedoes. The guys congratulated me; one of them slipped me a special "grammy" in a vial as a gift. Dave, especially, seemed to be in his element. I know there are a couple of photos kicking around of them from that evening, although I don't think they sought out the cameras. At the time, posing in black tie would have ruined their wild rock image.

I sat with the Doobies and Nicolette. Sitting and waiting through award announcements and performances got tedious, in part because you've got that edgy feeling because of the anticipation of the awards you and your friends might win. Early in the evening, Rickie Lee Jones won for Best New Artist. She looked more surprised than anyone in the room that she'd won. It was a great achievement for her and for Warner Bros. At that moment, it felt very good to have played a role in getting her signed.

About halfway through the show the Doobies played "What a Fool Believes" live onstage, in their tuxes. Mike, I know, was nervous as hell singing and playing a grand piano on such a big night. But it was cool to see those guys up there as a capstone to their amazing 1979.

Kenny Loggins and Smokey Robinson presented the award for Album of the Year. The Doobies' *Minute by Minute* lost to Billy Joel's *52nd Street*.

The big one for me was Producer of the Year. Larry Butler won. I was disappointed, but *The Gambler* had been hotter than a gasoline fire in summertime for months. It was a well-deserved win for Butler.

My final opportunity to win a Grammy that night would be for Record of the Year for "What a Fool Believes." We all sat, anxiously awaiting the verdict. Up on the stage, Herb Alpert and Kris Kristofferson read the list of nominees. Then Kristofferson tore open the envelope.

"The Doobie Brothers!"

I leapt out of my seat, elated. Along with Mike, Tiran, Pat, and Keith, I walked onto the stage. After a prodding from Mike, I spoke first, Grammy in hand.

Smiling, I said, "I produce these guys. I've been doing it for nine years. It's been a long time. I'd like to thank Warner Bros. for sticking with us a long time, and our engineer Donn Landee. We couldn't have done it without him."

The Record of the Year win followed the evening's overall trend. By the end of the night, "Minute by Minute" had won Best Pop Vocal Performance by Duo, Group, or Chorus. Along with Record of the Year, "What a Fool Believes" was recognized as the Song of the Year, making Mike and his co-writer Kenny Loggins the winners in that category. Mike also won Best Arrangement Accompanying Vocal(s) for "What a Fool Believes." For the band, and for me, these were our first Grammy wins. It was an incredible moment, especially when considering all the things the band and I had been through over the past twelve months.

For me, one of the most important things about that night was that I was able to thank Donn Landee from the dais. I meant exactly what I said. I couldn't have done it without him. If I could have cut my award in half, I would have given him an equal share. It meant a lot to his family that I did that, I learned afterwards. I recently came across a letter from his parents, thanking me for mentioning him when I won the Grammy. I remember getting it a week or so after the broadcast.

I don't think Donn has gotten enough credit for the success of the bands we recorded together. From my perspective, the working relationship between Donn and me is akin to the one between producer George Martin and engineer Geoff Emerick, the pair that made magic in the studio with the Beatles. Emerick was probably the most brilliant engineer of all time, and Donn Landee in my mind is right there with him. Martin could have never done those albums as well without Emerick at his side. Martin was able to concentrate on the arrangements and work with the four Beatles because of Emerick's abilities. With Donn and me, it was the same thing. So I always felt like it was Donn and me, *together*, who'd done the work from our side of the glass to win the Grammy. I didn't feel like *I* did it.

When you're a producer and you have that kind of right-hand man, it's invaluable. That's why I said what I said about Donn at the Grammy Awards.

Around this time, I gave Donn another token of my appreciation. As Van Halen's producer, I was contractually entitled to receive three points on the sales of their albums. (Incidentally, a non–Warner Bros., independent producer riding a similar hot streak to mine at that time would've demanded five points and a healthy advance to do a record. I *never* took an advance.) Decades later, when some of the guys in Van Halen complained about their record deal, they would grumble, "Well, three points on our albums went to Ted." What they don't realize is that I started giving one of my three points to Donn. Even if he wouldn't accept the title of co-producer, he deserved the extra compensation. The band didn't know that. So I wasn't getting that three percent. I got two; Donn got one. That was the right thing to do, because without Donn, those records wouldn't have become timeless classics. He deserved it.

I was thinking about someone else that night too: Tommy

Johnston. I felt conflicted about winning, because without Tommy, there would have been no Doobie Brothers. That's a fact. He should have been up there with us, but he couldn't be, of course, because he'd left the band. I *hated* that aspect of the band's situation.

The rest of the night was a blur. I went to some of the Grammy afterparties. I sat with Dylan and the legendary producer Jerry Wexler.

After it was all over, the headlines were everywhere from the *New York Times* to *Billboard*. The Doobies had followed up a No. 1 record with a huge night at the Grammys. Once something like that happens, everyone in the industry is all over you like a cheap suit. Bands started calling, asking me to produce them. Magazines wanted interviews. Your whole professional world changes, because you've won the industry's highest award.

In many ways, Mike's world changed a lot more than mine. I was over at Mike's place when the superstar songwriter Burt Bacharach showed up. He was playing songs on Mike's piano. I was blown away, because when it comes to pop songwriting, Bacharach is the *cat*. He's one of the most talented composers ever to walk the planet.

Mike was dumbfounded. Here's Mike, a guy who four years earlier was living in a garage after he'd been thrown out of his apartment because his Fender Rhodes made too much noise. Now he's writing with Bacharach? It was amazing for him. You just don't run into genius like Bacharach every day, and Mike was as aware of that as anyone. It was an incredible moment for him, but well deserved.

Still, both of us were on the same wavelength when it came to the new degree of fame that the Grammy award delivered. That started the night we won. When we got our Grammys, our feeling was, *Did somebody make a mistake? Who voted wrong?* Mike and the Doobies and I won for songs from an album that none of us thought was as good as *Fault Line,* one that left a good portion of the band dissatisfied artistically. So to win for "Minute by Minute" and "What a Fool Believes" seemed so unlikely that on some level it did all feel like a bit of a fluke.

The other thing is that back then there was no kind of big fame that came from being a producer. Sure, my profile increased, but ultimately it was the artists who deserved the spotlight, and that's how things went in 1980. That was more than okay with me, because I garnered my satisfaction from working behind the scenes to help them achieve greatness.

I think having that state of mind keeps you safe from having a big head.

Chapter 11

AND THE CRADLE WILL ROCK . . .

Because the making of *Minute by Minute* was such a grind, it's almost easy for me to gloss over the work I did on Van Halen's second album. In terms of the speed at which we got songs on tape, there isn't much of a comparison between the Doobies and Van Halen. They were totally different animals. So let me step back to December 1978 and recount what happened.

That month culminated an incredibly busy and successful year for my artists and me. *Van Halen*, which had come out in February, had peaked at No. 19 on the *Billboard* Top 200 and had sold more than two million copies by year's end. Nicolette's debut arrived in record stores in late September, and "Lotta Love" had broken big at radio and was headed to the Top 10. Then Donn, the Doobies, and I had persevered through the marathon sessions needed to complete *Minute by Minute*, which was scheduled for a December release.

My last major task of 1978 was to make a second record with the Van Halen guys. They got off the road in December. I went and met with them over at Dave's place to talk about tunes. Man, what a difference a year makes. When we'd last been together, they'd been an unproven act. Now they were stars.

If they were upset about their financials or the state of their deal with the label, they didn't let me know it. My relationship with them was great; I almost felt like a father figure to all of them, especially Ed. But here's the thing. When you take on that role, that's a double-edged sword for a producer. The guys want to get it right to please you, but they also on some level think you're an asshole because you're the authority figure ultimately calling the shots as they make an album.

Still, they couldn't have been more agreeable or enthusiastic as we got prepared to return to Sunset Sound to record *Van Halen II*. We had a tight schedule, but the guys were ready to go, despite being road-worn after their world tour.

We went back into Dave's basement. We spent a lot of time down there — more time than they probably remember. That's an important reason why we could work so quickly in the studio. It meant that we didn't need to write much in the studio and, consequently, I didn't have to blow through their budgets, which I always tried to keep low.

They were so cooperative and efficient when we worked. We had their 1977 demo to use as a starting point, and Ed and Dave always had a few song ideas for us to woodshed. Working with that pair was amazing. Al was really good too. He was always quick to pick up on where I was going.

You couldn't find a better working environment for a band than Dave's basement. Nothing could have been that good — a rehearsal hall, a studio, a soundstage. We worked in a room in this big concrete basement. It was perfect for us. We could get locked in together, because working down there felt like being on the moon. There were no distractions. It was so exciting to collaborate with them as they put together these phenomenal tunes, stuff that at that point no one had ever heard but soon would be blasting out over the airwaves.

At some point, the synchronicity of it all hit me. Four of the five of us lived in the same town, Pasadena (Mike lived down the road in Arcadia), pretty much four blocks from each other. Ed, Al, and I could drive a few minutes from where we lived and be in this basement and make magic. I really never put that together at the time, but what are the odds of this arrangement happening organically? Astronomical. It would be like if George Martin and the Beatles had all lived in the same neighborhood in Liverpool.

Anytime a hot band is working on their second album, the specter of a sophomore slump always looms. There's that old cliché — a recording artist has their whole life to prepare to record their debut and then a year to do the follow-up. Now Van Halen had a lot of good songs, but naturally I'd picked what I thought were their best songs for their first album. So when I listen back to *Van Halen II*, I remember that a few of these tunes were nail-biters for me when we were rehearsing for the sessions. I just didn't know if we'd get them to settle in properly before we ran out of time in the studio. Compared to those on the first record, I thought a number of these songs were marginal.

Even though it turned out to be a barnburner, I remember thinking "Somebody Get Me a Doctor" was an iffy song. When we were working on it in the basement, it just didn't feel like it was going to sit right. I didn't know if it was going to make the cut.

But when we got into Sunset and cut "Doctor," it all came together. The ironic thing about recording it was that Dave was on crutches. He'd broken his foot. The guys were out in the room, tracking together, and he was in the vocal booth, leaning on his crutch while singing into the mic. Of course, his injury just added to the vibe.

Donn's magic is all over "Doctor." The reverb on Dave's voice is really good; I think we used the echo chamber at Sunset Sound for his vocals. Donn set the decay just a little longer. It made Dave sound lonely, like he was yelling for help.

And Ed's solo is brilliant. It's one of those that he'd worked out in advance rather than coming up with it spontaneously in the moment. You can hear all those little parts — those little kicks — Ed, Al, and Mike had worked out together.

Another great track from *Van Halen II* is "You're No Good." I think Alex, to this day, believes we cut that one because I was a fan of Linda Ronstadt's version, which was produced by Peter Asher and was a big hit for her in 1975. Look, I love Asher's work on it; I'd known him since my Harpers Bizarre days when he was in Peter & Gordon and think he's a brilliant producer. I think it's a *perfect* record.

But "You're No Good" was Dave's idea. Dave said, "Teddy, let's do that old Betty Everett hit."

I said, "Which one?"

"'You're No Good.'"

"Hmm, I dunno. Linda *just* covered it. Her version is great."

"So what, man. We'll scare people with ours."

Dave was dead-on right about making it menacing, because that's exactly what we did with it. We made it scary, in part because the chorus is in a minor mode; in fact the whole tune is dark. Ed was a true genius for coming up with that arrangement.

I do remember that even after we'd worked the song up, Ed wasn't certain it was right for Van Halen. After Dave wanted to do the song, Ed said to me, "What do you think, Ted?"

I said, "Yeah, well, if it's been a hit once, you're halfway there."

That was true then, and it's true now. It was a principle I learned from Lenny when he produced Harpers Bizarre. If the public picked up on a song once, and then you cover it, there's a significantly better chance that it will be a hit a second time around. It's like making a safe bet when you're gambling. That quote's been attributed to me to explain the numerous covers Van Halen did over the years, but the initial impetus for doing "You're No Good," just like "You Really Got Me," came from the band rather than from me.

When we worked on the song in the basement, I got an idea for how to give the song an ominous feeling, one that captured the rage that a catastrophic heartbreak can generate in a spurned lover. For the chorus, I pushed Dave to unleash these blood-curdling screams as Ed did some searing unison bends on his high strings. I didn't tell them this, but what I had in mind was what movie audiences heard during the shower scene in Alfred Hitchcock's *Psycho*, with its screeching strings and tortured screams from Janet Leigh's character as she's being stabbed to death. I wanted Dave and Ed to recreate that same unsettling vibe on tape. Next time you listen to the chorus of "You're No Good," think about that scene, and you'll get what I had in mind.

I think it is the best version of the song ever recorded, in part because it features my very favorite Ed Van Halen solo. I'd asked him to make it scary, and he did just that. His solo embodies all of the angst and anger of the song's lyric, and while it is an understated part, Ed still threw in his little trademark musical gymnastics. Ed made that song smoke.

Even though we rehearsed extensively before we entered Sunset, the band and I still could create on the spot. Like "Jamie's Cryin'" during the first album sessions, "Dance the Night Away" was a work in progress for *Van Halen II*. In fact, I recall that the tune was worked up in the studio.

I remember everyone was really positive and optimistic when we cut that particular track, and the recording captures that perfectly. Ed's riff and chords sounded happy, so I gravitated towards that song idea because that upbeat vibe in their music is one of the things I liked to put forth on their albums. Dave and I always worked well together when it came to pop-sounding material because we'd grown up listening to a lot of the same pop songs in the fifties and sixties.

But we had to glue it together. The pieces we had were great
— the chorus riff, for instance — but it was like an incomplete
thought rather than a full-blown idea. When we worked on it, I
wrote the chorus melody for "Dance the Night Away." Now I'm
not good enough to come up with reams of sophisticated musical
ideas, but I had my moments as a writer. This was one of them.
And for the outro, I suggested Dave sing the same melody as the
chorus of Bruce Channel's "Hey Baby." I figured that line had
worked well for Tommy Johnston at the end of "Black Water,"
so why not go back to the well?

I did a lot of that kind of writing with my artists, because as
a producer, I felt my job was to contribute freely to the creative
process. One thing I wouldn't do when I did that was *ask* for
writing credit or publishing. I didn't take any credit despite contributing to "Dance the Night Away." The same thing followed
when it came to helping them nail down melodies for other songs
on their records, or when it came to working with Dave when he
didn't have any lyrics for a track and needed a spark to fire up his
creativity. There's an old music industry saying: "Change a word,
get a third." I never did that, much less anything more mercenary.
Hell, I knew of other producers who wouldn't even write anything on a record, and they'd want a cut of publishing from their
artists. I wanted no part of those kinds of arrangements.

In the end, it turned out to be a timeless track. Ed's harmonics
are beautiful. Dave's vocal is one of the best of his career. Mike
and Al delivered outstanding performances as well. The chorus is
infectious — I sang backgrounds with the guys — and you can't
help but be in a good mood when it's playing. I still hear that
thing in supermarkets; it's got this feel-good pop vibe to it.

On the last day of 1978, Kathi and I invited the Van Halen
guys over to our home in Pasadena for a family gathering on
New Year's Eve. Al, Ed, and Ed's girlfriend Kim did come by

and, to our surprise, they hung out with my family for a while rather than just stopping by for a few minutes and heading to another party.

After settling in, Ed laid eyes on my Ramirez acoustic. I'd bought it in Spain during my trip to Europe back in 1962. We sat on the couch in the living room and I watched him play these two-handed licks on it. I couldn't believe how powerful his playing sounded with no amplification.

It was as jaw-dropping as when I heard "Eruption" on the electric. What he played that night wasn't exactly "Spanish Fly," but he played all of these wonderful runs and chord patterns on acoustic that sounded like a complete left turn from what he'd done on "Eruption." So that's why we cut his acoustic solo, "Spanish Fly."

That night just reinforced my belief in Ed's musical brilliance. He played these unbelievable, innovative things on the Ramirez that we never put on the record. These were things I would have thought, before I met Ed, that a guitarist would not have been able to do on an acoustic.

Ed's a true musical genius. He could pick up any instrument and play it. Once he picked up a reed instrument in the studio — it might have been a bassoon or another double-reed instrument — and played it. I'm pretty certain this was the first time he'd ever tried to play one. To be sure, he didn't know everything about how it worked, but I thought, *Man, he's not even playing a stringed instrument, and he's making music and it sounds good.* Regardless of the instrument, he'd almost intuitively know what to do with it.

Van Halen II picked up where *Van Halen* left off. Their new album went platinum — one million copies sold — by May. "Dance the Night Away" hit the *Billboard* Top 20 in July, topping out at No. 15. Even into October, both of their albums were in the Top 100 in the *Billboard* Top LP & Tape chart. So they had a great 1979.

At the end of their 1979 tour, I saw their show in Phoenix. I'd catch them live whenever I could because I found that I'd pick up little ideas that could be used on their upcoming album. That night, I stood at the side of the stage and watched. In between songs, Dave launched into this rap about all the hot girls in the audience. He said something like, "You Arizona guys out there are some lucky fuckers! But hey, I get it! Everybody wants some, and I want some too! How about all of you?"

The crowd went *crazy*.

After the show I went backstage. I grabbed Dave and said, "Write that down in your notebook. That's a great idea for a song." That was the beginning of "Everybody Wants Some."

The development of that song is a good example of our working relationship. At the time, Ed had put together a little melodic chorded intro before the main riff of the song kicked into gear. I thought it was a good idea when we worked on it in the basement, but when we got into Sunset Sound in December 1979, I thought it was kind of lame. But it was all we had, so we went with it when we initially tracked it.

I don't remember what Dave's original ideas were for the song, but he and I didn't like them all that much. So when Dave asked, "Hey, Ted, got anything?" I reminded him of what I'd heard him say in Phoenix. His eyes lit up. He said, "Oh yeah!"

He flopped into a chair and started writing on a notepad. In less than ten minutes, while Donn was polishing the sound of Alex's tom-toms, he came up with a lyric pretty close to what ended up on the album. Now I wasn't surprised, because he has an uncanny ability to come up with words on the spot. He'd done nearly the same thing with "Jamie's Cryin'" back in 1977. His last-second writing bursts produced quality too, because what he came up with was both clever and unique. To top it all off, when he sang the words to me, he had the melody as well. When Dave was locked in like that, you couldn't ask for more as a producer.

The song had a steamy breakdown propelled by Alex's jungle drums, an atmosphere that Dave contributed to with his vocalizations. Hearing that gave me an idea that took me back to my childhood when I'd hang out at my grandfather's music store. I suggested we cop the drum intro of the Cadets' "Stranded in the Jungle." They were a fifties R&B group, and "Stranded" had been one of my favorite records when I was a kid. Alex's drumbeat worked wonderfully as an opening for the song, and so we scrapped Ed's chorded intro.

Even though Dave's first passes at his vocals were usually pretty rough, I always wanted Dave in the vocal booth when the other three guys were laying down tracks together; I firmly believed that Dave needed to sing with each and every take. He'd settle in after a while, and Donn and I would get some good performances from him on tape. At the end of the recording process, we'd comp his vocals from his multiple takes as needed or, if necessary, bring Dave back in the studio to repair any bum notes on his live takes.

This approach of having the vocalist always sing along while the instrumentalists recorded their basic tracks is not something that I always had my other acts do, but Ed, Al, and Mike *really* played off Roth as he did his thing. I'd watch him in the booth, listening to those guys as they recorded. It was like having the Big Bad Wolf cartoon character in full view of, and in the headphones of, the other three guys, and that was especially true for "Everybody Wants Some." It made the vibe great.

What we got on tape from Dave was always memorable. His ad-libs were hilarious. He interjected all of these X-rated asides during the song's breakdown. Donn and I sat in the control room and cracked up, listening to all of these lines that Dave put on tape. The three other guys were out in the studio having a blast too, while Dave's spouting all of this stuff. Dave's tongue-in-cheek approach to recording that song kept us all loose. Of course we had to edit out almost all of his lines, but you can still get a taste of them on the record. He was just a genius when it came to all of this stuff.

The *Women and Children First* sessions also presented my first opportunity to hear Ed play keyboards in the context of Van Halen. One day I came into Sunset 1 to record a song called "And the Cradle Will Rock . . ." Donn and Ed had set up a Wurlitzer electric piano through his Marshalls; Ed was pounding out the song's great riff, over and over. I was completely knocked out by how nasty it sounded. Hearing that for the first time was one of the highlights of my whole studio career — I loved it!

Dave then showed me what he'd come up with for lyrics. I was blown away by his idea. Another artist would have written some trite lyrics about looking for girls on a Friday night and the song would have been forgettable. Not Dave. He wrote something timeless and classic.

The song's message is heavy. It speaks a truth about the journey from childhood to adulthood that is pretty much universal. It didn't matter if you were fourteen when you heard the song or forty — you understood how rough teenage life can be when your parents are on your case and you feel misunderstood. The mass appeal of Dave's message is what made it an anthem.

The album's final track, "In a Simple Rhyme," is an overlooked classic. I love Ed's 12-string guitar work on it, and the bridge part — right before the solo — let the guys have their "Won't Get Fooled Again" by the Who moment on record.

But Ed's solo is the real showstopper. He's playing "outside" the chord changes. The chords are going by, just like that, and he's playing this insane free jazz. It's pretty genius stuff. A lesser player who was confronted with those chords would have stuck within their structure rather than taking such an adventurous approach.

When we were working on some of the acoustic songs for *Women and Children First*, I had an idea to add a mandolin to one of them. We were set up in Studio 1. Donn was behind the board and I was with him in the control room. Ed was sitting on a stool in the studio, playing some licks. We started rolling and, without warning, Ed yelled, "Fuck!" He stood up, screaming, "Ted! I hate this fucking thing!" He lifted the mandolin above his head and smashed it to bits. He tossed away the neck, bellowing, "Fuck you, Ted!" He stormed out, slamming the studio door behind him.

I was aghast. I racked my brain, thinking, *What could have happened to make him so angry?*

After an uncomfortable moment, I looked over at Donn. He was looking at me like he was at a loss to explain Ed's tantrum. A few seconds later, Ed came back into the studio, saying, "Hey, Ted, I'm just kidding." He and Donn burst into hysterics; they'd set the whole thing up. I shook my head at them, grinning,

Taking a break during Van Halen's *Women and Children First* sessions, January 18, 1980. BEN J. ADAMS/RHINO ENTERTAINMENT COMPANY, A WARNER MUSIC GROUP COMPANY.

because they'd fooled me completely. The three of us laughed even more after Donn rolled the tape back and played it. All of it was captured on Donn's recording; the wood smashing, Ed's cursing, and our laughter when Ed returned to the studio.

That incident is a good reminder to me about how special things were for the six of us. You had Donn, Ed, Al, Dave, Mike, and me all locked in on the exact same goal: to make great records, even under the pressure of deadlines and label expectations for one hit after another. Despite those external stressors, everybody was still having a hell of a good time.

In early 1980, Warner Bros. Records was negotiating with the Who to bring them into the fold. A few months earlier, Mo had invited me to dinner at his home when he hosted the Who's Roger Daltrey, and now to close the deal, Mo and I had scheduled a meeting with Pete Townshend in London. Mo liked to have me to meet with artists we were trying to sign because I could speak to the recording process in a way that he couldn't, since he didn't deal with the technical aspects of making records.

Because I had a couple of days when I didn't need to be in Los Angeles before going to Europe, I decided to fly to Paris on the Concorde before I went to the UK. After Mo and I met with Pete, I planned to fly back home to do some final vocal repairs and vocal overdubs on *Women and Children First*, which the label was expecting imminently.

I checked into Hôtel Plaza Athénée. It's this beautiful hotel situated right in the heart of the city. A day or so after I arrived, I was getting ready to head across the Channel when I got word that the meeting had been delayed for a week.

I called Mo and said, "What do you want me to do?"

"Just stay there. I'll call you when I want you to come over to London. It's going to be about a week."

In the meantime, though, I had to get the Van Halen record done.

So I called the guys and told them to come over so we could get into a studio and get to work.

The situation wasn't ideal, but we made the best of it. I recorded the Van Halen guys in a big Paris studio. The heat didn't work, so it was cold as a meat locker. Its layout was unwieldy too. The studio was one floor down from the small control room, so you couldn't see the musicians when you sat behind the board. I worked in those tight quarters with a French engineer and an interpreter.

At night, the five of us went to the discotheques. Paris's disco scene at the time was unbelievable. We hung out in all the biggest and hippest places, but unlike in the States, nobody knew who we were; nobody recognized the guys. Those nights were surreal and a ton of fun. We'd order champagne by the bottle; we were partying hard.

Whenever we decided to head to another place, we'd grab our bottles and head out the door. Walking through Paris did little to dampen our enthusiasm. I remember Mike and Al started banging on the hoods of the slow-moving cars at intersections. They scared the hell out of people. They were just clowning around, but at least one driver got so spooked that he jumped out of his car and ran off, leaving it idling in the street.

One other thing I remember from Paris was the guys talking excitedly about their trip over on the Concorde. At the time, the Concorde was the most technologically advanced and fastest passenger plane in the world. I'd flown on it many times, but that had been their first flight. Al and Dave had an idea — which we never followed through on, unfortunately. They wanted me to figure out a way that Donn and I could record the engines on the supersonic plane when the pilots engaged its reverse thrusters upon landing. When those things fired off, the noise was unbelievable. If we'd put that sound on record, it would have blown speakers.

In any event, we got the Paris overdubs completed. The guys went back to Los Angeles and I headed to London for the meeting. Pete Townshend talked about the Who's new material and played us some old *Tommy* outtakes. Mo made the deal.

Released in March, *Women and Children First* became Van Halen's third platinum album in a row, even though they didn't end up with a big hit single like they'd had with *Van Halen II*.

In the spring and summer of 1980, I produced what would be the final Doobie Brothers studio album of this first stage of their career, *One Step Closer*. I knew things were coming to an end for the band — in fact, they'd split within a couple of years. One major disappointment for Donn and me was that he had to pass on engineering the record. Heavy rains had caused mudslides in the Malibu area in early March, and his home was engulfed in mud. Understandably, he had to take time away from work to dig out and rebuild.

Even though I'd be without Donn, I had confidence going into the sessions, because I'd drawn up a good plan for the album. I traveled to the Doobies' rehearsal place for the pre-production meeting, ready to share my ideas. When we sat down, though, the guys blindsided me with their own plan. They told me that every member of the band, all seven guys, would sing lead on at least one track. In addition, they told me that every member of the band would write at least one song for the record. In effect, they were all caught up in an *esprit de corps* thing.

I said, "No, I can't agree to that plan. Mike, Pat, and Corny are going to sing the tracks. Nobody else. And I'll pick the songs, like I always do."

They got crazy mad. They insisted that all of them wanted every member of the band to contribute equally in songwriting and lead vocals.

I said no again.

The room exploded. They told me they were going to fire me. I said, "Go ahead!" They'd concocted an insane idea. You can't have an album with seven different lead vocalists. I said *sayonara* and walked out of the rehearsal facility.

After the meeting, Mike called up Lenny. He was apoplectic, saying that they had a brotherhood and that I was wrecking the camaraderie in the band. Lenny talked Mike off the ledge, and eventually all the other guys came to their senses too. They agreed to do it my way.

The major change I did undertake was phasing Corny in as a new element in the band's sound. He'd been my friend since we were little kids, and he was a supremely talented guy. I really wanted to give him a chance to enjoy some time in the spotlight. For example, on the title track, I had him sing co-lead vocals with Mike and I featured his saxophone playing too. Take a listen to that song; it's a good one. Keith, the country singer Carlene Carter, and John wrote it. Keith, Mike, and I sang backgrounds.

The album did well for them, going platinum in November 1980. To be sure, it wasn't the runaway success that *Minute by Minute* had been, but it did, in October, reach the *Billboard* Top 5 and generate a Top 5 *Billboard* single, "Real Love." As the final studio statement for that era of the Doobie Brothers, it was a nice way to bring their great run to a close.

These days, when I listen to Van Halen's fourth album, *Fair Warning*, I think about what was going on Ed's personal life as much as about the album we made together. When we started pre-production in November 1980, it was a time of unease in the band, because Ed and his girlfriend, the television actress Valerie Bertinelli, had gotten very serious. By this time Van Halen had built up a reputation as four whiskey-swigging bachelors who rejected any semblance of a domestic life. But Ed and Valerie loved each other; that was obvious. Would they take the plunge?

By December 1980, we'd started working on the album at Sunset. I was in the break room, grabbing a cup of coffee, when Ed walked in and sat down. He looked sad.

"What's wrong?"

"Al and Dave don't want me to get married."

His face was creased with pain.

I said, "Ed, that's terrible. How can they say that? It's *your* life. Tell them to fuck off."

He didn't answer.

"Ed, if you want to walk away from all of this, I will walk out with you. I don't give a fuck. Marrying the woman you love is more important than Van Halen. Fuck the band. I'll back you to the hilt." It was a very emotional moment for me, because I had such affection for him. I hated to see him suffer.

For the record, I got the impression that Dave's opposition to Ed marrying Valerie was way more intense than Alex's. Alex was probably just trying to encourage his younger brother to keep his wits about him and not do anything impulsive as he was falling in love with Valerie. Dave, I felt, had a more self-serving motivation. My read was that Dave didn't like all of the press attention that Ed (and Valerie) had garnered.

Ed, in effect, called Dave and Alex's bluff. Soon after, he and Valerie announced they'd set a wedding date: April 11, 1981.

I mention this situation around Ed's relationship with Valerie to underscore how much I cared about Ed as a person and wanted only the best for him. Until the waters between us got choppy when we were making *1984*, we always got along well. That's why I'm always taken aback when people claim that Ed tried to take control of the production on *Fair Warning*.

Part of that myth, I think, grew out of stories about Ed and Donn sneaking into the studio in the middle of the night to record solos without my knowledge or approval. That's all bullshit. If they were trying to be surreptitious, they did it in an odd way, since they used to tell me that they planned to work through the night. They told me because they knew I didn't have a problem with it.

We'd be wrapping up for the day at Sunset, and Ed might say to me, "Do you mind if we stay in the studio tonight and work on some stuff?" I'd say, "Fuck no. I'm leaving to go to dinner. I will be back tomorrow. Do whatever you want. I'll check in with you guys then." So there was never any covert shit.

Other times, Ed would call me at night and say, "Hey Ted, Donn and I are going to meet at the studio." I'd say fine. Ed and Donn loved the studio, so I didn't blink an eye when they wanted to log some extra hours inside Sunset. On those nights, they'd record some parts. I'd listen the next day. Some of it we'd keep and put on the album, some of it we discarded. He and Donn didn't sneak around.

For me, I'd do whatever it took to get a record right. The same thing went for mixes. If they didn't like the mix, I always offered to do it again. Every time I'd ask, the four guys would say, "No, it's okay." Really, at this point in time, the guys in Van Halen, Donn, and I all were on the same page.

The other thing is that back in those days, Donn and I were joined at the hip. I didn't care and was happy to have them work, because everything Donn and I did together turned out great.

I knew, too, that Ed might sometimes benefit from working without me, the producer, in the vicinity. This was a trick I'd learned from Lenny. If as a producer, you have an artist who is truly up there, truly gifted, you cut them some slack. So when Ed would say, "I'm going to do some stuff with Donn," I'd sense that he was feeling the pressure and needed some room to breathe.

I think people make a mistake when they assume ability goes hand in hand with confidence. There wasn't a better guitarist walking the Earth in 1981 than Ed Van Halen, but I could tell that he'd sometimes get nervous around me when we were working in the studio. When I was gone, he loosened up. My goal was to get great performances on tape and to oversee the making of an album that the band and the label would love, not to micromanage every second in the studio.

I'd announce to the guys that I was leaving Sunset and going to my office over at Burbank. And that's exactly what I'd do.

After a couple hours, I'd call Donn and say, "How's it going?"

"It's going good."

"Great."

I'd be making calls or taking meetings in my office for a few hours, knowing that Donn had it under complete control.

Of course, there were lots of engineers who could run a session without a producer standing next to them. But when it came to sparking and capturing the creativity of guitar players, Donn had a special gift. For years, long before Ed and Donn met, I'd watched Donn have intuitive connections with Lowell and Ronnie. Hell, when we worked on the Montrose records, I'd tell Donn to huddle up with Ronnie before we started the day's work. As a producer, when you're getting results thanks to a brilliant engineer and guitar player, you learn to stay out of their way.

Fair Warning ended up more moody and heavier than Van Halen's earlier albums. Even though once again they hadn't written a pop song like they'd done with "Dance the Night Away," songs like "Unchained" remind me of how prolific and special the songwriting partnership was between Dave and Ed. Ed came up with this incredible riff and then Dave paired it with these fantastic lyrics.

The thing is, there were lots of heavy metal bands that put monster riffs together with memorable lyrics. But none of them could match Van Halen's songcraft and humor. The breakdown of "Unchained" underscores what helped separate Van Halen from their competitors.

On the day we recorded the song, I had an important meeting I needed to go to after the session, so I was wearing a nice suit. We did some recording and then took a break. In the control room, Dave and I tossed ideas around for the post-solo break-down. During that conversation, Dave started busting my balls about how sharp I looked in my suit.

That's when I suggested to Dave that he sing the line about the suit. That comes from "Shoppin' for Clothes," the 1960 R&B single by the Coasters. I love the Coasters! Every single song of theirs is so lyrically visual, thanks to the songwriting team of Jerry Leiber and Mike Stoller. Their words for that tune are almost like the storyline for an animated cartoon. In fact, I think I played that very song for the brothers when they were at my house for New Year's Eve back in 1978.

Now when we cut the vocal for the breakdown, Dave blew his line. We had a back and forth through the talkback as we prepared to recut the part. Then one of the guys, maybe Alex or Dave, suggested that we add an exchange, one between Dave and me to the song. After we recorded it, we all busted out laughing when we heard the playback. Those tongue-in-cheek lyrics — coupled with that monolithic riff — makes "Unchained" the best example of what I mean when I say that Van Halen was a heavy metal band with a sense of humor.

Following along with what we'd done with "Cradle," we had another couple of keyboard songs on *Fair Warning*. Ed came up with this dirty-sounding riff on an Electro-Harmonix Mini-Synthesizer, which became the foundation for the album closers, "Sunday Afternoon in the Park" and "One Foot Out the Door."

Those songs were both experimental for Van Halen. It was Ed, searching for sounds. He has an uncanny ear and could visualize things he wanted to hear. Occasionally, when he was trying to push the envelope, I couldn't decode and translate what he was after. I don't think he ever knew how frustrated I felt when he would try to articulate a sound or feeling to me and I couldn't dial it up for him. I always wanted to make him happy.

Meanwhile, Dave was kind of spinning his wheels on the lyrics to "One Foot Out the Door," so I pitched an idea to him.

Back in 1977, Lenny and Russ Titelman were producing Gregg Allman. Lenny was so aggravated that Gregg could never arrive to a session on time. Lenny, sitting in the studio with Russ, would constantly call Gregg's place, trying to get him in the building. Cher, who was in a relationship with Gregg at the time, would answer the phone. She'd yell for Gregg. He'd pick up, and Lenny would say, "You're late, again. When are you going to get here?"

"Oh, in an hour or so," Gregg would drawl.

"You've *got* to get here before then," Lenny would insist.

"I've got one foot out the door, man." That was his way of saying he was on the way. He'd say that to Lenny a lot.

When Lenny and I talked, I'd ask him how things were going. He'd say to me, "Goddamn Gregg's always late. I call, and he tells me he's got one foot out the door."

So I'd said that phrase to the guys and asked, "How about this?" I thought it fit well with the way we worked in the studio, since we always seemed to be on a tight deadline.

Dave said, "Okay, I'll write around that idea."

A lot of things came together like that.

Shortly before *Fair Warning* came out, Valerie and Ed got married in Westwood. Val and Nicolette had become good friends, so Nicolette served as Valerie's maid of honor. Even that day, I remember there was static between Dave and Ed. Ed had asked him to be a groomsman. Dave refused. It was a power play by Dave, one that didn't leave Ed and Valerie feeling great. After the reception, there was a party with the Van Halen and Bertinelli families, and the cast of *One Day at a Time*, at the Beverly Hills Hotel. I don't think Dave attended.

The year ended on a rough note for me. In October, an interview I did with *BAM*, the San Francisco music weekly, came out. I was on the cover, which was emblazoned with a headline that called me a "superproducer."

The interview documented a wide-ranging conversation that covered my entire career. When Van Morrison came up, I said I liked him and that he's an unbelievable talent. But I also said, in jest, that I'd never work with him ever again, not even for three million dollars cash. I went on to joke about his penchant for firing his musicians, producers, and managers. Then I said something like "He even fired his wife and kids!"

At the time, this journalist and I were having lunch with drinks and we were in a festive mood, so my tongue got loose. When my comments were printed and I read them, I was horrified. I got even more upset after I was told that Van had read the interview. It pissed him off, and I don't blame him. I felt terrible then and still feel terrible now about what I said. I was joking — exaggerating for effect — but that's not an excuse. Van's a *really* good guy and we went through a lot together. I learned how to make records and the value of a first take when I produced him. He was the artist who gave me my first hit record as a producer. If he hadn't given me a chance, I'd not have met Bill Church and Ronnie Montrose, half the guys in Montrose. He was there when things got dicey when Kathi went into labor with my first-born child. Those were all important events in my life. So for me, those words are one of those things in life I most regret. He deserved better from me. I'm sorry, Van.

Chapter 12

JUMP

In late 1981, the Van Halen guys approached me with an unconventional idea for their next release. Rather than starting work on a new album, they told me they'd like to put out Roy Orbison's 1964 No. 1 smash "Oh, Pretty Woman" as a standalone single early in the coming year.

At the time, I had no idea that this song choice had been the outcome of an argument between Dave and Ed. Dave, from what I learned later, wanted to cut the 1964 Martha and the Vandellas hit "Dancing in the Street." Ed didn't like that idea. He thought Orbison's tune, with its prominent guitar riff, would be a better song for the band to cover. Ed won that debate.

The other important point here is that when they came to me, they'd already decided to film a video for the song. In some ways, it sounded to me like the video was the driving force behind their idea for a single. Obviously, promotion is critical, but in my view, it wasn't more important than the music itself. To think otherwise is to put the cart in front of the horse.

When we talked, it became clear that Dave and Al were the guys in the band who most wanted to make that video. They were storyboarding it, working on the wardrobes, and doing all of this production stuff. They were consumed with it. To me, putting so much energy into a video when we could be working on the music seemed like one big waste of time, but that's what the band wanted.

Because they'd committed themselves to doing the video, we didn't discuss their song choice much at all. I never wanted them to do that song. I didn't like it, even when Roy Orbison did it. If they wanted to redo an oldie, I could've thought of ten better song ideas. So at the time I thought it was totally wrong for Dave as a vocalist and Van Halen as a band. It still sounds wrong for them to me, but they'd settled on it.

So Donn, the guys, and I went into Sunset. We tracked three pieces of music: the Orbison tune, the Roy Rogers and Dale Evans cowboy ditty "Happy Trails," which would serve as the B-side of the single, and an instrumental, "Intruder." The band needed "Intruder" for their video soundtrack, which, as storyboarded, required more than the three minutes that the Orbison tune encompassed.

The sessions went well enough, but the fact that the band members prioritized the video over the songs gave me fits. Al and Dave were *obsessed* with the video being right. They wanted "Intruder" so the video would work, so we were doing all this crazy stuff for that instrumental in the studio. I just wanted to work on the song side of things, you know? All of this meant that the whole "Pretty Woman" video project was a big nightmare for me.

In early February, Van Halen released the video and single. I remember the band got a lot of free publicity after the video was banned by MTV and by broadcast outlets in Japan and Australia, because it starred a cross-dressing guy. The bigger news from my perspective was that "Pretty Woman" took off on radio. It began

Alex and Dave working on the set of Van Halen's "Pretty Woman" video, January 1982. DONN LANDEE.

An outdoor shot from the set of Van Halen's "Pretty Woman" video, January 1982. DONN LANDEE.

to chart in February, eventually peaking in April at No. 12 on the *Billboard* Hot 100.

The band probably didn't think that "Pretty Woman" would be a big hit, but it was. When you put out a hit single, you better have an album to go behind it, because nobody — the company, the act — makes any real money on a single. The only reason to sell a single was to sell an album, and then a tour. That's how rock bands made their money, not by cutting stand-alone 45s. Incidentally, it's not dissimilar to the situation I'd been through with Harpers Bizarre when "Feelin' Groovy" charted in early 1967. Lenny, in response, got us into the studio so we could make an album to capitalize on our hit single.

I'm sure those guys thought that by releasing a single and video, they could temporarily pause the annual album/tour cycle that they'd been on since 1977. But instead, the word came down to me from Mo and Lenny that Warner Bros. wanted a new Van Halen album within *weeks*. Van Halen's management agreed. So the message to the band and me was "Okay guys, you've got a hit. Let's get moving. Go into the studio." So I got called in to gather up the troops and expedite things. *Diver Down* was rush recorded in March in order to chase their single, meaning we had to get the album into stores as soon as possible so we could take advantage of the hit we had out there.

This wasn't ideal. The processes I'd put into place when we'd made the other albums now had to be tossed aside to get this thing done. In the past, I'd spend hours watching rehearsals in Roth's basement in order to pick songs (I'd categorize the songs: *Yes, No, Maybe*) and work on arrangements prior to entering the studio. Of course, I would have wanted to do our usual thing for *Diver Down*: rehearsals, prep, demos, and *then* go in and lay the album down. But now that was impossible. I wasn't ready to go into the studio with them. As a result, a lot of stuff on *Diver Down* we just threw together. It's no surprise that we ended up doing five covers on it. As their producer, that frustrated me, because Dave and Ed were a great songwriting team. They could write everything from pop tunes like "Jamie's Cryin'" and "Dance the Night Away" to rock anthems like "Ain't Talkin' 'Bout Love" and "Cradle." We just didn't have enough time to work on the record.

Still, I think the album has some standout moments. Ed had a bunch of really beautiful guitar stuff like "Cathedral." And God, he played just like Segovia on the introduction to "Little Guitars."

I have fond memories of cutting the jazz oldie "Big Bad Bill (Is Sweet William Now)" too. It was Dave's idea. I had never even heard the song before and I have a very broad knowledge of songs. It's a perfect tune for him, and he sang *great* on it. Ed's damn great too; he played chords just like he was a guitarist in Benny Goodman's orchestra, or like Tommy Tedesco, the first-call session cat. Al played brushes! And the guys suggested that Al and Ed's father, Jan Van Halen, play clarinet on it, so we had three Van Halens on the song. I really liked the outcome, and thought it added another dimension to the band.

Despite the rushed pace, the sessions went smoothly and everyone seemed happy with what we'd laid down. When we got stuck on something we probably would have worked out in Dave's basement on prior albums, Ed would say, "How about this?" He'd play something for us to fill in what we needed to patch over, and we'd lay it down.

The general good feeling about the album remained unchanged, as far as I know, for the first few years the record was out. But around 1985, Ed began to complain about the cover tunes on *Diver Down*, especially the one he'd rejected before we even started working on the LP: "Dancing in the Street." Ed seemed irked that we'd used a Minimoog synthesizer riff that he'd written for "Dancing" rather than letting him hold onto it for a future Van Halen original.

I love Ed, but his complaints about the song are hard to stomach, especially considering how things actually went down.

During the sessions, Ed played me the synth part that became part of "Dancing in the Street." So we recorded it. Understand, this was a riff only — there were no chords, no lyric, and no melody — so it wasn't a song.

So I asked Dave, "Do you have a melody?"

"No."

Dave worked with what Ed had recorded, but he couldn't come up with anything.

Dave and I always bounced ideas off each other, so I tried to find a starting point, but I was stumped too.

I'm thinking, *What are we going to do with this thing?* Because if we can't get a handle on it, it's going to go in the can, meaning it won't appear on *Diver Down* and may, in fact, never end up on a Van Halen album.

Because Ed's riff was in a minor key, something finally clicked. I loved "Heat Wave" and all the other things Martha and the Vandellas had done. So I said, "We can make Ed's riff work for 'Dancing' if we change the chords on the original version just a bit." We tried it, and it worked. So in the end, we recorded the song that Dave had wanted to put out as a single rather than "Pretty Woman."

It was, for the record, the first and only cover tune that Van Halen recorded on my watch that was *my* idea. They brought "You Really Got Me" and "Ice Cream Man" to me back in 1977. "You're No Good" was Dave's idea. The other copy tunes on *Diver Down* came from the band, not from me. But I still stand by what I said when we were making *Van Halen II*: if you redo a hit, you're halfway there.

So, yes, when I pushed for "Dancing," I did have airplay on my mind. "Pretty Woman," which we'd include on *Diver Down*, had already charted, so it was critical to have another potential single to pull from the album. I didn't hear another hit when I listened to the songs we'd cut, so I thought doing a proven tune was the right move. It's also important to remember that *Fair*

Warning had sold more slowly than any of their prior albums, so it was critical, as their producer and as a Warner Bros. executive, that I did everything I could to make this album bend their sales curve upwards.

At the time, no one in the band complained. Ed never said, "Hey, wait a minute. I don't want to do what you guys want to do here. Let's hold on to this riff." If you're not happy with something, why not say so at the time?

As a producer, you've sometimes got to make decisions that may rub an artist the wrong way. That happens as part of the creative process: the producer has to have the final word, otherwise the recording process becomes chaotic. But that doesn't mean that I believed in saying to my artists, "Hey, fuck you guys. *I'm the producer.* You've got to live with it. It's my way or no way at all." I always wanted to keep lines of communication open, so there could be understanding, if not consensus, when difficult moments emerged in the studio.

But the thing is, Ed was really pleased with the song at the time. I'd remember it if there was a disagreement. In fact, if I had an unhappy artist, I've never forgotten it. If Lowell George or Mike McDonald, for example, didn't like something, I'd be unhappy too. Like Ed, they were my friends, and so I'd work to find a compromise. I never had a bad time making the first five Van Halen albums with them.

At the time, I remember thinking that if we had more time, the song would have been better. I wasn't completely happy with it, especially with when they went into the b-section — it never sounded right to me. But we were all just trying to make a deadline. It was do or die, and we needed the track for the album.

But when I listen now, I've come to love it. Al played so great on it. He just *nailed it down.* Listen to it — now that's a groove. The solo on "Dancing" is fantastic too — those are very hard chord changes to play over. Ed was initially kind of puzzled, but he did it great. I think the track stands up well after all these years.

Reading Ed's after-the-fact comments, my take now is that Ed came to feel that Dave and I had overstepped our bounds. Dave and I had both pushed for "Dancing" and had liked the idea of using Ed's keyboard riff on the song. Ed, at the time, never told me he wasn't happy with what we'd done with the song. But mulling it over four decades later, I think it's clear that this incident was a big reason why he'd seek more creative control going forward.

We wrapped recording in March. When Donn and I sat down to mix, the two of us were under tremendous pressure since time was so short. Donn bore the brunt of this burden. We'd be rushing to finish a song and he'd get frustrated, telling me, "I gotta take a walk." I'd sit in the control room and wait for him to return. I don't know exactly what he was thinking, but looking back, my gut tells me that he felt anxious because I wasn't doing enough to let him know what I was after with the mixes, and because we didn't have enough time to mix things as well as we would've liked. He was a perfectionist, and that's a big reason why he is an extraordinary engineer. But we didn't have the time to make the mix perfect.

Despite all of our challenges, *Diver Down* was a hit; importantly, it sold more copies and did better on the charts than its predecessor, *Fair Warning*. *Diver Down* entered the *Billboard* Top 200 on May 8, topping out at No. 3, and would remain on it well into 1983. "Dancing in the Street" would run up the *Billboard* Hot 100, topping out at No. 38. As always, the guys hit the road in the summer to support their album, with plans to tour North and South America through early 1983.

In the interim, Ed had befriended the English fusion guitarist Allan Holdsworth. Ed had been a big fan of his since the late seventies, so much so that Holdsworth had significantly influenced his playing style. Holdsworth had moved with his band to Los Angeles in 1982, and Ed started hanging out with him. They jammed a couple of times, once at the Roxy. Ed was in awe of him. In fact, Ed was so turned on by Allan's playing, and so appalled that a guy as talented as Allan didn't have a major label deal, that he asked me to consider signing him.

In May, I went to Reseda and saw Holdsworth and his band at a nightclub called the Country Club. He was amazing — a rare talent with a unique voice on the instrument. He was one of the very best guitarists I've ever seen in my life. He didn't have the musicality — the ability to write anything from pop to hard rock — that Ed and Clapton had. But as a soloist? He was untouchable. I didn't love everything about his band, but as far as I was concerned, I was there to scout Allan. I talked to him after the show and said I'd like to get him on Warner Bros. and produce him. He was enthusiastic. Soon after, I signed him to a multi-album deal. Ed was ecstatic, maybe even happier than Allan.

I don't know what, if anything, Ed and Allan had discussed about working together in the future before I got involved. But I do know that by the time we did the deal, Ed expected to be deeply involved and work alongside me on Holdsworth's record. He wanted to co-produce and play on it. Because Ed was so jazzed about Allan's talents, and because I thought it would give a chance for Ed to work on the other side of the glass, I was happy to co-produce with Ed, even though I typically didn't like those kinds of production arrangements. But as far as I was concerned that was the plan, and I know Allan and I specifically discussed Ed's involvement before the deal was hammered out.

So the three of us, soon after, came together for our first production meeting. We met at Ed's house. So we all sat down, and Ed spoke about playing on the record and his ideas for songs. I offered up my take too.

Allan said, "Well, okay, first off though, I have a request."

Ed and I both nodded and said okay, sure.

I'm thinking he'll want to record in a certain studio, or that he wanted to suggest dates for our work to begin.

Nope.

"I don't want you guys in the studio with me."

"What?"

He said, "Well, I want you guys to produce me but not be in the studio while I'm recording."

Mouth agape, Ed looked panicked.

Ed had talked this guy up to no end, and now he has made a totally insane request.

So I told Allan, in my most diplomatic tone, that I wasn't sure that was going to work for us.

Ed then asked how Allan expected him to play on the record — and solo alongside Allan — if he wasn't going to be in the studio while Allan recorded?

Allan then said, though he'd apparently been open to the idea initially, that he didn't want Ed to play on the record.

After Allan left, Ed and I were both out of sorts.

"Ted, what the fuck are we going to do?"

I told Ed I'd try to talk some sense into him.

Ed said, "Can you believe this guy? He's nuts!"

All we could do was shake our heads and laugh, because, honestly, it was so off the wall all you could do was laugh.

After that, things got worse. As I'd do on any project, I started making suggestions and putting a plan in place for the record. He fought me every step of the way. We clashed on everything from his band lineup to his musical direction. He didn't get it. My job as a producer was to expose his abilities to a wider audience and to sell albums for Warner Bros. He seemed to have no interest in doing any of the things that I thought might get us closer to that goal.

Before long, Ed bowed out, which I would have done as well — if I hadn't signed him on Ed's recommendation!

One big area of disagreement between Allan and me involved vocals for this album. I had intended to make an all-instrumental record with him, but Allan wanted lead vocals on few songs. We fought about it, but he just wouldn't budge. After a while I gave in and let him have his way.

The whole thing turned out to be one giant headache. I left Holdsworth to his own devices in the studio much of the time, because working with him was so difficult. Rather than doing an album, Warner Bros. released the project as an EP called *Road Games*. It sank without a trace upon release.

Around the same time Ed was heading out on the road on the *Diver Down* tour, he called me with some surprising news. He told me he'd started construction on a small studio in the backyard of his Coldwater Canyon home and hoped it would be complete within a year. Donn, working along with a well-respected studio designer named Howard Weiss, was going to pick out the gear and wire it up for him.

When we talked, Ed described it to me as a facility where he could work up his song ideas at home in a more elaborate way than he could when he used his four-track Tascam recorder. I could tell he was jazzed about the project. I was happy for him.

When he came home on tour breaks, Ed would come down to my condo in Century City and pick me up so I could see 5150 while it was under construction.

Driving with Ed was always an adventure. He'd pick me up in the middle of the night in his brand-new Porsche Turbo. He'd then take the long way home to show off what his car could do. He used to fly through North Hollywood or Century City with me in the passenger seat, scared to death. He'd hit 80-plus mph on local streets.

These rides turned my knuckles white, every time, but to some extent I enjoyed them because Ed was an excellent driver. In fact, he could've been a professional racing driver. I say that as a racing fan who grew up watching the Pebble Beach Road Races. In later years, I'd also taken laps in a Scarab racing car, as it was put through its paces at the Laguna Seca course. Ed was as talented as, if not more talented than, the driver who'd pinned me to my seat in the Scarab.

After he got my heart rate up, we'd get to his place and walk around inside the studio. As you'd expect, it was a mess inside, like any construction project would be in its early stages.

Ed walked to where the control room was going to be and talked about what he and Donn had planned for equipping it. If Donn was there, he'd give me the technical lowdown on the gear he'd ordered.

Donn's abilities here didn't surprise me in the least. Not only was he a genius with sounds, but he also had a remarkable technical facility. The best way I can explain it is that he was like an expert pilot who knew how to build a plane from the wheels up.

I'd look around. Ed would ask, "Ted, what do you think?" He wanted me involved in the process.

I'd say, "It's going to be a great studio."

Years later, I read interviews suggesting that I wasn't enthusiastic about Ed building 5150. Nothing could be further from the truth. I was *never* against him building it. Still, I saw it as Ed's *home* studio, because when it was first being built, we never talked about recording the next Van Halen album at 5150.

In late summer 1982, I was unwinding in my condo. I rarely smoked weed, but I did smoke a couple joints for whatever reason on this one night. I was stoned out of my mind, well after midnight, and I collapsed on the couch. I was clicking the remote and came across this crazy cartoon movie called *Fritz the Cat*. I was all alone and laughing.

In the middle of it, my phone rang. Even in my condition, I knew that if someone had this number and was calling this late it was likely an important call. I muted the TV and picked it up.

"Hello."

"Teddy?"

"Yeah?"

"Hey man, how ya doin'? It's Q."

It took a couple seconds for me to process. It was Quincy Jones.

I stifled a laugh, took a deep breath, and tried to gather myself.

"Oh, hey, Quincy."

I burst into hysterics.

"Teddy, you okay?"

I couldn't stop laughing.

"Yeah, I'm just watching a funny movie."

He was asking me how I'd been, trying to have a normal conversation. I'm doing my best not to laugh, covering the receiver.

Quincy, by this point, had probably figured out that I was in an altered state of mind.

"So, hey, man, I want to get Eddie Van Halen on this Michael Jackson record I'm doing. Can you give me his number?"

"Ah. Ummm. Yeah, okay."

I laughed again. There I was, stoned, and I couldn't focus since I didn't usually smoke. But I came up with Ed's number, somehow.

Soon after, Quincy called Ed and invited him to record a guitar solo on "Beat It." He and Donn did the session at Westlake Audio in Los Angeles. Several months later, Ed's solo was all over the radio and MTV after the song topped the *Billboard* charts.

Quincy's work with Michael Jackson inspired another memorable incident in my career. During the early eighties, Prince was one of the label's rising stars. I struck up a conversation with him one day at the Burbank offices, and he asked if he could use the stereo system in my office to listen to some rough mixes. I said sure.

Since I was at the studio so often, I gave him free rein to come in and use my office. I told him about the back way into my office, so he could come and go discreetly. He'd enter the building through the rear loading dock. He'd walk through the mailroom and right into my office, which was located in an out-of-the-way spot on the lower level of the building. He'd hunker down in there when he had to spend a day at our headquarters.

One day in early 1983, he showed up and I happened to be there. He told me he wanted to talk about something. I said sure, and shut the door.

He sat down, looking really out of sorts. When I asked what was wrong, he said, "I *have* to find a way to knock Michael out of the No. 1 spot." At the time, his album *1999* was selling very well for us and he was a big star, but as he explained, it was driving him crazy that *Thriller* was breaking all sorts of sales records. I knew that his goal was to surpass Michael's success, because he'd told the executive team that very thing in a number of meetings I attended.

I listened until he ran out of steam. "So you really want to top Michael, right?"

He nodded. "Yes."

"Well why don't you get Quincy Jones to produce your next album?"

His eyes got wide, his face turned red. He sprang out of his seat and, for a second, I thought he might hit me. I wasn't much worried about that, though, because Prince was about as slightly built as any guy I'd ever met, but still, he'd become unglued.

He screamed, "I produce my own records!"

I tried to calm him down, telling him that Quincy had his finger on the pulse of the R&B and pop marketplace, and so he was the exact right guy to produce his next record. I couldn't believe this idea had set him off, because I honestly thought Quincy and Prince would've made a dream team.

He stormed out, still yelling. About a year later, his next album, *Purple Rain*, became a runaway success. He had in fact produced it himself.

Around February 1983, Van Halen came off the road. It was time to start getting ready to work on a new album; we all agreed to start cutting tracks around late April.

At that time, construction on 5150 was still ongoing. Donn had rewired the board they'd purchased and gotten the studio up and running, though, so Ed could use it for demoing tunes.

In March, however, Van Halen accepted an offer to headline the massive US Festival's Heavy Metal Day, which would take place in San Bernardino, California, on May 29. The payday here would be huge for them, so it made sense to take the gig, but the timing meant that our studio work would be disrupted and delayed.

I don't recall exactly when this conversation happened, but sometime before April, Donn and Ed told me that they'd like to track the new record at 5150. Donn was confident that, even though it was tiny when compared to a place like Amigo, and its interior was still unfinished, he could get everything on tape and sounding good. Ed saw it as a win-win. He could work in his own backyard without the band having to spend $200 per hour hiring out Sunset, and our recording schedule could be flexible. The thing Ed didn't say, but surely factored in as well, was that we'd be working on his turf, where he'd have more control over the process.

This idea took me aback. I didn't think 5150 was going to be where we'd make an album. Ed wasn't thinking that either, best I could tell, when construction started. I just thought it was going to be a place where Ed could work up tunes.

I wasn't sold on the idea. 5150 was still in a state of semi-completion. It was jerry-rigged. Donn had it running, but it looked like a half-finished construction project on the inside. There were exposed two-by-fours and wires running everywhere. The patch bays weren't color-coded yet, so only Donn could decipher the inputs and outputs; he had them memorized. On its face, this made 5150 seem like an inhospitable place for me to produce a record.

The control room, likewise, wasn't right for me. It was so cramped that you could barely get up and stand behind the board while someone else was sitting at it. I liked to stand up in the back of a control room and listen to playbacks through the monitors. That wasn't really feasible at 5150. Whenever I was in there, it felt like I was working in a bathtub — everything was so confined. The other thing was that when Donn and I sat at the boards in Amigo and Sunset, he was always on my left. At 5150 he'd sit on my right. That really felt off to me.

Nevertheless, the control room had one memorable feature that perfectly captured Ed's warped sense of humor. In between two pieces of glass they'd used for the control room window, Ed had entombed a piranha with a cigarette jutting from its toothy mouth.

The tracking room itself, I thought, was too small as well to make a Van Halen album there. The recording area at 5150 was 17 feet by 23 feet. By comparison, Sunset 2 was 34 feet by 40 feet. So while there was space for a full drum kit at Ed's place, you couldn't properly isolate the drums from other instruments when Ed, Al, and Mike tracked live. In a bigger room, like Sunset 2, we'd put the drums in a corner, mic them, and put gobos — portable acoustic barriers — around Al's kit so there wouldn't be much leakage when Mike, Al, and Ed played together. Donn and I had done that same thing with Little Feat.

Alex, to his credit, found himself a workaround. He decided to record with a Simmons electronic kit rather than traditional acoustic drums, as he'd done on the prior records. This rendered any leakage concerns moot, since there was no need to get an ambient drum sound on tape when using Simmons pads.

Neither Donn nor I was thrilled about Alex's infatuation with Simmons drums. But his choice did make sense to me, because their disembodied sound fit with a new Van Halen sonic identity that Ed and Donn were chasing. I'd listen to things they'd recorded, and they'd talk about this whole "Brown Sound" thing, which they were getting on tape at 5150. Donn and Ed were really onto something cool and unique. But it was not the kind of thing that was pleasing to my ears. It didn't sound live enough, like it did when the guys played together at Sunset. Now Ed did have an EMT plate reverb in 5150, which did generate some warmth, but you couldn't manufacture a traditional "live" sound in that room. It was deader than a doornail in there. There was no ambiance, no big room sound. As a result, everything started to sound the same; you couldn't use the room to color the sound you'd get on tape. It just became too processed-sounding. But that was a matter of taste, because Donn, Ed, and Al loved what they heard on tape when they recorded at 5150.

Everything else aside, the sticking point for me was that we had access to world-class studios like Amigo and Sunset Sound. So why would we record at an unfinished backyard studio? Think about it. The Rolling Stones could have built the best private studio in the world, right in Mick's backyard, but instead they still came to LA to work at Sunset. Zeppelin, Elton John, the Beach Boys — they all recorded at Sunset.

The other key point, which had me worried, is that during my career I'd visited a number of home studios owned by big artists. They always had a clubhouse feel to them. There was no need to keep a sense of decorum and focus when working in them, as was necessary during sessions held at leading professional studios like Amigo or Sunset. It's almost as if the "home" aspect of a home studio, regardless of how sophisticated and great sounding the studio was, made it difficult to be productive. So that weighed on me after Donn, Ed, and Al suggested we record at 5150.

Eventually, though, I said yes because Donn and Ed were so excited about the new facility. Ed always wanted me to be happy with it and Donn wanted it to work for all of us too. Donn was just as enthusiastic as Ed. So I was willing to give it a try, even though I had reservations.

Despite my unsettled feelings about using 5150, I felt like Ed and I were in a good place when we started work in April. One particular incident illustrates this well, I think. Before we even started recording, we met at 5150 for a pre-production session. This was the first time the five of us were going to have a meeting at Ed's studio.

So we were standing outside of 5150. Suddenly, Dave said, "Ted, could you excuse us a minute?" They all went into the studio without me and shut the door.

I didn't think anything of it at that moment.

A few minutes later, the door swung open, and out came Ed.

His brow was furrowed and he looked miffed.

He walked a few steps away from the door. I followed. Now facing me, he leaned in close.

"I can't fucking believe what Dave said to you about staying outside! I'm sorry, man."

Ed was mortified, but what Dave did hadn't bothered me. I thought they just wanted to have a private conversation, but Ed was all rattled by it. He was mad at Dave.

Thinking back, I'm sure Ed wanted to make sure that I felt, as always, like I'd be involved in every aspect of making this Van Halen album, even though we were working in his backyard. Our earlier conversations had made him aware that I had misgivings about 5150, so I think when Dave told me to wait outside, Ed was worried that I'd think that he planned to keep me at arm's length now that we were working at his private studio.

But honestly, that whole exchange was an outlier when we started the record. Nothing was tense or weird. Everything was fine.

In the days that followed, Ed played his song ideas for Mike, Al, and Dave and me. These included a number of synthesizer pieces, including the demo for what would become "Jump." Ed had played this same demo for everyone a year or two prior.

I know Ed has said in a retrospective interview that I immediately loved "Jump" and didn't have much interest in the other songs that ended up on *1984*. He's mistaken.

Dave and I, at least, hadn't liked it much the first time we heard it, and I still wasn't sold on it. I liked his other synthbased riffs and ideas even less. Donn and Ed must have played us thirteen other keyboard riffs after "Jump." One of those, incidentally, was the genesis of "I'll Wait." I remember Dave and me looking at each other and just cringing at most of these pieces as we thought about them in the context of Van Halen.

When we were done listening, Ed advocated for "Jump." I was honest. I said, "Wait a minute. I signed a heavy metal band. When Van Halen uses keyboards they should sound nasty, like they do on 'And the Cradle Will Rock . . .' or 'Sunday Afternoon in the Park.' They should shatter your senses and make your ears bleed. This riff sounds like keyboard playing you'd hear between innings at a baseball stadium. So I'm not crazy about it."

What gave me pause about "Jump" was my instinctive sense of what defined the Van Halen *sound*. When I produce an artist, I get a feel for what will likely work — and not work — on an album, especially when I've done five with them.

To me, Van Halen wasn't a pop group. Yes, they'd done "Dance the Night Away" and "Pretty Woman," but that was as far afield from their raucous, primitive nature as I wanted them to go. "Jump" was *way* too pop to my ears. I wanted them to stay edgy and raw.

As I tried to explain to Ed and the guys, it wasn't that I was "anti-keyboards." Remember, I was completely knocked out when Ed played me the piano riff for "Cradle" at Sunset Sound. Ed had played keyboards on "Dancing in the Street." I know it sounds like an odd comparison, but the "Jump" riff didn't sound like Ed's "Ain't Talkin' 'Bout Love" riff. That's the stomping, powerful sound that I thought they should keep pursuing. Even though *Diver Down* served its purposes, it was too pop for me.

I liked the *Fair Warning* stuff better. I thought these guys should stay right in that pocket, and not go pop.

The other point I tried to get across that day was about Ed's guitar playing. I think Ed recalls this debate as Dave and I wanting to keep him locked into "guitar hero" mode for the sake of his image. I can't speak for Dave, but that wasn't where I was coming from. His image had nothing to do with my view. Here's the thing. Ed's a guitar genius. No one has ever played or ever will play the way that he did on electric guitar. You immediately knew it was him playing something, and he had profound things to say on the instrument. Guys tried to copy him, and none of them came close. He was like Parker and Tatum. Ed's right in there with jazz guys like that; they are generational talents. But, to me, any competent keyboardist could have *played* that keyboard riff. You can't say the same about anything he *plays* on guitar.

But Ed, to his credit, told me I was wrong about "Jump" not working for Van Halen. He said, "Ted, I've been listening to a lot of classical music and playing keyboards and this is what I came up with. I really like it." He didn't say it, but I also knew that Donn had been encouraging him to stretch out musically, to follow his muse and write on keyboards.

I could see Ed had a big personal investment in the song, and had worked hard on it. So I said, "Okay, fine. It's a start. It doesn't really float my boat, but let's see where we can go with it." Again, this was Ed's taste versus mine. He wanted to work on it, so I was game. What I didn't say was: *Let's not do the song.*

I left, went home, and went to bed. Then around three in the morning, the phone rang. I let it go to the answering machine, but the volume on it was up, so I could hear the message after the beep.

"Hey, Ted!"

Ed and Al.

"Wake up! We're still here. We've got something great for you to hear."

They held the phone up. I could hear "Jump" playing.

They sounded jazzed, so I called right back. Ed said he'd come and get me at my place in Century City.

If I'm not mistaken, Ed did in fact pick me up and take me up there to hear it.

It turned out that Dave and Mike had gone home too, but Ed, Alex, and Donn had stayed up all night. They'd recorded basic tracks for three songs from *1984*: "I'll Wait," "Drop Dead Legs," and "Jump." The first two were unfinished ideas, rough sketches that would need to be much more fully fleshed out if they were going to end up on the record.

But in the case of what became "Jump," Ed and Al had really improved it from the demo. Donn played it a few times. As I listened, it really put the hooks into me. The brothers had the riff and the rhythm nailed down tight. And the verse keyboard parts that Ed had recorded — even if what I heard that night wasn't a completed composition — were very close to what ended up on *1984*. Donn, working with Ed and Al, had gotten greatness down on tape.

So here we were, again, in a similar place to where we'd been on the prior record with Ed's keyboard part that became "Dancing in the Street." We had a seed of something with tremendous potential, but chords and a riff aren't a *song*. Without lyrics and a melody, you don't have a song. As much as Ed says, "I wrote it," the "Jump" track at that moment in time was just a well-developed *idea* with great promise.

When I next saw Dave up there, maybe later that same day, I pulled him aside and said, "There's something here. Let's do something with it. Listen to it and go write some lyrics."

For whatever reason, Dave had good luck with lyrics when he wrote in his cherry-red 1951 Mercury convertible. So soon after we had both heard the new version, we climbed into the backseat of his car, which he'd parked outside of Ed's studio. We listened to the "Jump" instrumental on the tape deck. Dave put his feet up on the front seat, with a clipboard across his legs. He'd scrawl down ideas, rewinding and replaying the tape from time to time.

Then he'd show me what he'd written. I'd give him my feedback. Then he'd write some more and show me. This went on and on.

It wasn't as though inspiration struck like a bolt out of the blue. Dave came up with some stuff that didn't work, but within an hour, he came up with the "Jump" lyric.

I wasn't crazy about what he'd written. It gave me pause, because I thought "Jump" was about suicide. Honestly, I thought it was too rough, too heartless. I interpreted the message as, "Yeah, go ahead, loser, jump. Kill yourself!" I kept thinking about this old Dudley Moore and Peter Cook "Derek and Clive" black comedy song about a guy screaming for help from an upper-storey window of a burning house. They sang it with a line that called on the guy to leap to his death. It had that vibe, and I couldn't get that out of my head.

So I said, "I don't know. I don't like the idea of you singing about encouraging someone to jump out of a window."

"No, no, no! That's not what I mean, Teddy. I mean you've gotta find your nerve. Take a chance! Ask that fine girl across the room to dance, even though she might say no. You're worried, 'cause she might turn you down, but life is all about rolling the dice and going for it — take a leap of faith and jump! Get it?"

Dave also pointed out that his line about a jukebox would make it clear to everyone that the song had nothing to do with suicide.

Explained that way, it all made perfect sense. "Jump" was about taking bold action in the face of humiliating failure. Dave knew that even when you're a wildly successful person who appears super-confident, self-doubt always looms. Basically, he said that it all came down to the fact that *everyone* shares the feeling of insecurity.

When he told me that, I said, "Wow, that's great!" Those lyrics were all Dave, just writing those things down. If Dave hadn't come up with those words, "Jump" never would have had the same impact.

This whole sequence was a perfect example of what made Van Halen special. Ed had written this out-of-left-field piece and Dave had, basically in one sitting, come up with lyrics that you could sing along to in an arena, but with a message that expressed a deep and profound truth. I'll say it to anyone who will listen: Dave was a genius when it came to writing rock lyrics.

Dave did a couple more minor rewrites, but even without them, his lyric was fantastic.

Soon after, he recorded vocals.

By May, preparations for the US Festival began to intrude on our work, but we all busted our asses to get "Jump" perfect before those guys had to go into live performance mode. I worked on it really hard. We recorded overdubs; Ed cut solos. Donn did rough mixes, and I'd listen, over and over. I'd suggest edits, parts, and guitar lines, but really, we were just trying to improve something that was already very good. Ed had its essence together after that night he picked me up to hear it.

We'd mix it a million different ways. Ed would mix it. Donn and I would mix it. The three of us would mix it. And then we spliced stuff together. That guitar solo is so amazing, because God, those chord changes in the second half of the solo section that he played over are so weird.

Ed and Donn experimented quite a bit as well. Donn miked up Ed's Lamborghini a couple of different ways, capturing the lope of the idling engine and the roar of the exhaust as Ed stepped on the gas pedal. They toyed with the idea of putting the engine sound on "Jump" as I remember.

As it came together, one thing was clear to me: it was catchy as hell. That actually made me uneasy, strange as that seems. I was afraid this was going to be the end of Van Halen, because when I heard "Jump," I imagined it on the radio. I'd always loved what Van Halen *represented*, and here was this weird-sounding thing, a departure from what had made them great. Now I *knew* (well, I thought I knew) it was a hit, but I thought, *Oh my God, Van Halen is over, sonically at least,* because the abandon of Van Halen had just disappeared into pop city for me. As their producer and a fan, I wanted them to stay true to their core character as a band.

Starting in May, we took a break. Donn worked with those guys to mix and edit the audio and video from their US Festival performance, which was going to be broadcast on cable TV and on the radio. Ed, too, had to deliver the soundtrack for the forthcoming *The Seduction of Gina,* a TV movie starring Valerie. He and Donn worked on that as well.

We reconvened later in the summer. We cut "Hot for Teacher," which I *loved.* I remember thinking its groove had a couple of rocky spots; it wasn't locked down as tight as it could be. Take a listen to the ascending section during the guitar solo. It feels a

Ed Van Halen poses with a Steinberger Bass inside of 5150, circa 1983. Note the unfinished nature of the facility and the presence of Alex's electronic drums, which became a big sonic component of *1984*'s Brown Sound. DONN LANDEE.

bit uneasy. But as I'd learned when I worked with Van Morrison, when artists get that *great* of a performance on tape, leave well enough alone. Tinkering around the edges with it was only going to make it less frenetic and powerful.

I was with Dave when he worked on the lyrics. He sang it a couple of times with some lyrical variations before the final version emerged. He also had a brilliant idea to give the track a middle-school vibe. Dave set up a little classroom in the studio with bottles and cans on some school desks. Donn set up a mic and rolled tape, while the guys were wisecracking and knocking shit over, sitting at these school desks. So for the verses, there was a bunch of background noise — you can hear the bottles clanking around. It gave the track this sense of humor, like the Katzenjammer Kids. I loved what he did — it was great. We had a blast doing that stuff.

Donn and I also worked with Alex to create his trademark drum intro for the song. There's one thing about the drum part that's flown under the radar. If you listen to the *very* beginning, it doesn't sound like a drummer; it's too random a pattern. That's because the first five seconds are the Lamborghini exhaust, *then* Al's electronic drums come in. The song begins with *bumm, blu-lu-lum, bumm* — that's the telltale engine lope, that high-octane growl that signals you've got something big under the hood. It's unmistakable to me, since I'm so car-crazy. It took Donn a *lot* of time and work to match up the sound of the Simmons drums to the sound of the idling engine.

We likewise laid "Panama" down around this time. It's one of my favorite things I ever worked on with Van Halen. It's just an *amazing* song. In fact, if "Panama," rather than "Jump," had been the first single off the album, that would have been okay with me.

Back in 1983, I didn't realize that Dave was writing about a racecar — a dragster — nicknamed the "Panama Express." But that's all part and parcel of Roth's gift as a writer. His lyrics are phenomenal — just think about the way he could write so abstractly, with that imagery. "Panama" could have been about a chick, a car; it could have been about anything.

I'd helped Dave with lyrics plenty of times in the past, including with "Jump," but this one was all him. The writing process for it, in fact, reminded me of the way "Ain't Talkin' 'Bout Love" had been done. It was something magical to be a part of, because that kind of creative partnership, one that is so fruitful, is rare. Dave heard Ed's great riff and chord changes, and did the rest — melody and lyrics.

Van Halen got a ton of well-deserved attention for Dave's charisma and Ed's guitar playing. But Dave's lyrical contributions were an essential — but underappreciated — part of what made Van Halen so great. Dave had a different fix on things. It's as if he viewed the world through his own demented kaleidoscope.

Let me give you an example of how he marched to the beat of a different drum. I remember one day I got up there, and he was parading around in the studio, back and forth in that small space, in a kilt, playing *bagpipes*, before we got to work. He wasn't playing them well, either, because he was learning how to play them. He didn't care what I, or anyone, thought about it. That's who he is. He looked at everything around him like it was a huge cartoon. His words, and his unique way of seeing the world, were a big part of why that band was special.

All this time, by the way, Mike's the Rock of fucking Gibraltar. The guy never missed a beat. His bass playing was always superb. He did everything right, including singing backgrounds with that unbelievable voice, which was a big part of the Van Halen sound. You couldn't ask for a better bass player to go with that guitar playing. His instincts were perfect. I know he wishes I coached him up a bit more, but honestly, he was perfect. He never made mistakes and he knew exactly how to leave room for Ed's frenzied guitar playing. Regardless of the drama or deadlines, Mike was great.

By the end of August, we'd cut the basic tracks for eight songs. Because work had slowed in the summer, my plan was to cut three more songs, as well as overdubbing, mixing, and mastering sessions. We'd deliver the album to the label in late October so the album could be released in the last week of the year.

Even though I had a schedule for completion, I was anxious about finishing the record on time. Things had moved so slowly to this point; we'd never gotten back to that old Van Halen pace of knocking tracks down — bang, bang, bang — like we'd done on earlier records.

To be frank, I didn't think Ed and Donn were taking the deadlines as seriously as they should. To get everything squared away for the album, we needed to start overdubbing by a certain date. We'd need to work up rough mixes for each track after we'd finished overdubbing, then turn to final mixing. Donn and Ed, obviously, knew this as well as I did.

This was, in part, a product of working in a home studio. 5150 was in Ed's backyard, and was always available to us. That freedom to blow off deadlines, to be honest, drove me crazy. But it's almost certainly true that if we'd been working at Sunset Sound or Amigo, we might not have gotten "Jump" right. Ed and Al worked on it in the middle of the night, with Donn behind the mixing desk saying, "Just keep going. That's great!" You could work for long uninterrupted stretches of time up there. So I do understand that recording at 5150 did contribute to the success of the album.

But deadlines matter. When we worked at Sunset Sound or Amigo, we *had* to stick to a schedule, because back in those days another artist had the studio booked the day after you were scheduled to leave. Sure, you can move to another studio in town, but as a producer, you want to avoid that if possible. Working beyond deadlines wastes time and money. No one, including me, wanted to keep the meter running unnecessarily while making a record because the bills could pile up quickly. That costs the artist and the label money. This is why I'd gotten the first five Van Halen albums finished on deadline and under budget.

At 5150, none of those factors were in play. If someone doesn't show up for a session, or a bass part doesn't get cut, it doesn't cause any immediate pain. There's always tomorrow, right? Since we never need to vacate the premises, let's not just have one drink. Let's have a bunch, 'cause the couch is great for sleeping it off.

Another reason why we ended up behind schedule was that Ed simply refused to stop writing. Now I know it's counterintuitive, but when Ed kept coming up with new things, I'd get agitated.

"Ed, you can't keep writing forever."

"I know. But I just came up with something new."

He'd then play me these works in progress.

There's a point as a producer where you *have* to say, "Hey, we could go on working on the album this way for the next ten years. We've got to focus in and pick from the ten or twelve things we have." Even Al agreed with that at the time. He helped me get Ed to switch gears.

The wild card, with a lot of this, was Donn. He saw that Ed was at an absolute creative peak. So he'd stay up all night with Ed and encourage him to keep working and creating. And that's what Ed would do. They'd seemingly never go to bed. They'd work overnight. Then during the day, Al, Mike, Dave, and I would show up at 5150, and Donn and Ed would work with us. Then when we left Donn and Ed alone again, they'd keep going. After a while, that kind of zombie existence is going to hollow you out. And that's exactly what happened.

Over time, it became difficult for me to get into a good working headspace with them. I'd wake up around six. I'd play some tennis, and be in my office in Burbank by nine. I'd visit with my assistant and see what I needed to do to clear my desk. I'd arrive at 5150 by noon. I'd be excited to dive into whatever track we were trying to finish. But many times when I'd get up there, nothing productive would be happening. Some days, after Ed *had* to crash after a few days of no sleep, he wouldn't get out of bed until four p.m. If Ed was awake, he'd sometimes be fried and wouldn't be eager to get after it. This is assuming no one else was running late or couldn't make it. Regardless of what we accomplished, I'd have to leave in the early evening — I couldn't stay there past midnight and be able to function at my desk the next day.

Thing is, I knew that Ed was capable of coming up with riff after riff and idea after idea if he kept working. That's one of the things that made him great — not only was he a technical genius when it came to tone and playing, but he could write like a motherfucker. He'd come up with things like "Panama" and "Hot for Teacher." Everyone who has ever heard them knows they are great.

Still, not *everything* Ed came up with was good. Donn knew how to get what Ed had in mind on tape *really* well. But that's because his primary talent was as an engineer and not as a producer. That's *not* a knock on him. I could run the board at 5150, but I could have never gotten anywhere close to what Donn got on tape, because I'm not an engineer. I didn't know how to do a lot of things with the board and, likewise, Donn in some cases wouldn't know what to do with a song idea. Sometimes, there'd be stuff they'd spent hours getting on tape. I'd hear it the next day, and think that they'd been spinning their wheels, because I would have rejected the idea outright for the time being. We'd put it in the can, and maybe come back to it the next time around. Again, my focus was on finishing *1984*, not encouraging Ed to remain locked in writing mode for as long as he felt like it.

As I've said, my objection wasn't about them working without me; I just wanted them to get the *right* work done. Even back on the earlier albums, when Donn, Ed, and I would be at Sunset, I could see those guys were working well, and that Ed was in a good frame of mind. I'd say, "Guys, I'm going to go work with Nicolette over at Amigo. Lay down some stuff. Work as late as you want. I've approved to pay for an open-ended session." You see, part of a producer's job is to know not only when an artist needs your input but also when it's best to leave an artist alone. You can't stay on top of them all the time. You've got to let them breathe. So those guys tracking at night during the *1984* sessions, when I was home asleep, was fine with me. But I did want to work when I got there during the day.

And so that's how I got caught in the middle. I didn't want to squelch Ed's creative impulses, because I was his friend and his producer. I also understood that Donn was trying to facilitate Ed's musicality. But deadlines were getting ignored, and I couldn't get all of us on the same page. I could feel it kind of unraveling up at 5150, even though *1984* turned out to be their biggest album. I didn't have my hands around it.

So, yes, all of this did cause friction between Ed and me. Things never got heated, but there was tension between us, even though all I was trying to do was make sure we finished the record on time. I came to realize that Ed, and Al too, had started seeing me less as a collaborator and more as the individual who wanted to limit their freedom to do what they wanted with the record. We'd hit that spot where I'd gone from the father figure who showed you the ropes to an authority figure looking to control you.

As Labor Day came and went, things started to slip out of my grasp. It reminds me now of when the waters would rise on the San Lorenzo River in Santa Cruz when I was a kid. You look out the window, rain's sheeting down. You run down to the river, it's angry and churning, dark and rising. You're worried, but you're thinking, *The storm will pass. And as long as we keep filling sandbags, we can keep the water at bay and prevent the flood.* Yet in the back of your mind, you know the outcome is beyond your control, regardless of how hard you work to prevent the worst.

It's still hard for me to put my finger on why the teamwork broke down. Donn and Ed started to hold themselves apart from Dave and me when we went up there. It was almost like we were interlopers when we'd show up to work. Had resentment been brewing because Dave and I hadn't embraced Ed's keyboard-based song ideas? Because I'd not been enthused about recording at 5150? Because of what happened with "Dancing in the Street"? At the time I didn't know what was at the root of it all.

The other factor here was that Dave and Donn were like oil and water. I can't really explain it because neither of them said anything to me about it. But I could sense it. My read on it was that Donn had limited tolerance for Dave. Of course, Donn was a professional. He wasn't there to get into a pissing contest with Dave. We'd made five albums together without sparks flying. The same went for Dave. I don't know what his issue was with Donn, but he didn't seem to click with him all that well. None of this helped matters when it came to getting the record done.

As Ed and Donn did more of their marathon sessions, things began to go sideways. They got into this weird space. Those two just fed on each other. I don't know fully why, but they seemed to think that Dave and I were against them. It was crazy.

The tension when we were all in the same room was bad enough, but on a few occasions, Dave and I arrived at 5150 only to find that those guys weren't in shape to work, so we'd cancel the whole day's schedule. Other times, we'd find ourselves locked out of the studio. I'm glad Dave wrote in *Crazy from the Heat* that he and I waited, waited, and waited for Ed and Donn. Donn, Al, and Ed would be working until three a.m. Al would leave, then the sun would come up and it would be just those two guys sequestered.

Other times, we'd show up to work and Ed would be alone, locked in his house, and wouldn't come out. That was the really bad part of it all. Here you have someone who has been up all night, and you can't get in the studio to work. We'd sit on this bench and wait and we'd waste a day. It was so frustrating.

Dave was never the bad guy with all the drama surrounding these sessions. He did his homework. On the occasions he didn't, say, have his lyrics finished, he was better on the fly than any artist I ever worked with in the studio. He always had his shit together. He'd come ready to be productive and to work.

Once again, this kind of stuff never would have gone on at Sunset on my watch. Yes, we'd have fun during the earlier album sessions. We'd indulge a bit. Guys would do the occasional bump, some drinks to keep things loose, but on my sessions you had to be restrained and discreet. When you go to a studio like Sunset or Amigo, you recognize that they are semi-public places, so everyone has to behave. There's a certain decorum that you absolutely have to maintain. Once you step out of that situation and you are in your own backyard, in your clubhouse, you can do whatever you want, whenever you want. Moreover, when we worked at Sunset or Amigo, everyone knew we were paying by the hour to use the studio, so no one even thought about no-showing for a session there.

The other thing that played into all of this was Valerie. She was more concerned than anybody. When I would get up there to Ed's place, she'd grab me and say, "Ted, God only knows what the hell they are doing in there. They've been in there all night. They haven't come out." Or she'd call me and say, "Ted, they've been in there for two days. Can you come and get them out?" She was beside herself.

So there was noticeable tension between her and Ed. Look, married couples fight all the time. Kathi and I had our disagreements, but I wasn't trying to produce an album in my backyard while keeping house with my wife. But that's what Ed was trying to do while working at 5150. The lack of separation between home and work up at Ed's place hurt our ability to remain focused and productive.

Probably the worst moment for me came out of the blue. In the late summer, I came up to the house to work with Ed. He unlocked the studio door and came outside. He looked terrible. He'd been up for days; he was shitfaced, absolutely whacked out of his skull.

I asked him something about the record.

We exchanged words. He made clear he didn't want or need my help in the studio that day. Rather than argue with him, I left.

Making this record was turning into a nightmare.

We still weren't done, though, so soon after, I was back up at 5150, trying to put my personal feelings aside, so I could stay focused on finishing the album.

One piece we kept circling back to was the still unfinished, synth-driven song idea that became "I'll Wait."

We'd laid it down weeks earlier without a vocal guide — meaning we didn't have even a rough melody or lyrics — because it was something Ed, Al, and Donn liked.

To be frank, it hadn't grown on me since I first heard Ed's demo back in April. It slogged along, like a jeep stuck in the mud.

Maybe I had it all wrong, but I just didn't love Ed's new keyboard stuff, in part because I thought it diluted what made Van Halen distinctive.

As a producer, I was used to Van Halen as this great signature situation. You've got this eclectic mixture of brilliance. You've got these great lyrics and this great guitar playing. I'm hearing this song idea that, to me, is going to sound like Van Halen copying other, less talented acts. I actually thought it sounded like Argent's "Hold Your Head Up." It was kind of a forgotten song by 1983, but still, I was listening to Ed's idea, thinking, *Will people hear that too?* I thought they would. Van Halen shouldn't ever sound like they are copying someone else.

I tried to be upfront with Ed about my views on what became "I'll Wait," but with our relationship at a low point, it seemed like Ed was taking things I said personally. And — I think because this piece seemed to encapsulate the Brown Sound to them — it seemed very important to Ed and Donn that we do everything in our power to get it on the album. So I put my reservations aside and worked with everyone on getting it together.

But just like we'd been through with the "Dancing in the Street" riff, Dave couldn't come up with a melody or lyric to go with Ed's keyboard track.

I was stumped too.

Then Dave approached me with an idea. He said, "Hey, Ted, can you ask Mike McDonald if he'd be willing to take a crack at this with me?"

Dave and Mike didn't know each other, so I called Mike. He said he'd be happy to sit down with Dave and work on it.

I'm not sure Dave and the other guys appreciated what a coup this was for them. Mike was one of the most successful pop song-writers in the recording industry. He'd written hits as a solo artist, as a member of the Doobies, and with stars ranging from Carly to R&B superstar James Ingram. At that time, Quincy Jones, who had done *Thriller* with Michael Jackson, wanted to produce Mike. Everybody was after him.

So one early fall day, the three of us met at my office in Burbank. We played a tape of the demo. Mike sat down at a keyboard and he and Dave began bouncing ideas off each other. The way I remember it, Ed had the chorus written in chords, but Mike came up with the chorus melody, the song title, and contributed to the lyrics. After months of getting nowhere, Mike's input paid immediate dividends. That's how "I'll Wait" became a song.

I didn't love everything we'd cut, but in addition to things like "Jump," "Panama," and "Hot for Teacher," I thought Van Halen had come up with some great album tracks. I lreally liked "Drop Dead Legs" and "Top Jimmy." The whole band was at their peak, but I loved Dave's lyrics on those tracks. His writing is so ethereal. A lot of times, like on "Panama," and "Jump," you're not sure exactly what he's writing about. It's kind of like reading e. e. cummings or T.S. Eliot's "Prufrock."

I knew the keyboard songs were going to make a stir, but I just didn't know what the public's reaction would be to such a radical change of sound. It would be a new Van Halen, with a change of address, from Mean Street to Pop City.

Some weeks later, mixing began. In the past, Donn and I had almost always worked alone. Now, though, Ed, and occasionally Al, joined us as we mixed the 16-track recordings from our sessions down to two-channel stereo masters. This wasn't a welcome development, but it was hardly unexpected since Ed *owned* the studio.

Mixing by committee turned everything upside down. In the past, Donn and I had simpatico tastes for Van Halen's sound, but now Ed and Al had their hands on the board too.

At first, I had hopes that Al would be able to retain his objectivity. During the summer, for example, he had helped reel in Ed and Donn when they made suggestions that seemed more likely to get us further behind schedule. Put another way, Donn and Ed would be on Pluto, and Al would bring them back to Earth.

But when we mixed, those three guys became of one mind. For example, on "Girl Gone Bad," I didn't like the preliminary mixes. I thought the drums were too loud, and I said so. But Al wanted the drums to be higher and higher in the mix, and Donn and Ed agreed with him. I love the song, but not the mix. If you listen to the kick drums, they're pushed up too high, for me. That was the result of Al and Ed being in Donn's ear. That was just the way it was.

By the end of October, the mixing sessions wrapped. At least, that's what Dave and I thought. On the prior albums, Donn would now take the mixdown over to Amigo and start cutting reference lacquers, which we'd evaluate in order to assess the album's sonics and to get all the tracks uniform-sounding, while I started sequencing, or setting the running order of the album's songs. Once we'd finalized everything, Donn would master the album, the last step in the process before we delivered the album to the label.

I'd had to push some deadlines back, but if we rushed things along, we could still get *1984* in stores by the end of the year.

I moved on to working on other projects, and waited to hear from Donn and Ed.

But for whatever reason — maybe because they'd barely slept for weeks and had lost perspective — Donn and Ed kept working in the studio. Were they remixing without telling me, the producer? I'm still not sure, but they apparently still weren't finished with the album.

Now, initially I didn't know this was happening. Donn had never missed a deadline for Warner Bros. Records before. Never.

I started calling up to 5150 after Donn missed the deadline for cutting the lacquers. Then the mastering deadline came and went.

The calendar now says November, and I'm wondering, *What the hell are they doing?*

I'm getting more anxious by the day because, while I had a safety *copy* of the multitrack tapes down in Burbank, Ed and Donn still had the multitrack *master* tapes and, of course, I needed them to deliver the *album*: the stereo mixdown of *1984*.

This was a big problem. First, Warner Bros. didn't take kindly to non-delivery of their very valuable property — in this case, an album from a band that had a streak of five straight platinum records going. Second, without the mixdown, the album couldn't be mastered, which brought the whole production schedule to a standstill. Third, if, God forbid, a fire had consumed 5150, destroying the mixdown and the multitracks, we'd be utterly fucked. We'd have to start mixing from scratch using my safety, an analog *copy* of the multi-track master tapes. Because analog replication by its very nature involves some sonic degradation, we'd be risking releasing an album with noticeable audio flaws.

Obviously, as a Warner Bros. Records senior vice president and the album's producer, I felt responsible for this mess. And do understand, not a day went by when it wasn't the foremost thing on my mind, because I was constantly fielding calls from other label executives, telling me that their departments couldn't fulfill their tasks related to *1984* until the album got delivered. Putting all of the insanity of the last few weeks aside, the bottom line was this: Donn and Ed had those tapes, which belonged to Warner Bros. I had to get them to turn in the tapes.

After getting Ed on the phone, I'd drive over to his place. Ed would buzz me through the gate. I'd drive to the top of the hill, park, and go and bang on the studio door. Ed would answer, sheepishly telling me that Donn had the tapes and wasn't around.

Initially I had no inkling of what was afoot here. I thought Donn had just gone off the rails. But then years later in an interview, Ed said something like, "We hid the tapes from Ted. He'd tell me he was coming up to the house. Donn would take the tapes and get in the car and leave the studio. Then when Ted showed up, I'd put him off when he'd ask about the tapes. He'd leave, and Donn would come right back to the studio with the tapes."

After all these years, best I have been able to figure out is that they wanted to run out the clock to assure they'd have the final say on the mix. This way, even if I'd *wanted* to "pull rank" on them and remix the album, there'd be no time to do so.

Look, I understand those guys were in a paranoid state of

mind, but it's difficult for me to understand why they'd take this tack after all of our years of working together.

If they were upset with the mixes, or anything at all, why didn't they just meet with me at 5150 and have a discussion, rather than running away with the tapes? They could have just said, "Ted, come on in. Sit down. Let's discuss this." We could have talked about it. We could have listened to different mixes, and they could have told me, "We don't agree with you." We could have hashed it out.

That's why I think they thought I'd close them down. But at first, I just wanted to see what was going on up at 5150, since, much to my surprise, they'd not delivered the album on schedule. I wasn't coming to seize the tapes from them. I just wanted them to quickly tie up any loose ends and deliver the album so we could master the record.

Frustrated, I finally took matters into my own hands. During the second week of November, I grabbed Warner Bros. chief engineer Lee Herschberg and entered Sunset Sound with the 16-track safety reels. Working as quickly as we could, we mixed *1984* from scratch since I had to take seriously the idea that Donn and Ed might not turn in the album at all. Dave came in and sat with us for stretches of time too, since he wasn't feeling welcome up at 5150 either. At the time, I wasn't laughing, but in retrospect it's amusing that in mid-December, *Billboard* reported that Lee and I were working on the new Van Halen album at Sunset Sound, with nary a mention of Ed, Donn, or 5150.

It was soon after Lee and I finished that Donn suddenly showed up, unannounced, at Amigo Studios. When he came in, Lee and a few other people were in the office with me. It was a bit like seeing a ghost.

Donn stood in front of me, clutching the *1984* master reels. All Donn was supposed to do was bring in the tapes, so we could master *1984*. Donn came in to master the album himself, but he was in no shape to do it. He'd been up for days; he was just manic and all messed up, sweating and crazy.

I told him I wanted the tapes.

"No!"

To emphasize his point, he reached back and slammed the door so hard the doorknob broke loose and skittered across the linoleum floor. He was holding the tapes in his arms, across his chest, yelling, "I'll throw them in the ocean!"

Everyone else melted away, leaving us alone. I walked right up to him and yelled, "*DONN!*" All my frustration from the past few months surged through me. I was ready to fight. I didn't care what it came to, because he had the master tapes.

We argued, I think about mastering. Donn wanted to master the album right then and there, but I wasn't going to let him, because he wasn't in shape to do it.

No punches were thrown, but after some more back and forth, he put down the tapes and left.

I didn't want to escalate things, so I had the album mastered, using their mix. (Donn, I believe, came back a day later, when he was in a better frame of mind, and mastered *1984* himself, just like he'd done on every previous Van Halen album.) Plus I knew that the mix that Lee and I did, which was done by the seat of our pants from the safety copies, wasn't going to be as meticulously prepared or sonically vibrant as the one they'd obsessed over for weeks.

Finally, on January 9, *1984* reached record stores, more than a week late. As always, the liner notes said *Produced by Ted Templeman and engineered by Donn Landee.*

Despite the fact that the album's sold more than ten million copies, I don't love it. "Hot for Teacher" and "Panama" are great, but I'm still not crazy about "Jump." To be frank, it's hard for me to be objective about it because I can't separate the experience of making the record from the songs themselves. A lot of times, when I hear "Jump" and "Panama," I get a weird feeling, because I remember thinking on many days while we were in the studio, *Okay, I need to make sure we make it through today's session so we can get this song finished.* Things at 5150 weren't as happy as they sound on the record.

But Ed does deserve massive credit for the success of "Jump." Dave and I had our doubts, but Ed was on the money. In fact, the thing I got most right after my initial listens to Ed's idea was that "Jump" sounded like it should be played at sports arenas. Today, you can hardly go to any sporting event without hearing it.

I understand now that Ed needed to grow as an artist. From building the studio to the keyboard songs, he took things in directions that I didn't necessarily get at the time. Donn got it though. Everyone knows about the tight connection between Ed and Al when it came to making music. But here's how I'd explain it in terms of Donn and Ed: at the time, they had the same kind of brotherly connection when it came to capturing sounds and performances on tape.

Putting all the drama aside, Ed created an anthem that was a No. 1 hit record for five weeks in a row. I never would have guessed that would happen. He wouldn't have either, but still, through that song he dreamed up a grander vision for Van Halen and found a new way to connect with the band's audience. As a result, Van Halen got bigger than ever.

When I think about my role in making the record, I can't help but wonder what I could have done differently keep things from getting so toxic. But still, I'm proud I succeeded in bringing out the best in the band. Because things were so volatile, I had to think on my feet all the time. On prior records, the sessions were organized and I could keep things on track. Up at 5150, I couldn't get a hold of the process — it was like grabbing lightning — so if something's working, we had to seize it, and get the track recorded right then and there, because who knew what tomorrow would bring?

Really, the fact that the album came out at all seems like the biggest achievement. Making it was an incredible ordeal because of all of the craziness going on at 5150. I don't think they ever would have finished the record by themselves. In fact, I *know* that it wouldn't have come out if I hadn't been part of the process.

Chapter 13

SPLIT

I don't remember whether I was at home or at the office, but I remember my most unpleasant conversation with Mike McDonald like it was yesterday.

Soon after *1984* came out, he started calling my assistant, saying it was urgent that I call him. She said he sounded very agitated, very upset.

When I got him on the phone, he gave me an earful.

He was angry, telling me that he just found out that Van Halen hadn't credited him as a songwriter for "I'll Wait."

I tried to calm him down, telling him he had to be mistaken. I'd been there with him when he and Dave came up with the melody and lyrics. Everyone in the Van Halen camp knew they'd finished off the song together.

The reason I thought Mike was misinformed had to do with the way songwriters document and protect their work. There are deliberate steps songwriters follow when it comes to music publishing and copyrighting. They have to register the songs they've written with a performance-rights organization like ASCAP so they can collect royalties. When there are co-writers, percentage splits are determined carefully. They have to assign their songs to their music publisher, in this case Van Halen Music.

So I said, "Are you sure?"

"Yes I'm sure!"

He'd seen the songwriting credits on *1984*. His name wasn't there, but Edward Van Halen, Alex Van Halen, David Lee Roth, and Michael Anthony's names were there. He was furious.

"How could those guys do that to me?"

Of course, I felt outraged on Mike's behalf. He'd bailed Dave out, and had done Ed, in particular, a huge service by filling in the blanks on Ed's unfinished song.

I told him this was the first I'd heard of it, that I had no idea. I don't think he believed me.

I told him I'd make some calls and find out what happened.

When I got off the phone, I felt awful. Mike was one of my best friends. The thing is, Ed and I were very close, but I didn't socialize with him. Mike and I were buddies. We were the trouble twins. We traveled together, we hung out. We'd room together when the Doobies rehearsed up north.

I immediately called over to the Van Halen offices. I got the runaround.

Soon after I called the label's Legal Affairs office. The lawyers there were just getting up to speed on what happened, but were looking into it.

The bottom line was somewhere along the line between Mike, Dave, and me sitting in my office and the final run-up to the album's release, somebody or some group of people in the Van Halen camp didn't want Mike to have a writer's credit on the record. Mike was mad, and who could blame him?

Even more infuriating was the way certain people in the Van Halen camp reacted. They got their hackles up, acting indignant at the notion that Mike deserved a share.

As upset as I was for Mike, there wasn't much I could do to

fix it. It was a dispute that would need to be settled by lawyers and the label. Mike's attorney took it up with Warner Bros. and the band; I just put my head down and worked on what I had on my plate.

As a result of all this bullshit, my relationship with Mike was damaged. There was a level of trust we'd always had, going back to the times when Mike had offered me writer's credit after I'd made the smallest suggestions when we kicked around his song ideas. I never took him up on it, but he was so generous and thoughtful, I can understand why he felt betrayed. Even though I had nothing to do with the credits on *1984*, I'd put Mike and Dave in the same room. Really, he'd done it as a favor to me. He didn't know the guys in Van Halen. So when Mike got stiffed, it affected my relationship with Mike.

At the close of 1983, Sammy Hagar hired me to produce his upcoming album for Geffen. Back in 1980, Mo had signed a deal with David Geffen to finance his label, so working for Geffen Records, rather than Warner Bros. proper, wasn't an issue. As it happened, I'd known David since my Harpers Bizarre days, when he was an agent for William Morris.

John Kalodner, Geffen's A&R point man, spearheaded this project. He was kind of an odd duck, walking around in a white suit like John Lennon, but he saw that the market for catchy hard rock, or pop-metal, whatever you want to call it, hadn't been fully tapped by record companies. So he grasped Sammy's growth potential. I'd have chances to work with him again later in the year as well on another album.

Sammy and I hadn't collaborated since Montrose's second album, *Paper Money* — something like a decade had passed — but I was excited to get back into the studio with him. We'd decided to work up in the Bay Area at Fantasy Studios. I can't recall why we settled on that studio, but it wouldn't have been my first choice. I know Sammy had done some recording there in prior years. From my perspective, I'd always rather work at a studio where I really know the board and the echo chambers, and how each room is going to sound. I also had to fly back and forth between LA and Berkeley, which wasn't ideal.

Before we got rolling, I had to find an engineer for the project. Because things had gotten screwed up between Donn and me, I thought it would be best for us to take a break from each other.

For me, of course, this situation wasn't ideal. Donn and I had been partners for a long time, and now I needed to find a new engineer and then go to work in a studio I'd never worked at before.

One of the first people who came to mind to help me in my search was Bob Clearmountain. At that time he worked out of the Power Station Studios in Manhattan, and he's one the best engineers in the world. I thought he might have some suggestions for me, so I called him.

"I need a young, hungry, talented guy to engineer for me at Fantasy for the upcoming Sammy Hagar record. Who do you recommend?"

He told me about an engineer he'd been mentoring named Jeff Hendrickson. Jeff had been Bob's second on great-sounding records like David Bowie's *Scary Monsters*, Bryan Adams' *Cuts Like a Knife*, and Sister Sledge's *We Are Family*.

Jeff and I talked. Jeff was blond and skinny, a twenty-something standing over six feet tall. We hit it off, so I hired him. When Jeff and I did pre-production for the album with Sammy at Fantasy a short time later, it was obvious that Clearmountain had steered me in the right direction, because Jeff is a producer's dream of an engineer.

After all of the bullshit surrounding the Van Halen record, working with Sammy in the studio was a breath of fresh air. Sammy was so enthusiastic and fun. You couldn't help but have a good time when you were around him. He had nicknames for everyone, from the guy who worked security at the studio to Jeff and me. For instance, Jeff had a habit of greeting people by saying, "Hey, good buddy." Sammy ran with it and started calling Jeff "Big Buddy" — a nickname so durable that thirty years later I'm still more likely to refer to Jeff as Big Buddy than his given name. At first Sammy dubbed me "Grandmaster Buddy" before deciding that he preferred to call me "Champagne," because I liked to sip the bubbly in the studio to take the edge off things. Sammy, that sneaky bastard, even put that nickname in the album liner notes. I laughed hard when I saw that.

This project also gave me the chance to reconnect with bassist Bill Church. I'd met him back in 1971 during the *Tupelo Honey* sessions, and then he'd played bass on the first Montrose record. Church, like all the other guys in Sammy's band — Gary Pihl, David Lauser, and Jesse Harms — were total pros in the studio.

My work on *VOA* is a good example of my approach to working with artists. A big part of my job when I was producing a record involved A&R: assessing the quality of an artist's songs and choosing the right ones for his or her record. That's why I almost always had my artists do a demo before we cut tracks.

There's a give and take involved in this process. I'd make suggestions and look for areas of agreement between the artist's vision and my vision for the record. When there's disagreement, a producer has to work to find common ground. If an act isn't happy with a song, it's not going to come off well on the album in most cases.

But at the same time, a producer may need to try to push an artist to take a risk. When you see potential for growth, ideally, you'll be able to steer a band down a new and suitable creative avenue without them feeling as if it's a producer's power play at work. So I always tried to nudge my artists forward rather than prod them. If I've done my job well, they'll appreciate the guidance.

Ultimately, it all comes down to this: a producer should strive to get an artist's individuality on tape. That's why the albums I cut with my different acts always sounded different from each other. For instance, the Van Halen albums don't sound like the Doobie Brothers records, even though I used the same studios and same engineers. Likewise, I wasn't going to try to make Sammy sound like Van Halen, even though their audiences did overlap to some extent. You see, some producers think of music fans as fast-food consumers. Once these producers hit on a formula that sells, they want to standardize it. That's why they have a characteristic sound that shows up on all of their albums. Perhaps the best example of this is producer Phil Spector's trademark Wall of Sound. That wasn't my thing. When it came to sonics or songs, I didn't want to make cookie-cutter records. I wanted the artist's personality to define their album.

By taking this general approach, I wanted to make their unique talent available to the listening public. I was trying to put my artists in the best possible light for listeners to appreciate what gifts they had to offer the world. If the artist's personality comes through on the album, I know I've done my job. That's just as important as getting great-sounding, appealing songs on an album.

So let me explain how all of this worked in Sammy's case. Sammy's a high-energy guy. He's a jock. He was a boxer when he was younger. When I was working with him on *VOA*, he and his buddies used to do things like run up steep hills and ride bikes to stay in shape. That spirit reminded me of the camaraderie I experienced while playing high school football back in Santa Cruz. That was the vibe of the *VOA* project. So my plan, like I tried to do with all my artists, was to let Sammy be Sammy.

So that's how I approached things. Like all artists, Sammy did some things better than others. Sammy's a great singer and writes good rock songs. Rick Springfield took Sammy's "I've Done Everything for You" to the *Billboard* Top 10 in 1981. That's an example of what Sammy, when he's at his best, is capable of delivering.

But Sammy's writing wasn't consistent because his lyrics sometimes lacked depth. We didn't have a ton of time for pre-production for this one, so I didn't kick lyrical ideas around with Sammy as much as I might have liked to do. So we ended up recording a song called "Dick in the Dirt."

But here's why I green-lighted that tune. Sammy's enthusiasm is so infectious and the humor so direct that it's hard not to smile when you hear it. It's locker-room humor, which works for him, because to some degree it reflects who Sammy is as an artist and a person. That said, Randy Newman's not going to cover it anytime soon.

Lyrics aside, Sammy was incredible in the studio. He played great guitar and he sang even better. He's always on pitch, and when I'd coach him, I became really aware of how versatile he was as a vocalist. He'd sing lines for me that sounded like Sly Stone or James Brown. He had so much soul, and so much energy when he sang like that. There was this untapped potential in him, a side of him that I couldn't really showcase within the confines of hard rock.

After we'd work, and maybe the guys in his band and I looked a bit tired, he'd have the perfect ways for us to recharge. I remember one time he said, out of the blue, "Let's order some spicy ribs!" He had a huge platter of BBQ delivered to the studio. He'd be slapping me on the back, laughing as he said, "Come on, Ted! Get yourself some of these hot, spicy ribs!" He'd take a big bite, wipe the sauce off his face and yell, "Whew! These are *hot*!" He had this infectious enthusiasm that was incredible.

I just wish every project could be as fun as it was to make Sammy's albums. With Sammy, you have great musicians and a great vibe, every day. Sammy could have just crashed his car on his way to the studio, and he'd still be upbeat and in a good mood. You know, Sammy's like a guy who's been through the school of positive thinking. He was part cheerleader, part quarterback, the whole nine yards. Big Buddy fell right into place in all of this. He was easygoing, smart, and fun.

Jeff and I decided to mix in New York at the Power Station Studios. One appealing aspect of that arrangement was that I could spend a couple of weeks in Manhattan. I'd been there many times since my first visit back in 1962, whether it was to see Linda perform on *Saturday Night Live* or to play with Nicky at the Bottom Line.

But that was less important than the chance to mix at the Power Station. Located in Hell's Kitchen, it had opened in 1977 and was in fact the site of a former Con Edison facility. I wanted to work there because of how great the albums that were recorded there sounded. Take the first couple of Chic records. (Jeff had, in fact, worked as an assistant engineer on those landmark releases when he was apprenticing under Clearmountain.) "Le Freak" and "Good Times" just knocked me out. I couldn't wait to get behind the board in there.

In 1984, I could feel the energy when I walked into the place, in no small part because the studio was defining the sound of the eighties. I could sense that when Jeff and I worked there for the first time. For instance, the Power Station, a new band that featured some of the Duran Duran guys and the singer Robert Palmer, were recording their first album. They could've gone to any studio in the world, but they chose the Power Station. Hell, they liked the facility so much that they named their band after the studio. Then when I'd leave for the day and turn on the radio, I'd hear things that had been recorded there, like David Bowie's "Let's Dance." In a lot of ways, it felt to me like the east coast's Sunset Sound.

Of course, I never would have mixed there if Jeff hadn't been my engineer. He'd been working there since about 1978, so he knew every piece of equipment in that place. It showed too. Jeff dialed up a great soundstage on Sammy's record. He had a vision for how he wanted the records to sound; he was creative and had confidence. He needed direction, of course, but he was a self-starter and once he was rolling, he came up with great results. The guitars shimmered, the bass thumped, and the drums popped. Sammy's voice sounded powerful. I thought it was a unique-sounding LP.

When we weren't mixing, Jeff was my tour guide. I checked out every inch of the place. Like Sunset, it had great live echo chambers. These were rooms specially built to enhance reverberation. At Amigo, and of course at 5150 and other smaller studios, you had machines to generate the same effect — plate reverb units like EMTs — rather than echo chambers. I'd always loved Sunset Sound's live chamber, so this place really felt like home.

Around that same period, I had the opportunity to spend time in Manhattan with a rising star: Madonna. At the behest of my friend Seymour Stein — who'd signed her to Sire, a Warner Bros. subsidiary — and the rest of the executive team, I arranged a meeting with her.

At the time, "Jump" had already been to No. 1, and *1984* was selling like crazy, so I was an ideal person to chat with her about the label's strategy for her forthcoming album, *Like a Virgin*. In particular, I was asked to convey the label leadership's thoughts on her next single.

Now her first album, which had come out the previous year, had gone gold. She was recording the follow-up with Nile Rodgers at the Power Station.

My job was to suggest that she release "Material Girl" as the first single instead of "Like a Virgin." At the time, some of the marketing people at the label thought "Like a Virgin" was too edgy and might not get widely played on MTV and the radio as a result.

So I met her at this new nightclub called Private Eyes. We got a booth, sat, and talked. She was friendly and nice. I tried to explain the politics of the issue at the label, rather than giving her a heavy-handed trip as a Warner Bros. vice president.

She listened thoughtfully, and said, "Well, what do you think I should do?"

I said, "To be honest, I don't care what you do. I'm just delivering the message from the company."

"What's your opinion?"

"You're the artist. You probably know best."

In the end, she went with her gut and pushed for "Virgin" as the first single, which was an absolute smash.

I don't remember when during the course of 1984 Dave and I started discussing a solo EP release, but by the early summer we'd gotten the project underway.

We both agreed about its parameters. We'd record the Beach Boys' "California Girls," Louis Prima's "Just a Gigolo/I Ain't Got Nobody," the Edgar Winter Group's "Easy Street," and a big favorite of both of ours, the Lovin' Spoonful's "Coconut Grove." Four songs, all covers. It was stuff that Dave liked but had no place in Van Halen.

In fact, we'd avoid anything that sounded like hard rock. There would be no heavy-guitar riffs or jungle drums. It was going to be a totally different musical ecosystem: all pop-vaudeville meets big band.

In other words, other than the fact that Dave would be on vocals, it would be the antithesis of Van Halen. That was the bottom line for us, and the most important thing to Dave was to do something that would never detract from or compete with Van Halen. We didn't want to get in the way of the band, at all. Even the artwork was supposed to be like a cartoon. It was all meant to be tongue-in-cheek and fun.

When I suggested we record at the Power Station, Dave was enthusiastic. After mixing *VOA*, I was particularly eager to do a project there from beginning to end. And I knew that with Big Buddy at my side, we could make a kickass-sounding EP.

At the time, I saw all of this as beneficial when it came to the future of Van Halen. I figured this would help Dave get this stuff out of his system and give him a clean slate from which to start the next Van Halen record.

My other major motivation was to wake Ed up. I was genuinely scared for him after experiencing the craziness up at 5150. I thought that if he saw Dave and me working and creating, he might take a hard look at himself and find the strength to straighten up. Honestly, I wasn't sure if I was going to be involved in the next Van Halen album, but I didn't want to stand by and do nothing while he struggled. My paramount concern was seeing him get healthy.

I can't definitively speak about Dave's innermost motivations for the future of Van Halen. I believe that he didn't have any interest in leaving the band when we worked on *Crazy from the Heat*. If I'd gotten even the slightest sense that he saw this as step one of David Lee Roth's post–Van Halen solo career, I wouldn't have done the record. I never, ever wanted to do anything to threaten the future of Van Halen. I can't emphasize this enough.

That's why, as a label executive, I thought the EP was a good move. It would keep Dave working and creating, we'd sell some records, and it would keep Van Halen, via Dave, in the public eye for a few months in early 1985. I believed that block of time would be valuable because it would give Ed a chance to get himself together without the pressures of writing, recording, or touring.

In preparation for the sessions, I hired Edgar Winter to be my point person for Dave's studio band. I'd worked with him on the first Mike McDonald solo album, and he proved to be a multi-talented, monster musician. Dave was a big fan of his too, from way back.

Edgar helped me put the rest of the band together. I hired vets like John Robinson on drums and Sammy Figueroa on percussion. Willie Weeks, who'd done a stint with the Doobies, played bass. Sid McGinnis, who later became a fixture on *Late Night with David Letterman*, did a lot of the guitars. It was an incredibly solid band.

Once Dave got off the road in July, I started counting down the days. Dave was motivated and I knew he'd knock down the tunes like we'd done with Van Halen in the early days.

Dave came in primed for action. His voice was in shape despite months on the road; it had a bit of smoky grit to it, which was perfect for the tracks. He was prepared and worked hard.

After working with him on so many records, I knew how to get a vocal performance out of him. We cut the tracks live while Dave sang, getting multiple takes of vocals on tape. His humor and exuberance were front and center on "Gigolo," "California Girls," and "Easy Street," and he gave me a somber, moving vocal on the melancholy "Coconut Grove." When you listen and close your eyes, you can see the palm trees swaying.

Edgar Winter was the lynchpin of those sessions. He and I arranged the tracks. He played keyboard and sax on "Easy Street" and "Gigolo," and keys on "California Girls." I often had him double Willie's parts with a synth keyboard to kick up the bass, which he did perfectly. Listen to the album in headphones; those walking bass lines are so funky. It doesn't get any better than that. He did his parts in one take. There are not many guys who can lay down great Fender electric piano, play regular piano parts or B-3 organ, or lay in all the saxophone parts. Then he'd turn around and sing backgrounds with me on "Easy Street" and "Gigolo." He was like a musical Swiss Army knife. Any ideas I had for the different tracks were possible with him. Edgar is an amazing musician and brilliant in the studio. And he's such a sweet guy and a pleasure to produce. I loved working with him.

And Big Buddy, now recording on his home turf, got sounds on tape to die for. Take a listen to that first couple snare hits on "Gigolo." That was a drum sound that only Jeff could get in that room at the Power Station. That was perfect, too, because I didn't want even the drums to sound like something off of a Van Halen album. When I heard the drum sound Jeff got on "Gigolo," I was so happy I actually did a little jig around the studio.

I also had fun in the studio with percussionist Sammy Figueroa. On the first day he came in to record, I met with him to go over his parts.

"So for 'Easy Street,' what are you thinking?"

"What if I just throw a bunch of cans around?"

He reached over to a nearby table and grabbed two or three empty Coke cans.

Dropping them, they clattered around on the polished wood floor.

He stared at me, waiting for my verdict. I went into producer mode, trying to encourage him to try something else without criticizing him.

"Ah, well, I dunno, Sammy. That wasn't what I had in mind. How about —"

"Oh, I'm just messing with you, Ted!"

He was shining me on — I didn't know it. He nailed his parts too.

It did take me a while to get into the New York groove. I remember one of the studio guys saying, "I'm going to go get a pie. You want some?"

I'm thinking: Pie? That's a weird choice for dinner.

"Nah, I'm good."

Thirty minutes later, I'm sitting there, and he walks back in with a pizza box. I thought he'd be coming back with a cherry pie, because I didn't know New Yorkers used the word pie for pizza.

One night when we were working late, Eddie Anderson, Dave's imposing bodyguard, looked at Dave and me and said, "Let's take a walk."

Dave leaped up, ready to go.

I stayed seated, because this seemed like a very bad idea. The Power Station is located in Hell's Kitchen. Whenever I was out on the street, especially at night, the scenes reminded me of *West Side Story* meets *The Warriors*. During the eighties, there was a bit of menace in the neighborhood.

"Shit, in this neighborhood? Someone will try to kill us," I said to Eddie.

"Nah. That's why I'm here. Let's go. Hopefully somebody will give you trouble and I can take care of it."

Needless to say, I didn't feel scared while walking around the city with a guy like Eddie. He went everywhere with us, whether it was to the bodega or a restaurant.

Actually, other than our walks and our studio sessions, I didn't spend a ton of time with Dave in New York. He'd come in to the Power Station, do his parts, and leave. In fact, I spent more time shooting the shit with Jeff and the other engineers than I did visiting with Dave.

In contrast, I hung out with Edgar quite a bit. He and his wife had this huge apartment in the city. We'd go to their place and have a drink, and then head out for dinner. The three of us would eat at Mr. Chow's Chinese restaurant on 57th Street. We'd order tons of great food and hang out until they kicked us out at closing time.

When we wrapped up in New York, I was so happy with what we'd accomplished. Dave left New York in August to go back on the road with Van Halen. We planned to release his EP in January, approximately a year after *1984* had arrived in stores.

Around the same time I recorded Dave in New York, Geffen released *VOA*. Sammy's first single, "Two Sides of Love," did reach the Top 40, but "I Can't Drive 55" broke the album. He did a great vocal on the song, and the lyric absolutely represented the essence of Sammy — fast cars, good times, and testosterone. He did a memorable video that went into heavy rotation at MTV right out of the gate. He got to race his Ferrari in it, helping to make the song an anthem for every lead-footed driver in America. When I listen to "I Can't Drive 55" today, I think it sounds great. I was a bit surprised by how much radio airplay it got, but I think the video spurred the radio adds. Either way, it does have that fun Sammy vibe. The video — I love watching it. It absolutely was the driving force for sales

Sharing a laugh with Sammy Hagar and his band as they are presented gold records for *VOA*, late 1984. (*seated from left to right*): Geffen Records executive John Kalodner, Sammy, me, keyboardist Jesse Harms. Gary Pihl, Sammy's guitarist, holds the gold record award.
TED TEMPLEMAN COLLECTION.

of that record, which went gold by the fall. Between *1984* and *VOA*, I was having another good year.

In the fall, Lenny, who was now the president of the label, called me and said, "Clapton just submitted his new record. Come up and listen to it."

This album, which would be entitled *Behind the Sun*, had been recorded in Montserrat and produced by Genesis's Phil Collins. It was Eric's second for Warner Bros., but his first working with Phil. There was a lot riding on this album for Eric and the label. Warner Bros. had experienced a financially tough 1983, so Lenny and I and all the other execs hoped he would be able to build on the modest sales success he'd enjoyed with his prior album, *Money and Cigarettes*.

I went up to his office and listened. Afterwards, he said, "So what do you think?"

"I don't love any of it, except for a couple of songs."

Lenny had a similar opinion. He didn't think much of it.

I wasn't in the loop for what happened next; what I heard after the fact from Lenny was that soon after he and I met, Lenny called Eric and told him that he and Phil needed to rework and resubmit the album.

Eric took this as an affront. He spat back at Lenny, "Well, if you don't think it's good enough, why don't you produce it?"

Lenny said, "Well, okay."

I'm not sure if Eric expected that answer.

When the dust settled, Eric agreed to record a few new, more commercial songs to substitute for the ones we felt were weak. Eric would come to Los Angeles to work on tunes to replace the ones that Warner Bros., by way of Lenny, was rejecting.

Lenny then called me and said, "Why don't you and I do these new songs with Eric?"

Even though I didn't love working as a co-producer, even when partnered with my best friend, I quickly said yes, because I knew it was important that he and I collaborate on this record. Lenny and me both working on the album sent the message to everyone in the company, all the radio people, and the decision makers at MTV that Warner Bros. viewed *Behind the Sun* as a key release for 1985. When the label president and a senior vice president co-produce an album by an artist of Clapton's stature, it gives the record a better chance to succeed.

The way Lenny described his conversation with Eric, it sounded like Eric was throwing down the gauntlet — challenging Lenny to put his money where his mouth was. I didn't really care about the politics of it all. I just went into the project to do what I do.

In terms of working with Clapton, I had mixed feelings, to be honest.

I absolutely loved Cream, particularly the way Ginger Baker, Eric, and Jack Bruce played together as a trio, perhaps even more than I liked their songs, which were good, of course.

And I'd probably met Eric in passing back when Harpers Bizarre was on a TV show with Cream in the late sixties, but I didn't know him at all.

But because of my fondness for George Harrison, with whom I'd become good friends after he signed a deal with Warner Bros. in the seventies, I had a preconceived dislike of Clapton. George's wife, Pattie Boyd, had left George for Eric back in the seventies, which had hurt George a lot, even though George and Eric remained friends. So when George and I talked about Eric as a musician, George made it clear that he thought Eric was the world's best guitarist. But when the personal stuff about Eric and Pattie came up, I could see the sadness in his eyes. With his voice trailing off, he'd drop his head and say, "Oh yeah, the Clapper." George was a really sensitive, nice guy who'd been through a lot of hurt because of that love triangle.

But once I spent time with Eric during pre-production, I put all of that prejudice aside. Eric's a gentleman and an extremely nice guy, so we got on great. Like all of us who came of age musically during the British Invasion, Eric adored the Beatles. He and I swapped stories about seeing them live. I told him about the times I'd seen them in the Bay Area. I particularly remember Eric's eyes lighting up as he recounted what it was like to see the Beatles before they became the biggest band in the world. When he was in the Yardbirds, he gigged with them in the UK a few times. He told me he'd watch as John, Paul, George, and Ringo would lock into this massive groove and just *kick ass*. He loved watching them play.

To start the process of finding a few more radio-friendly songs for Eric's album, Lenny had sent Eric a demo tape of songs written by a Texan named Jerry Lynn Williams.

Williams had a history with Warner Bros. He first got on my radar in the late seventies when he auditioned for Lenny and me. We signed him because he was an excellent piano player and an amazing songwriter. In 1979, he cut an album for Warner Bros. Along the way, he caused Mo and Lenny endless headaches, because he was a very difficult person. So Warner Bros. dropped him from the roster soon after his record came out.

But good songs are good songs, regardless of the personality of the songwriter. Eric loved the Williams material. After some discussion among the three of us, we chose three tunes for Eric: "Forever Man," "See What Love Can Do," and "Something's Happening."

We did the album at two Hollywood studios, recording the vocals at Lion Share Studios and the instrumental tracks at Amigo. The great Lee Herschberg ran the board for us.

When we got into Amigo, I watched Eric set up his rig. When I'd previously asked him what he was going to record with, he told me he intended to use two Pignose amps, in stereo, and a funky Gibson guitar. I learned later that he'd recorded with Pignoses on some earlier albums, but when I listened to him play through it all that day, I didn't like his tone at all.

This was weird to me. Here's Eric Clapton, an unbelievably great player. He was every bit worthy of his status as a guitar idol. But to my ears, he didn't seem very attuned to his own sound.

So I approached him and said, "I don't like this. Let's try something different."

I floated the idea that he record with a Fender Stratocaster instead of a Gibson. I also suggested that we get a Fender Bassman top and a Bandmaster cabinet in the studio and see how he liked that combination. I'm not a very good guitar player, but after years of working with great guitarists, I had an almost instinctual feel when it came to dialing in great tones.

He smiled at me, laughed, and said, "Whatever you want, *you bloody colonist!*"

I didn't get the joke.

Colonist?

Oh, he's referencing the American Revolution.

I'll never forget that. He called me a colonist.

That became a running joke throughout the sessions. Whenever I asked Eric to do something, he'd say, "Well, all right, you bloody colonist!"

We'd all crack up.

When I came back into the control room, Lenny gave me a sideways look. He whispered, "Are you sure you want to do this? That's *Eric Clapton.*" But as a producer, I'm thinking, *Yeah, Clapton's one of the all-time greats, but right now he's just the guitar player on a record I'm trying to make. I'm the producer.* Eric and I both had our roles to play, and it was my job to work with him so he'd sound as good as possible on the record. Working with Eric was no different to me than when I'd worked with gifted players like Ronnie or Lowell. As a producer, you can't get intimidated just because you're working with a true legend with otherworldly talent.

So I called SIR and ordered the gear. I got him some wonderful vintage Fender guitars and good amps to try out. We put together an updated rig, and he liked it.

During pre-production, Lenny had this idea, which sounded like a risky one to me: let's call Williams up and invite him to come to town and work on Eric's record. I expressed reservations to Lenny because of Jerry's reputation for wild living. I didn't know all the details of Clapton's sobriety, but it was my understanding that he'd been clean for a while, so for us to bring a potential junco partner for Eric into the studio seemed unwise.

When we broached it with Eric, he was very enthusiastic. Eric really wanted to meet Williams and thought playing the songs with him would really breathe life into the tunes. Williams, likewise, jumped at the chance. I didn't like the idea, but since I was co-producing with Lenny, and Eric was so gung-ho, I gave in to it.

Now to be fair, none us knew when we hatched this plan that Williams was going to show up so strung out and fucked up. Once Jerry got into the studio, I thought about how Jerry's lifestyle was going to affect Eric, but at this point there was no turning back. Eric was thrilled about recording with Jerry.

Williams was big — well over six feet tall and huge across his chest and shoulders. He was built like a bull. He was also loud and abrasive.

But I want to give him his due. Jerry was a brilliant musician. He played killer piano and guitar. He was just a natural songwriter, and remained so throughout the course of his life. Even decades later, I had the Doobies cut one of his songs, with Bob Clearmountain engineering, called "Back to Louisiana," which has never been released. When you heard songs like that, you knew that the guy just had a genius for songwriting, despite his other issues.

You'd think that after years in the business I'd be able to handle those types of situations without difficulty, but it was tough to be in the same room with Williams. Maybe it's because of my experiences growing up with my alcoholic uncle up on the hill back in Felton, but Williams and I didn't get on, at all. Meanwhile, he and Eric hit it off like long-lost brothers. They became fast friends which, regardless of my personal feelings about Williams, at first appeared to be an okay situation for Lenny and me.

Along with Williams, Lenny and I recruited all of the best session players to play on the record. We hired John Robinson, who'd played drums on *Crazy from the Heat*, and drummer Jeff Porcaro and Steve Lukather from Toto. We also hired bassist Nathan East, keyboardists Michael Omartian, James Newton Howard, and Greg Phillinganes. In fact, they were a lot of the same guys who'd done the first Mike McDonald solo record with Lenny and me, so we were all familiar with each other. All those guys were total pros and a pleasure to produce.

I remember the session went quickly. We cut the three songs that appeared on *Behind the Sun* plus another Williams song called "Loving Your Lovin'," which remained in the can until it was released a few years later on the *Wayne's World* soundtrack. We also did additional backgrounds for some of the Collins-produced tracks.

Eric was really cooperative, but Jerry was very difficult. He was unorganized and undisciplined, and rarely sober. He was so big, loud, and brash that he'd hijacked our schedules and would, at times, seem like he was going to totally wreck the project. For Lee, Lenny, and me, it was a real problem, because this guy was big *and* drunk. I mean, he'd set a case of beer down next to himself before he'd even pick up his guitar to play.

I certainly didn't have a problem with a guy having a few drinks in the studio, but I never tied one on during sessions. After the 1984 sessions, it was frustrating to deal with this kind of chaos again.

The worst moment for me transpired when Williams and I ended up alone. I was getting ready to leave the studio bathroom. The door flew open, slamming against the doorstop. In charged Jerry, looking crazed. As I started to step around him to leave, he muscled himself in front of me. He then pressed me against the bathroom wall.

He pulled out a vial and spoon and did a bump.

When his eyes returned to focus, he stared at me.

"Do a bump, *man!*"

"No, Jerry. Not now."

I tried to step away, but he pushed me back.

He filled the spoon again and put away his vial.

"Do this bump."

I shook my head.

Grabbing my face, he tried to push the spoon up my nose. I was twisting my head, so it ended up in my mouth. Somehow that satisfied him, and he let me go.

Working with Clapton reminded me a bit of what it was like when I worked with Van Morrison. When artists of that stature are in town recording, other big stars take an interest. I remember one afternoon before we'd started recording with Clapton, the studio secretary told me that I had a phone call.

"Who is it?"

"Eddie Van Halen, holding for you on line one."

I picked up the phone.

"Ted, Ted? It's Ed. Are you in the studio with Eric Clapton?"

"Yes. Do you want to say hi?"

"Yeah!"

Suddenly he'd have second thoughts.

"Oh, hang on, wait a minute. I'm kinda nervous."

I'd encourage Ed, and then put Eric on the line. Ed was big admirer of Clapton, so I knew he was thrilled to talk to him. Ed called a few times. He'd ask for me first, hoping to talk some more to Eric. Sometimes when he called I could tell he was buzzed, but I knew that was because he was so nervous about talking to Clapton.

Looking back on those Ed and Eric moments, it's just another reminder of how my relationship with Ed continued despite our disagreements during the making of *1984*. He was my friend; we'd had difficulties but, as far as I was concerned, that was in the past.

Meanwhile, even though the songs we recorded with Eric came together well, it wasn't an easy process for me. I'm a lousy co-producer. It creates too much indecisiveness in how I approach things. I always end up second-guessing myself, whereas when I produce alone, I don't take votes or overthink things.

To do my best work, I need to lock in on a track and try to make sense of all the moving parts, from arrangements to performances. During the Clapton sessions, I'd be in the midst of that process, and Lenny would want to talk about an aspect of the song, say a bass fill, one that I'd already made my peace with. "Have you thought about this part?" Because I so trusted Lenny's judgment, I'd start second-guessing myself and I'd have to circle back to where I'd begun. In the end it would quickly become information overload for me.

It was especially challenging when I was trying to coach one of the musicians and that happened. It didn't have anything to do with Lenny, who was my lodestar when it came to production and, like me, was trying to make a great record. It just didn't work for me. Lenny sensed my unease, so he would do things like let me handle the drummers. He'd say, "Ted, just go and take care of it." I'd then go and talk John Robinson or Jeff Porcaro through their parts. In retrospect, it probably would have been better if we'd clearly defined our specific roles as producers on these songs before we began.

On the other hand, it was interesting to collaborate with Phil Collins and think about how the songs he'd done with Eric fit in with the ones we were tracking.

Of the three songs that Lenny and I produced that ended up on *Behind the Sun*, I like "Something's Happening" best. Man, that song had really gotten stuck in my head when Williams first played it on the piano for Lenny and me. He was so talented as a writer.

Eric's version has its charms, and I enjoy listening to it, but as the producer I can hear its flaws too. Jerry and Eric sounded wonderful when they sang together. The high background part I believe is Jerry. The snare sound, too, is interesting. It's very deep — it almost sounds like a tom-tom. But I think Lenny and I didn't get the feel right; the song just doesn't move right for me. It's just a mistake we made, as co-producers, but I can hear the problem with the groove now; I should've heard it then.

I initially liked "Forever Man" significantly less than "Something's Happening." Even after "Forever Man" was a big hit for Eric, I'd turn it off when I heard it on the radio. But I've come to like it more over the years. It's a good little song, with some wonderfully soaring, liquid solos. His voice sounds especially rich on that one too.

For me, the most significant stamp I put on this record was layering on the percussion. For instance, on "Something's Happening," I played shaker and tambourine. But really, my calling card as a producer, perhaps more than anything other sonic element, was congas and timbales. I'm almost embarrassed because those instruments are on almost every album I ever did (except the hard rock stuff like Van Halen). But I always wanted them on my records because I just loved the way they musically moved things along.

I actually played the timbales on "Forever Man." I wasn't a virtuoso, but I'd played them live at things like the Lowell George Memorial Concert. I remember cutting that song live in the studio and having a lot of fun with the rest of the musicians. I could see Eric smiling while we were all playing, which felt good.

Towards the end of the sessions, Jerry, Eric, and I were at the studio. I was assembling the desired takes and comping some vocals. They continued to get on fabulously. They told me they were going out to dinner and would be back in a bit. I kept working. After a few hours, I wondered what the hell happened to those guys but didn't think much of it.

The next day, Eric and Jerry were MIA. No one was particularly concerned with what Jerry was up to beyond the fact that we knew we'd likely find Eric with Jerry. The whole thing was a drag, though. Here we are trying to finish a record, and we've got staff from Warner Bros. paired up with Eric's manager Roger Forrester, trying to find our artist.

This went on for two, three days. Nobody knew where they were. Roger was worried sick, as were Lenny and I. We're sitting at the studio, spinning our wheels, because we need Eric to finish up his overdubs.

Finally, Roger, who had my assistant in tow, tracked them down at a luxury hotel in Westwood. After he knocked and got no answer, Roger asked hotel security to open the door. When Roger and my assistant got in the suite, they didn't see Eric, but Jerry was sitting naked on the floor of the main room, surrounded by empty liquor bottles, a bunch of blow, and a couple of hangers-on.

Roger, to his credit, didn't lose his very British sense of humor, despite the serious nature of the situation. He stood there staring at the pathetic sight of Jerry, fleshy and loll-eyed. And then he yelled, "Eric? Eric! *I told you this would happen to you if you drank again!*" I know how it went down because my assistant filled Lenny and me in after the fact.

So that's where Clapton had gone. Those guys were partying their asses off, which sucked for a number of reasons, not the least of which was that Eric had been sober for years.

Eric's indiscretions took the wind out of our sails for a week, but we managed to get him back into the studio and finish the record.

In the early fall, Dave, Big Buddy, and I worked in Los Angeles at Lion Share Studio to put the finishing touches on *Crazy from the Heat*. Our first priority was to finish Dave's vocals. Jeff and I had done Dave's vocals the same way that Donn and I had done them. At the Power Station we had him sing each song a few times. At Lion Share, we now comped his vocals (we constructed master vocal performances for each song from the multiple vocal takes he'd done in Manhattan) and did vocal repairs: we had him sing certain parts of the songs again to patch up flaws in his performances.

I remember feeling aggravated with Dave because he was in such a rush. He was eager to get finished because he was heading to New Guinea in October on one of his Jungle Studs trips.

Dave's timing wasn't good. Here we are trying to finish the project, and he's leaving the country for nearly a month. It was totally irresponsible of him, because we weren't anywhere near finished. We had to do all of these overdubs, and the artist wasn't around for any of it. Basically he went on vacation while Jeff and I were finishing all the work on the EP. There was a certain vacancy in his head, but he was a big star at the time.

To give "California Girls" the lush harmonies that had made the original so timeless, I reached out to two of the best singers I knew. I first called Christopher Cross, whose first two records had sold big for Warner Bros. and who had one of the smoothest voices in the business.

I then asked Christopher to reach out to Carl Wilson of the Beach Boys to see if he'd sing with him on the song. I'd not talked to Carl for years, but I'd first met him when I was a member of the Tikis and we opened for the Beach Boys at Foothill College back in 1964. Christopher was nice enough to make that call, and Carl agreed, so we got both of them together in Amigo Studios. It was great to see Carl after so many years. He was the same sweet person, and he said his brother Brian was excited when he heard the news that Carl was singing on Roth's version. That gave me a thrill. I wish Brian could have joined in too, because beyond his talent, he's as nice as Carl. At the time, though, he was wrapped up in his therapeutic-professional relationship with his psychologist Dr. Eugene Landy, who had Brian on virtual lockdown. Carl and I talked about Brian's phenomenal record as a songwriter. Carl got a distant look in his eyes, almost like he was thinking back on their whole career, and said, "That Brian sure is something." I could only nod in agreement. Back in the sixties, Brian and the Beach Boys were neck and neck with the Beatles, and that was a testament to Brian's genius.

Carl and Christopher made a great team. The harmony vocals on the song were spot-on perfect.

When Dave came back to the States a few weeks later, he had some good stories about his adventures. He danced with the local people and painted himself up. He told me about the differences in food between villages in New Guinea. The conversations were fascinating.

When the EP came out in January, I was very surprised at the splash it made. Dave's right-hand man, Pete Angelus, who's an immensely creative person, and Dave, put together these two hilarious, memorable videos for "California Girls" and "Gigolo" that took MTV by storm. Now I knew Jeff and I had captured some outstanding performances by Dave and everyone else and that we'd made a great-sounding little record, but Jesus, when "California Girls" and "Gigolo," two novelty songs, started running up the charts? I didn't expect that. On paper, Christopher Cross, Carl Wilson, and David Lee Roth together, in 1985, didn't seem like the formula for a Top 5 hit. So it took me totally off guard. Suddenly Dave, the solo artist, was all over late night TV, MTV, and the radio. I'd underestimated the EP's appeal and, by extension, Dave's appeal. He made himself even bigger than "Jump" had made him.

Then next thing I heard, Dave and Pete wanted to make a comedy movie, starring Dave. Initially I was told the movie would be a Van Halen project, but to be honest the idea didn't excite me at all, especially after the "Pretty Woman" clusterfuck. I'd been around Hollywood enough at this point to know how difficult it was to get a script green-lighted. So for there to be this focus on making a movie, which could all be for naught, just seemed to me like something that would stand in the way of getting the next Van Halen album underway.

The other thing I was hearing through the label grapevine was that the other three guys in Van Halen, particularly Al, didn't think much of Dave's solo project. I didn't see it coming, but looking back it's clear now that, particularly for Al, the EP was one of the dealbreakers when it came to putting up with Dave. He hated it then, and I'm sure he hates it now.

Because the EP so angered those guys, in retrospect I wish I'd avoided doing it. My intentions were good, but it didn't have a salutary effect on Ed's personal situation and it certainly didn't have a good effect on the band itself. Like I've said, I thought it would keep Dave happy, keep the band (by way of Dave) in the public eye for a few months while the four Van Halen guys worked out their differences and Ed got himself right.

And again, I wasn't hellbent on producing the next Van Halen record. My attitude was that 1984 had taken a lot out of us all, and if Donn and Ed wanted to do the next album themselves, so be it. I had a number of projects in the pipeline — the next Mike McDonald solo record, the next Sammy album, and Jeff and I were about to get Aerosmith rolling again. In fact, in the spring of 1985, when Van Halen was coming apart, I was focused on pre-production for Aerosmith's next record. At this point, I just wanted to see the four guys in Van Halen reconvene, work out their differences, and keep the band going.

It was in the spring of 1985 when I got a call from John Kalodner. He asked me if I'd work with Aerosmith on what Geffen Records hoped would be the band's comeback album. (The band had fallen on tough times by the late seventies and had seen its commercial prospects decline sharply in the eighties.) I had worked on Sammy's record for Geffen, so it made sense that John would seek me out again. I was especially intrigued because I'd be producing the band's original lineup: vocalist Steven Tyler, guitarists Joe Perry and Brad Whitford, bassist Tom Hamilton, and drummer Joey Kramer. I also talked to their managers, Steve Barrasso and Tim Collins, and they too sounded enthusiastic about my participation.

Soon after, I flew into Boston to meet with the Aerosmith guys. I drove to their rehearsal space, which was in a suburb of Boston called Somerville. They practiced in this bare-bones but cavernous garage. In fact, it was big enough that they could pull their cars inside of it.

I remember one of the guys, I think it was Joey, had a Saab parked inside their facility. When I saw his car, I admired its unique lines and told him I liked it. He chuckled.

He said, "Thanks. You know, a Saab's a drinking man's car."

"Why's that?"

"It's got a curved roof. When you roll it over, you end up back on your wheels."

Jokes aside, when they played, they showed that they still had it. Like all superlative bands, there was this chemistry — this alchemical magic, especially when they settled into a groove.

When we talked afterwards, I said that while I liked their early records, I didn't think their runaway-train, rhythmic interplay had always been properly captured on record. It turned out that they were big fans of my Montrose records, especially the debut. I told them I wanted to produce them and get that live Aerosmith dynamism on tape.

Soon after I returned to Los Angeles, I inked a deal with their management and with Geffen Records to do the album, which would be entitled *Done with Mirrors*.

Since the band was Boston-based, I traveled there a few times in April to do pre-production. I stayed in this great little hotel in Cambridge, overlooking the Charles River.

Over the next few weeks, we'd meet in Somerville. I spent a lot of time rehearsing them. The more I did, the more jazzed I became about doing the record. Tyler's an amazing talent; he could sing his ass off, and even when he'd just scat along with some new jam the band had cooking, he sounded great. Perry's the composer of a riff — "Walk This Way" — that's right there with "Satisfaction" in my mind.

At rehearsals I saw Joe come up with a bunch of promising ideas. At the same time, he and Whitford meshed so seamlessly, you could tell they'd played together forever. You had a rock-solid rhythm section to support the two guitarists. Hamilton doesn't miss a note, and Kramer's a human metronome. Watching them play off each other, in fact, reminded me of the Sausalito nights at the Ark back in '66 when I saw Buffalo Springfield.

When we shared ideas, I made it clear that I was less interested in their string-laden ballads than their shambolic, swaggering rock stuff. I wanted to get that explosive rawness, reminiscent of the Stones, with two slashing guitars and a sassing Tyler, on tape. What I didn't want was something slick, polished, and pre-packaged, overthought and overproduced.

The other thing I saw as essential was keeping the focus on the band as a whole. Aerosmith was a well-synchronized unit with no weak links. These were all high-performance players. It wasn't a situation where a virtuoso player or a magnetic lead singer carried all the other guys in the band.

That's the lightning I wanted to catch in a bottle.

After we'd firmed up their new songs, the six of us got in a room at Collins and Barrasso's office in Boston to talk more formally about plans for recording.

Now a day or two before, I'd met with Steven to talk arrangements. We'd discussed a number of things, including the fact that I thought we might need to tweak a guitar part in one of their new songs once we got in the studio.

As soon as Joe arrived at the meeting, he looked pissed off.

He said, "So, Teddy . . ."

"Yeah?"

"Ah, what is it about my guitar playing that you don't like?"

"What?"

"I hear you don't like way I play."

Steven started to fidget. He had a mischievous look on his face.

"Who said that?"

"Steven said you don't like the way I play."

I glared at Steven.

"What the hell is going on here? I didn't say that, Steven."

Steven smiled and hemmed and hawed before backtracking, saying he must've misunderstood what I'd said to him.

I told Joe and the rest of the guys what I'd said to Steven, observing it was an arrangement issue which had nothing to do with the way any of them played.

But you see, Steven was a shit-stirrer who liked to push people's buttons. So he turned around and told Joe I didn't like his playing. He loved getting under Perry's skin.

In any event, that episode highlighted their very different personalities. Steven was usually loose and laughing. Joe was much more serious.

Those guys showed me around Boston. They knew all these hole-in-the-wall places to eat. They knew all the great restaurants, especially the seafood places. We had a great time when we hung out, but I remember some of the conversations transpired without smiles. They told me about how they'd fallen from the pinnacle of success. Both Steven and Joe had really bottomed out, and had lost all of their money — millions — and fast cars and huge houses along the way. Joe told me stories about watching his favorite pieces of furniture, including this gorgeous antique desk, being taken out the front door by debt collectors. He said, "That's never going to happen to me again." So there was a steely determination there.

Those guys, particularly Steven, had at least taken some steps to overcome their demons. But they weren't totally sober, and of course I wasn't sober either. Still, I tried to be supportive and to keep myself in check around them. I went with them to AA meetings in the Boston area, including at the McLean Hospital's East House, where Tyler's had recently gone to rehab.

So no, I wasn't a perfect influence. We'd sometimes stay up all night and party while we worked. But those guys did have it in their mind to go straight — although I think what was most paramount in Tyler and Perry's minds was avoiding a return to their darkest days of addiction.

In June, the guys, Jeff, and I got together at Fantasy and started recording. As I've explained, it wasn't my favorite studio, but Collins and Barrasso wanted us in Berkeley rather than Los Angeles or New York. The two managers seemed to think that those big cities offered up more potential temptations to the guys. But come on — Berkeley is twenty minutes from Oakland, where you could score dope at the drop of a hat. So in the end, the location didn't keep any of us clean.

Still, the bigger issue for me was the studio itself. If I'd had my druthers, we would have used Sunset or, even better, the Power Station, the studio that Jeff knew inside and out. I kept thinking about the killer snare sound Jeff had gotten on "Gigolo." As I knew firsthand, Fantasy was not the Power Station.

So while I understood management's concerns, and wanted to be supportive, it didn't do wonders for my ability to produce. To me, sitting behind the board in the right studio was as important as sitting behind the wheel of the right car at the starting line in a Formula 1 race.

When we first got into Fantasy, we stumbled out of the gate. What they'd played perfectly in rehearsal felt stiff and out of synch when we recorded.

So I performed a little sleight-of-hand. I put Tyler in the booth and the four other guys together in the big room. Jeff would be in the control room, behind the board. I'd then announce to everyone through the talkback that I was going out to get something to eat. I'd say that while I was gone, they should run through the songs again so we can keep smoothing out the rough edges.

Meanwhile, without telling the band, I'd gotten Jeff all ready to record. I went as far as to have Jeff disconnect the red record lights in the studio. I'd make a production of leaving the control room, waving to them through the glass. A few minutes later, I'd crawl back into the room with Jeff, beneath their line of sight. I'd duck beneath the console while they blasted away. Jeff kept a poker face while they ran down their tunes. They thought they were just rehearsing. Meanwhile, Jeff's sitting there, nodding to the beat, recording as we ran down all the tunes.

When they finished, I'd emerge from under the board.

I know some of the guys later questioned my approach, but experience was my teacher. As a recording artist, I learned how easy it is to choke once the red light illuminates. I didn't want those guys to overthink things; I'd already heard them firing on all cylinders back in Somerville. I wanted it raw and I wanted it real and we did get great live takes on tape. The truth of the matter is, once they got rolling, they could stand alongside any band I ever recorded, in terms of being able to play as a unit in the studio.

Looking back, though, I didn't do my best work as a communicator or technician on *Done with Mirrors*. For example, I didn't explain to Joey why I wanted a close-miked, thumping drum sound for the record rather than the live, ambient sound he wanted. It had to do with the fact that we weren't working in a room, like Sunset 1, that was conducive to getting a big, booming drum sound. That came back later to haunt me. I also couldn't dial in an identifiable guitar sound for Joe. In that case, I was really focused on getting a trashy, almost punk sound on record, rather than making sure his guitar sounded distinctive. In terms of that unified, ragtag Aerosmith sound, I got close to what I wanted, but in general, I missed my mark on a few things on *Done with Mirrors*.

The other challenge was that Steven and Joe didn't quite have their songwriting mojo back. I kept waiting for those guys to come up with a couple of vintage, instant-classic Aerosmith songs, and it didn't happen. We redid "Let the Music Do the Talking," a great tune that Joe had cut on one of his solo records. But a lot of stuff, especially Steven's lyrics, got finished at the last minute and wasn't quite as good as it could've been. Even though I bought them as much time as I could, we didn't end up with a song or two strong enough to break the album at radio.

Still, I think a lot of the material was solid. "Shame on You," is a great, funky track, with a classic Aerosmith cock-of-the-walk riff. "Gypsy Boots," which reminded me a bit of early Zeppelin, is another one I thought smoked. Tyler — with Perry on backgrounds — sang great on it, and his jive-talking, breathless delivery, when coupled with the Aerosmith locomotive beat, captured what I saw and heard when I'd rehearsed them back in Somerville.

Maybe my favorite on the record was "My Fist Your Face." That one is so goddamn good; I love the groove. I remember Steven came to me after he'd written the lyrics and explained that they documented his time at McLean's East House, so it's a song about recovery from drug and alcohol abuse. He sang about praying for relief from the tortures of addiction, and about the different people he met in rehab, particularly a character he dubbed Julio Afrokeluchie, who was one of the only guys in treatment with Steven who didn't try bolting the barn. Before we recorded vocals, he'd tell me the story behind his lyrics. Every one of his songs on this record came from some event that happened to him. That was one of the things I liked best about working with Steven. As a lyricist, he reminded me of Roth. They both had a real way with words.

I had so much fun with the Aerosmith guys, both in and out of studio. Almost every morning, Steven would slip a note under my door at the Fairmont with some sort of witty comment. One day, I remember he came in to record vocals. He's stretching out his back and groaning.

"What's wrong? Did you throw your back out?"

"No, man. She had me tied up all night in my hotel room in a hammock."

I didn't ask.

After we had the album mostly completed, we all went to Los Angeles to finish things up. I don't remember why we booked Can-Am Recorders in Tarzana, because it was another studio that I hated. I'd done some of Sammy's record there and it was no fun to have to go back. I didn't like the way it was set up, ranging from things like where the speakers were in the control room to how the big room was baffled. I'm guessing Jeff and I used it again because it was the best available studio we could find in Los Angeles for the days we needed to work.

Still, we managed to have a good time there too. By far the most memorable moment of the entire recording process happened there during a vocal session. Steven had some very enthusiastic female companionship at the studio that day. Before things got too crazy, I placed gobos — acoustic partitions used for preventing bleed between instruments while recording — in the booth, so from where Jeff and I were sitting in the control room we could only see him from the waist up.

We rolled tape. Steven sang along to the instrumental track in his headphones. He stood at the mic while his friend went down on him. When Jeff soloed his microphone, you could hear him singing, *and* all of these other noises. Jeff and I laughed so hard we could barely breathe. We actually kept that take. If you pulled the multitracks today and soloed that vocal, you'd hear *everything* that went on while he was singing. It was true old-school rock 'n' roll.

At Can-Am, too, I remember I'd get calls from Dave. He'd be asking things about his movie, about me doing the soundtrack. I wasn't into the idea of doing a film. I just didn't give a shit about that stuff. I didn't want to get mixed up in the movie world, and even soon after, when I did work on films like *Lethal Weapon*, I did it because of politics at the label, not because I loved soundtrack work.

When I look back on Dave's movie ambitions, I can say for sure that when Dave first talked to me about it, Dave and I never had a conversation about him quitting Van Halen. I never wanted Dave to leave that band. *Ever*. But once that movie thing really got going in early 1985, his head blew up. Then he wanted to be a movie star. That became his dream. I wanted to make music — hence the EP — and keep Van Halen going for the long haul. Once he started with that movie thing, that's when he and I didn't collaborate as much, because making a movie held no attraction for me.

Now, you'd think, considering how monumental an event it became, that I'd remember where and when I was when I heard Van Halen had split. Hell, I don't even remember who told me. All I know for sure is that I found out while I was working on the Aerosmith record. At that point, the press hadn't gotten wind of the breakup, so I know someone in Van Halen's orbit called and told me. The fact that I don't recall many specifics tells me that I didn't think it was going to be a long-term, much less a permanent, parting.

Meanwhile, I stayed busy. Along with finishing the Aerosmith and Mike McDonald records, I started pre-production for Sammy's next album for Geffen. We planned to start recording it in September.

Sometime shortly after I heard the Van Halen news, maybe around mid-June, I called Sammy to discuss the follow-up to *VOA*. In more than a few interviews, Sammy has said that apparently I told him during that conversation that Dave had recently left Van Halen.

I don't remember saying it to Sammy. But if I did, I only mentioned it in passing, because it had nothing to do with why I called him. I can say that with certainty, because here's the absolute, unvarnished truth: *I never, ever would have wanted Sammy, or any other singer, to join Van Halen in 1985*. I wanted Dave in that band, period. And I wanted Sammy on his own, because he had built some solid momentum on his last record and I was looking forward to helping him take the next big step forward in his career.

Soon after, Sammy and I talked more extensively about his next album. I asked him to consider taking an artistic left turn by working up some sixties-style R&B songs. The thing is, when he first got on my radar when Ronnie Montrose had hired him as a vocalist, I heard him sing soul tunes, stuff by James Brown. In fact, that's the direction I thought Sammy was going to go in after Ronnie disbanded Montrose, because Sammy is a unique talent who can, in fact, sing like Robert Plant *and* James Brown. But he really wanted to do hard rock, so he pursued that sound during the decade that followed his stint in Montrose.

I explained to Sammy that I envisioned making a contemporary-sounding record, but one that had its roots in Stax/Volt and Motown. To really make things cook, I wanted to hire the Tower of Power horn section and drummer David Garibaldi to back Sammy. I emphasized to him that his versatility as a vocalist hadn't fully been explored on record yet. Everyone knew he was a monster hard rock singer, but as his producer, I knew he could also sing like Wilson Pickett, or even like a bluesman, if given the right material to showcase those talents.

One comparison I made was the live album I'd done with Van Morrison, *It's Too Late to Stop Now*. That's the kind of band situation, and repertoire, I had in mind for Sammy. I knew Sammy was a Van Morrison fan, so I thought that *Too Late* would be a good point of reference for him. So that's what I wanted to phase in for Sammy, because I saw some untapped potential that could be the basis for a great new chapter in his career that would broaden his popular appeal as an artist.

Sammy was noncommittal and seemed underwhelmed. I asked him to keep an open mind, and said that of course I'd produce his album regardless of whether my initial ideas appealed to him.

Over the coming weeks, I remained confident that a Van Halen armistice would be coming soon. When Dave and I talked, I made it clear that I hoped they'd work things out, even though his movie project seemed to be the most important thing in the world to him that summer.

I had good reasons for my optimism. Look, there's nothing unusual at all about band infighting. There's almost always some sort of unease among band members. It can run from simmering resentments and petty jealousy to explosive anger and physical violence.

I'd seen it myself in the bands I produced.

So my gut feeling was that they'd all come to their senses soon and that Dave and Ed would patch things up.

I was wrong.

At the height of summer, I got word that Sammy and Ed had met through Claudio Zampolli, who owned a repair shop in Van Nuys where they got their Italian sports cars serviced. Ed and Al had called Sammy, and he made a beeline for 5150 and rehearsed with Mike, Ed, and Al. It went well, and now they'd invited him to join Van Halen.

Sammy Hagar arrives in his Ferrari on his very first day visiting 5150, summer 1985. Not long after this photo was taken, the other guys in the band would invite him to join Van Halen. DONN LANDEE.

I was not happy.

Neither was David Geffen. Sammy, who was one of Geffen Records' bestselling artists, owed Geffen Records three more releases. Now, along with being a *great* A&R guy, David Geffen has always been relentless in pursuit of his own ends. David wasn't going to release Sammy from his Geffen contract so he could waltz into Van Halen — a Warner Bros. act — without David getting a significant cut of any Van Halen–Sammy album.

There was another complicating factor involving the two companies. David Geffen wanted to do another distribution deal between Warner Communications and Geffen because the current contract, originally signed in 1980, was set to expire around the end of the year. But Mo made clear he wasn't going to rubber-stamp another Warner-Geffen deal just because one of our company's key acts, Van Halen, wanted a Geffen artist to join its lineup. So a stalemate developed between David and Mo, and for some weeks it wasn't clear whether Sammy was going to be able to join Van Halen.

Eventually, however, both deals got resolved in terms favorable to David. Geffen Records hung on to Sammy as a solo artist for one more album, and would receive a percentage of the sales of the next Van Halen album, assuming Sammy sang on it. David also got a new, five-year deal from Warner for Geffen Records.

Now, I can't blame Sammy for wanting to join Van Halen. They were America's biggest band and were coming off their most successful album and tour.

But the thing is, what Sammy did isn't much different than the guy who puts the moves on a wife who has recently separated from her husband. That kind of outside influence, coming when feelings are raw and unsettled, just kills the chance for any reconciliation. Sammy, in effect, gave the three Van Halen guys something to embrace as they said goodbye to Dave. Again, I respect Sammy as a musician and consider him a friend, but I truly believe that if Ed hadn't connected with Sammy through Claudio, Dave would have returned to the fold and Van Halen would have eventually repaired itself.

But now, with Sammy in the picture, both sides dug their heels in. Dave had resolved to do his movie with Pete Angelus and was putting another band together, and Sammy and the Van Halen guys were acting like quadruplets reunited after being separated at birth.

Now, I knew Ed and Donn wanted to produce the record on their own, but as I recall, Lenny convinced them that they still needed an outside ear in the studio with them.

Soon after, I had a lunch meeting with Sammy and his longtime manager, Ed Leffler. Over beers and tacos at a restaurant in North Hollywood, Sammy came to me at the behest of Van Halen.

"Come on, Ted, let's all of us do this Van Halen thing. Produce the record for us."

The question hung in the air.

I sighed and said, "No, I don't want to do it."

They both looked shocked.

I can understand why. Because I'd had a long and successful relationship with both Sammy and Van Halen, I became an obvious choice to them as a producer.

But what Sammy and Leffler, and Ed and Al for that matter, couldn't seem to fathom was the deep attachment that I had to the band that I'd signed, meaning Dave, Ed, Al, and Mike.

Without Dave, the band wasn't going to feel right to me. For all of the enthusiasm I had for Ed's writing and playing and everything that Mike and Al contributed, I also put tremendous value on what Dave brought to the table. With a different singer, Van Halen's sound and feel was going to change. I wanted that original Van Halen vibe, the one that I'd fallen in love with in 1977 and had kept me excited about working with them album after album. In that sense, it wasn't so much a question of whether

I wanted Sammy to join Van Halen, because I didn't want any other singer in that band.

After I said I didn't want to do a Van Halen album with Sammy singing, Leffler and Sammy both got agitated. Sammy was really upset. He said, "Ted, you've *got* to produce this!"

I said, "Look, I just can't do it. It's not personal, but without Dave, it's not Van Halen to me."

After I said that, Leffler lost it. Glaring at me, he growled, "This is my big chance!"

"I am not going to do it. Period."

The lunch didn't end well. Those guys left in a huff.

This meeting generated a lot of fallout. When Leffler and I next talked, he told me that Sammy felt that I'd really let him down by not leaping to produce the Van Halen record, and that my idea about Sammy doing R&B had "broken Sammy's heart." I didn't quite get why Sammy was so upset about the latter. I had this honest-to-God, impassioned vision for Sammy — of this James Brown, Soul Band, rock 'n' roll thing — and I pitched those ideas because I wanted him to evolve as an artist, and somehow he felt insulted. He took it personally, thinking that I didn't like his rock material, which wasn't true. I saw a growth opportunity, and of course I wouldn't have suggested it if I didn't think Sammy had the requisite chops. But Sammy has this blue-collar, lunch-pail mentality. He's a rocker at heart, and that's the space he wants to occupy as an artist.

I also told Leffler, and Sammy too, that I just couldn't get past the fact that they'd be calling themselves Van Halen without Dave in the band.

Soon after, I got wind of the subsequent conversation between Ed and Sammy. Ed called up Sammy to find out why I didn't want to produce them. He told him, "Ted said it's not Van Halen to him with me singing with you guys." Ed said, "Yes it is! My name — my brother's name — is Van Halen!"

I'm sure my hangup about the band name hurt and insulted Ed and Al, but that wasn't my intention either.

Sammy lobbied me some more. He really wanted me to produce the record. So I bent a little, and said, I'd do it *if* they changed the band name. Then I could live with it. I was thinking that maybe with Sammy in the mix, the vibe up at 5150 wouldn't be so dark, and making a record with Ed, Al, and Mike could be fun again.

I can't overemphasize the fact that I *loved* working with Sammy. His energy, optimism, and vocal expertise — he's an absolute monster in the studio — always made him a joy to produce. So that was my final offer. Change the name, and I was on board.

I said, "Well, call it Van Hagar, or something else, and I'll do it."

So I threw them a bit of a curveball there.

I wasn't trying to be difficult. It was just how I felt. I remember Lenny backed me on this, going as far as visiting 5150 to try to convince them not to use the name Van Halen. Ed was indignant, saying, "Hey, it's my name."

So they pushed back, and said they didn't want to change the name, but that to me was a symptom of the issue — one I couldn't get past. It wasn't Van Halen. It was Sammy and those three guys, you know? The original Van Halen, to me, represented something singular. There are a lot of aspects to this, but when you really get down to brass tacks, Van Halen isn't Van Halen to me without Dave and Ed, together. In my mind they were like Led Zeppelin, the Rolling Stones, or the Beatles. You can't have Zeppelin without Page and Plant. You can't have the Stones without Jagger and Richards. You can't have the Beatles without John and Paul.

Those guys didn't want to change the name, so ultimately I said no.

Later on, they suggested that I didn't want to produce their album because I'd "chosen" Dave over Van Halen. That wasn't true. And it also wasn't true that scheduling interfered. I could have done both records, because at that moment in time, Dave was knee-deep in his movie project and was nowhere near a recording studio.

I can only imagine how those guys felt. First Dave quits, and then I turned them down. I suspect Ed, in particular, felt betrayed and abandoned, but I don't think he saw things clearly. He came to believe that Dave and I thought, "Forget Van Halen. Let's just focus on a solo career for Dave." But that wasn't what it was about at all.

What really drives me crazy is that Ed seems to have lost sight of the fact that Dave and I did the EP because we just wanted to work. On multiple occasions we'd go up to 5150 and we'd get nothing done. I still don't think Ed has the faintest inkling that our frustrations during the making of *1984* were a big part of why Dave and I did the EP. I think Ed thinks we just wandered off and went to do our own thing at the Power Station. It's kind of crazy to think of this part of the Van Halen breakup saga as a misunderstanding of our motivations, but that's what happened.

In any event, the die was cast, and they'd broken up. Now I know it's hard to grasp in retrospect, because they stayed split for decades, but in 1985 I had hopes that the original lineup would reunite once their respective album cycles completed. I know Lenny thought the way I did as well. I thought maybe they'd each do one record — Dave as a solo artist, those guys with Sammy, and then we'd have a reunion of the original lineup. That's what I wanted to happen.

In the meantime, they blamed a lot of it on me. Years later I read an article that quoted Sammy saying something to the effect of "Since Dave was the enemy when I joined Van Halen, Ted Templeman became an enemy to us too." The brothers directed a lot of ire at me because I worked with Dave. I think Ed and Al were always afraid of losing Dave, and then when he left, they blamed me because they thought I stole him away.

In the summer, Dave started putting together a band. Beyond being David Lee Roth, his movie project was the perfect enticement to get the greatest players, because they'd both cut songs for its soundtrack and appear in it with Dave. The first guy he recruited was the virtuoso bass player Billy Sheehan. He started looking for a guitar player next.

One guy I pitched to Dave was Billy Idol's guitarist, Steve Stevens. That summer, I'd signed him as a solo artist to Warner Bros. Records. My son, Teddy, had turned me onto his killer playing on Billy's records and then later I came away impressed after I saw him play live with Billy in Santa Barbara. One big reason I wanted to work with him was that he'd been influenced by Ronnie Montrose's sonic innovations — those out-of-this-world ray gun effects from Montrose's "Space Station #5" — which he'd used on Billy Idol's hit "Rebel Yell." I knew Steve was preparing to take the next step in his career, so I suggested him to Dave. Unfortunately, Steve and Dave couldn't make the scheduling work between Dave's movie plans and Steve's commitments to Billy Idol.

After that, Billy Sheehan put former Frank Zappa guitarist Steve Vai on Dave's radar. After Dave told me he was considering Vai, I endorsed the idea. I made a point to scout the best emerging guitarists on the rock scene, so I'd heard Vai's *Flex-Able* solo album, which was great in its Zappa-esque craziness.

So soon after, Dave and I got together for a quick meeting, in a parking garage of all places. He put a boom box on his car fender and played me a beat-up, noisy cassette of Vai's best stuff. We listened to a few tracks and talked. At the end I said to Dave, "Yep, that's the right guy."

I was less involved in his selection of drummer Gregg Bissonette. But once Dave informed me Gregg had played with jazz legend Maynard Ferguson, I was sold. I knew that any drummer who could land that gig was going to be a killer.

Meanwhile, I was finishing up Aerosmith. The final steps of the process, unfortunately, ended on a sour note. Jeff and I had mixed the record at the Power Station in August. It was being mastered, so it was on its way to release. Around September, Joey Kramer got a test pressing and called me at my Santa Barbara place. He started yelling at me, "The drums suck! I hate them!"

He just reamed me, so I lost my temper. Soon I was yelling back, "Fuck you, Joey! Fuck you!" I'll never forget it, because it was so out of the ordinary. It was one of the only times I really had a knock-down, drag-out fight with an artist.

Truth be told, he had a right to be mad. In the studio, he told Jeff and me that he never much liked the sound of the drums we'd been getting on tape. If I'd been working at Sunset, I'm sure I could have made them sound much better. He thought they sounded screwed up, and Jeff and I weren't able to fix it in the mix.

Later on, I ran into him. He said, "I'm sorry about yelling." I said, "Me too." He's a good guy, and what a monster he was in the studio. Honestly, Joey's one of the best rock drummers I ever worked with, and could have been a studio session player. I wish I could have done better by him.

We had big expectations when the record came out in November, but it didn't chart as well as we hoped. It crested at No. 36 on the *Billboard* Top 200. Without a big single, it's hard to expect more out of a straight-up rock record.

A sheet of lyrics given to me by Steven Tyler of Aerosmith, soon after the release of *Done with Mirrors*, November 1985. TED TEMPLEMAN COLLECTION.

After the record didn't set the world afire, I started to spend a lot of time second-guessing myself about its songs and sound. I had this killer band, and the album didn't connect. So I didn't like *Done with Mirrors* much in the aftermath of its release. But decades later, I've come to love it. In fact, it's one of the few records out of the dozens that I produced that I will regularly listen to these days.

I like it now because it's so stripped down. A lot of the guys in the band wanted to dress it up more, but I wanted it to be more live and raw. It's got this abandon to it, and to me, that's the essence of Aerosmith's greatness.

By the fall, Dave was going great guns on his movie. I'd agreed to produce the soundtrack, but Dave and Pete were handling a lot of the initial legwork. Dave was working on finding artists to contribute music to the film, which he'd pair with the original material that Steve and Billy were writing.

At the time, I was hearing whispers that his movie deal was on thin ice. I had enough friends and contacts in Hollywood to know that it wasn't unusual for movie deals to get torpedoed, so I took the rumors seriously. In addition, when I went to our weekly A&R meetings, I'd hear doubts from my colleagues that Dave could have a successful recording career without Van Halen. All of this just reaffirmed my belief that Dave needed to get back in Van Halen.

Eventually, what I feared might happen with Dave's film came to pass. He lost his deal at the tail end of the year. Dave and I talked and came up with Plan B. Instead of doing a movie soundtrack, we set out to make a rock record with his new band.

I got together with Steve, Billy, Gregg, and Dave, and went right back into the basement at Dave's house. His band was just killer. I was blown away by the musicianship. These guys were the best of the best. They could play anything from fusion to funk, from metal to Motown. The band did lack a songwriter as talented as Ed but, let's face it, how many guys can write like Ed? Still, we had some good originals and could flesh out the record with some killer covers.

Now even though we'd stayed away from anything resembling heavy rock on the EP, I thought, let's go balls-to-the-wall with metal and stack that alongside the big band, vaudeville stuff that had been on the EP. I figured we could make an album that could tap into Van Halen's traditional sound, kind of like *Diver Down* meets *Fair Warning*. The album we'd make could never match a Van Halen album by the original four guys, but I wanted to try to get as close as we could. With Billy, Steve, and Gregg, I knew I could do it all. Thus Dave and I wanted to make a record that would continue the Van Halen tradition of performing material that ranged from thumpers like "Romeo Delight" to sing-alongs like "Happy Trails."

That said, I didn't want to dial up an Ed-like guitar tone for Steve or make Gregg's drums sound like Al's. I wanted to keep it in a different space, sonically, altogether, while still capturing that Van Halen spirit. Inevitably, there were going to be comparisons, and so I didn't want to sound like a carbon copy of the older Van Halen albums.

And to be sure, Dave didn't and I didn't want it to sound anything like the new, synth-heavy stuff that Ed had been writing recently. We wanted it to be loud and leering, fun and ferocious. All of this lit a fire under us and got Dave's and my competitive juices flowing.

So Jeff and I and the guys went back into Fantasy in late November. We started by laying down "Tobacco Road," "Goin' Crazy," and "Shyboy." As Jeff and I always did, we tracked everything right off the bat, so we could get the basic tracks down on tape. These guys were so good that a lot of the instrumental stuff that ended up on the record came from these first takes.

"Shyboy," in particular, was just killer. That one's a good example of how we tried to allude to Van Halen without cloning it. Listen to the guitar, for example. Steve's playing is technically masterful, but I think in terms of tone and approach it was in a different zone from Ed's. Gregg, too, didn't play like Alex. He was great in a totally different way. So I wanted to keep it in a separate space, sonically, altogether.

One interesting side note: I heard later that when Ed first listened to "Shyboy," especially that insane ending Billy and Steve put together, he got upset, because it was so over-the-top technically brilliant that he interpreted it all as a personal challenge to him. Now I don't think Billy and Steve sat around trying to think of ways to outdo Ed, the best guitarist in the world, but "Shyboy" was Dave's effort at one-upmanship, to be sure.

We also did the basic tracks with Dave's band for Sinatra's "That's Life" at Fantasy. It was a fun song to get on tape. To evoke the spirit of the original, I hired the Sid Sharp Strings, a veteran string section that had worked a million big sessions, including the Beach Boys' *Pet Sounds*, to accompany Dave and his band. To record the strings, I rented the same Hollywood room that Sinatra used back in the sixties: Western Studio 1. (By this time, however, United Western had changed its name to Ocean Way.) Lee Herschberg, who'd engineered some of those very same Sinatra sessions at Western that I'd witnessed ran the board while Jeff assisted. Most of the young engineers at the time, including Jeff, had little to no experience recording an orchestra. Lee, in contrast, had been doing those kinds of sessions before I ever got into a recording studio, so it was a no-brainer to get Lee involved to work with Jeff.

To be honest, Dave didn't deliver a technically great performance on "That's Life." But with Dave's singing, it was never about his chops. It was about bravado, enthusiasm, and personality. In addition, that song allowed him to showcase a different facet of his talents — it was Big Band, rather than Big Rock, Dave. It was in a lot of ways far afield of anything Van Halen would have ever done, but still had that Van Halen spirit.

In the first months of 1986, we paused work on the album. I can't recall all the details, but I know Dave and Pete had sued

CBS for breach of contract, and had to do depositions and what-not, which ate up a lot of their time. I also seem to recall that Dave was searching for another company to pick up his movie project and continue where CBS had left off, so those efforts may have distracted from the recording process as well.

Around the same time, I got a call from Ed. He asked if I'd help him and Donn sequence their new album. I said sure. Soon after, Ed and Donn visited me at my Burbank office and played *5150*, the forthcoming Van Halen album, for me. We talked about the tunes and I gave them my suggestions about how they should order the album's songs.

After all of the fire and fury surrounding the Van Halen split, it might seem odd that those guys would come to me for advice. But I'd sequenced all of the Van Halen albums — and pretty much every album I ever produced or co-produced — so it made sense that they'd come to me for an outside opinion. Ultimately, it underscores that even though there were bruised feelings and egos involved on all sides, when the chips were down I always tried to help Donn, Ed, Al, Mike, and Sammy. We had our differences, but I never had any lasting animosity towards them.

In the late spring Dave told me he was ready to resume. We reconvened at the Power Station and finished the bulk of the album there.

The scene at the studio hadn't changed. In the lounges and the hallways, you'd rub shoulders with the hottest stars and producers. I remember seeing Cyndi Lauper and Dave sitting around, laughing, while I was mixing. It was like listening to two stand-up comics doing their routines right next to me. They had me in tears — she's as witty as Dave. Nile Rodgers was working in another room in the facility. There was always a ton of star power in that place, which gave it a special atmosphere.

At the Power Station, we cut another set of songs, most notably "Yankee Rose," "Big Trouble," "I'm Easy," and "Ladies' Nite in Buffalo?"

That last song is one of the highlights of my career. Sultry and laid-back, it conjures up a perfect languid summertime vibe, thanks to Dave's brilliant lyric about cruising in the darkness with the top down, the cool night air blowing through your hair.

This track, too, really showcases Vai's abilities. He's so goddamn talented! Paradoxically, his only real weakness as a player was that he was so methodical. A schooled musician, he'd write charts before we recorded a note. He'd also create these very elaborate demos, with all of these interlaced parts, guitars stacked on top of guitars. Oftentimes I felt this kind of approach affected his ability to be spontaneous.

I don't think he realized how good he was, and he was so fastidious about everything he would do. I'd have him play live in the studio, and he'd always have a certain amount of abandon on his first take. But he didn't realize the value of that. He always thought he'd fix it, or double it, not seeing that the vibrancy of that one-off live take was magical.

That's pretty much what happened when we cut "Ladies' Nite." Steve presented me with a demo for the song with quite a complex arrangement. I tried to steer him away from an instrumentally dense approach, explaining that I didn't want the song to come off sounding orchestrated instead of live. He wasn't very receptive to what I was saying.

So I approached the "Ladies' Nite" session in a manner not dissimilar to the way I'd handled things with Aerosmith. I announced that I wanted to record a rough version, telling Steve that he'd be able to add his multiple guitar tracks at a later date. So we recorded it live — Dave sang while the three guys played.

Afterwards, I took a tape of "Ladies' Nite" to my hotel room. I listened back, and thought, *Damn, the musicianship is just perfect.*

Gregg, Billy, and Steve had just nailed their parts, and Dave had delivered the perfect breathy, laid-back vocal. I was so happy.

So now I had to tell Steve that I'd pulled a head fake on him. The next day, I let him know his guitar part — which at that point was just a single track — was great, and we should leave well enough alone. He looked at me like I'd lost my mind, but I eventually convinced him. We may have added a couple of guitar overdubs to flesh things out, but for the most part the guitar on that song is Steve's live performance.

Because the new generation of studio equipment had gotten so complicated, Jeff and I took a different approach to mixing than the one Donn and I had followed for years — really, up to the making of 1984, when everything changed. Prior to then, when I mixed with Donn, we'd start by working together at the desk. Then I'd leave him alone for a few hours, so he could take a crack at it by himself. He'd get a rough mix down that he liked. Then some hours later, I'd join him at the board again, and we'd work together. Donn would take a break, and I'd mix alone for a while. He'd return, I'd leave again, and he'd continue mixing. I'd come back once again, and we'd work some more. Before long, we'd be on the same page about how we wanted things to sound and we'd be done.

By this time, though, the technology had surpassed my technical abilities. I couldn't run the board at the Power Station, for instance, on my own. So Jeff and I didn't trade off like Donn and I had done. Jeff did a lot more of the mixing on his own. Then I'd come in and give him feedback on what I liked or didn't like about what he'd come up with for a mix. That approach worked well, especially because I thought it was helping Jeff prepare for a future career as a producer. So Jeff was making a lot of the calls that I would have made in the past.

Before the record came out, I went down to a soundstage for Dave's video shoot for "Goin' Crazy!" I saw Pete Angelus, who was overseeing the shoot. Then this actor, dressed in a fat suit and dripping with gold chains, lumbered up and started talking to me in character. I played along, laughing with him and Pete. After a minute, the actor said, "Ted, it's me! Dave." I had no idea. You couldn't even tell it was him inside that thing! It was really hilarious.

When I heard the record after it was mastered, I was really pleased. I thought *Eat 'Em and Smile* sounded amazing. That was a testament to how great Dave and the guys performed, but also to Jeff's abilities. I never directly heard this from the Van Halen camp, but I think it probably surprised the Van Halen guys and Donn both that I was able to go to a different studio with a different engineer, and oversee the making of a record that stood toe to toe with what was coming out of 5150, and one, in my opinion, that was sonically *better* than what was coming out of 5150.

The other thing I thought was that *Eat 'Em* was the *exact* record to get Van Halen back on track, because I knew it would be difficult for any honest observer to believe that Dave didn't remain committed to the heavy rock Van Halen had done on their early records when they heard things like "Tobacco Road" and "Elephant Gun." So any narrative that the Van Halen guys might latch onto about how Dave didn't want to rock anymore after Dave's EP came out would completely fall apart after they heard *Eat 'Em and Smile*.

Dave's album arrived in stores in July. At that point, Warner Bros. had already reaped the benefits of Van Halen's 5150 hitting No. 1 on *Billboard* in April, right after its release. Van Halen's singles, too — "Why Can't This Be Love," "Love Walks In," and "Dreams" — would likewise perform extraordinarily well during 1986. Now, this stuff wasn't to my taste, but Ed and Sammy really connected with their audience and the album was a monster. By the end of the year, they'd sold three million copies.

Dave's record would eventually peak at No. 4, with "Yankee Rose" winding up in *Billboard*'s Top 20. It sold considerably less, somewhere north of a million copies. It was a success, but of course as measured against Van Halen, it didn't deliver the same type of commercial benefit to Warner Bros.

In late December, Dave played the Los Angeles Forum. His tour was doing well; he was playing arenas and drawing a Van Halen kind of crowd.

Backstage before the show, I bumped into Sylvester Stallone. It was a cool moment, because he's just about the world's biggest action star, and he actually recognized me. He was a soft-spoken, very nice guy.

Before Dave hit the stage, Stallone asked me if we could watch the show from the sound booth at the back of the floor of the Forum. I said sure.

So we stood out there while Steve, Billy, Gregg, and Dave were onstage doing their thing. The crowd was going apeshit. Suddenly, there was a quick flash and a massive explosion in the air above the booth. *BOOM!* Some dumbass had tossed an M-80 firecracker from the upper deck. Stallone freaked out. He yelled in my ear, "Let's get out of here!" It scared the shit out of him. Sure, it was upsetting and it was too close for comfort, but his panicked response was kind of funny, considering that Stallone was playing all these fearless, war-loving characters like Rambo at the time.

I calmed him down, and we stayed in the booth. It was worth waiting around, because on that tour Dave did this great sleight of hand onstage. There'd be a puff of smoke by the drums, and he'd disappear. Unbeknownst to the audience, the roadies would quickly slip him into an Anvil case and start wheeling him away from the stage. Meanwhile, Billy, Gregg, and Steve did this wild, extended jam. When it ended and they went into the next song,

Dave would be at the back of the arena on a platform, right near the sound booth. It was a cool trick and the crowd ate it up.

After the show was over, I couldn't help but think that the brothers probably hated the fact that Dave was doing as well as he was without them. I never spoke to Dave about this either, but I'm certain he was equally surprised that Ed, Al, and Mike could plug Sammy into Van Halen and remain a huge, big-selling act without him as the ringmaster of the Van Halen circus.

When the two albums had run their course, I hoped against hope that there would be a reconciliation between Dave and rest of Van Halen. *5150* and *Eat 'Em and Smile* had both gone platinum so neither Dave nor Ed and Al would be approaching the other party, hat in hand, begging for a reunion. I thought that with Dave and Van Halen's profiles now higher than ever, Van Halen would be bigger than ever if they joined forces again.

And because Dave's record had showcased their talents so well, Billy, Steve, and Gregg were all in the perfect position to pursue new projects. I knew they'd be fine without Dave, and I know they knew I'd help them the best I could going forward. My whole thing was to get Van Halen back together.

But Ed, Al, and Dave didn't see it my way. The brothers, best I could tell, remained aggrieved because they thought Dave had left them in the dust back in 1985. Plus, they'd sold a ton of records with Sammy, whom they loved. Dave, for his part, was plenty pissed off at Ed and Al too, and even though I knew Dave wanted to find a way to get back with Van Halen, his ego was such that he'd never admit it.

So my whole plan that I'd hatched while we were doing *Eat 'Em* — to find an opening to convince Dave to get back with Van Halen — never amounted to anything. That was tremendously disappointing.

Chapter 14

BACK TO 5150

At the end of 1986, I started talking to the Aerosmith guys about doing their next record. They'd deserved a better effort from me and I desperately wanted to redeem myself for not doing my best work on *Done with Mirrors*. Those guys, too, wanted to get it right. Joe and Steven had gotten sober and were eager to make a great Aerosmith record. So all of us wanted a second chance.

My birthday is in October. Steven sent me an unbelievably raunchy and hilarious birthday card that year.

I went back and forth with Steven and Joe a bit more. We started kicking around ideas; in effect, we'd initiated the pre-production process. That said, they needed to hash it out as a band and with their management before we finalized things. I told them to let me know what they wanted to do, because I wanted to do the record.

Shortly afterwards, I got a call from Collins. He said, "The guys are ready to go. They want to know if you'll do their record." We'd get started early in 1987. I told Collins that I needed to check about my schedule, and I'd be back in touch very soon.

As excited as I was about Aerosmith, I felt compelled to visit with Roth to see what he had planned in terms of a follow-up to *Eat 'Em*. I'd produced every recording he'd made since 1977, so I felt a certain degree of loyalty to him.

So I called Dave. I said, "Dave, do you want me to do your next record?"

He said yes, telling me that he wanted start work in early 1987.

This meant that his record would conflict with the Aerosmith record.

I told him that.

"You're sure we're on? This is really important because I'm going to give up the Aerosmith record to do a record with you."

"Yeah, we're on. I guarantee it."

So I called Aerosmith and said, "I can't do it."

I was bitterly disappointed, but Dave and I had a long relationship and an enviable record of success.

In January, Dave called me and said he wanted to meet about his new record. He asked me to come to his office in Hollywood. He had this threadbare, dumpy place over on Sunset Boulevard.

He ushered me in before sitting behind his desk. We talked for a minute and then, out of the blue, he went into executive mode.

"Ah, Ted, I think I need a new producer."

Needless to say, I was pissed. I tuned him out as he talked for another minute or two, and then I left.

Right then, Dave picked my pocket of a million dollars, easily. But I wasn't all that upset about the money. At the time, I had more money than I could've ever fathomed when I was a kid running barefoot through the woods up in Felton.

I made records, spent precious time away from my kids and wife, because I loved the music. My days were all about making records. I'd go to my office at Warner Bros. in Burbank in the mornings, Amigo in the afternoons, Sunset Sound in the early evenings, and then go home.

I had beautiful houses I didn't get to enjoy. I'd buy these

Ferraris and Porsches, and barely had time to drive them. I never went on vacations. When I traveled, it was for work. I didn't do anything other than work, most of the time. So what good was more money to me?

Sure, I was pissed Dave fired me. But more than anything else, the way he did it pissed me off. Here he is behind a desk, terminating me like I was like a guy who'd done a bad job painting his house. He was a prick about it.

Even worse, I suspect Roth fired me when he did so I *couldn't* do the Aerosmith record. I was an asset to him when I was helping him sell records, but when he decided he fancied himself a producer, he was sure as hell going to make sure I didn't go to work for the competition.

So all those endless hours of work, fighting through bad take after bad take, planning and dreaming with him about how to make great music — it was all behind us with not even a thank you.

Here's the thing. It bothered me less that he fired me than it bothered me that he blew my chance to do another album with Aerosmith. I *loved* working with them, in no small part because they were such amazing musicians. And they've got Steven Tyler, another genius lyricist. So this whole episode was a bitter disappointment.

Ultimately, it all worked out well for the Aerosmith guys. I was happy for them that *Permanent Vacation* became a smash, and I thought Bruce Fairbairn, whom they picked to produce the record when I bowed out, did a very good job. A hit is a hit, and he delivered. He also produced an album that was more overtly commercial than *Mirrors*, which was more in line with what Kalodner wanted. From an A&R perspective, he was looking for something else than what we gave him on *Mirrors*, that's for sure.

While all this played out, Lenny asked me to work on the soundtrack of the forthcoming Mel Gibson and Danny Glover buddy picture, *Lethal Weapon*. Doing soundtrack work wasn't exactly my cup of tea, but I did it to be a good team player.

In any event, I needed to find a Warner Bros. rock artist to perform the title track for the film, which had been written by Michael Kamen. I ended up selecting a young, promising Canadian quintet called Honeymoon Suite. Jeff and I did the song with them, which ended up playing during the end credits of the film and appeared as the leadoff track on the soundtrack.

Early in 1987, some old friends decided to do some good works. The Doobies organized a reunion to do a short tour to raise money for some charities, most notably causes that supported Vietnam vets. Keith Knudsen and Bruce Cohn got the ball rolling by reaching out to former members, and within a few weeks they had commitments from almost everyone: Tommy, Mike, Pat, Jeff, Tiran, John McFee, Corny, Bobby, Chet, Mike Hossack, and John Hartman. Bruce soon organized a short tour consisting of a dozen dates in May, including a culminating performance at the Moscow Rock 'n' Roll Summit. This would be their first time back together since their farewell tour in the late summer of 1982.

They were nice enough to ask me to participate. So I joined them onstage in San Diego and at the Hollywood Bowl and played the congas alongside Bobby LaKind. It was great to be around all of those guys again; it brought back so many memories when we played songs that covered the band's full history, from early hits like "China Grove" and "Black Water" to the later singles like "Minute by Minute" and "Real Love."

The tour was very successful. The shows were packed and the audiences were rabid, much to the surprise of some of the guys, including Pat, who'd concluded that the rock scene considered the Doobies dinosaurs. Perhaps best of all, the tour raised something like a million dollars for charity.

In the wake of the shows, my sister, Roberta, began floating the idea that the Doobies should consider writing and recording a new album for Warner Bros. She put a bug in my ear about it, and I started calling the guys around July. Mike McDonald, at that point, was fully invested in his own solo career and didn't have an interest in returning to the fold permanently, so I looked to reconstitute the *Toulouse Street* lineup of the early seventies.

As the pieces fell back into place with the Doobies, the Honeymoon Suite guys invited me to produce their third album, *Racing After Midnight*. All of us had good chemistry when we worked on the *Lethal Weapon* soundtrack, so I agreed to do it. During pre-production, when those guys were in writing mode, I got Mike McDonald to help them polish one of their songs, "Long Way Back." In the end, the project got delayed because the band's singer, Johnnie Dee, got hit by a car at LAX in December 1987, just as we were finishing up the record.

Unfortunately, in part because the Honeymoon Suite project got bogged down, I had to pass on the Doobies. At that point, they had interest from Geffen and Capitol, so I wasn't hanging them out to dry. Ultimately, in March 1988, they signed with Capitol. That made good sense for them because at that time Joe Smith, who'd been instrumental in signing them to Warner Bros. back in 1970, was now president and CEO of Capitol.

Soon after I finished up Honeymoon Suite's album, Roberta gave me a tip about a Sunset Strip pop metal group called BulletBoys. She was militant about them, because she thought they were reminiscent of Van Halen, and so she pushed me hard to go see them. So I went down to their rehearsal room, which was in a rough part of Los Angeles, and listened to them as they ran through their material. Their drummer Jimmy D'Anda recalls that I arrived there in my black Rolls Royce. I don't remember that, but Jimmy swears it's true. In any event, they played their songs for me that day, and soon after, I signed them.

Before we went into the studio, we demoed their tunes. Then I rehearsed them for a week or so, and picked the songs for the record. We ended up going into the studio in the summer of 1988 with more loose ends when it came to arrangements and writing than I usually felt comfortable with, but I thought the guys were up to the task.

To be honest, the thing I liked least about them were their lyrics. They were a bit too in-your-face for my taste. I didn't like the words to songs like "Hard as a Rock" and "Kissin' Kitty." They were too graphic, too sexual, but they did fit with their overall vibe.

Jeff and I worked at One on One Studios in Hollywood. Toby Wright, who has gone on to have an amazing career as a producer and engineer, served as the second engineer.

It was fun working with those guys. They were young and hungry, and honestly, I almost always got my best results as a producer when I worked with new, unproven acts from their first album forward than I did when I worked with established bands that had released prior albums with a different producer. I remember they had a version of "For the Love of Money" by the O'Jays. I thought, *Wow, this is a great tune for them.* So I worked on the arrangement, starting with the drums. I had Jimmy D'Anda, their drummer, play a backbeat. As we pieced it together more fully, I jumped on his drums and showed him what I had in mind. That's what I loved doing — disassembling songs, considering the strengths and weaknesses of the different parts, refining them, and reassembling the tunes. Nicolette had her own funny metaphor for my arrangement process. She used to call it "rearranging the refrigerator."

What stands out most in my mind is the tremendous job Jeff, with Toby Wright's assistance, did on mixing and engineering one of their best songs, "Smooth Up in Ya."

At that point, I had to leave Jeff to his own devices when it came to mixing, because as I've mentioned, the board had gotten so complicated that I was a bit out of my depth. But I knew we'd be in great shape. After all those years of working at the Power Station, Jeff could do these things with the board that I couldn't dream of doing. He could dial up all these great sounds. So after I got Jeff started in the morning, I went to my office. That evening, Big Buddy called me and said, "I think I've got it." I went over there, and he played it for me.

I remember sitting there in the control room of One on One, listening to a playback of the song. He'd been at it for hours on end. He was totally exhausted. I listened, offering suggestions about tweaking this part or that part. Throwing me a desperate look, he said, "It's perfect. Please let's leave it be. It's right." He was totally drained. He was pale and I thought he might pass out from the hours of stress and concentration. When I hear the song — with those great performances from all the guys, plus Jeff's mix — it gives me the chills. All of it does. He was right. It was perfect. And the fact is, he couldn't have gotten "Smooth" right with me sitting there saying how about more of this and less of this. He needed to do that mix on his own.

For all of the talk that Ed and I didn't get along after we made 1984, we worked together again in the studio before the eighties ended.

At the close of 1989, Ed called me. He asked if I could help him produce the second album by a radio-friendly rock act signed to Warner Bros. called Private Life. They had a female keyboard player and vocalist, and a great guitar player, Danny Johnson, whom Ed had known forever. He and Donn had done their first record, but from what I recall, at this point Donn and Ed had stopped working together, leaving him without an engineer and partner to work on the record. I said sure. I brought Jeff Hendrickson and Lee Herschberg in to engineer, and we recorded it at One on One and Amigo.

I don't think we'd even finished the basic tracks on the record when I got an unexpected call from Valerie. It was New Year's Eve, 1989. Sounding panicked, she told me she needed me to get to their Coldwater Canyon house immediately. Ed had gotten into a heated argument with her father and he'd punched Ed in the face. He hadn't meant to hit him as hard as he did, but regardless, Ed was in a bad way. Valerie, understandably, was incredibly distraught. I hauled ass from my Santa Barbara place to their house. When I got to see Ed, he looked horrible. The side of his face was purple and blown up like a balloon. I helped her get Ed into the car and we raced to the emergency room at St. Joseph's hospital in Burbank.

I stayed with them that night while she put the wheels into motion to get Ed into a month-long treatment program for substance abuse. It's a reminder to me, when I think back, of how much affection I had for Ed. I love the guy. I did and would still do anything for him. I hated to see him like that, but I was proud that he was willing to stare down his demons.

Once Ed got well and got his life back on track, Jeff, Ed, and I went back into One on One with Private Life. One thing that I recall was that I encouraged them to cut a cover of Van Morrison's "Domino."

During this period, Ed and I hung out a lot. That's when we were going to AA meetings. We'd go to what was called the "Musicians' Meeting" over on Lankershim Boulevard in Hollywood. It was good for me to go to these meetings for my own personal health, but I also enjoyed them because the scene was always interesting. You'd go into the meeting and see lots of old friends who were trying to get their lives back on track.

At that time, I was going through stretches of abstaining from alcohol. I'd get sober for a year, then I'd backslide. A big part of that was cocaine, because before I did coke, I had no interest in drinking. In other words, before I turned thirty-five, I almost never drank. But when I started using cocaine, I'd drink some champagne or wine to take the edge off my high. So cocaine and alcohol were an insidious combination for me.

At the same time I was finishing Private Life with Ed, Jeff and I were also doing Mike McDonald's forthcoming record, *Take It to Heart*, as well. During pre-production, I had suggested that Mike cover the Percy Sledge song "When a Man Loves a Woman," which had been a No. 1 hit back in 1966. I got the idea after seeing Mike do it at this small venue, the Wiltern Theater, in Los Angeles back in December 1985. His performance just *killed* me. It was magical. The audience was paralyzed — spellbound. Mike, meanwhile, had no idea how great he did that song. It was a song he was born to sing, and it would fit perfectly on his new album.

So we'd started laying it down in the studio. Mike had sung it a couple times. It sounded great.

On a break, Toto's Jeff Porcaro, who was playing drums on the session, walked over to Mike and me. He looked at Mike and asked, "You really want to do this song?"

Mike got this deer-in-the-headlights look.

Mike said, "No."

Right then, I knew it was over. I was so pissed off.

Now understand, Porcaro was a studio god to everyone from huge stars like Mike to the second engineers just getting started in the industry. But in some ways Mike was especially susceptible to Porcaro's opinions. Along with appearing on scores of hit albums, Porcaro had played on those early Steely Dan albums like *Pretzel Logic* and *Katy Lied* — that's the same time period when Mike had gotten his first big break when Fagen and Becker of Steely Dan hired him to sing backgrounds. So when Porcaro said what he said, Mike took it as gospel.

I wanted to choke Jeff, because it wasn't his place to chime in there like he was co-producing the record. But I could understand why Mike McDonald didn't want to do "When a Man Loves a Woman." When you listen to Percy Sledge sing it, there's such intensity. It's almost like sacrilege to cover it.

Anyway, I couldn't stay mad at Jeff for long, because the truth is, very few guys could play drums like him.

One of the special moments on this album for me was getting Jeff, Mike, and one of my heroes, saxophonist Stan Getz, to play on "You Show Me." I'd been an admirer of Getz since I was still in elementary school, when I first heard his incredible playing on some of his early records. Along with Bud Shank, whom I had play on Carly's album, Getz was one of my favorite jazz players. Mike had written this impassioned, heartfelt tune, one that, when you listened to him sing it, you could tell was coming from a deep place. As soon as we demoed it, I thought of Stan. His playing was lyrical, smooth, and gorgeous.

Getz was one of these elite musicians who wasn't going to bother playing a session for a straight union rate. When I called him, he agreed, as long as I fulfilled his requests. So I had to send a Cadillac limo to Malibu to pick him up, and provide him with bananas with no brown spots and a certain kind of yogurt so he could snack in-between takes, or it was no deal. Van Halen's no-brown-M&Ms backstage rider request was simple compared to what Getz wanted.

But there was no question whether I'd get him what he wanted. When it comes to sax playing, there's nothing like Stan Getz. He's as identifiable as Miles Davis or Ed Van Halen. He's unbelievable, and he didn't disappoint in the studio that day.

Something unsettling did happen when I was working on the record with Mike. I think Mike and I were in a control room together at One on One. Out of nowhere, Ed showed up. I'm not sure what he was up to that day; maybe he'd come down to visit someone who was recording in another room. He spotted us, so he came into the room smiling. "Hey Mike! Hey Ted! Howya doin'?"

Mike looked uneasy. I made small talk to try to dispel the awkwardness. It was all so uncomfortable for me, because Mike and I had both tried to put the "I'll Wait" issue behind us. It didn't come up, but it was the elephant in the room. Even stranger to me was the fact that it wasn't like Ed was trying to smooth things over with Mike; it was more like he didn't remember what a big ordeal that had been for Mike and me.

In January 1991, Ed called me. Out of the blue, he asked me to come work at 5150 with producer/engineer Andy Johns to help finish the in-progress Van Halen album. He said, "Ted, can you come in and crack the whip?" In other words, he wanted me to help them get things in order and make sure their record got delivered to the label in a timely manner.

After making 1984, I certainly could imagine how things up at 5150 could have gotten off schedule once again. Ed's a brilliant, creative guy but he was never very organized or focused on deadlines. Those tendencies only get exacerbated when you record in a home studio. When you're making a record in a room that you own, there's no mounting rental costs like there would be at a big-name, professional facility to help keep an artist focused on finishing an album.

Still, I was taken aback — in no small part because he had Andy up there. Andy had worked behind the board for everyone from Led Zeppelin to the Rolling Stones, so I was surprised they'd need a co-producer. When I heard they'd hired Andy, I figured it would be a nonstop love affair, especially with Al, who'd grumbled to me over the years about how we never got a Led Zeppelin drum sound on a Van Halen record. Andy had conjured up Bonham's mighty beats on "When the Levee Breaks," so he was the right guy for that job.

I said yes.

If you'd asked me, the day before I got this call, whether I'd ever produce a Van Halen album again, I'm sure I would have said no. But here's the deal. Those guys, Ed and Al, did have something of a complicated relationship with me. Periodically they'd get themselves all worked up about something that happened with *Diver*

Down or the mix on one of the early albums and complain to a journalist. But when we all got in the same room, they'd behave themselves — no matter what. Always. Plus, like I did with all my artists, I showed them the same respect in return. I'd always listen to their ideas, and when they asked for help, I gave it. So when Ed ran into a jam, whether it was with his private life or this record, he'd call me, because he knew he could count on me.

Almost immediately after I spoke to Ed, Sammy called. By this point, all the stuff we'd been through back in 1985 was water under the bridge. Since then I'd spent time with him in the Bay Area. I'd been to his home in Mill Valley a couple of times. On one of those visits, he took me to a mountain bike shop that he owned, Sausalito Cyclery. I was really impressed with it; it was huge and bustling with activity.

When we talked about the Van Halen record, he had a less cheery view on what was going on at 5150 than Ed. Andy had apparently erased a couple of things by mistake, including one of Sammy's vocal tracks, and tried to hide it from the guys. When Sammy found out Andy had wiped one of his vocal performances, he lost his shit.

Sammy's one hell of a singer, so he wasn't angry because he thought that he couldn't get another great vocal recorded. You could drag Sammy out of bed, put a mic in front of his face, and he'd give you killer stuff. His ire grew out of the fact that artists feel a tremendous sense of accomplishment when they get something great on tape. I'm sure Sammy felt exactly that way about what he'd sung, only to find out later that it had been erased. Sammy's an easygoing guy, but even he has his limits. He was *pissed*. He refused to record any more vocals with Andy.

Ed, sensibly, suggested that Andy and I get together and discuss how to finish the record. I'd not met Andy before, so I told Ed to give Andy my number.

Andy called. I'd barely said hello, and he started insulting me. He was enraged that Sammy and Ed had called me. I'd been in the business a long time, but this was the most abusive call I've ever endured. He spat insults, calling me a "fucking little blond asshole," which of course I knew was his attempt to scare me off the project. I'm not sure if his main motivation was ego, territoriality, or money — by co-producing, I'd be cutting into his take — but beyond the fact that I wanted to help the Van Halen guys out, I had a responsibility as a Warner Bros. senior executive to do whatever I could to get the record done.

After he realized he wasn't going to be able to dissuade me from co-producing, I suggested we meet for lunch. He chose the place.

As soon as the *maitre d'* at this restaurant eyed Andy, I could tell he'd encountered him before. The establishment wasn't anywhere near full, but he said they had nothing available. When I pointed to the open tables, he leaned in and said, "I'm sorry, but *he* can't come in here." I couldn't imagine meeting Andy in public again, so I pressed the issue. Exasperated, he said, "Okay, sir. I am going to put you in the very back." It wasn't hard to figure out that the management didn't want Andy around other customers. Once we settled in, Andy proceeded to tell me that he'd be in charge of the sessions and that I was a terrible producer, all while he drank himself into a stupor.

Even though my first meeting with Andy had been a miserable experience, I showed up at 5150 soon after and worked right alongside him in that small control room, listening to what they'd gotten on tape to date. The whole time, Andy was giving me grief. He was just unhinged. It was not fun.

So my next task was to finish Sammy's vocals. I seem to recall the two of us considered doing them at Ocean Way in order to steer clear of Andy. But eventually we decided to record at Ed's place.

Because Sammy wouldn't work with Andy, I called in engineer Lee Herschberg. To avoid a scene, Ed and Al must have talked some sense into Andy, or found a way to keep him away, because he generally vacated the premises while Lee and I worked with Sammy. It still was a weird deal, because the general atmosphere was that we were working surreptitiously, in a way that wouldn't end up on Andy's radar. Anytime you're trying to do something when you're working on an album, which is supposed to be an all-in team effort, and you're kind of sneaking around, it's not a good thing. But it was what we needed to do to get the vocals done.

In the studio, Sammy kept his eye on the ball — which at this point meant getting this record *done*. We'd get together and go over his lyrics. I'd offer suggestions and we'd kick around ideas as we revised. Then he'd do his vocal. If there was something he didn't like, or I didn't like, or we both didn't like, about the way he sang something, he'd fix it on the spot. He was very professional and very organized, which, when you're surrounded by reels of tape and trying to see the way forward to finish a record, is a producer's dream. There was attention to detail and a focus that was superb.

If memory serves, those guys were largely finished with the instrumental tracks when I got involved in the project. So once we finished the vocals, we did some punch-ins and overdubs, and then Andy and I set out to mix.

It was not fun. When Andy would come in to 5150, he was such a huge presence, especially in that small control room. He was like a giant grizzly bear. He was confrontational and gruff, but Ed loved him and Al wanted his Bonham drum sound.

Sammy, despite his issues with Andy, did his best to bro with Andy as much as possible. Andy, meanwhile, insulted Sammy on a regular basis. Sammy was always trying to keep it together so we could finish without the sessions blowing up. Sammy's a real pro.

I tried my best to get on with Andy. Occasionally, he'd relax a bit and talk to me as a peer. He was a well-read, knowledgeable person — a bright guy. But alcohol was his nemesis.

While his guard was down he told me he was under enormous financial pressure. He'd overextended himself, and was worried that the bank was going to foreclose on his home. So I gave him twenty-five thousand dollars, no strings attached, to pay his debt. He was a good guy at heart, but he was a very insecure person.

Somewhere along the way — I don't remember if this started before or after I started working on the record — Ed and Andy became drinking buddies. Al was sober at this point. Andy would hang at the studio with Ed and get hammered. Eventually the session would end. We'd offer to call him a cab. He'd say he was fine to drive. He was so big and strong that none of us could've taken his keys away, so that was out of the question. He'd clamber into his Cadillac convertible and drive down Ed's driveway. Ed, Al, and I would just shake our heads, because more often than not he would hit the retaining walls on his way down to the gate. You'd hear *bang, bang, bang,* one crunch and scrape after another as he ping-ponged from wall to wall.

As far as the songs went, I liked some of them better than others.

I dig "Spanked," especially the mix Andy and I did on it. Ed, who played bass on the intro, delivered a kickass performance here. His bass sound is so interesting; it sounds like a stumbling, drunken dinosaur. Sammy's lyrics, about calling up a sex hotline, were tongue-in-cheek and funny, but they remind me why I had reservations about Sammy joining Van Halen. His writing on "Spanked" would've fit perfectly on his *VOA* album; in my mind, they just seemed out of place in the context of a Van Halen album.

I liked Sammy's writing on "Top of the World" better. Sammy helped make that one commercial; it has a straightforward chorus that everyone could relate to when they listened, and it serves up the kind of effervescent, optimistic Sammy Hagar lyrics, especially in the first verse, that I prefer. To me, Sammy is at his best as a singer when he sounds like he's having the greatest time of his life. That's how he sounded on "Top of the World."

Despite all of the problems they had during the making of the record, by the time we wrapped up, Sammy and Ed were in heaven. He and Ed had a bromance going before that word was ever coined. Those guys loved this album. They thought we'd all done great work together. Sammy was a one-man cheering session through all of it; I can't overstate how important it is to keep things upbeat and fun while an album's in progress, because some days are going to be tough, even under the best circumstances. Sammy always knew how to keep everyone smiling, and I had enormous admiration for the way he rose above the issues with Andy to get the record finished.

The record, *For Unlawful Carnal Knowledge*, came out in the summer of 1991 and was an instant smash. Debuting at No. 1 in *Billboard*, the album sold millions. "Right Now," in particular, became a phenomenon at MTV.

To celebrate their success, Van Halen invited me to attend a couple of awards shows. In September 1992, I went to the MTV Video Music Awards over at UCLA's Paulcy Pavilion. Those kinds of shows are always as much about people watching as they are about the awards presentations. I remember Howard Stern, who was promoting his new movie, was walking around in a costume with his ass cheeks hanging out of cutouts in his pants. That was memorable. After the show, I saw Steven Tyler. We were talking, and then Sammy spotted us. He joined our conversation, and then those guys proceeded to compare notes about me while I stood right next them. They were busting my balls, basically saying, yeah, he's a pain in the ass as a producer. It was a funny moment.

After I finished the Van Halen album, I produced the soundtrack for the comedy movie *Wayne's World*. As I've said, I never loved working on movies, but it was a fun project. I had the BulletBoys cover a Montrose song that I'd produced back in 1973, "Rock Candy." I blew the dust off Eric Clapton's "Loving Your Lovin'," a Jerry Lynn Williams song that Lenny and I had worked on during the *Behind the Sun* sessions. I also oversaw the recording sessions for the numerous musical transition pieces, played by a band of session guys, that director Penelope Spheeris wove throughout the film.

But the best part of the whole experience was getting to know and produce the vocals of the film's female lead, Tia Carrere. She played Cassandra Wong, the singer of an up-and-coming band, so she sang a few songs for the film soundtrack. When I met her, her beauty was overwhelming. Man, she's a total knockout. When we talked, I realized that she was going to be a dream to produce, because she was nice, unaffected, and interested in learning how to become a professional singer.

The recording sessions were a bit harried, because she had a rigorous shooting schedule and so we always had to work around what Penelope had planned. But Tia rolled with the punches. On days we worked, she used to come pick me up at my Century City condo in her convertible and drive me to the studio, so we'd have time to talk about what I had planned for the day. After our sessions, she'd drive me back home.

She wasn't a trained vocalist, but she was a hard worker who was a pleasure to produce. She was always so up, funny, and bouncy. As a result, the studio musicians were happy as can be. So for the soundtrack, I produced her vocals for the Sweet's "Ballroom Blitz," Private Life's "Touch Me," plus Dwight Twilley's "Why You Wanna Break My Heart." I was so proud of her when we were done, even more so when I went to the premiere and got to see her performing them on the big screen.

Chapter 15

IT KEEPS YOU RUNNIN'

In the fall of 1992, the culture at Warner Bros. started to change in ways I didn't like. It became particularly noticeable after the chairman and co-chief executive of Time Warner, Steve Ross, died in December of prostate cancer at age sixty-five. He'd been a fixture at the company since 1972 and had been instrumental in leading it to the heights of success. In addition, he'd played a key role in the merger between Warner Communications and Time in 1989. At that juncture, the new conglomerate, Time Warner, was the world's biggest media company. I'd matured as a record producer and executive under his tutelage and considered him a friend. It was a big loss for all of us.

Mo maybe took it harder than anyone at the company. He'd lost his close friend, but he'd also lose the sense of relative autonomy that had helped him make Warner Bros. Records such a special place to work. For decades, Mo, chairman/CEO of the label, had reported directly to Ross (and after the Time Warner merger, Time's CEO Gerald M. Levin and Ross). But after Ross's death, that arrangement came under scrutiny. Levin, perhaps understandably, saw it as peculiar that Mo didn't report to his direct superior, Robert Morgado, who was chairman of the Warner Music Group (WMG). Aloof and impassive, Morgado wasn't a record man. As far as I could tell, he wouldn't have cared if he sold toaster ovens instead of CDs. He was a numbers guy all the way, so Mo didn't respect him. Within the formal WMG corporate hierarchy, the heads of Atlantic, Elektra, and Warner Bros. Records reported to Morgado. In practice, Mo answered to Levin alone, and paid Morgado little heed.

All of that soon changed. In late 1993, Mo met with Levin to discuss his next contract, suggesting that Lenny, then president of Warner Bros. Records, should share CEO duties with Mo for a time, until Mo stepped aside and Lenny took over. Levin rejected Mo's succession plan, and added that he expected Mo to report to Morgado.

Mo bristled.

In July 1994, Morgado made his own move. Creating a new position within the company, he named Atlantic Records CEO Doug Morris the president and CEO of Warner Music US, effectively making him Mo's superior. This was a poison pill to force Mo's — and Lenny's — hand.

All of this started the clock ticking down to the end of the Warner Bros. I'd known. Mo refused to sign his new contract, and by October, Lenny had made a momentous decision as well. As president of Warner Bros. Records, he still seemed like the logical person to become the next CEO of the label. But he told Morris, Morgado, and Levin that he wouldn't be re-upping with the company either. Mo's and Lenny's contracts would expire by the end of the year. As a result, Danny Goldberg, who'd been Nirvana's manager before becoming an Atlantic Records executive, would get the nod as the new CEO of Warner Bros. Records, replacing the irreplaceable Mo as of January 1995.

As they prepared to depart, I spoke to Lenny about what was next for him. He was noncommittal. He and Mo had everyone in the industry trying to woo them, so he was weighing his options. Back in October 1994, David Geffen had left Geffen Records and formed DreamWorks SKG, an entertainment company, with film studio executives Steven Spielberg and Jeffrey Katzenberg. Soon after, rumors began to swirl that Lenny and Mo were headed there once their contracts lapsed.

I asked Lenny again about his plans. He told me, confidentially, that he and Mo were in fact going to join DreamWorks. Now around this time, I got offered a very lucrative deal from another label. It was tempting, because it was a *big* money deal. Danny Goldberg had also offered me a big promotion and a title inside the company. I told him I'd mull it over as I considered my own future.

I called Lenny. I asked him, "Is there a place for me over at DreamWorks?"

He said yes. So I didn't take the promotion that Danny offered, and passed on the offer from the other label too, because things seemed locked in at DreamWorks.

As much as I felt loyalty to the Bunny and was flattered by Goldberg's offer, I knew things were never going to be the same without Lenny and Mo. There'd been so much turmoil and uncertainty. In April, Goldberg hired Howie Klein and Steven Baker as the new presidents of Reprise and Warner Bros. Records, respectively. Then in May, Levin forced Morgado out and replaced him with the former head of HBO, Michael Fuchs. Fuchs in turn fired Morris in June, and followed that up by forcing Goldberg out in August, replacing Danny with Russ Thyret. I liked Russ. I'd known him for years; he'd worked for the company for decades. But needless to say, things at the top of the company had gotten totally dysfunctional. It was nuts.

I'd been with Lenny and Mo my whole career and wanted to keep working with them. Lenny was my best friend and my mentor. Plus their leadership had shaped the company's unique culture. Hits were never the primary thing for Warner Bros. It was all about signing and nurturing quality artists, because Mo and Lenny knew that great artists, given time to create, would eventually make the company money. That was Mo and Lenny's thing. Like Louis B. Mayer and Irving Thalberg, the legendary MGM movie impresarios of the 1920s, Lenny and Mo favored substance and potential over instant results. They didn't chase trends — they set them.

In early October, the news became official. Lenny, Mo, and Michael Ostin, Mo's son, became the newest members of the DreamWorks team.

So I bided my time, worked, and waited for the other shoe to drop.

But I never got the offer from DreamWorks.

For me, it was a terrible feeling, because I felt like Lenny had let me down. I wish he'd said from the start, "It's *not* a guarantee. It *may* not happen." After I didn't get the job I knew, instinctively, that over the prior months he probably just couldn't bring himself to tell me that there wasn't a position for me at DreamWorks. But he should have just told me the truth, because my options became limited after the fact.

I tried to make the best of it. As an executive vice president and veteran producer, I often got the call to give the final seal of approval on new releases. Thyret, in his role as CEO, and I would do listening sessions, even for established artists. For instance, we'd go and meet with Rod Stewart and his team. Those meetings were almost always formalities. You sit down, have a drink, and listen to an artist's new songs. The protocol is that everybody's supposed to go, "Yeah, it's great."

The same thing happened when Van Halen finished *Balance* with Bruce Fairbairn. I went up to 5150. All the guys were there, along with Ray Danniels, who became their manager after Leffler died in 1993. Trying to be objective, I listened to their new album as an executive, not as a guy who'd produced a bunch of their albums. I made a few observations and asked some softball questions, because as a producer myself, I knew that what ended up on the record needed to be between the guys and their new producer. No producer wants a label executive making a power play after a record's about done, especially one who'd previously produced the band in question. The Van Halen guys had a streak of platinum records going back to 1978, and Bruce was a pro, so they didn't need my nitpicking or endorsement.

In the past, I'd kept my mind off of any personal problems I faced by working all the time. That approach stopped working after the DreamWorks debacle. During most of the nineties, I'd had long stretches of sobriety. But once Lenny and Mo left me behind, I found myself getting depressed.

At night, I just couldn't face the reality of the situation. I'd lie in bed, unable to sleep. But I knew if I took a shot of something, I could escape. It took very little for me to get drunk; I'm a real lightweight. My father was half Cree Indian. I'm not sure if that's why alcohol didn't agree with him, but either way, he passed that trait along to me. In college, I'd have a couple of sips of beer here and there, but I couldn't handle much more. When I did consume more aggressively, my face and neck turned all red, and I felt terrible. My body didn't like alcohol at all.

Remember, cocaine was probably the only reason I started drinking at all. I'd do a bump here and there during marathon sessions to keep my motor running, but after being high for hours I'd get anxious. To take the edge off, I'd drink a bit of wine or champagne. And yes, Sammy called me Ted "Champagne" Templeman. I'd just sip away at it while I worked. I wasn't getting drunk. A bottle of Emerald Dry would last me two or three days. You can hear the Van Halen guys joking about my affinity for that brand in the "Lotta Drugs" send-up of Nicolette's "Lotta Love" that they put together with Donn in 1978. So I wasn't an alcoholic back then. I was just using alcohol to manage the effects of cocaine.

But now, when I wanted to knock myself out for the night, regardless of whether I'd done coke, I'd down two tequila shots, and it was lights out. It was a terrible way to live, but it's what I needed at the time to make it through.

One bright spot for me in mid-1995 was signing a Los Angeles neo-swing band called Royal Crown Revue. There was a big swing revival going on in Los Angeles. These guys had been around for a while, playing the clubs up and down the Southern California coast, and they'd performed one of their songs, "Hey Pachuco!," in the 1994 Jim Carrey movie *The Mask*. Their manager, Dave Kaplan, had turned me on to them, so I went down to the Brown Derby and saw them.

Their energy and sound took me back to my days seeing the Kenton band and all the other jazz acts I'd obsessed over as a schoolboy. They'd updated Louis Jordan's jump blues of the forties and given it a fresh nineties twist. They had this big-band vibe; they swung and had these great horn arrangements. Their material ranged from Sinatra swing to Gene Krupa jungle beat numbers. Musically, every guy in the band from the horn players to the bassist was a terrific player. The drummer was as good as the jazz players I'd admired when I was a kid. So working with Royal Crown Revue gave me a chance to make my first real jazz record.

In the summer, I took them into the studio with Lee Herschberg, who probably knew better than anyone walking the Earth at that point how to get the band's retro sound on tape. The resulting record, *Mugsy's Move*, emerged the following year. It hit the Top 10 on the *Billboard* Top Jazz Albums chart, but didn't cross over into the pop charts like we'd hoped.

In October 1997, as I was doing Royal Crown Revue's second album, there was another big leadership change at the label. Robert Daly and Terry Semel, who'd become the co-chairmen of WMG in November 1995 after they won a power struggle with Fuchs, hired Phil Quartararo, formerly of Virgin Music, as president of Warner Bros. Records. He'd report to Thyret, who remained CEO of the label.

Phil's main claim to fame was that he'd been leading Virgin when the Spice Girls became huge. I liked Phil, but he was a marketing guy. At Virgin, they'd sold a ton of records, but his was not a track record that inspired serious artists to look to him for guidance.

After he came aboard, Phil, Thyret, and I would all be around conference tables with Warner Bros. Records' highest-profile talent. Whether it was Neil Young or Bette Midler, they'd look to me rather than them for advice, because I was a musician who knew how to make records. This was just the way it was. Back in the eighties, I'd meet with George Harrison, John Fogerty, and Paul Simon when they were making records for us — musicians like to talk to other musicians and producers when it comes to making records.

Phil didn't like this dynamic at all, even though it wasn't unusual in my experience. I remember Miles Davis came to the Burbank offices one time for a meeting regarding a potential record deal. I'm in the room with Mo, Miles, and other Warner Bros. executives. Mo had been speaking for a few minutes about what Warner Bros. could offer Miles.

Miles, who could be blunt as hell, interrupted Mo.

"Hey man, are you a musician?"

Mo said no.

Miles shook his head in disgust. "Then why the hell am I talking to you?"

In December 1997, I got a call from Nicolette's husband, Russ Kunkel. He told me that Nicolette had died of cerebral edema. I fell to my knees, speechless. I hadn't had much contact with her in recent years, but she held a special place in my heart. She was only forty-five, and had a young daughter.

A flood of memories came rushing back to me. When I was producing her records, her parents came to Los Angeles to visit her a few times. Kathi and I hosted them at our homes in Santa Barbara and Malibu. Another time or two she brought her little sister Heather up to my house on Lake Arrowhead. Donn Landee and I, Nicky and Heather, and my son, Teddy, all spent time together up there, in and out of my boat. Heather was practically like a daughter to her. Nicolette never stopped talking about Heather and was so protective of her. In fact, I remember when Nicky used to pick me up to go to the studio or over to the Warner Bros. offices in Burbank, out of habit she'd reach an arm across the passenger seat every time she stopped at a light. She'd learned to do that as

Nicolette, my son, Teddy, her sister Heather, and me enjoying a day at my Lake Arrowhead house, 1979. TED TEMPLEMAN COLLECTION.

a teenager when she'd drive Heather, then a toddler, around in her car in Kansas City. I miss her a lot.

Early the next year, Bette Midler asked me to work on her new Warner Bros. record. This felt good, because her presence at Warner Bros. was a part of Mo's legacy. Before he was forced out, Mo had lured her away from Atlantic Records. It was a classic Mo signing. She was a singular talent, one who regardless of music fashion or her latest sales trends would thrive at a label that supported her vision for her art. Gregg Geller of Warner Bros., as I recall, did A&R for the record, and as a result, she and I had some great material at our fingertips.

Counting myself, the record featured six different producers, including Arif Mardin, who'd collaborated with Bette for years.

Bette is an absolutely wonderful singer. She's totally distinctive — you know it's her by the time you listen to one verse — and she's a wonderful stylist. She puts her own spin on everything she sings.

I was thrilled to be working with her, but I found the sessions very stressful because I never really built a rapport with her. It's funny. Her stage persona was this take-charge, take-no-shit lady. So when I heard stories, before we went into the studio together, that she screamed and yelled at people while she recorded, I believed them.

But that was all completely untrue. She was very focused, serious, and thoughtful. She was quiet, almost meek, when we recorded. It was almost like she was intimidated by me in some odd way. I don't know why. She'd sing while I listened from behind the mixing desk. When she finished her take, I'd offer some suggestions through the talkback. There would be long awkward silences. I never quite connected with her the way I did with Nicolette, Linda, or Carly.

Although I recorded most of her vocals in Los Angeles, we did some work at Right Track Recording in Manhattan. One of those days, I got a call from my sister. She said that our father had been experiencing chest pains and had been taken to Huntington Hospital in Pasadena. He'd had a mild heart attack. The good news was that he had been stabilized, and that his doctors expected to be able to send him home in a few days.

When I got off the phone, Bette could see I was upset. She asked me what was wrong and I told her. We were facing a deadline, so I said, "It's okay, let's finish the session and I will go back to Los Angeles tomorrow."

She shook her head in an empathetic fashion. She said, "Ted, go home. If something goes wrong at the hospital and you're not by his side, you'll never forgive yourself. We're just making a record. This is your father we're talking about. Go to the airport. I'll go home and relax for a few days. Go be with your father."

She was so right, and so kind. I will never forget that day.

I produced three songs for her. "Song of Bernadette," a tender piano ballad, opened the record. Her performance was full of pathos. She did a great job on it.

We also did another ballad, a Ben Folds song, "Boxing." That's a track I really love.

The third track was "One Monkey Don't Stop No Show," made famous by the R&B legend Big Maybelle. Released back in 1955 on Okeh Records, I'd first heard it in my grandfather's music store back in Santa Cruz, so I was all in on doing this song.

As I started pre-production, I had this idea to have Royal Crown Revue back her on the record. She loved the idea, and she hit it off with them right away. The Royal Crown guys and I worked up a jazz-swing arrangement for the song that, truth be told, was a bit of a departure from what she usually did on record. She was nervous about doing it. So I got her to loosen up by giving her a few shots of Southern Comfort. It worked like a charm. Once she settled in, she delivered a sultry, defiant performance. We then got it on tape fast — *bang* — just like I'd learned to do with Van Morrison and Van Halen.

I brought in a lot of old and new friends to work on the record. I called Gregg Bissonette to play drums on "Boxing" and "Song of Bernadette." Lee Herschberg and Jeff Hendrickson ran the board for me.

In the fall of 1998, soon after the label released Bette's *Bathhouse Betty*, I got a call from a friend who worked in New York for Warner Bros. She said, "Ted, I hate to be the one to have to tell you this, but I'm worried you're going to get fired. I overheard some lawyers talking in the office. One of them said, 'There's going to be some firings at the label.' I heard them say your name, Ted."

Early the next morning, on November 20, my home phone rang. It was Russ Thyret, asking me to come to his office at eleven a.m. When I got to the company headquarters, there were hordes of people standing in the parking lot. Some Warner employees later said there'd been a bomb threat, but that was just a cover story concocted after the fact. I suspect Russ had set off the fire alarm so no one else would be in the building when we met. So everyone was outside milling around, worried about a fire. The Burbank police and fire departments, sirens blaring, had responded to the scene. It was all a surreal sight to see.

I ducked in the back way, the same way Prince used to sneak into the building way back in the early eighties.

I went to his office and sat down.

After I did, he sighed, "We've known each other forever. This is the hardest thing I've ever had to do at the company."

"What is it?"

"I have to let you go. I'm sorry."

It got quiet.

Finally, I asked, "So what are you going to do with my salary — book it?" In other words, was Warner Bros. going to use me as a tax write-off?

"I'm just going to pay you out."

In effect, he was going to pay me to go away. He then proceeded to tell me what the company's buyout package entailed.

"Excuse me for a minute, I want to call my lawyer."

I went into an empty office down the hall and called Allen Grubman, who'd been my attorney for many years. I explained that Warner Bros. Records had offered to pay me a million dollars a year, for the next five years. But the agreement also included a non-compete clause, so I wouldn't be able to work anywhere in the industry for that stretch of time.

I said, "What do you think?"

"You're gonna get five million bucks. What can I say about their bad judgment? It's their loss. Look, if you want to litigate it, I can make their life miserable. But I'd take the deal."

When I left the building, I had to walk past all the company's employees, people I'd worked alongside for decades, in some cases. Everyone understood what had happened. It was a horrible few moments for me.

So that's how I got fired.

Now I could speculate about internal company politics, about the motivations of certain individuals, but I'm still not sure why, after I'd delivered hit after hit for the company for decades, I got fired. What's even more difficult for me to understand is why the company was willing to pay me more money per year than I was making in annual salary for the label, not to work for the label. If I'd kept working for Warner Bros. Records, the company would've paid me less per year while making income from my efforts as an executive and a producer. It just didn't make any sense to me.

So in my last dealings with Warner Bros., stretching back to my days with the Tikis, the company stipulated that I wrap up my ongoing projects for the label.

Making the best of things, I tied up loose ends. In December, Bette and Royal Crown appeared together on the *Billboard* Music Awards. In one of my last official acts for Warner Bros. Records, I flew to Las Vegas. Working out of a remote truck parked outside the Hard Rock Hotel & Casino, where they performed, I helped dial in the live sound for their rendition of "One Monkey." We didn't have much time for rehearsal but they all did great. Eddie Nichols, Royal Crown's singer, danced and sang backgrounds with her, but Bette, naturally, stole the show. She put on a bawdy, sexy performance. Those guys were the perfect backing band for her. I loved putting that together.

Soon after that wrapped, I got a call from a shipping company. This company had been hired by the label to pack up my Burbank office. Everything that I had in there, all of my gold and platinum records, my desk, my family photos, had been put in crates and loaded into a truck. I had it all delivered to my home in Montecito, and told the shipping company to unload it into my garage. After dedicating my life to the company, it felt so awful to have my career at Warner Bros. Records conclude in this manner.

So that was the end for me at Warner Bros. Now maybe for some people, a golden parachute like mine would've been a dream. But for me it was a nightmare, and it almost killed me.

Since I was a little kid, I'd been obsessed with making music. Now that part of my life had been cut off, like I'd lost a leg. I couldn't work in a recording studio. I couldn't work in the industry, which had been the center of my day-to-day life since the mid-sixties, in any capacity. It felt like a part of me was slowly dying.

I kicked off my forced retirement by buying a luxury condo at the Dorchester on Wilshire Boulevard. It was an elite address, but what was that worth? I thought of myself as a failure.

I had nothing to do, or had nothing that seemed worth doing, all day, every day. In retrospect, I can see how insidious depression can be. An outsider could've looked at my life and thought, *Here's a guy who has plenty of money. He has real estate investments, gold and platinum records on the wall, high-performance cars, and a wonderful family.* But I didn't think about that stuff. I couldn't even think about my family from a levelheaded perspective. I felt disconnected from Kathi, which wasn't her fault. I'd drive up the coast to see her and the kids on the weekends, but I felt like I needed to be by myself. I didn't want them to see me when I was this sad. I just didn't feel comfortable in my own skin.

I felt so lost that all I wanted to do was go into my condo, pull the shades closed, and do whatever would come to me to not make me feel the blackness. Depression changed my relationship with music. I could only stand to listen to certain kinds of music. Of all things, I'd listen to the Ray Conniff Singers. They were an easy-listening vocal group that had hits when I was a kid. They hadn't entered my mind in years, but when I started ruminating about my childhood, I remembered them. When I played their albums in my condo, it brought back happy memories of visiting the home of my childhood friends Fred and Bruce McPherson when we were all kids. Their parents played the Conniff Singers all the time, so hearing those records kept me out of the darkness.

My coke consumption grew as well. Once you've snorted your brains out for hours, you can't sleep and you're climbing the walls. I'd mix vodka and milk and just down it, because I just wanted to knock myself *out* — I didn't care about anything else. Just to sleep. I couldn't find anything else that would work. So my drinking got worse. I'd come to a few hours later in the middle of the night. I'd feel horrible, so I'd take another shot of something, mixed, because I couldn't stand the taste of alcohol. I'd pass back out.

It's incredible how depression can consume you. All I wanted to do was escape — from everything. It came to a point where I'd drink at night to go to sleep, and I didn't care whether I woke up or not. When you're trapped in that mindset, you're not thinking clearly. Of course I loved my family. I didn't want to hurt them and yet it didn't even really register to me how much my kids, for instance, would miss me if I passed away. You lose all perspective on things. I didn't think about the successes I'd had, or the fact that pretty much everyone who works in the entertainment industry is going to face a reckoning at some point along the way. I'd lasted more than three decades with one company, rising from a lowly tape listener to senior vice president and then executive vice president. It was an incredible run.

After I'd been living there for a couple of months, I was in the Dorchester lobby getting my mail. I bumped into a woman who lived on my floor. She said hello and we talked. In a gossipy voice, she told me that the actress and singer Julie Andrews also lived on our floor. That night, that conversation about Andrews brought back a long-forgotten memory.

Back in the mid-eighties, I bought a beach place out on Broad Beach Road in Malibu. The person I bought it from was Robert Wise, who directed *The Sound of Music* and *West Side Story*. As we closed the deal, he and I became friends. I remember we talked a lot about Julie Andrews, because as a producer, I admired her gorgeous voice. He told me a story that I loved. He said that when they filmed *The Sound of Music* in Europe, it rained regularly, so the cast and crew endured a lot of days when they couldn't shoot outside. He said Andrews was like a second mother to the children. While waiting for the weather to clear up, she entertained the kids on the set by singing just like she did as the character in the film. I thought, *What a kind person she must be.* That story made the movie a little more magical in my mind and made me admire her even more.

After hearing that Andrews was my neighbor, I kept thinking I might bump into her. Then one day I heard a woman singing to herself when she was walking down the hall. It was her, but at that moment, I couldn't think of a good excuse to fling my door open and say hello. A couple of other times, I heard her having conversations while she walked past my door to and from the elevator; she had a very distinctive voice so you knew it was her.

I *so* wanted to meet her, but in the weeks that followed, we never crossed paths.

And then one day I woke up with a tremendous hangover.

I could barely get out of bed and I hadn't shaved or showered in three days. I opened the door to my condo in my underwear to get my newspaper. I bent down into the hallway, and when I looked up she was right there. She goes, "Oh, hello there." It was so awkward. I froze and went back inside without saying a word. I was mortified.

All this time went by, and I didn't think I had a real problem with alcohol or drugs. Of course, I knew I was drinking a lot, but denial is a powerful force. I rationalized my behavior by telling myself that I'd earned the right to have some fun after so many years of endless work.

But my drinking was accelerating. A friend of mine came by to see me. I was *really* a wreck, but I'm sure I told her I was doing great. She saw the state I was in and somehow convinced me that I needed to get help. *Right away.* She took me to the Huntington Hospital in Pasadena. I figured I'd be in and out after a checkup, but I was in such bad shape that the doctors admitted me and started trying to stabilize me. From there I went into Las Encinas Hospital's Recovery Center in Pasadena for treatment. It was a facility with a long history. W.C. Fields and Clark Gable used to go there to dry out.

After I got released I had a period of sobriety that lasted many months. But then I slipped again. I didn't immediately start drinking heavily, but in the end my experience was just like that old proverb: *First the man takes a drink. Then the drink takes a drink. Then the drink takes the man.* That one drink led me down a path to insanity once more.

I'd bottomed out again and, thank God, the same friend intervened. I was drinking all of this vodka and doing tons of blow. I thought I was fine, but the truth was I was literally dying. She took me back to Huntington Hospital. It was Halloween night. I remember because as I was being admitted, the nurse was dressed as Minnie Mouse and the physician as Groucho Marx. I wasn't all that clear-headed when I walked in the door, and a welcoming committee dressed like that didn't make things any less confusing. This time around, the doctors kept me in Huntington for four days. I had all of these IV tubes in me to prevent acute alcohol withdrawal seizures, because if you go cold turkey after heavy drinking, you can die from seizures.

I went to treatment at a Los Angeles facility called the Hills, this time for almost two months.

Ultimately it was no one's fault but mine that I drank.

With years of sobriety under my belt, I've tried to make sense of why I fell into such a pit. I think one big cause of my troubles started when I had to move my family out of Los Angeles. The smog and pollen in the city put my son in an oxygen tent, twice. After the second time I moved my family to my home in Montecito so he could breathe cleaner air. I'd spend my weeks and many weekends in the city, living in my condos in Century City, away from my loved ones. That's when I started to use alcohol to dull the pain, because before I moved them, I never drank all that much.

The other thing I've come to understand about myself is that I experienced a lot of trauma in my life that I never processed properly. For instance, my childhood growing up in the woods was a frightening time for me. I had to be in close quarters with my drunk uncle. He was impulsive, loud, and unpredictable. You could never relax when he was in the vicinity. Then there were the mountain lions, rattlesnakes, and my car crash, which should have killed me. The other traumatic event was the hijacking. I truly thought I was going to die that day in the air. I know now that those things gave me PTSD, a condition that still affects me to this very day. All of these things haunted me during my darkest days.

Chapter 16

BROTHERS

Around 2007, I called Pat and Tommy. I hadn't talked to them in a while and I wanted to reconnect. They invited me down to a Doobies rehearsal. When I watched and listened, I felt both nostalgic and energized. Playing with Doobie vets Mike Hossack and John McFee, I thought Pat and Tommy, the whole band, sounded amazing.

I spoke to Tommy afterwards, and asked they'd been writing. The answer was yes. I asked if they had plans to make a record. Tommy said not really, but then he suggested he and I get together and listen to what he'd written over the past few years.

Soon after I went to Tommy's house in Northern California and ran through the songs he thought would be suitable for a Doobies album. I liked a lot of the stuff he'd written.

And then I sat down with Pat, and he too had some great tunes.

After we talked, the guys decided they wanted to do another record with me behind the board — this would be our first studio album together since 1980's *One Step Closer*, and the first time I'd be working with Tommy since 1979 when we did *Everything*

You've Heard Is True. Likewise, this would be the first time I'd worked with Tommy and Pat together on an album from front to back since we did *Stampede* back in 1975.

When we decided to collaborate, I wanted them to know that this wasn't about money for me. I didn't take an advance — if it sold, we'd all make money. At that point, there was no record deal, so the band fronted all of the money for the album. I wanted to make a record with them because I love those guys and I thought they still had a lot to say musically.

One of my first tasks was to pick the tunes. Back in the old days, when those guys were coming off the road and running right into the studio so we could finish a record, we often had to piece songs together at the last minute. This time around, Tommy and Pat had a huge backlog of song ideas and, for better or worse, without a deadline dictated by a record company, we could take time and let the songs take shape over a longer timeline.

As we worked through them, I actually ended up writing a couple of lyrical things with Pat. One was "Chateau," which was a look back at their early days playing for crowds of bikers at the Chateau Liberté. I can still remember what it was like when Lenny and I saw them those first times, jamming onstage while these hairy, beefy guys in greasy jeans and leather, with their motorcycle mamas hanging all over them, danced and drank. That shared history was something that I kept thinking about as we worked on the songs — about how many years I had with these guys, and how far we'd all come since we first met back in 1970.

I also came up with the idea of revisiting one of my favorite Doobie Brothers songs, "Nobody."

I had always thought that song should have been a hit, but Lenny and I hadn't gotten the production and mix right when we first cut it back in 1971. And even after Donn and I had remixed it and Warner Bros. had released it again as a single in the fall of 1974, it still hadn't connected the way I thought it should.

So for *World Gone Crazy* we decided to rebuild it, in a lot of ways from the ground up. For instance, Pat wrote a new acoustic intro for the song and John wrote a new banjo picking part over the top of it.

So we worked up demos, and that started the ball rolling on what would become *World Gone Crazy*. For the basic tracks, we worked at Sunset Sound. There's still no better studio in the world.

During pre-production, I'd put together a list of session players I wanted to use to play certain parts on the record. I'd call in some old friends and make some new ones.

I used Lenny's son Joey Waronker, who is a fabulous drummer, on a track called "My Baby." At this point in his career, he'd already done sessions for Beck and served as the touring and studio drummer for R.E.M.

I also once again hired Gregg Bissonette. A master technician, Gregg is also one of the funniest people you'll ever meet. When he came into the studio to record "Young Man's Game" and "World Gone Crazy" he spent the first fifty minutes telling us all jokes. When he finally settled behind the kit, we ran down the songs twice before listening to the playback. Ask any drummer I've ever worked with — I'm an obsessive when it comes to getting drum parts right. Each time, he'd nailed his parts and so his work was done. Both times it was like we paid for fifty minutes of standup and ten minutes of drumming! He's the greatest. If I was going into the studio tomorrow and needed a drummer, I could call him and he could come in the next day and knock the part out, no problem. He's Ringo's longtime touring drummer. Is there any better endorsement for his abilities?

We cut the rest of the record in a few other studios, including two home studios in Hawaii. Pat has a studio over there, as does Mike McDonald. Pat had written a song called "Don't Say Goodbye." I helped him finish off the lyrics. We both thought it would be perfect for Mike to sing on, so he and Pat got together in Hawaii and recorded the song. What was also nice about this reunion of sorts was that Mike's wife, Amy Holland, sang on it as well. Any record that you've got Mike, Tommy, and Pat all singing on together is just magic. There's nothing else like it. Of course, it felt so good to me to have Mike and Tommy working together; that made things feel like they'd come full circle for the Doobies, and was a good reminder to the world that any talk about a rift between Mike and these other guys was utter bullshit. There were strong friendships and mutual respect undergirding their work together.

Pat also recruited Willie Nelson, whom he also knew from Hawaii. He collaborated with Pat in writing the ballad "I Know We Won," and then Willie sang the song with Pat on the record. Willie was stoned when he did his vocals, but he delivered!

Little Feat's Billy Payne, who'd been playing on Doobies records since *Toulouse Street*, played Hammond B-3 organ and piano on a bunch of tracks on the record. Having him take part just felt right.

Since the Doobies didn't have a full-time bass player, I called in Bob Glaub. He'd played on a number of my productions, including the Carly Simon record, Tommy's solo record, and Nicolette's first two albums. He was drop-dead perfect as usual.

One song that I loved that didn't make the final cut was "Going Back to Louisiana" by Jerry Lynn Williams. I hired Bob Clearmountain to work on it and spent thirty thousand out of my own pocket on studio time to finish off the track. It's a killer. I hope one day the Doobies will release it.

We finished the record up in the summer of 2010. Released in September on HOR Records, *World Gone Crazy* peaked at No. 39 on the *Billboard* Top 200 chart. Our reworked version of "Nobody" connected too, and got played on VH1 Classic and Country Music Television.

To date, it's the last record I've produced. If it turns out to be my last musical statement, I'm glad it was a product of a collaboration with some of my dearest friends in the business.

GREG RENOFF

The summer of 1984 was my Summer of Van Halen. The quartet was everywhere: on the radio, in the pages of *Rolling Stone*, and on MTV after "Jump" topped the charts. After overdosing on *1984*, I bought their other five albums. Immersing myself in their catalog, Van Halen became my favorite band.

As much as the memorable songs and electrifying performances on Van Halen's albums captured my imagination, I also found *the sound* of their albums incredibly compelling. Through my Walkman's headphones, they sounded like I was in the room with them while they played in the studio.

At that time, I knew only the basics about the role a record producer played in the making of an album. I understood that producers ran recording sessions; they were most responsible for the way a band presented its sonics and songs on an album. Now I'd heard enough records to know that some, like those by Van Halen, sounded way better than others in my collection. Investigating further, I'd read Van Halen's album liner notes. I'd see: PRODUCED BY TED TEMPLEMAN.

Since I owned every Van Halen album, I decided to buy more albums produced by Ted Templeman. On subsequent trips to the record store, I'd look for his name. In 1985, I bought two new releases, Aerosmith's *Done with Mirrors* and Eric Clapton's *Behind the Sun,* because Ted worked on them. I'd also discover that Sammy Hagar's *VOA* and David Lee Roth's *Crazy from the Heat* were Ted Templeman productions. I remember I was quite surprised that these four records sounded nothing like Van Halen's Ted Templeman–produced albums. Moreover, none of the four sounded like the others. Nonetheless, all of them sounded good to my ears.

Years later, after I became a historian and author, I remained a devout Van Halen fan. Those two basic elements of my identity birthed *Van Halen Rising*, my history of the band's origins and rise to fame.

In June 2014, while I was in the final stages of researching *Van Halen Rising*, I conducted a one-hour interview with Ted. By now I knew he was the individual who not only produced Van Halen, but also discovered and signed the band back in 1977. Soft spoken, he came off more like an unassuming emeritus professor than a vainglorious Grammy-winning superproducer. When I mentioned that two of Van Halen albums he produced (*Van Halen* and *1984*) had sold well over ten million copies each, and that an act he plucked from obscurity became the vanguard for an entire generation of 1980s hard rock bands, he lavished praise on the band members.

Ted did, however, want to talk about how much he loved making records with a band as talented as Van Halen. Ted explained his basic approach to recording Van Halen, which was to have the four guys play live together while the tape rolled. He particularly credited others for the group's studio magic, emphasizing that without the lyrical brilliance of Roth, the musicality of Edward Van Halen, and technological genius of Donn Landee, their albums wouldn't have become such stone-cold classics.

When I asked Ted about his philosophy on producing, he stressed that his main job was to highlight his artists' talents so they can shine in the spotlight. He said, "As a producer, I always thought of myself as a lighting man. Some producers, like Phil Spector, had a sound. He'd produce different artists, but all of his albums sounded the same. I *never* wanted a sound. I wanted to make timeless recordings with great sonics, but ones that were unique enough that people had to ask: 'Who produced *Stampede* by the Doobies?' 'Who produced that that Nicolette Larson hit?' I wanted to keep the focus on the personality and musicality of my artists, rather than putting *my* stamp on them." This explained why the albums he did with different artists were sonically distinct.

A year or so later, I sent Ted a pre-release copy of my book. He was effusive with his praise — probably the greatest compliment I could get as a historian who wrote about Van Halen. Ted then kindly agreed to appear with me at a book event in Pasadena, answering audience questions and joining me in signing copies of *Van Halen Rising*.

A few days later, Ted and I got on the phone again for the first time since our initial 2014 conversation. I asked him about his wider career. He told me about growing up in Santa Cruz as jazz-obsessed drummer and trumpeter and how he helped form the sunshine-pop act Harpers Bizarre, which scored a Top 20 hit in 1967. He shared his memories of his remarkable musical life: seeing Sinatra and Elvis record in Hollywood in the late sixties, watching acts he'd championed, like the Doobie Brothers and Nicolette Larson, rise to stardom, and serving as a sounding board for stars like Pete Townshend and George Harrison in his role as a Warner Bros. Records vice president.

In the weeks that followed, Ted and I frequently talked and emailed. He told me compelling, eye-opening, insightful stuff, the kind of insider tales that thrilled me as a historian and a fan. After Ted shot to fame as a Warner Bros. Records pop star in 1967, he found himself just three years later working for the company as a fifty-dollar-a-week tape listener. His first production effort, as co-producer of the Doobie Brothers' debut, was a sales dud. By 1979, however, he'd produced two No. 1 hits for the same group. (He'd add a third with Van Halen's "Jump" in 1984.) By 1996, he'd risen to executive vice president and seen two albums he produced, *Best of the Doobies* and *Van Halen*, cross the ten million album sales mark; two years later, the company let him go, ending his thirty-two-year relationship with Warner Bros. Records. Across all these conversations, my biggest takeaways evolved from Ted's explanation of the *work* of a record producer: his best technical practices, his mastery of the psychology of studio performance, his most memorable mistakes and biggest successes.

The more I thought about our conversations, the more I came to believe that Ted's life would make for a great biography.

In the fall of 2015, I asked Ted if he'd be willing to partner with me on his autobiography. After assuring him that I'd do a deep dive into the studio work he'd done with the artists he'd produced, musicians he still counted among his closest friends, he agreed.

Soon after, Ted invited me to interview him at his home. On my first visit I was struck by the fact that this didn't look like the home of a record producer. There are no gold and platinum records anywhere; instead a number of well-curated European paintings hang on the walls. Only his office offered visible signs of his past achievements. A few photos of Ted working in the studio adorn the walls. Surprisingly, his Grammy award for Record of the Year ("What a Fool Believes") was nowhere in sight. (Eventually, I asked Ted to show it to me. It sits quietly on a shelf in the living room.)

Over the next few years, our conversations continued as I researched the book. I became particularly interested in Ted's shift to record production in 1970. A musical prodigy, Ted grew up obsessed with R&B, pop, and jazz. On any given day during his teen years he'd listen to recordings by James Brown and Stan Kenton, by the Beatles and Miles Davis, by the Supremes and Tito Puente, dissecting their arrangements and pondering their sonic architecture. He'd explain that one constant irritant to him was the poor sound — indistinct bass, thin-sounding drums — that he heard on a lot of records.

As a trumpeter, Ted logged his first live performances in elementary school. While he loved performing instrumentally (he'd later add drums to his repertoire), circumstances demanded in 1967 that he step out from behind his drums and sing lead for Harpers Bizarre. That latter experience, of fronting a band, made him increasingly aware that while he enjoyed playing supporting roles onstage, he didn't want to pursue a long career as a pop vocalist. "I didn't have the chops to pull that off, so I hated singing lead. I also hated the whole pop-star scene, especially the non-musical aspects of performing."

Even though he felt uncomfortable as a recording *artist*, Ted explained that he loved the recording *process*. He recounted how he'd do double duty while making the Harpers Bizarre albums. When he wasn't being recorded, he'd spend time on the other side of the glass. He'd apprentice under his best friend, Harpers Bizarre producer Lenny Waronker, and two of the best engineers ever to haunt a studio, Lee Herschberg and Donn Landee. Those experiences, from learning how to select and arrange tunes to the intricacies of mixing and mastering, made him a studio junkie, even after his band ran its course.

Along with Waronker, Landee, and Herschberg, Ted feels particularly indebted to the late Warner Bros. executive Joe Smith. In 1970 he not only green-lighted the signing of the Doobie Brothers, he also endorsed the idea of Templeman and Waronker co-producing their debut. Shortly thereafter, Smith introduced Ted to Van Morrison, setting off a chain of events that led to

Ted serving as co-producer on Morrison's *Tupelo Honey* and *St. Dominic's Preview.* "Joe really helped me out," Templeman says. "He saw potential in me and gave me the opportunity to prove myself."

Ted also went to pains to explain how much he still appreciates Morrison taking him on as his co-producer. During those sessions he'd see the wisdom in the Irish singer's hell-bent-for-leather approach to recording. When he'd listen back to takes, he'd realize that while there were imperfections, there was magic on the tape. He'd apply these lessons to his future studio endeavors. "Get it on tape," Templeman says. "If a band's performance gives you goosebumps, no one's going to hear one bum bass note during the second verse. George Martin knew that. There are mistakes all over the Beatles albums." This exact philosophy is what animated his rapid-fire approach to recording Van Halen.

That said, Ted made clear that he never had a one-size-fits-all approach to making records. Because of their more densely textured arrangements, Little Feat and the Doobie Brothers required a more time-intensive manner of recording. Ted's favorite example in this category was the seemingly interminable sessions in pursuit of an acceptable version of the Doobie Brothers' "What a Fool Believes." In the end, however, the results spoke for themselves: a No. 1 song and slew of awards for the band at the 22nd Annual Grammy Awards.

Making records also gave Ted the chance to musically collaborate with his artists by pitching in from behind the scenes, like he'd done before he moved out from behind the drums in Harpers. During our conversations, Ted put a number of his unheralded *musical* performances on some of his most successful production efforts on my radar. He played timbales on Clapton's "Forever Man," Hammond organ on Montrose's "Rock Candy," tambourine on Hagar's "I Can't Drive 55," and most famously, drums on the Doobies' "What a Fool Believes." I'd likewise learn that Ted went uncredited on a number of albums. For instance, Ted doubled Edward Van Halen's background vocal parts on numerous early Van Halen records, which played to Ted's strengths. "My voice sounds best when I'm boosting up and supplementing another singer, not when I'm in the forefront," he told me.

Ted likewise loved to give the artists he worked with a chance to perform as session players or special guests on albums he produced. He'd enumerate a long list of examples for me. He'd bring Little Feat's keyboard player, Billy Payne, into the studio to play on a number of Doobie Brothers' albums. Years before Edward Van Halen soloed on Michael Jackson's "Beat It," Ted let him run wild on Nicolette Larson's "Can't Get Away From You." She'd return the favor by singing backgrounds on Van Halen's "Could This Be Magic?" Ted's teamwork-minded approach hit its fullest development in 1976 when he brought in Doobies and Little Feat into Sunset Sound to back Carly Simon on her covers of their songs on *Another Passenger*. And when David Lee Roth hit the wall during the writing sessions for the song idea that became Van Halen's "I'll Wait," Templeman paired up Mike McDonald and Roth.

Outside the studio, Ted further collaborated with his artists by joining them onstage. In 1979, he went on the road with Nicolette Larson's band, singing backgrounds and playing percussion. That same year, he'd play timbales and percussion during the Lowell George benefit at the Los Angeles Forum, and drums on "What a Fool Believes" with the Doobies during the No Nukes concerts at Madison Square Garden. He enjoyed these moments immensely, he said, because it made him feel like he was working side-by-side with his artists, who also happened to be his friends, in pursuit of a common goal, rather than lording over them as their "producer."

As I approach the end of this process, I've been thinking about what I've enjoyed most on my journey with Ted from the idea to write this book to its publication. To be sure, hearing the story of his incredible life, firsthand, has been the experience of a lifetime. But what's been most satisfying on a personal level has been the opportunity to *learn* from him. My favorite moments have been sitting alongside him as he'd play me both songs he'd produced and the songs that inspired him, hearing his insightful commentary as music filled the room. Practically everything he played for me was new to my ears. He'd pull up recordings by pioneering Black performers on Okeh Records. He'd find b-sides of Supremes singles that he'd heard as a kid. He'd spin tracks by artists drawn from a kaleidoscopic array of genres. Moby Grape. Hank Williams. Royal Crown Revue. The Beau Brummels. Modern Jazz Quartet. Nicolette Larson. The Animals. Stan Kenton. Big Mama Thornton. Michael Bloomfield. Steely Dan. The Daily Flash. The Four Freshmen. Ike Turner. The Coasters. Tower of Power. The Animals. My head spun trying to keep up, but every time we talked, I'd become a better student of music.

When I think back on those hours with Ted, I'm reminded that in the summer of 1970 Ted came close to leaving the music industry behind for a career as a teacher. While we're all glad that didn't happen, I don't think Ted, even with his dazzling achievements as a producer, ever left that other vocational aspiration fully behind. Thank you, Ted.